THEY WILL HAVE THEIR GAME

THEY WILL HAVE THEIR GAME

SPORTING CULTURE AND THE MAKING OF THE EARLY AMERICAN REPUBLIC

KENNETH COHEN

CORNELL UNIVERSITY PRESS
Ithaca and London

First published 2017 by Cornell University Press

Printed in the United States of America

Library of Congress Cataloging-in-Publication Data
Names: Cohen, Kenneth, author.
Title: They will have their game : sporting culture
   and the making of the early American republic /
   Kenneth Cohen.
Description: Ithaca : Cornell University Press, 2017. |
   Includes bibliographical references and index.
Identifiers: LCCN 2017012929 (print) | LCCN 2017015937
   (ebook) | ISBN 9781501714207 (epub/mobi) |
   ISBN 9781501714214 (pdf) | ISBN 9781501705496 |
   ISBN 9781501705496 (cloth : alk. paper)
Subjects: LCSH: Sports—Social aspects—United States—
   History—18th century. | Sports—Social aspects—
   United States—History—19th century. | Popular
   culture—United States—History—18th century. |
   Popular culture—United States—History—19th
   century. | United States—Civilization—1783–1865.
Classification: LCC GV583 (ebook) | LCC GV583.C6155
   2017 (print) | DDC 306.4/830973—dc23
LC record available at https://lccn.loc.gov/2017012929

Cornell University Press strives to use environmentally responsible suppliers and materials to the fullest extent possible in the publishing of its books. Such materials include vegetable-based, low-VOC inks and acid-free papers that are recycled, totally chlorine-free, or partly composed of nonwood fibers. For further information, visit our website at cornellpress.cornell.edu.

CONTENTS

ILLUSTRATIONS

ACKNOWLEDGMENTS

We live in a world where sport is often presented as a microcosm of life. But spending seventeen years on this project has made me see my life as a microcosm of sporting culture. Like all the professionals detailed in the coming pages, I have depended on the generosity of many "backers" who will never see a fair return on their investments. They gave their time, intellectual capital, and emotional support, and I strung them along for years with paltry updates on my slow and hardly linear progress toward this final product. I can only hope that it, and my sincere thanks here, are enough to keep my account open with them.

The list of creditors must begin with the archives and public offices whose grants made this study possible. The American Antiquarian Society, the Historical Society of Pennsylvania, the Library Company of Philadelphia, the New Jersey Historical Commission, the University of South Carolina, and the Virginia Historical Society all provided warm and efficient venues for the otherwise isolating and unpredictable experience of historical research. I was particularly fortunate to have received seven years of financial support in various modes from the University of Delaware and the Winterthur Program in American Material Culture affiliated with it. I completed my dissertation with a yearlong fellowship at the McNeil Center for Early American Studies, where I joined a long list of scholars who benefited from the sharp criticism and good cheer of their fellow Fellows as well as the incomparable Dan Richter. I am thankful for two Faculty Development Grants from St. Mary's College of Maryland, which helped me tie up loose ends at archives and pay for the images referenced in the text.

In addition to institutional support, friends and friends-of-friends graciously housed and fed me, and helped secure access to additional source material. Ann, Alec, and Wendy Sarratt helped out in Richmond, New York, and Chapel Hill, respectively. Hunt and Callee Boulware did the same in Columbia, South Carolina. Nic Butler, Lisa Reams, and Gary Smith guided me in Charleston. Roger Stanton and my sister Heather Cohen helped me navigate the

University of Maryland's library system. John McCoy generously located and polished the image of the obscure baseball card in the Epilogue.

I follow in the footsteps of many a sporting entrepreneur by saving my most flagrant welshing for the people I owe the most. Paula Treckel introduced me to early American history and encouraged me to study sporting culture. She could not have known that her stint as my advisor would last more than two decades, but I am grateful that it has continued even into her retirement. I owe at least as much to Cathy Matson's tireless attention. Her detailed suggestions mixed pointed critiques with supportive urging, while her own meticulous research and constant advocacy of mine have provided a model for professional scholarship and mentorship. Michael McGandy's interest in this project never faltered, even though he first inquired about the manuscript ten years ago. No doubt it would still be unpublished if I had not received patient guidance from him and Bethany Wasik at Cornell University Press. Finally, my parents bantered with me over arguments and offered encouragement whenever my confidence faltered. Their role as coaches was fitting, since their enjoyment of history and sport led to my own interest in marrying the two.

I accumulated smaller but no less crucial debts to dozens of colleagues who read portions of the text over the course of its evolution, and who readily discussed the subjects it addresses. Like many of the sporting culture participants in this study, we formed community through debate. Particular thanks go to Zara Anishanslin, Rick Bell, Gretchen Buggeln, Steven Bullock, Ben Carp, Toby Ditz, Paul Erickson, Russell Field, Simon Finger, Matt Garrett, Ritchie Garrison, Dallett Hemphill, Woody Holton, Mike Huggins, Cathy Kelly, Julie King, Christian Koot, Anna Leipsic, Brian Luskey, Will Mackintosh, Brian Murphy, Jess Roney, Jaime Schultz, Brandi Stanton, Bill Wagner, Jenn Van Horne, and my colleagues in the History Department at St. Mary's College of Maryland. Of course, whatever I have taken from others' comments and suggestions, any errors are my own.

It is a truism among scholars that we all stand on the shoulders of those who came before us. But this project's topical and chronological breadth simply would not have been possible without relying on existing but separate historiographies related to theatre, horse racing, tavern-going, and gambling. Works by Melvin Adelman, Rosemarie Bank, Ann Fabian, Odai Johnson, Heather Nathans, Steven Riess, Susan Salinger, Nancy Struna, and Peter Thompson directed me to sources and provided a foundation for my thinking about sporting culture as a whole. I do not always agree with their interpretations. Yet, like the experience of attending sporting events in early America, this work derives its meaning from negotiating with others—sometimes borrowing from these scholars, and sometimes challenging them.

Even when I tried to take a break from this project, my own sporting background meant that I was often engaging in the latest version of the culture I was studying. Plus, it turned out that my friends in the sports world wanted to share their own valuable insights. Thanks to Scott Grzenda, Mike Singleton, Mike Dickey, and my former coaching colleagues in the Olympic Development Program, as well as my friends at Special Olympics Southern Maryland, H Street Runners, and Watkins Rec, all of whom shared good ideas during my supposed down time.

Rebecca Levy was, and remains, the exception. Our long runs together were never about sporting culture, and she continues to broaden my vision and sense of adventure now that we spend most of our time together running after our daughter. This book, and everything I do, is better than it would have been without the perspective she brings to my life.

THEY WILL HAVE THEIR GAME

Introduction
The Meaning of Sport

In November 1797, twenty-nine-year-old English architect and artist Benjamin Henry Latrobe visited his friend Bathurst Jones in the Tidewater Virginia hamlet of Hanover Town. The two men shared a connection to Thomas Jefferson. But while Latrobe applauded Jefferson for having "spread actual and practical democracy and political equality" in the country, he also complained about how political democracy bled into everyday social relations and undermined respect for "superior talents" in America. The visitor's unease with egalitarianism explains why he was so struck by the nightly entertainment offered by his host in Hanover Town: hanging out in tavern billiard rooms.[1]

Latrobe was critical of these destinations before he entered them. He thought the game of billiards made it "impossible for the mind to catch the most distant entertainment or improvement," and so two tables in a town of seventy-five residents signaled their vapidity. Yet, after two evenings, he concluded that not everyone in attendance was unenlightened. "Mr. Mansen, a merchant, Mr. Bathurst Jones, Dr. Lyons, and a french Gentleman Mr. Vial are very agreeable and most respectable men," Latrobe wrote in his journal. "When the whole town is assembled every evening at the billiard room they appear in contrast to the rest." As Latrobe phrased it, "the other Inhabitants show themselves more void of rational employment and sentiments, and though it seems invidious to condemn a town in the lump with so few

FIGURE I.1:   *Billiards in Hanover Town, Virginia,* Benjamin Henry Latrobe (1797), ink and watercolor on paper, courtesy Maryland Historical Society.

exceptions, yet I think justice would not be done, if any commendation for industry, sobriety, understanding or good temper were conferred upon them."

What surprised Latrobe was not the overwhelming number of boorish locals but their lack of regard for the handful of refined gentlemen present. In the billiard room, the base majority gave no special treatment to their apparent betters. "As every face is known and every acquaintance intimate, ceremony and even politeness have disappeared," Latrobe concluded with chagrin. Familiarity had bred contempt for distinction, and, what was more, the town elite appeared to accept it even as they continued to demonstrate their superior cultivation "in contrast to the rest."[2]

The scene made such an impression on Latrobe that he rendered it in watercolor, a format he reserved for the observations he considered most emblematic of the young republic. (See figure I.1.) *Billiards in Hanover Town* portrays a four-handed game, involving two teams of two men each. The participants run the social gamut, with a gentleman in a dark suit and white stockings foregrounded alongside a player whose bare feet and torn pant cuffs allude to a harder life and lower standing. Across the table from these two stands one nondescript player and another donning riding boots and a greatcoat—a level of dress in between that of the first two players. No matter how you imagine the teams, they breach lines of rank and class. Moreover, other men of wealth, one wearing stockings and another in an older-fashioned suit coat, watch from behind the table. The picture illustrates Latrobe's comments and evokes the observation of another English traveler in Virginia at the same time, who was similarly amazed by tavern billiard tables in Norfolk, "which are crowded during the whole of the afternoon and till late at night. To these (in this land of equality) any person is admitted," the visitor noted, "and you sometimes see there a collection of curious characters, some of them not of the most respectable cast; but still, when it comes to their turn, they will have their game, notwithstanding there may be some of the first people in the country waiting to play."[3]

This book explains why places like billiard rooms hosted such democratic experiences, as well as how those experiences nevertheless rarely undermined the hierarchy that distinguished "the first people in the country" from everyone else. Indeed, as the ensuing chapters illustrate, billiard games in post-Revolutionary Virginia were just one expression of a widespread "sporting culture" that simultaneously promoted egalitarianism and hierarchy on the Anglo-American mainland between 1750 and 1860.

Across this span of time and space, scores of other writers echoed Latrobe's observations—and his sentiments. At taverns, the hearthplaces of early American sporting culture, refined travelers in Boston, Philadelphia, New York, and Richmond from the 1720s straight through to the 1850s all decried "the circumstance of having the taverns thus infested" by "a few bad characters" whose presence soiled "the Society they meet with there."[4] Other prominent public sporting culture venues, including theatres and racetracks, witnessed similar mingling and objections to "the circumstance of a lady being seated in the same box, side by side, with the individual who fitted on her shoes in the morning or dressed her hair in the evening."[5] Sporting culture was not static, and the following pages detail its changing contours over time. But an examination of leading sporting venues reveals them to have been persistent places of self-assertion and social contest. This behavior drove the country's "most respectable" inhabitants to incessantly complain but also constantly negotiate with their challengers. As with the Hanover Town elite, who accepted mingling and familiarity in their local billiard rooms without losing their elevated positions in society, the negotiation at sporting culture sites produced a sense of equality that ultimately supported rather than undermined existing hierarchies of wealth and power. In many ways, then, the early history of sporting culture in America offers an exploration of the origins, nature, and limits of democracy in the nation's formative years.[6]

Defining Sporting Culture

This book focuses on a constellation of activities linked under the banner of "sporting culture." But what was sporting culture? Early Americans would not have known. The term was invented just in the last twenty years by historians whose research has grouped together nineteenth-century activities and behaviors previously studied only separately. These researchers have described gambling, racing, and theatregoing as related components of a hypermasculine urban milieu responsible for fomenting libertinism, prostitution, and misogyny. Their studies have explored sporting culture as the hub for an aggressively masculine heterosexual discourse that perpetuated men's power and provided an escape from the constraints of mainstream Victorian "respectability."[7]

My investigation builds on the work of these pioneering scholars but broadens its scope in two ways. First, I trace sporting culture's origins back to the mid-eighteenth century, offering a more detailed narrative of its rise before the emergence of the nineteenth-century forms that have received more attention. The evidence presented below suggests that the discourses, behaviors, and even the much-studied impresarios of the mid-nineteenth century, such as P. T. Barnum, mark the end of sporting culture's formative period rather than its beginning.[8] Second, this project examines the evolving structure of several public sporting events, instead of focusing on the sex trade and the discourses that described participation in it. By combining research in published sources, diaries, and court records with an examination of financial accounts, business correspondence, and architectural evidence, I put the organization of sporting culture in dialogue with reports of experiencing it in order to deepen our view of its breadth, evolution, and internal tensions.

The book's organization reflects this effort to interrogate the relationship between producing and participating in sporting culture. The narrative is broken down into three chronological units, divided by major shifts in the financing and staging of sporting events. These shifts did not happen at the same time or pace in all places or activities, so the units overlap a bit. Each unit features two chapters. The first focuses on the production of activities in a given era, and the second concentrates on the experiences of participants in that era. The resulting story line reveals how the plans of producers (elite investors, professional managers, and performers) were constantly challenged and appropriated by ordinary participants.[9] In turn, these challenges and appropriations drove producers to adjust their plans in an effort to keep control. Each major wave of adjustment initiated new modes of financing and staging events, which only renewed various participants' efforts to challenge and appropriate them.

The focus on sporting culture's negotiated nature adds breadth to the argument that its origins lie in the urge to resist emerging Victorian sexual mores. The evidence presented here shows men engaging in sporting culture to try to turn a profit, make valuable friends, and secure political power. In sum, the narrative that follows both reiterates and then goes beyond sporting culture's promotion of virility to outline its impact on the wider economic and political culture of early America. More than just the basis for a fringe subculture, public sporting activities helped establish modes of democracy and capitalism that became cornerstones of mainstream American life.[10]

Exploring this bigger history of sporting culture requires addressing a large swath of chronological and geographic territory. The narrative distributes coverage evenly over time, but the exigencies of research led me to draw evidence more heavily from the major Anglo-American cities that existed throughout the period from 1750 to 1860. Consequently, examples from Boston, New York, Philadelphia, and Charleston dominate, while evidence from Richmond, New Orleans, and rural spots from upstate New York to western Kentucky appear periodically to help illustrate both local variations and the generally similar evolution of sporting culture's core traits.

Like geographic locations, the full range of sporting culture activities simply cannot be covered in a single book. So, as with cities, events that left behind more evidence receive the greatest attention. This means an emphasis on horse racing, theatre, and tavern games such as billiards, cards, and backgammon. I discuss prostitution and sexual behavior as they relate to these activities. However, I have not covered brothels and the sex trade separately here because my intent is to complement and expand the existing literature by delving more deeply into the most common public sporting events and tying together their largely separate historiographies. Other forms of public sport, such as cockfighting, footraces, and, later, baseball and boxing, left smaller imprints on the historical record before 1860 than the three primary activities noted above. As a result, I consider them only occasionally, to help chart differences and similarities between activities over time, just as underrepresented locations help demonstrate variation and commonality from place to place. Overwhelmingly, though, the evidence exhibits more congruencies than deviations across space and different kinds of activities, so the story line privileges the evolution of an overarching Anglo-American sporting culture that was punctuated but not fractured by local, regional, and activity-specific differences.

An introduction to the concept of "sporting culture," and how this study approaches it, still leaves unexplained what, exactly, was "sporting" about a culture that encompasses several activities not considered as "sport" today. After all, modern definitions typically apply the word "sport" to "athletic competition," in contrast to "games," which are competitions not requiring athleticism. Theatre and sexual behavior typically fall outside both categories. Yet these categories are ahistoric theoretical constructions devised by anthropologists and sociologists in the middle of the twentieth century.[11] In early America, the terms "sport" and "sporting" had much more expansive meanings, some of which implicitly and even explicitly considered all these activities to be related. This period usage justifies grouping together what we might otherwise consider unrelated activities today.

To be sure, British and American dictionaries printed between 1750 and 1860 reveal the root of sport's modern meaning. Starting as a noun for "diversion" and "play" in the early part of the era, the word came to imply leisure, or "action not imposed; not work" by the mid-nineteenth century. In addition, "sport" was a verb interchangeable with "play." In this form, the word had no fewer than fifteen definitions in the 1770s, ranging from "to do anything trickish" and "to act with levity" to "contend at some game." These meanings persisted into Noah Webster's dictionaries of the 1830s, where verb forms of sport and play signified an intent "to trifle" or "to toy." Despite the variety of entries, themes of unpredictability, competition, and performance tie them together.[12]

Dictionaries provide only a cursory test of a word's meaning, but period use of the term "sport" suggests some key similarities to the themes in dictionaries. On one hand, writers referred to physical activities from skating to cockfighting to fishing as "sports," whether or not competition was involved. In contrast, billiards and card-playing were typically called "games." In this sense, the noun "sport" denoted the athleticism at the core of today's definition. Hence, there were "tumultuous sports" and "manly sports," but no "calm sports" or "female sports." These applications offer a reminder that, by the early 1800s, "sport" already was associated with a particularly masculine brand of physical performance rife with the exertion and competition proper women were supposed to avoid.[13]

On the other hand, common use of the word "sport" also referred to a quality of pleasurable uncertainty in any particular competitive event. For example, consider Maryland planter Edward Lloyd's 1772 letter to his son-in-law John Cadwalader regarding plans for an upcoming horse race:

> I shall certainly send . . . my Posthumous Mare, and the Horse I purchased from Mr. McCardy, should you make the purse 100 Guineas, Horses and Mares aged to carry ten stone, otherwise it will not be worth my while to send my chattle up, they being young, cannot have the least chance of winning. In short, if you do not fix this weight, you may make

a present of the money to Nettle, who must win easy, and of course give
the spectators little sport, which I imagine will not be very agreeable to
some of your subscribers.

Here, the word "sport" implies a degree of desirable competition. Unless Cadwalader can ensure the handicap weights Lloyd recommends, the race will
not be close, and a blowout provides "little sport." In contrast, Lloyd concluded,
"you may be afraid I will give you good sport, should you make the weights
as I have desired." Reports of nineteenth-century horse races apply the term
similarly, complaining about the "indifferent sport" of lopsided or low-quality
races and lauding the "fine sport" of well-contested events.[14]

This use of "sport" does more than describe athletic exercise or competition. It communicates a preference for the dramatic tension of uncertainty and
risk. Not surprisingly, then, "sport" and "risk" were often connected in references to gambling. In his published response to a horse racing challenge in
1763, Long Island breeder A. W. Waters declared he would race his horse only
if a certain proposed judge was a bettor and not a presiding official: "for tho'
I do not like the Man, I have no Objection to his Money, if he dare Sport it,"
Waters wrote. Likewise, actor Sol Smith recounted a steamboat card game he
observed in the 1830s, in which one player tried to revoke an escalating
wager. "'Take back your last bet,' [he] urged—'it is too much for either of us to
lose; I begin to think I have been rash—take it back and let us show our hands
for the money already down.' 'No!' said Hubbard [his opponent]—'if you mean
sporting, put up the hundred or back out and give me the money.'"[15] To "mean
sporting" and to "dare Sport" meant "to embrace risk." In fact, professional
gamblers who claimed not to cheat constantly called themselves "sportsmen"
in order to distance themselves from the term "gambler." The distinction lay
in the "sporting" willingness to accept risk and potential defeat. A "gambler"
was "a cheating gamester" who rigged contests to eliminate risk and ensure
victory because he wagered to win, not for the thrill of the competition. So,
in period use, "sport" referred to the structure of an activity as well as a more
broadly applicable relish for trying to prove oneself in unpredictable and fair
competition.[16]

At first glance, theatre might not seem to fit under either definition. Yet theatre is essentially unpredictable. Nobody knows how a live performance will
come off, or whether the audience will applaud or boo. The uncertainty was
even stronger in early America than it is now, since rules geared to silence audiences and keep actors from adjusting a playwright's lines—rules that created the sober play-going experience of today—only began to take hold at the
end of the century under investigation here. For most of the era, audiences

felt that buying a ticket to a play was just like buying a drink at a tavern or placing a wager on a card game or a horse race. In all these cases, spending or risking money purchased the right to express an opinion and pursue a good time. Accordingly, theatre-goers pelted and shouted at musicians and actors, trying to craft their version of a pleasurable experience by commanding music and lines that reflected their opinions on issues ranging from foreign policy to the power of the rich. Just as importantly, spectators of all stripes challenged each other in an effort to prevent rivals from shaping a performance they would find less enjoyable. The result was a theatre environment every bit as conducive to uncertainty, competition, and risk-taking as the ones at taverns and racetracks, right down to the riots and brawls that were common in early American playhouses. No wonder period observers thought theatre audiences "behaved as if they were in a tavern," and moral reformers figured a proponent meant "by 'a well managed theatre' the same as he would mean by a well managed horse race, a well managed gambling house and a well managed brothel." Seventeenth-century writers, including Shakespeare, had specifically called theatre a sport. Though this usage did not appear in Anglo-America, people there clearly thought that theatre, racing, and tavern games all possessed similar "sporting" qualities rooted in the enjoyment of competition and risk.[17]

Sporting Culture and Power in Early Anglo-America

Although competition and risk were central to understandings of "sport" in early Anglo-America, the formation of a sporting culture based on those elements was not inevitable. It was a purposeful choice, made largely by empowered white men, to construct sporting culture around traits that encouraged engagement within their ranks and helped to define them as a group despite internal class and ethnic divides. Crucially, the choice was not unanimous from the beginning. It was the product of prolonged negotiation across class lines in colonies where the white male population enjoyed broader enfranchisement than in England, and later periods saw them further expand their suffrage at the expense of other groups. The context of suffrage is important to note because the process of building sporting culture both reflected and served political ends.

Benjamin Henry Latrobe witnessed at first hand the political value of turning sport into a vehicle for bringing white men together. After complaining in his journal about familiarity across class lines in the Hanover Town billiard rooms, he described the behavior of one other gentleman who showed up: Meriwether Jones, his host's older brother and an active politician. Noting that "Mr. M. Jones was here in his own town and among his own constituents," Latrobe then confessed that despite his distaste for mingling across class lines, he "could not help admiring the facility with which he [Jones] adapted his manners and conversation to the understanding, habits, and tempers of the company." Naturally, Latrobe was most impressed by Jones's ability to limit his accommodation, so that his "superiority, however, in intellect, in sentiment, and in habitual gentlemanly conduct, appears even when, as one of the people, it is almost necessary to be one of the rabble." Jones drew no censure from Latrobe, though the traveler criticized other elites for similar behavior, because even Latrobe could understand why an elected official might need to "adapt his manners" and almost "be one of the rabble." As Latrobe put it in the conclusion to his journal entry, "in nothing is art so easily discovered, and so ineffectual when detected, than in condescension." By courting voters where his peers played billiards with their barefooted neighbors, Jones used sporting space and the environment it created to present himself as a refined gentleman who nevertheless was approachable and willing to engage with voters whose lives were very different from his own.[18]

Meriwether Jones was hardly alone in applying sporting culture to politics. In every period of the early American era, politicians used sporting culture as a tool for winning and rallying supporters. By the nineteenth century, sporting elements had become such core components of American electoral politics that politicians no longer "stood" for election, as they did in English parlance. They "ran" for office, and elections were described, even pictured, as races (see Figure 6.2).[19]

This metaphor, like Meriwether Jones's agile politicking, had a purpose. Both used the egalitarian atmosphere associated with white masculine sporting culture to present candidates as competitors eager to engage with fellow citizens who possessed less wealth, less refinement, and lesser connections than they did. So, if the beginning of Latrobe's journal entry describes the tavern billiard room as a place where hierarchy was challenged, its concluding portrayal of Jones illustrates how sporting events also entrenched inequalities of power among white men. Elites like Jones won support and garnered power by engaging in democratic sporting environments. Sporting culture cut both ways, informing a sense of equality and the construction of hegemony in early America, because white men crafted it into an accessible arena where they could negotiate authority among themselves. On one side, nonelite white men used sporting culture to pressure elites to accept engagement and give up exclusivity. Meriwether Jones demonstrated this concession when he "adapted his manners" to win political support. Jones's behavior illustrated what Alexis de Tocqueville observed some thirty-five years later—that wealthy and well-connected elites kept power in American democracy because the "population does not ask them for the sacrifice of their money, but of their pride."[20] Yet sporting sites were key locales not just because they encouraged this sacrifice, but also because they helped limit it to pride. For their part, elites used the democratic opportunities of sporting culture to foster the sense of a level playing field for all white men. In billiard rooms and other sporting spaces, white men's shared right to access and engage made elites seem more like other white men, and thus made differences in wealth and power seem less unnatural and more reflective of superior ability and character. The legitimating power of the sporting framework explains why leading politicians and merchants created discourses likening politics, and later business, to sport.

White men of all ranks made sport about unpredictable competition and risk-taking partly because they thought those elements would help them press each other for concessions of influence and power, and partly because the specific association of those elements with white manhood helped them limit the contest to themselves. Historians of masculinity have noted that "it was in essence the ability to face risk with equanimity that made a man's reputation" in the Anglo-American world of the eighteenth and early nineteenth centuries. Reputation, often described in terms of "honor," reflected a man's status among other men. That status affected his ability to secure friends and credit. In turn, the capacity to build expansive networks and economic wherewithal underwrote white men's claims to patriarchal authority over women, children, servants, and slaves. It was precisely because they were supposedly more rational risk-takers, capable of evaluating and successfully negotiating opportunity, that colonial and early national law concentrated political and economic rights in the hands of white men. So the pioneering scholars of "sporting culture" were right to focus on masculinity as its driving force. White men both constructed and defended their power by proving manliness in sporting settings. But sexual behavior was far from the only way they did so. Many forms of competitive risk-taking among white men—in commerce, betting, and physical challenges to prove superiority (including sexual behavior)—demonstrated and legitimated their empowerment. Indeed, refusing to participate in risk-taking, or recklessly and repeatedly losing, marked a man as no man at all but rather an "unmanned" failure and "a great loser" more akin to allegedly irrational or noncompetitive white women and African Americans. Making competition and risk the central elements of sporting culture helped white men turn it into a vehicle for demonstrating the shared masculinity that justified their privileges, encouraged negotiation within their ranks, and restricted others' full inclusion in society.[21]

The following chapters trace the process of building this sporting culture. The story begins in the early eighteenth century, when public sport consisted almost entirely of "rough" events and venues attended by all sorts of men. These settings occasioned little respect for social distinction, not unlike the billiard rooms in Hanover Town that shocked Latrobe years later. Then, in the 1750s and 1760s, the aspiring colonial elite started to sponsor new "genteel" sporting experiences designed to publicly distinguish them through more refined performances and exclusive spaces. The elite hoped these new events and venues would strengthen their ties to each other and expand their influence by impressing their presumed inferiors with their superior sophistication. As chapter 2 details, however, genteel sport inspired more resentment than deference from nonelites. So, when the Revolutionary crisis drove Patriot gentlemen to seek popular support in the late 1760s and 1770s, they distanced themselves from unpopular elitism in part by backing away from genteel sport.

Chapters 3 and 4 cover the decades after the Revolution, when wealthy and well-connected men renewed the initiative to entrench elite status through genteel sport. This time, though, they responded to previous challenges by anchoring genteel sport in profitability rather than nonremunerative sponsorship. They aimed to present themselves as a republican meritocracy who proved their worthiness as leaders by succeeding in competitive marketplaces, in contrast to the previous generation of would-be colonial aristocrats who based elite standing on birth and inheritance rather than accomplishment. Yet their profit motive quickly pushed elite investors and professional managers to choose between distinctive exclusivity and selling wider access to it at an affordable price that would maximize revenue. The demand for profit, combined with pressure from nonelite patrons who clamored for affordable access to all sporting spaces as befitting the new republic, led investors to gradually concede their hopes for deference through exclusivity. They opened up access to genteel sport while they also continued to enjoy rougher venues. The increased cross-class interaction and competition produced by this concession explains why the gatherings at Hanover Town taverns looked to Latrobe much as they would have appeared fifty years earlier, before the initial introduction of genteel sport.

However, elites soon began to apply sporting productions and discourses to broader commercial and political ends, using the democratic feel of sporting culture to help support their claims to power. First, politicians such as Jones used sporting settings to link themselves to their constituencies. Then, in the decades after Latrobe's observations, elites began to present the republic's economic and political systems as sporting grounds whose level playing fields likened them to ideal liberal marketplaces where the best men won and their apparent superiority legitimated their wealth and influence. Still, the elements of cross-class accessibility and competition required to make anything seem "sporting" pushed elites to concede claims to social authority that were not rooted in proving themselves. This negotiation, in which elites conceded exclusivity and claims to unquestioned authority in return for a culture that revered them as winners worthy of keeping economic and political power, laid the foundation for the white male republic as well as the values of capitalism that justified growing inequality within it.[22]

In the early decades of the nineteenth century, the disorderly nature of cross-class negotiation led white men to tighten restrictions on the participation of white women and African Americans. Increased accessibility brought fights to places where politeness had outlawed them in the past, as well as assertions of gentility in places previously presumed not to be genteel, and white men reacted by banding together to limit the potential for inversion. Reputable white women, who had previously seen taverns as an unfortunate necessity of travel, now risked disrepute by visiting such rough sporting spaces, and hotels sprang up as polite heterosocial alternatives. At the same time, African Americans were excluded from genteel sporting spaces. Some cities even passed laws requiring theatres to segregate or ban blacks. Enforcement was not uniform, and plenty of individuals tried to ignore these rules, but in the absence of sporting spaces clearly distinguished by differences in accessibility and behavioral norms, white men fixed others as either genteel or rough while guaranteeing for themselves the freedom and opportunity to pursue all the empowering possibilities of manhood by competing, taking risks, and making connections in both raw and refined ways.

In the 1830s and 1840s, the popularity of contentious sporting settings created a crowded sporting marketplace that ironically drove investors and professionals to find ways to reduce competition among themselves, even as they continued to provide competitive experiences for their patrons. Their solutions included consolidating ownership of sporting ventures in fewer hands and specializing their facilities to reestablish the difference between genteel and rough sporting settings. But whereas many early venues had included spaces fostering both genteel and rough sport, most now invited one or the other. In chapter 5, I argue that the specialization, accessibility, anonymity, and centralized control of this new stage in sport's development represents the beginnings of "mass culture" in America and marks the end of sporting culture's formative period. Chapter 6 then explores how this early version of mass culture produced a kind of "cultural mobility" among white men, which they translated into a "mass politics" that sealed the social boundaries of the republic by uniting white men through their unique freedom to assert themselves in the fullest range of both sporting and political settings, despite the realities of widening inequality and hardening class lines in the antebellum period.[23]

Given this outcome, sporting culture might seem like nothing more than the early republic's version of ancient Rome's circuses. But sporting culture was not a simple ruse by which investors and politicians duped the masses into accepting their power. For one thing, challenges issued in sporting spaces did not always stay there. Few men extended their gains from sporting activities into a significant rise in economic or social standing, but some did. Just as importantly, some elite men lost enough status and wealth from wagers and other sporting investments to fall out of powerful circles. More often, personal confrontations and larger-scale riots produced prosecutable assaults and even spilled into the streets, where they occasionally took on an air of outright class conflict. That sense of class conflict was almost always fleeting. It tended to dissolve into cross-class partisan action or individual encounters, because the majority of nonelite white men got what they wanted from sporting culture without resorting to class action. According to the evidence in the chapters that follow, they wanted two things. First, they wanted to protect their place in society by preventing others from challenging their empowered status as individual white men. Second, they wanted to use that shared status to prevent elites and their allies from turning class formation and economic inequality into unquestionable social hierarchy and cultural authority. Though not revolutionary, these goals also reached beyond the confines of sporting events.[24]

If realizing these goals still seems small in comparison to the power elites secured through sporting culture, it is only because today we take for granted the right to contest class and status. Early Americans did not, and the concerns they expressed about winning or losing that right represent a second reason not to view the negotiation at the heart of sporting culture as a sham. After all, if sporting confrontations meant so little, why would planter and colonial racehorse owner John Tayloe II worry so much about bowing to popular pressure to race his horses, or "sacrificing my Judgm[en]t to a parcel of boys in sport," as he put it? He could not abide the appearance of inferior men dictating his sport to him because it signaled a limitation on the authority he presumed to possess as an elite Virginia planter.[25]

For generations, men like Tayloe tried to create sporting events and venues that would grant them power without requiring them to mingle and face challenges ranging from infiltration and verbal affronts to physical assaults of thrown food or punches. Elites would not have worried about the demands of the populace, and they would have recognized projectiles of rotten produce as nothing more than sour grapes, if they had felt that accepting confrontation at a sporting event was a minor concession. Instead, they knew these challenges represented a public demand for accessibility and engagement that checked their desire for simple deference to their leadership, and so they fought to prevent them.

Meanwhile, ordinary participants constantly feared that elites might succeed in using sport to avoid challenge and expand their authority. Opponents saw nothing less than freedom and democracy at stake in elite plans to "infallibly degrade the spirit of the people by instilling into it a reverence for pride and arrogance," fostering a conviction that "you are one less noble than he who is sitting in the box above," and suggesting that a poorer man's "pleasures may be withheld without his peace and liberty suffering." Opposing exclusive seating as a vehicle for constructing an unapproachable and unquestionable elite was the goal of those who would "acknowledge no superiors, but such as by their merits and virtues can prove themselves so." From the perspective of nonelite white men who defined themselves by their right to strive, accepting the legitimacy of a wealthy elite that had to prove itself in the face of challenge was quite different from accepting the legitimacy of one so revered that it did not have to engage.[26]

The story of ordinary white men driving elites from a social order built around class toward one prioritizing race and gender is hardly new among historians, but tracing it through sporting culture draws new attention to sport's political importance and the insights it offers into broader debates over the nature and evolution of power in the early republic.[27] For example, the vast majority of histories covering specific sporting activities in this period frame them within the context of social stratification over the course of the nineteenth century, typically concluding that "interclass participation was virtually nonexistent" by the time of the Civil War.[28] In contrast, the scholars who invented the notion of "sporting culture" describe participants as a "heterogeneous mix of wealthy and poor, educated and ignorant, fashionable and ragged." The evidence presented here suggests that the "sporting culture" picture of participation in the sex trade more accurately represents public sporting events as well. Rather than securing power by building class division, sporting culture helped minimize the impact of the class divide and provided a place where "the hard work of hegemonizing" could be carried out in close quarters.[29]

This interpretation is attributable largely to a difference in sources. Most histories of public sporting activities rely on diaries and mainstream published materials such as manuals, tracts, standard newspapers, and books written by foreign travelers. The analysis below combines such evidence with an examination of financial, architectural, and court records, as well as sensational sporting guidebooks and underground newspapers known for detailing real episodes of cross-class engagement.[30] The financial evidence, partly uncovered from club and company records but largely mined by identifying individual investors and then tracking down accounts and correspondence in their personal papers, shows how producers reacted to pressure from participants by increasingly catering to the widest possible audience and gradually withdrawing their plans to minimize cross-class interaction.

Analyzing sporting space helps explain how this shift played out for participants. Venues with similar floor plans, architectural finish, and furnishings generated similar descriptions of behavior, revealing how sporting spaces established "frames" of "rough" or "genteel" experience that set the ground rules for interaction. The collapse of these distinct frames in reaction to increased accessibility in the post-Revolutionary years provides valuable context for understanding why racial and gender lines stiffened at venues in the same period: because the disintegration of the spatial order motivated white men to limit who could take advantage of it. Additionally, the reconstruction of distinct rough and genteel spaces in the antebellum years explains how historians of sport have missed the persistence of cross-class interaction: because they have relied too heavily on accounts from travelers and reformers who mistook a space's behavioral norms for a shared class background among its habitués. Considering accounts of mingling within the context of the evolution of sporting space makes clear how the power of a space to guide behavior obscured cross-class interaction if observers were not looking for it.[31]

Indeed, the persistence of sporting settings where a range of white men negotiated solidarity through risk-taking and confrontation suggests that historians have granted too much weight to the mountains of largely unheeded reform-minded literature in the nineteenth century. Relying on this literature has helped produce conclusions that exaggerate class lines at sporting events and the degree to which reform "respectability" eventually "tamed" rough sport.[32] Similarly, a fuller range of sporting culture evidence suggests that, even in the colonial period, the concept of "gentility" never successfully created the degree of distance and deference between classes that its architects desired. Overstating the influence of both gentility and respectability obscures the fight against elites' and reformers' cultural authority as well as its negotiated outcomes.[33]

Of course, vice-ridden, disrespectful, and contentious cross-class interaction was not unique to sporting culture. Gentlemen in Anglo-America complained about it almost from the moment colonization began, lamenting how common men courted by politicians during elections "become inflated and imagine themselves of great importance." Likewise, elected militia officers grew frustrated when every soldier "supposed himself equal to his commander." Affronted or aspiring "lower sorts" also turned away sheriffs attempting to prosecute them, insulted ministers whose teachings offended them, and occasionally accumulated enough money to match their superiors' dress and accoutrements.[34]

The trend only became more common after the Revolution unleashed a vibrant rhetoric of equality and, in the words of one jaded magazine editor, "gave tars and tailors a civic feast and taught the rabble that they were all viceroys." The nineteenth-century revolution in ready-made clothing multiplied the number of self-proclaimed viceroys who could afford to play the "vulgar upstart" and crash previously exclusive seating sections, not only in theatres and at racetracks, but in posh gaming houses, hotels, and stores. Far from decrying these situations, merchants across the country promised to multiply them with prices so low "every sober mechanic . . . can make as good a display, when he chooses, as what are called the upper classes."[35]

Sporting sites would have been just another set of venues sparking these kinds of remarks, were it not for the elements of freedom and choice that distinguished them. Travelers, shoppers, and pedestrians could not avoid brief contact with insouciant inferiors, and laws of various kinds limited the challenge to hierarchy in the workplace, militia, and many religious institutions in early America. But, to a greater degree than almost any other setting, sporting events were regular and unregulated gatherings of a broad public that was willfully and freely engaged. Springing from traditions of festive inversion that dated back to the holiday celebrations of medieval and early modern Europe, neither law nor tradition nor economic necessity compelled hierarchy or even attendance. If elites had refused to accept contested and egalitarian atmospheres at sporting events, the very people they wanted to impress could simply have chosen to deny them the assent they wanted by staying away. Sporting culture was a particularly important venue for securing power precisely for this reason. Winning acceptance there symbolized a willing and freely given assent, the holy grail of hegemony.[36]

Assent is the prize driving elites, and their negotiations with ordinary participants, in the following pages. The desire for it led to the construction of the white male republic and a political culture geared to mask and preserve the widening inequalities of wealth and power concomitant with the rise of capitalism. Yet because hegemony requires some degree of concession from those in power, achieving assent also required accepting challenges from outside elite circles. Those challenges first surfaced in tavern billiard rooms where poor white men refused to cede their place to their supposed betters, but the same spirit later brought challenges from the likes of Jackie Robinson and Billie Jean King. This study explains how sporting culture bred such complex and contradictory outcomes, telling the story of its emergence as a crucial battleground where the humble and the high-flown fought to define the very nature of their society, their economy, and their state.

PART ONE

The Colonial Period

CHAPTER 1

The Rise of Genteel Sport

You can get a sense of sporting culture on the British mainland in the 1760s by comparing two of the largest and best-known taverns in Charleston, one of the densest tavern markets in the colonies. Robert Dillon's two-story brick public house stood in the center of town. It had doubled as a courthouse and a theatre in the 1730s, before separate structures were built to serve those purposes. Dillon maintained the facility's prominence when he arrived thirty years later, welcoming classical music concerts, meetings of the elite jockey club and more inclusive mutual aid societies, as well as a diverse clientele of merchants, shopkeepers, and artisans looking to make deals. In sum, Dillon's tavern was a site for orderly social gatherings and business. Sometimes refined music set the tone. More often, it was a game. "There are very few there at any time but those who are playing Back Gammon," noted one guest, who likened the tavern to coffeehouses built specifically to facilitate business. Indeed, coffeehouses everywhere were particularly known for backgammon. Visitors to New York even complained about the "vile practice . . . of playing back-gammon (a noise I detest), which is going forward in the public coffee-houses from morning till night, frequently ten or a dozen tables at a time."[1]

Nobody confused Benjamin Backhouse's waterfront tavern for a coffeehouse. It was mostly made of wood and was built in so many stages that its façade looked far less symmetrical than Dillon's. Like Dillon, Backhouse hosted performances—they just tended toward the carnivalesque showman who promised to "eat red hot coals out of a chaffing dish" instead of classical music. Clubs came to Backhouse's, too, but rather than mutual aid societies it was the Beef Steak Club, patterned after a namesake in London which brought together artists, actors, and gentlemen committed to self-indulgence. The local Sons of Liberty were regular guests as well, mixing powerful propertied men, local artisans, and sailors whose shared opposition to British trade policies occasionally led to threats and violence. Such gatherings led Backhouse's critics to call the place "The Bacchus on the Bay," linking a play on the proprietor's name to his tavern's licentious reputation.[2]

Also like Dillon, Backhouse used games to fuel the air of his tavern. He offered guests three backgammon tables, but distinguished his place by having one of the city's ten public billiard tables. Backgammon was played in pairs on small boards, fostering personal relationships. In comparison, twelve-foot-by-six-foot billiard tables required their own rooms, where anyone could come in to watch, comment, and wager. Billiards' ability to create impromptu

Figure 1.1.   Like Latrobe's watercolor sixteen years later, this study for a later print shows the social mix common to tavern billiard tables in Britain and America. The centerpiece is a poorer shoeless player about to offer his more advanced cue to a higher-class player using a traditional "mace." Spectators of various middling and upper ranks gamble on the match and appear amused by the social inversion of the moment. *Tavern Billiard Match*, William Henry Bunbury (1781), ink on paper, courtesy The Lewis Walpole Museum, Yale University.

communities of diverse men who gambled, argued, and competed with each other was well known enough to prompt satirical drawings and prints in Britain (see figure 1.1).

Games, then, were a valuable tool in a crowded tavern market. Backgammon helped Dillon craft an emphasis on exclusive groups and polite, if noisy, sociability while Backhouse's billiard table encouraged a more inclusive and aggressive environment.

Yet the differences between taverns had not always been so great. In fact, the effort to create such distinctions in the middle decades of the eighteenth century significantly altered not just tavern life but all of colonial sporting culture. The seminal change came after land speculators and merchants at the top of colonial society had accumulated and concentrated wealth as never before in the mid-1700s, thanks to booming trade with the Caribbean, imperial war supply contracts, and a spike in immigration that drove demand for land. Putting some of their burgeoning resources into new sporting venues and events was one way they hoped to forge a more distinctive, exclusive, unified, and powerful colonial elite. Dillon's tavern exemplified this movement.[3]

By the time Dillon took over the facility in 1762, taverns like his had multiplied up and down the Atlantic seaboard, alongside a host of new purpose-built playhouses and racetracks. A rift widened between these refined venues and rougher ones like Backhouse's. Both settings persistently attracted a diverse range of white male patrons. What differed was how those patrons interacted and behaved in each type of sporting setting. Exploring how and why elite colonists aimed to construct distinction through sport unveils the alluring opportunities they saw to craft class, profit, and political support through sporting culture. It also reveals the seeds of the tension between hierarchy and democracy that drove the development of sporting culture over the course of the ensuing century.

"But We Were Interrupted"

Dr. Alexander Hamilton experienced colonial taverns before the distance between Dillon's and Backhouse's widened in the 1750s and 1760s. The son of an administrator at Edinburgh University in Scotland, Hamilton followed his brother to Annapolis, Maryland, in 1739, at the age of twenty-eight. There, the erudite apothecary quickly won acclaim for his physick and his wit, and parlayed his popularity into an elected seat on the city council in 1743. The following summer, Hamilton went north to escape the Chesapeake humidity, which he blamed for a spate of illnesses. Like most colonists, he visited taverns regularly while traveling. But unlike most, he kept a detailed diary, which now provides a droll assessment of public houses from Maryland to Maine before the era of Dillon and Backhouse.[4]

For the most part, Hamilton did not enjoy colonial taverns. He particularly disliked the unavoidable interaction with people he deemed inferior. In Philadelphia, just a week into his journey, he "observed several comical grotesque Phizzes at the inn where I put up." Hamilton correlated his company's ugliness with their intelligence, claiming they "talked there upon all subjects, politicks, religion, and trade, some tolerably well but most of them ignorantly." He reacted by distancing himself from the crowd. When he "discovered two or three chaps very inquisitive," he refused to respond and they ended up "asking my boy [Hamilton's slave Dromo] who I was, whence come, and whither bound."[5]

Two days later, Hamilton "dined at a tavern with a very mixed company of different nations and religions." Though "mixed," the company this time was not at a level where they could be passed off to Dromo, so Hamilton could not escape when "a gentleman that sat next to me proposed a number of questions concerning Maryland." Instead, he deflected. "In my replies I was reserved," the doctor wrote, "pretending to know little of the matter, as being a person whose business did not lie in the way of history and politicks." This was Hamilton's way. When confronted by "mixed company" in a tavern, he refused to engage and held his tongue until he could safely mock the group in his diary.[6]

Men from all sorts of backgrounds offended him. In New York a few months later, Hamilton left the city's first coffeehouse, "where were some rattling fellows playing at backgammon," and went with a friend to a tavern "to sup and have some chat snugly by ourselves." Once again, the inveterate familiarity of tavern life intruded. "We were interrupted by three young rakes who bounced in upon us, and then the conversation turned from a grave to a wanton strain," Hamilton rued. A "rake" was a young man of means, often from a reputable family, who enjoyed disreputable behavior. Once the rakes arrived, "there was nothing talked of but ladys and lovers, and a good deal of polite smutt." After dinner, Hamilton and his friend "went home like two philosophers, and the others went a whoring," but at the tavern there was no avoiding unwanted company.[7]

Hamilton could be social. He just reserved his geniality for exclusive settings in which he trusted and respected his companions. For instance, after his interfaith dinner at the Philadelphia tavern, he went to the town's coffeehouse and met an eminent local doctor who introduced him into a private club. The group spent the evening making fun of Cervantes, and Hamilton reported that the "conversation was entertaining." Select meetings of educated wits received rave reviews.[8]

What Hamilton disliked was mingling with people not like him. But no traveler could completely restrict tavern visits to club meetings, and social interaction with all sorts of people was a staple of tavern life everywhere in the colonies. Even The Corner, as Dillon's place was known before he arrived, hosted "Grotesque Characters." In supposedly puritanical Boston, too, reporters complained that "Gentlemen of Honor, Probity, Temperance, &c." could not evade "the Society they meet with" at taverns, which included "Sots and Tiplers, Reeling and Spewing on either side."[9] Throughout the early eighteenth century, town officials from Massachusetts to Virginia found themselves confronted by, and sometimes came to blows with, citizens who refused to defer to them inside taverns.[10] Contention crossed racial lines, too. Authorities in New York blamed interracial mingling at taverns for fomenting a slave rebellion plot in 1741, and officials everywhere feared a black population invigorated by the sense of challenge promoted by taverns. As a result, almost every colony banned tavernkeepers from serving slaves alcohol or allowing whites and blacks to gamble together at their establishments. The repeated passage of these regulations alludes to their frequent evasion, which underscores the broad popular understanding of taverns as places for contest across social lines.[11]

No tavern could guarantee the social selectivity and order Hamilton desired because colonial legislatures fixed the prices of tavern food, drink, and lodging at affordable rates in an effort to facilitate travel and trade. In addition, most colonial governments viewed tavern licensing as a kind of poor relief, especially for widows. Permitting indigent applicants to run a tavern was far cheaper than providing them with almshouse care. A market flooded by liberal licensing and constrained by price regulations created intense competition and narrow profit margins. Of course, all taverns were not equal. Bigger and better-appointed public houses often enjoyed prominent reputations. But keepers of small taverns could carve out niche markets among ethnic or occupational groups and take patrons away from larger establishments, which needed more income to meet higher operating costs. In this environment, no tavernkeeper could afford to turn away patrons of any rank. Hamilton discovered this fact when one publican saw he was "uneasy" around a gaggle of inebriated, foul-mouthed guests. The proprietor gave him a "trite apology," saying "that indeed he did not care to have such disorderly fellows come about his house," but "'Alas, sir!' added he, 'we that entertain travellers must strive to oblige everybody, for it is our daily bread.'"[12]

Yet men like Hamilton dominated government offices in every colony. Why did these powerful men allow taverns to become such cauldrons of cross-class commotion? There are two reasons. First, colonial taverns legally existed to support the local economy. Colonial assemblies and city councils were loaded with merchants and planters deeply interested in promoting trade, and in the absence of Europe's large exchanges and guildhalls, they turned to taverns to create centers for hiring and dealing both among locals and with "strangers" from out of town. Though local officials bewailed public drunkenness, they generally agreed to keep taverns accessible rather than alter them and risk losing the benefits derived from places that provided centers for business and a cost-efficient form of poor relief.[13]

Second, taverns presented powerful men with a setting where they could entrench their status and power through conspicuous public display. In a public room, or even marching through that room to a private club meeting upstairs, these men advertised their exclusive rank to the wider tavern community through their rich apparel and polite manner of sharing "the friendly glass." Hamilton thought club men undermined these claims when they began "to drink stoutly" and "talk bawdy," so the decorous doctor typically withdrew from conversation or walked out when even club gatherings headed in this direction.[14] Sometimes, however, drunkenness could yield positive results for aspiring leaders. In mixed company with the militia units they headed, or when campaigning for political support, savvy elites "treated" their inferiors with rounds of drinks shared alongside them. The frequency of this practice led John Adams to complain in 1760 that taverns had become "the Nurseries of our Legislators," and moral opponents everywhere urged that "We should not make our Publick Choice the Recompense of Private Favours from our Neighbours . . . nor may we exchange our Birth-right (and that of our Posterity too) for a Mess of Pottage, a Feast, or a Drinking Bout." But despite persistent arguments against "intoxicating the People to influence their Voices," those who rejected the practice invariably lost elections to those who embraced it. Simply put, most poorer men refused to support politicians who appeared distant or snobby by refusing to engage at taverns. So, successful politicians had a reason besides fostering business and providing welfare to preserve the inclusive nature of tavern society.[15]

The economic and political benefits of taverns stemmed from their roles as places where men bonded through displays that declared their shared claims to masculine power. Long before public houses became explicit venues for political campaigning, they hosted heavy drinking and prostitution, which symbolized men's physical and economic prowess. Association with these two activities kept most reputable women away from taverns in the sixteenth and seventeenth centuries, as Europeans defined proper womanhood in opposition to such behavior.[16] By the mid-eighteenth century, the addition of business and electioneering to the tavern experience only bolstered the tavern's function as a place where men announced their manhood, since English law had slowly entrenched men as the formal economic and political agents for their families. To be sure, some men had more power and wealth than others, but the attraction of the tavern was that it provided a place where all men could announce their inclusion in the community of empowered masculinity by engaging in manly behavior, regardless of their wealth or connections. In these settings, contesting the authority of a haughty magistrate, supporting a favorite candidate, sizing up an economic opportunity, indulging in drink, or competing against other men in some kind of game all announced a rough equality among the men who participated, even if that equality did not extend beyond the walls of the tavern.[17] Indeed, colonial tavern-goers announced their manhood by laying wagers on all sorts of tavern behavior, loading tests of physical masculinity with the extra heft of manly economic risk-taking. In Philadelphia alone, one man accepted "a wager to smoke above one hundred pipes in one day," and another bet on his ability to drink twelve pints of alcoholic cider in thirty minutes. That both men won their bets, but the first went to jail for gambling and the second died before leaving the tavern, says something about the value placed on proving manhood through tavern contests in eighteenth-century British America.[18]

This world of challenge consternated men like Hamilton, who lamented the presumptive inquiries and brawny competition it generated. The good doctor decried the common tavern "opinion that a man could not have a more sociable quality or endowment than to be able to pour down seas of liquor and remain unconquered, while others sank under the table." Nor was he the only one to feel the pressure to prove manhood by drinking heavily. Decades earlier, visiting Frenchman Durand of Dauphine had been astonished by the quantities his hosts expected him to swallow. "When they were not intoxicated they usually let me drink in my own way, & generally I just kissed the glass," he reported, "but when they were drunk they would have me drink at their will." On occasion, he even claimed he was "forced" to drink. Failing to meet expectations never jeopardized Durand's or Hamilton's overall standing in society. They possessed wealth, connections, and an etiquette that preserved their position among fellow elites. Still, tavern culture unnerved them because its less refined conception of manhood demonstrated the ways in which they were not superior.[19]

The centrality of raw, manly confrontation and competition at taverns explains why they were nurseries for games and sporting culture. On the most superficial level, sporting amenities were part of a publican's business strategy to attract patrons and lengthen their visits. But sport worked well in this role precisely because it fit the aggressive and competitive environment that had drawn men to taverns for centuries. As a result, well before the eighteenth century, taverns offered a range of games and sports. Cards and dice were universal, with draughts (checkers), ninepins, lawn bowling, and quoits (a game like horseshoes) widely available. Violent blood sports such as cockfighting and baiting also were staged at public houses throughout British America. Even when religious moralists in northern colonies such as Massachusetts and Pennsylvania explicitly outlawed some of these activities, regular updates "for the more Effectual Suppressing and Preventing" of them signals their persistence. So, while laws differed regionally, sport's role in contributing to the tavern's competitive fraternity did not.[20]

Although some elites strengthened their position by fully engaging in tavern masculinity, even men of this strain joined those like Hamilton in yearning for the option to sometimes prove superiority by holding themselves above mingling with their perceived inferiors. By the time of Hamilton's journey in 1744, his peers already were fashioning such opportunities through clubs as well as new forms of sport that would let them display the competitiveness of tavern manhood within a more refined and exclusive vision of masculinity. England had seen an explosion of such sport in the wake of the 1660 Restoration and the subsequent relaxation of restrictive Puritan laws. For instance, neither backgammon nor billiards were new in this era, but both became more prevalent among the restored aristocracy, who adapted them to expensively crafted boards and tables and saw them as markers of refinement in contrast to older tavern sports. These fashionable games first appeared in wealthy colonists' homes in the early eighteenth century. By the 1740s, more and more tavernkeepers supplied them in hopes of attracting lucrative clienteles or at least fostering more polite behavior from everyone.[21]

The difference between Dillon's and Backhouse's taverns makes clear that these games could help create distinct environments, but not always in the way tavernkeepers or aspiring elites intended. The case of billiards illustrates this point. Originally, billiards was not played with the cues used today. Players struck the balls with a shuffleboard-like "mace" that kept them from touching the pricy felted cloth on the table (see figure 1.2). In fact, the game's early rules forbid contact with the cloth, emphasizing delicacy and respect for the material. "This is a cleanly pastime," one manual explained, and so "Laws and Orders [are] made against lolling slovenly Players, that by their Forfeitures they may be reduced to regularity and decency." However, when the game took root in taverns, the competitive cross-class community that gathered there under-

TROISIÈME APPARTEMENT

FIGURE 1.2. *Troisième Appartement*, Antoine Trouvain (Paris, 1694), engraving on paper, © 2017 Museum of Fine Arts, Boston.

mined the goal of distinctive refinement. Victory soon outweighed courtesy, as players started using the narrower tip of the mace's handle to impart greater spin on the ball, and they began to lean over the table in order to shoot better with this new "Qu." Confrontations, arguments, and even assaults over disputed play soon marred the game's reputation in public houses and banished it to large but less reputable taverns—Backhouse's rather than Dillon's.[22]

Backgammon more successfully fulfilled its original intent. The game invited a detached and rational analysis of odds without reference to a player's physical ability. Its smaller equipment also fit on a tabletop, limiting spectatorship and permitting greater selectivity in opponents. As a result, there is little evidence of explosive arguments or violence over backgammon games, and period commentators clearly linked the game to the busy but businesslike air of coffeehouses. Considering that Hamilton had not correlated preexisting distinctions in taverns' size, finish, and amenities to significant differences in behavior, the rise of games such as billiards and backgammon appears to have played a crucial role in constructing the divergence patrons knew by the time Dillon and Backhouse entered the business.

Dr. Hamilton took his trip just before these differences began to crystallize. Upscale taverns and coffeehouses offered better food, finer tableware, and backgammon instead of billiards, but the risk of unseemly confrontation remained. Even ten years later, the keeper of a well-reputed Philadelphia tavern told a traveler not unlike Hamilton that "we are apprehensive it may not be so pleasing to thee to continue in a Publick House so hurried as ours sometimes is, tho' we do believe ours is not the worst of the sort." Such apologies came less and less from the keepers of upscale taverns in the 1760s, as they could virtually guarantee a more "pleasing" atmosphere. Unfortunately for Hamilton, his death in 1756 meant that he did not live to enjoy the firmer distinctions he so desired. For his peers, however, sport became an increasingly central tool for creating distinction, and not just at taverns.[23]

Building Genteel Sport

The same economic growth that swelled the number of backgammon boards and billiard tables also fueled a building spree in new sporting venues. Between 1750 and 1775, the five largest colonial towns raised at least eight new theatres, six new racecourses, and dozens of posh new taverns and coffeehouses. The high-end public houses looked like Dillon's. They were either built from scratch or converted from elegant mansions into enormous facilities with "12 fireplaces, 2 dancing rooms, and eight other good rooms." At the same time, theatres moved from abandoned warehouses and back rooms in taverns into two-story, three-thousand-square-foot playhouses replete with green rooms, permanent stages, and storage space for scenery. Jockey clubs also multiplied, setting up permanent looped racecourses that replaced old quarter-mile straightaways laid out by farmers on their land or by tavernkeepers on public roads.[24]

The wealthy funders of these facilities equipped them with distinctive spaces that literally elevated selected spectators over the masses without entirely removing them from public space. The new high-end taverns featured more private rooms upstairs and behind public rooms, while other types of venues offered less reclusive yet still exclusive spaces. Theatres, for example, included box seats. They hung at eye level to the stage, looked down on ground-floor "pit" seats, and—unlike the cheap "gallery" seats above or behind them—boxes stood low and forward enough for everyone in the theatre to see who sat there. Several playhouses granted box patrons even more attention by having them walk across the stage to get to their seats. The social value of these prime perches warranted the highest ticket prices, usually seven and one-half shillings, just over half of a laborer's typical weekly income. Racecourse stands functioned similarly. Originally developed to isolate judges and give them a better view, mid-century colonial jockey clubs followed English precedent and authorized additional stands "to accommodate Gentlemen and Ladies." The early examples were simple wooden "scaffolds" with stairs leading up to a covered platform. Like theatre boxes, they provided a better view and made occupants visible to attendees on the ground-level "concourse." The platforms also created additional secluded spaces beneath their elevated floors, where jockey club members met for exclusive meals on race days.[25]

The new venues reflected a larger change in the organization of sport. Previously, the majority of stage drama in British America had been "acted by some of the Gentlemen," usually military officers and elite young men enrolled at colleges. Likewise, owners or their younger relatives had jockeyed horses in competition. However, the new theatres and racecourses were accompanied by the rise of professional performers. Elite men backed these pros, and withdrew themselves into less exposed roles as judges, privileged spectators, and financiers of activities requiring much more investment and planning. As the leader of one newly arrived professional acting company from England put it, "a Journey by sea and land five hundred Miles is not undertaken without Money."[26]

The transformation of horse racing demonstrates how the expensive changes to sport involved the structure of the activity, not just the space that housed it. Until the 1740s, colonial racehorses were "quarter horses," named for the quarter-mile straightaways they sprinted in competition. These animals did not differ materially from the common horses predominant among the general population. Virtually all horses in seventeenth-century British America descended in one way or another from the stocky and powerful Irish hobby horse. As a result, craftsmen and small farmers could possess animals fast enough to challenge wealthy men's quarter horses. Into the early eighteenth century, richer men tried to exclude their poorer neighbors through steep wagers, but they could not resist the occasional urge to prove their superiority in direct competition against supposed inferiors. They also failed to prevent lesser men from racing their horses against each other, despite laws that set property minimums for entrants and court rulings that declared horse racing "a sport only for gentlemen."[27]

In the 1740s, wealthy men turned to the thoroughbred to successfully distinguish their horses and their racing. The result of crossing hobby horses with Near Eastern stallions in the late seventeenth century, thoroughbreds were taller, leaner, and renowned for endurance rather than explosive sprinting.

Following the model set by the English aristocrats who first developed the breed, colonial thoroughbred owners established looped courses and four-mile races to appropriately challenge their new steeds. More importantly, the small number of Near Eastern imports kept thoroughbred prices too high for middling and poorer colonists. By the 1750s, an expensive breed running longer races at more substantial venues had created a more exclusive form of racing. Thoroughbreds had helped wealthy men finally reduce poorer men to cheering for one of them.[28]

The men who wrought these changes to colonial sporting practices did so in an effort to express "gentility." Conceived during the Renaissance, "gentility" connoted a package of ideals intended to civilize life. Rather than determining superiority by raw power or strength, genteel men, or "gentle-men," displayed prowess through skill, wit, refined etiquette, and an expensive but not gaudy taste that set them apart from the masses. In essence, gentility privileged mental over physical ability in the hope of making life less brutal. More elaborate playhouses, scenery, costumes, and props—along with scripts "replete with wit and humour" demonstrating "purity of manners" instead of "low" physical comedy—heightened the gentility of theatrical perfor-mance, just as thoroughbreds gentrified horse racing by emphasizing endur-ance and the greater tactical possibilities of longer races over shorter dashes of pure speed. In addition, gentility encouraged heterosocial gatherings by refining brutishness out of social interaction. Believing the presence of "pure and amiable" women "polishes and sweetens that abruptness and asperity so natural to men," advocates for genteel sport combatted the overwhelmingly masculine tradition of tavern sporting culture and appealed to "Ladies and Gentlemen" in advertisements for theatre performances, thoroughbred races, and assemblies at elegant taverns.[29]

Commentaries suggest that the new genteel sport certainly appealed to as-piring gentlefolk. A British visitor to Williamsburg's theatre in 1771 referred to the experience as attending the town's "court," a comparison to the royal levees at the epicenter of genteel display. Contemporaries in Annapolis and Philadelphia more explicitly noted that "my pleasure and my surprise were therefore excited in proportion on finding performers" who were "genteel in their person and action" and "not inelegant" theatres where "the boxes are commodious and neatly decorated." Fewer diarists lauded taverns or horse races in such terms, though keepers of upscale inns clearly pandered to aspi-rants when they advertised "a genteel dinner" and explicitly referred to their establishments as "a genteel coffee room" or "that genteel and well-frequented Tavern." Philadelphia's jockey club voiced similar goals when it directed its stewards "to have the Ground in the daintiest Order" and required jockeys "each to appear in a neat Waistcoat, Cap, and Half Boots," all as a part of presenting "this noble Prospect of Sport."[30]

Genteel decorum reflected two potentially contradictory goals. On one hand, it promised to uplift all of society and make life for everyone more pleasurable and less rude. On the other hand, not everyone could afford the time and trappings required to meet genteel standards of behavior and appearance. By staging and demonstrating superior gentility at public sporting venues, would-be colonial elites intended to uplift everyone while distinguishing themselves. The end result, they hoped, would be deference, a recognition of their superiority and a willing submission to it. Certainly, sport was not the only tool used to encourage gentility and deference. Dress, homes, and landscapes all were designed with similar goals in mind in the eighteenth century. Still, the gentrification of sport is particularly noteworthy because sport previously had been connected only to a decidedly ungenteel tavern setting riddled with compromising social interaction. Genteel sports and venues aimed to keep the popular sense of accessibility and contest associated with traditional taverns, but constrain it in ways designed to build deference and limit the social risks of confrontation and competition with inferiors. Ideally, then, genteel sport would unite gentility's two goals, legitimating exclusivity and social hierarchy by earning widespread respect for having refined everyone's sporting experience.[31]

Achieving both goals required recognizing and respecting genteel performance. A coherent colonial elite would form in part by acknowledging each other's superior gentility, and in part by impressing those of lesser gentility with their superior display. Yet only a few individuals, typically those who were the most established and involved in politics, put in the time and effort required to win acknowledgment from both peers and populace. As a comparison of the sporting careers of James DeLancey Jr. and John Cadwalader makes clear, some men pursued acceptance from one group more than the other.

DeLancey was a New Yorker who inherited an understanding of sport's political utility. His father and grandfather had built and then ferociously defended the family's mercantile fortune by presenting themselves as opponents of arbitrary power. They dunned aristocratic debtors, fought taxes proposed by royal governors, contested the opinions of crown-appointed judges, and further advertised their populism through tavern politicking. Opponents warned the community of being "brib'd, or dram'd, or frolick'd, or bought, or coax'd, or threaten'd out of your Birthright (the right to vote)" by a family quickly becoming privileged in their own right. But such criticism fell on deaf ears, as voters appreciated the DeLanceys' willingness to mingle with them. The family's faction dominated the colony's elected assembly from 1740 to 1760.[32]

Given his forefathers' tactics, it is hardly surprising that James DeLancey Jr. "was all his days addicted to company and knew mankind well from the highest to the lowest orders." However, it took some time for the son to adopt his father's populist methods. Complaints about his tavern politicking are conspicuously absent from newspapers during his first run for the Assembly in 1761, an election DeLancey lost. He rebounded several years later once he embraced the old family approach. He entertained the raucous Sons of Liberty shortly after their formation in 1765, when few of his peers countenanced them. At the same time, his accounts start to show payments to men for "Collecting of Votes" and "Services during the Election," obscure and perhaps overly benign-sounding references to his modes of political persuasion, considering his brother Oliver had killed a man in a politically motivated tavern brawl and opponents claimed he "horsewhipped" voters to the polls. Tavern sporting events complemented these political "revels with low company." James staged so many cockfights that one political foe thought "Chickens yet unhatch'd shall curse D——'s Name."[33]

While James soon lost any early compunction about applying tavern sport to political ends, his taste for carousing did not make him less inclined toward gentility. His forebears' work allowed James and his brother to forgo "grubby trade" and live largely off loans and more prestigious investments in land. The brothers even sold the family's mansion in the city (fittingly, it became a high-end tavern) and built their own elegant country estates further up Manhattan Island. At home in any barroom, James' accounts nevertheless reveal at least four exclusive club dinners a week in the early 1770s, ranging from the conservative Ould Club to the modish Macaroni Club.[34]

Thoroughbred racing provided James with a way to be genteel and popular at the same time. As the only colonial member of the Jockey Club, England's preeminent and largely aristocratic racing organization, he used club contacts to import no fewer than nine full-blooded horses between 1765 and 1774. He then employed a full-time groom to oversee his racing stable, and cross-bred these imports to produce mares and stallions whose genes remain in every American racehorse today. One of his horses claimed the top purse at either Annapolis, Philadelphia, or New York—the colonies' three major race meetings—every year from 1768 to 1773.[35] His wins demonstrated superiority over his competitors, and did so in an accessible public setting filled with a range of potential political supporters. A 1773 New York newspaper report describing a ferry pilot, a merchant, and an apprentice who drowned together in the Hudson en route to a race in New Jersey indicates the breadth of male society DeLancey reached through racing. Its political value becomes even clearer in light of the fact that the major spring and fall races usually took place just weeks before elections. DeLancey's opponents castigated him for his genteel sport just as they did for his tavern cavorting, lumping together genteel and ungenteel sport when they claimed that a "Cockfighter, Horseracer, and Whoremonger" had no place in government. But though the new brand of racing excluded lower sorts in ways quarter horse racing had not, DeLancey's willingness to compete in public still recommended him over foes who avoided such settings. A mixture of rough and genteel sport helped DeLancey remain in power until the eve of the Revolution.[36]

In contrast to DeLancey, the case of Philadelphian John Cadwalader shows how aspiring gentlemen could use thoroughbred racing to earn acceptance among genteel peers without any concern for broad popular support. Cadwalader was one of Philadelphia's wealthiest men in the 1770s. He followed in the footsteps of his father, a respected local doctor who married into a family owning hundreds of acres of New Jersey farmland. His father was well enough off to provide £1,000 in start-up capital for John and his brother to enter commerce after they returned from touring Europe in 1763, but the young men struggled as the Seven Years' War ended that same year and the decline in imperial spending dragged the colonies into a recession. John only improved his circumstances in 1768, when he wedded Elizabeth Lloyd, daughter of Maryland councilman, tobacco planter, and ship owner Edward Lloyd III. Elizabeth's dowry added a plantation to John's portfolio, and her total estate worth £11,000 immediately placed the couple among the twenty richest families in Philadelphia.[37]

Within months of the wedding, Cadwalader joined the Philadelphia Jockey Club. His father-in-law raced extensively and his mother-in-law was a sister of Virginian John Tayloe II, who bred and raced on a par with DeLancey. Cadwalader also had his own reasons to pursue membership in the club, which put him in contact with top merchants, landholders, and government officials. As a newcomer to this circle, he took a more vigorous approach to membership than the club's silent majority. He actively organized match races on his in-laws' behalf, convincing members to pay funds beyond their annual dues in order to provide purses for these additional events. Such initiative led to his election as vice president of the club in 1772, a position tantamount to club leadership, since the presidency was an honorary position granted to the governor.[38]

Besides organizing the major races held for one week each spring and fall, Cadwalader bought, bred, and sold blooded horses from the Maryland plantation he acquired as part of his wife's dowry. Yet he never entered a horse of his own in a race before the Revolution. Unlike DeLancey, Cadwalader was not trying to impress the populace. He held no political office prior to 1776, nor had he run for one. His goal was inclusion in the city's most elite circles, so racing and beating peers mattered less than leading their Jockey Club. Only after the Revolutionary War, when he was an established gentleman and political leader in his own right, did he race his animals.[39]

The Business behind Genteel Sport

Whether those who invested in genteel sport prioritized political popularity or a place in the genteel elite, racehorses, courses, theatres, and elegant taverns were costly expressions of gentility. Benjamin Backhouse contracted over £300 in debts to expand his tavern, but a high-end public house built from scratch, such as Philadelphia's City Tavern, cost ten times as much. Purpose-built theatres required between £300 and £700. Racecourses were cheaper, since they usually went up on public land for which no rent was paid, but maintenance and prize purses still demanded more than £200 per year. These figures far outstripped the £50 annual rent for an average tavern at mid-century, and the cheaper price of staging plays in warehouses, animal baits at taverns, militia tournaments on open greens, or quarter horse races on public roads.[40] The roughly £300 minimum cost to build and run a genteel sporting venue for one year remained almost twice the value of the biggest annual tobacco crops, and exceeded the annual income of all but the wealthiest 5 percent of colonial merchants.[41]

To spread the burden of these costs, and to foster the genteel community the venues were designed to recognize, gentlemen pooled their resources through subscription drives that gathered pledges of financial support. Subscription efforts regularly attracted upwards of fifty signatures spanning the rosters of social clubs, philanthropic civic associations, and even rival political factions. Indeed, among the elite, only religious zeal marked the limits of inclusion, as devout Dissenters abstained.[42]

Sporting subscriptions typically were led by ambitious men on the cusp of middle age seeking to establish themselves. Twenty-nine-year-old and recently well-married John Cadwalader was only one example. He took over the vice presidency of the Philadelphia Jockey Club from thirty-year-old recently arrived Irish linen merchant Stephen Moylan. Cadwalader also oversaw the subscription for the elegant City Tavern while he led the Jockey Club. In Annapolis, leading young lawyers William Paca and Samuel Chase orchestrated the town's 1771 theatre subscription. Paca went on to become Maryland's governor and Chase earned appointment to the United States Supreme Court. But, perhaps not coincidentally, the thirty-one-year-old Paca won his first term in the colonial assembly while he led the theatre subscription, which was the first public project for the twenty-eight-year-old Chase. All of these men hailed from families of some, though not extraordinary, wealth. Genteel sporting projects offered them a proving ground where they could stake their claim to inclusion in elite society, build networks of clients and patrons, and demonstrate leadership.[43]

To accomplish these goals, ambitious subscription leaders solicited financial and social support from established gentlemen. Established gentlemen usually were older and already successful merchants, retired from trade, or crown-appointed officials. Government officers were especially important because they dispensed licenses and executed laws in favor of their pet projects. Actors could only perform "by permission" of the local governor. Likewise, the governor's membership helped the Philadelphia Jockey Club comply with a Pennsylvania law specifically forbidding horse races "without the governor's special license." Tavernkeepers, too, were more likely to receive and keep their licenses, as well as avoid prosecution for a "disorderly house," if they counted government officials among their friends. Even in the South, where there were fewer legal restrictions on sport, only government largesse and the concentration of wealthy and powerful colonists it attracted allowed the cozy capital towns of Annapolis and Williamsburg to build theatres and host races on a scale comparable to cities such as New York and Philadelphia, which were home to thousands more people.[44]

Though government officials were key participants, half of all known subscribers to genteel sporting projects were merchants, ship captains, auctioneers, retailers, and planters heavily invested in diverse commercial activities.[45] These men used sporting projects to bolster their business connections. As John Cadwalader was told when he wanted to raise some money in 1770, "Everybody will be at the Anna[polis] Races. You can there meet if any thing can be done, and put things in a proper order for business." Jockey clubs and races were such important mercantile nexuses that horse owners fronted subscriptions for business partners ranging from local planters to London merchants, using racing to strengthen their own relationships by strengthening others'.[46]

This integration of social and business networking could yield real benefits. Philadelphia theatre subscriber and hunting and fishing club leader Samuel Morris made a fortune in the Irish linen trade in the 1750s. However, in the 1770s he needed loans to cover losses incurred in trying out a new trade in grain to southern Europe. His assistance came from Levi Hollingsworth and Thomas Foxcroft, fellow sporting subscribers with whom he had not shared a business connection prior to subscribing. Merchants also cultivated clients from among their fellow subscribers. John Cadwalader purchased large quantities of wine, cloth, and sundry dry goods from fellow Jockey Club members with whom he had not dealt prior to membership.[47]

Genteel sporting subscriptions thus interlocked business and social interests, defining the genteel elite as a network of prospective trading and investment partners as much as a social cohort. Sport worked as a vehicle for vetting and admitting members to this network precisely because the aggressive opportunists at the heart of sporting projects recognized that sport and trade demanded the same appreciation for competitive striving and bold (though not reckless) risk-taking.[48] Of course, not every eager striver was admitted. The mercantile men who dominated genteel sporting subscriptions used the concept of gentility to filter applicants. In general, subscription fees were not high enough to prohibit master artisans or even journeymen from pledging. Annapolis's theatre project asked for five pounds, the Philadelphia Jockey Club required three pounds, and a subscription to Philadelphia's London Coffee House cost just one pound. But while craftsmen might join fire companies and other clubs or civic associations, upwardly mobile subscription leaders and their backers wanted genteel sport to foster more exclusive economic networks that would support the construction of a particularly mercantile genteel elite. So, with the exception of a few singularly successful and well-connected printers or brewers, occupational segregation was the norm.[49] Charleston's 1773 theatre subscription identified the target audience when it described "a catalogue already honoured with the notice of a number of the most respectable characters." Similarly, in Philadelphia, just two of the eighty-four subscribers to the Jockey Club were not merchants of some kind, government officials, lawyers, military officers, or owners of expansive agricultural estates. However, this nascent class line did not trace firm boundaries of wealth. Fully one-third of the Jockey Club's identifiable members were merchants under thirty years of age in the bottom or middle third of tax assessments. Despite a lack of wealth at the moment, these men's occupations and at least middling family backgrounds made them just the kind of young aspirants established gentlemen would admit to their circle of genteel opportunism.[50]

Andrew Orr and William Glenholme belonged to this group of young aspirants. They came to Philadelphia from Belfast in 1765, and, like most Irish merchants in town, the duo intended to specialize in the trade of American flaxseed for Irish linen. They were distressed when they arrived and found that market unprofitable. Unable to crack the dominance of leading traders already in place, such as John Nesbit, James Mease, and Samuel Morris, Orr went to Europe to scout new trading partners. The pair also added another Ulsterman, George Dunlop Jr., to their partnership in the summer of 1767. Dunlop's father was a wealthy and well-known merchant, and he boosted the partners' capital by securing over £2,000 in credit on English merchants.[51]

Apparently, Orr did not think Dunlop's capital and connections were enough. A few weeks after the new partner arrived, Orr sent a gray Irish thoroughbred named Northumberland to Philadelphia. The horse immediately elicited "a great many sayings about him," and, by extension, made the partners the talk of the town. In fact, the horse seems to have been part of a calculated plan to upstage the Ulstermen's chief rivals, all of whom participated in the city's sporting scene. Dunlop joined the Jockey Club, but Nesbit and Mease were members as well, and Morris was an avid supporter of theatre as well as a leader in the city's most exclusive hunting and fishing club. Yet none of these men ever entered a horse in a race. Seeking popular favor to heighten their visibility, the partners wanted Northumberland to help them challenge for commercial primacy.[52]

Like jockey club membership, racehorse ownership promised networking opportunities. Samuel Galloway, a Maryland plantation owner and trader in indentured and enslaved labor, used breeding access to his renowned racehorse Selim to generate and strengthen trading and political connections near his Annapolis home. Several names appear in Selim's stud records before they first appear in Galloway's account book, including Anthony Stewart, one of his biggest trading accounts in the 1770s. Orr, Dunlop, and Glenholme aimed to replicate Galloway's networking, but through racing rather than stud services. Their actions suggest that they believed racing victories could validate their reputations and produce the same connections others acquired through breeding, club membership, or marriage. Glenholme even described marriage and racehorse ownership as comparable networking strategies when he told Orr, "the Grey Horse is in good order but really costs more money to keep than a Lady would do."[53]

Cost was not the only problem. Neither Dunlop nor Glenholme knew anything about racehorse ownership. They initially relied on the groom who cared for the horse during its Atlantic crossing. But, as Dunlop later told Orr, "the damned rascal you sent over with [the horse] got drunk every day & at length gave him Mares [without our consent], so [we] were obliged to send him home." Openly admitting that "neither of us are Jockeys," Dunlop and Glenholme chose a new groom "by recommendation" from "every Bodie's opinion." "Our Friends thought us very happy in getting him," Dunlop wrote of his new employee. "He behaved very soberly & put that Horse in excellent condition. But the very hour before the Horse was to start [a race], the son of a Bitch got as drunk as a piper & was incapable of riding him. How to behave in this Dilemma, we could not think, [and] at last were resolved to [with]draw the horse from the race, but [did not], by the Entreaties & perswasions of our acquaintance who had laid considerable Betts and who said if he did not Run he would be deemed distanced by the Rules of the Turf."[54]

Dunlop's report contains two hints that the racehorse fulfilled its purpose, despite the comic debacle of its management. First, Dunlop refers to the "Friends" who recommended the second groom. Eighteenth-century philosophers and dictionaries defined "friendship" as a blend of "mutual sponsorship" and "warm affection." Of course, many men participated in genteel sport precisely to generate this mixture of economic support and social esteem. Considering that the partners only used the term twice to refer to people in America, and both cases referenced ties to Northumberland, the horse apparently helped the process of making and maintaining friends.[55]

Second, and providing further evidence of this point, the letter also describes an effort to cultivate a closer friendship from an "acquaintance who had laid considerable Betts." Explaining this effort first requires an understanding of racetrack gambling in the eighteenth century. Today's betting windows and paper tickets grant a privacy to racing bets that did not exist in the eighteenth century. Prior to the 1850s, racing wagers were public negotiations. A Virginia newspaper later recounted the process, describing how a famous owner in the early nineteenth century "paced about the field proclaiming in his firm manly voice and rapid articulation" the odds he offered on his horse: "'One hundred guineas upon the Sir Harry against the field.'" Any "taker" in the audience could reply. A taker might accept everything the proposer said, or adjust some of the terms. Then the proposer responded to the taker's offer. Negotiation went back and forth until one side quit or consented to the terms proposed by the other. A bettor accepted terms by saying, "Done!" and his opponent sealed the wager with a handshake and then repeated the phrase, saying, "And done!" Public bettors invented the phrase "Done and done!" and said it loudly, because they needed witnesses. After 1730, bets were not legally enforceable in Anglo-American courts. The only leverage to make a loser pay came from pressure applied by others who knew the bet had been made.[56]

The public nature of these bets freighted them with social demands and opportunities that differed dramatically from wagers placed on cards or backgammon, table games that required players to bet on themselves and rarely attracted significant spectatorship. In contrast, most gamblers at races and cockfights were not entered in the contest at hand. They could bet on anyone, and everyone was watching. Some gamblers simply wanted to correctly predict the winner and claim victory (and money) in public sight. Others took a more strategic approach, and used their bets to declare support for friends, publicly stating confidence in other men by betting money on them.

Virginian George Hume noted this function. "Money is so scarce, it is a rare thing to see a dollar," he wrote in 1754, "and at publick places where great monied men must bet on Cock fighters, horse races &c, ye noise is not now as it use to be—one pistol to 2 or 3 pistoles to one—it is now common to cry 2 cows & calves to one or 3 to one or sometimes 4 hogshead tob[acco] to one." Hume's phrasing makes the point clear. Even in a tight economy, great monied men *must* bet. They had no choice if they wanted to have influence. Particularly in places where waves of ambitious newcomers bombarded the ranks of the wealthy (as in Philadelphia), and in places where a small circle of established elites competed for political and economic influence (as around Hume's home in northern Virginia), public gambling presented wealthy and powerful men with a valuable means of building and sustaining networks of popular support.[57]

The setting, process, and social opportunity that distinguished these "public wagers" from other kinds of bets helps explain why the Philadelphia partners raced their horse after they had wanted to withdraw it. The bet laid by an "acquaintance," not a close "friend," represented an offer to build a friendship. The young Ulstermen had bought their racehorse to solicit just such an act. When the bettor heard about the plans for withdrawal, he quickly responded with "Entreaties and perswaisions" that convinced the partners to reverse their decision. The acquaintance explained that if Northumberland "did not Run he would be deemed distanced by the Rules of the Turf." Being "distanced" was a term describing defeat by more than a furlong—240 yards— and it was the benchmark of a shameful drubbing. A bet on a distanced horse reflected poorly on the bettor, who should have known better than to back an animal so far out of the running. Such a bet suggested recklessly seeking and supporting friends. In an economy comprised of daily decisions about extending credit to other men, a reputation for rash confidence in others was as damning as a reputation for not paying one's own debts.[58]

Since the same repercussions resulted from withdrawal and actually being distanced, the bettor thought the horse might as well attempt to salvage the reputation he had staked on it. The Ulster merchants accepted the bettor's appeal because they could ill afford to ignore large bets from acquaintances. Just as great moneyed men had to wager despite a lack of cash, Northumberland's owners had to race him despite likely defeat lest they appear selfish and untrustworthy, more concerned with saving their own face than with entering the mutual relationships capable of improving their business.

In the end, Northumberland slogged around the track to a distant last-place finish. The result probably brought some ridicule to the partners and their backers. Correspondence reveals no general expansion in local networking or any specific increase in "friends" after the race. Certainly, other factors may explain this failure, but the horse's performance did not help and may have contributed to the partners' growing isolation in Philadelphia's mercantile community. Fleeting references suggest that they felt spurned. After Dunlop died eight weeks later, Glenholme mentioned "officious persons" in Philadelphia whose "old way of pretended friendship" was ignored in favor of relying on the partners' extra-local networks.[59]

As the fallout from the horse's performance helped squelch budding connections in Philadelphia, and Dunlop's death doubled Glenholme's responsibilities for the ailing partnership, he turned away from racing and farmed out Northumberland to bolster a critical friendship in another place. Dunlop's father had introduced the partners to Waddell Cunningham, the largest flaxseed and linen trader in the colonies. By 1767, Cunningham had removed from New York to England and appointed two young Belfast-trained merchants to oversee his Manhattan business. Then Dunlop Jr. died, leaving Cunningham's men and the Philadelphia partners tied only indirectly, through Cunningham's relationship with Dunlop's father. Orr and Glenholme used Northumberland to strengthen their relationship with these men, the only American-based merchants they ever called their "friends."[60]

Cunningham's representatives apparently had a penchant for horse racing, perhaps because they, too, were young men on the make looking to develop connections in their new colonial home. The New Yorkers first helped locate and contract the riders and grooms who guided Northumberland to victory in the next year's Philadelphia Jockey Club Race. Glenholme then repaid these "good offices" by allowing the New Yorkers to enter the horse in the Long Island races—where he won again. After that, Cunningham's men oversaw the horse's care through the winter. Usually, thoroughbred owners charged a fee for letting someone else run their horse. But the partners' letters and accounts say nothing of payment. In fact, when contacted by a Philadelphian who wanted to lease the horse, the partners replied that they "have sent Northumberland to Long Island at the request of some Gentlemen" whom "we could not refuse."[61]

Cunningham's men ingratiated themselves with Glenholme and Orr by doing more than leading Northumberland to victory. The New Yorkers also granted the Philadelphia partners over £200 in credit during the winter of 1767–68, and did not press for repayment through the following winter even though the Philadelphians began to founder. By then, not even the horse's victories could win new friends for the troubled partners. Glenholme repaid small portions of the debt to the New Yorkers by purchasing goods for them in Philadelphia. As a sort of procurement agent for Cunningham's men,

Glenholme contracted many small debts to Philadelphia craftsmen and lesser merchants but kept open larger credit lines from their friends that enabled the pursuit of bigger returns in transatlantic trade. Cunningham's men did not offer this leniency in a simple exchange for control of the horse. Larger economic and social ties urged Cunningham and his lieutenants not to press for repayment. But the horse did represent the Philadelphia partners' collateral at a time when they could offer little else to demonstrate their friendship.[62]

Unfortunately for Orr and Glenholme, they needed more than one pair of friends. By the spring of 1769, the partners had defaulted on debts in both Europe and Philadelphia. Northumberland was sold at auction to satisfy creditors' demands, having provided a brief but insightful testimony on the ways in which genteel sport served practical business needs as much as social ones.[63]

"People of No Estates"

Genteel sport was also about business for people other than those funding it. The very creation of better-organized and more substantial genteel sporting venues reflected gentlemen's decisions to prioritize watching, judging, and financing over performing themselves. Specialized workers emerged to take their roles. It is not a stretch to call these workers "sporting professionals," since, like other types of "professionals," they tried to craft prestige and secure wealth and advancement by claiming a specialized skill set. But the very nature of genteel sport left sporting pros in a liminal position, from which most were unable to advance. While their jobs required close contact with genteel society and offered the allure of acclaim and even wealth, their dependence on gentlemen and public performance, as well as their itinerancy in moving from venue to venue, associated them with servants and vagabonds. As a result, sporting professionals existed in the interstices of colonial society, between the gentility and baseness, dependence and independence, and wealth and poverty that defined everyone in British America.[64]

David Douglass was perhaps the best documented sporting pro in the colonies. He managed a small acting company on Jamaica in the 1750s, having purchased a controlling share of the company after its first leader decided to return to England. Douglass then merged his company with a larger one that came to the island from the mainland in 1755, and took control of the combined group by marrying the widow of the larger company's director when he died less than a year later (as her new husband, he legally assumed control of the shares she inherited).[65]

Just how long Douglass had been a manager on Jamaica is unclear, but one of his first moves as the head of the consolidated company was decidedly untrained. Early in 1758, he brought the troupe to New York in hopes of tapping a city which had not seen professional actors for four years and which was flush with government spending amid the ongoing Seven Years' War. He no doubt envisioned his company's continued growth, and imagined applying the anticipated income from New York to forge an enormous colonial circuit covering all of British America. Yet he arrived in New York unannounced. However the theatre might abet genteel aspirations through cultivated performance, an unknown acting company's transience made its air of refinement seem like the ruse of a rootless thief who—as one newspaper put it—"steals the goose and gives the giblets in alms" before bolting to the next town. In 1753, Douglass's wife's first husband had done the same thing, arousing the same fears, and New York's officials only let the company stay after the manager pleaded "that as we are a People of no Estates, it cannot be supposed that we have a Fund sufficient to bear up against such unexpected Repulses." Without benefactors or at least ticket sales, the actors could not fund their requested departure from town.[66]

Douglass was similarly denied a license to perform in 1758. But instead of reacting by pleading, he orchestrated a thinly veiled circumvention of the ruling, opening "an Histrionic academy" in which performances were advertised as "lectures." The move only irritated city leaders more. On the verge of eviction, Douglass shifted course and prostrated himself before the local elite who controlled his company's fate. He printed a contrite public apology in the newspaper, claiming he "never once" planned "an affront on gentlemen on whom I am dependent for the only means that can save us from utter ruin." Douglass had learned an important point. Despite running their own companies, theatre managers needed friends among local authorities, most of whom wanted genteel sport to reinforce their power and not just operate as businesses bringing genteel performance to everyone.[67]

Douglass proved a quick study. When he left New York to start building the grand circuit of his dreams, he prefaced visits to new towns with published letters stating his company "humbly hope that the inhabitants will grant them their protection." The manager also cultivated overlapping networks of support up and down the entire Atlantic coast. He delivered letters between gentlemen, helping to support their vision of a trans-colonial elite while using his role as deliveryman to meet new backers who promised "to shew Every service in my power to him" and who helped him defend his own "pretentions to the name of a gentleman." In addition, he joined the Freemasons, whose meetings introduced him to even more middling and elite "brothers" in every place he performed. All these strategies enhanced his financial and political support networks as he moved through the colonies. Over the next ten years, Douglass successfully asked gentlemen in Williamsburg and Annapolis to build theatres for his company. Moreover, the contracts to build these theatres only gave subscribers a mortgage on the playhouses. Douglass owned them, and would have clear title once he repaid subscribers the amount of their subscription in free tickets. This amounted to an interest-free loan repaid in kind rather than in precious cash or bills of exchange. He later raised a theatre in Philadelphia on his own credit, without a subscription, in 1767. Shortly thereafter, he largely stopped acting and spent months traveling ahead of the company to prepare its future stops.[68]

Douglass's success bred confidence. He even began to pull back from complete statements of dependence. Where he once advertised each performer's "pleasure of waiting on as many Ladies and Gentlemen as he possibly can," he began to request "Leave to acquaint the Town that the ceremony of waiting on Ladies and Gentlemen with Bills at Benefits has been for some years laid aside in this Company." By the time he convinced gentlemen in Charleston to raise a new theatre in 1773, he was signing his contracts "David Douglass, Esq." The manager of theatrical temples to gentility was making a play to include himself in the colonies' genteel circle.[69]

Many other managers and actors were Masons, most used letters of introduction and public statements of submission to get started in a new place, and all companies performed similar material, but none equaled Douglass's success. Other troupes moved from town to town as much to flee creditors as to reach new audiences. Wherever they stopped, locals complained that "never were debts worse paid" than by this "set of idle wretches" who neglected sums owed to printers, wigmakers, and other shop owners. The theatre projects they initiated were seized by creditors or sold by disillusioned subscribers. Individual actors were regularly jailed for debt, and some ended up sleeping in playhouses.[70]

What set Douglass apart was an additional network of business partners. Besides gentlemen and Masons, Douglass worked with printers in every town where he performed. Some historians have speculated that Douglass had been a printer as a young man, before he took to the theatre. Whether this background guided him or not, he struck deals with printers who acted as ticket agents, and in return they used ticket sales to pay themselves for printing admissions and advertisements. Douglass further built on this relationship by empowering printers in every town to lease out his theatres while he was away, using the income to offset any unpaid debts left behind from his period in residence. The result was an ability to return to a city instead of being chased out by creditors.[71]

And yet, despite the unique array of networks behind him, Douglass was never financially or socially secure as long as he was tied to the theatre. Ticket sales varied from year to year and place to place, so he took personal loans from individual supporters to finance travel in America and periodic trips back to England for new performers and scenery. In 1769, he admitted that the unexpected death of "a great and honour'd Friend and Patron" resulted in "a change in our Circumstances." Financially strapped, he rushed to Philadelphia and begged for an unplanned season there, where he did not make enough money to repay his local printer, William Bradford. At the end of the season, Bradford refused "to send the Money" he had collected from ticket sales because Douglass was in arrears. The manager pleaded with him. "You are no Stranger to our very bad success this Season," he reminded the printer before he expressed his dilemma. "As I am oblig'd to carry the Company away directly to Williamsburg that I may not lose the June Court," he wrote, "and am much straitn'd for Money, you will very highly oblige me if you'll only Deduct the Bills &c. for the play out of it and . . . send me the Balance." He closed with optimism, hoping it would convince Bradford to fulfill his request. "We are getting very fast thro' our difficulties and I hope in a short Time to settle your whole acc[oun]t."[72]

No records tell whether Bradford sent the money. When Douglass arrived in Williamsburg, he received payment from his printer there, who had periodically rented out the theatre during the decade since he last visited town. Probably trusting Bradford to repay himself by leasing the Philadelphia theatre, Douglass spent the Williamsburg windfall on a carriage. Yet that purchase, too, was a momentary statement of status. He sold it before he left town for his next stop. Douglass only found stable wealth and standing when he left the theatre business. Pushed to vacate the continent as imperial tensions rose in 1774, he took his company back to Jamaica, sold his shares to his wife's son, and became a printer, eventually rising to the Governor's Council before he died in 1786. His obituary called him "a Gentleman," and he had resided on the finest street in the capital. He finished his life with the kind of wealth and standing he could only fleetingly claim while he was a sporting pro.[73]

Horse racing's professionals, grooms and jockeys, enjoyed more stability but less independence than theatre pros. In the colonial period, most jockeys doubled as grooms charged with caring for horses. The high cost of thoroughbreds in particular led gentlemen to pay well for men with the skills to strengthen and preserve them. Grooms came from England or Ireland and earned between forty and sixty pounds per year, with room and board covered by their employer. The total package was roughly equal to a plantation overseer's, and beat all but the top actors and managers, who also regularly experienced unforeseeable losses and costs from which grooms' contracts shielded them.[74]

The flip side of not having to cobble together a living from individual donors and ticket sales was that a groom depended heavily on the one gentleman who employed him. Few of those men were forced to liquidate their stables due to failure during their lifetime, so the job was usually secure until an employer died. But working for one man rendered grooms more like servants. In fact, several American owners required their grooms to wear liveried outfits like the servants of English aristocrats. Grooms brought from overseas were familiar with this kind of subservience, though it was amplified by the growing presence of slaves among the equine workforce in the late eighteenth century. Many leading owners hired grooms from the British Isles and then had them train slaves to do the job. By the 1760s, racing was remarkably integrated. Some slaves were head grooms, and horse races were one of the few genteel sporting events where whites and blacks openly competed against each other. While traveling to races and breeding sessions gave slave grooms and jockeys a greater degree of autonomy than most bondsmen, their presence also downgraded the prestige of horse work. So did the range of charlatans and runaway servants who used the guise of a traveling horseman to escape authorities and sell lame horses. The result was diminished status for white grooms and jockeys, illustrated by the colloquial use of "jockey" as an epithet for being overconfident or shady—akin to the reputation of used car salesmen today. Equine knowledge was valuable, but a career based on it was not reputable.[75]

Despite the very different conditions of their servility, both free and enslaved grooms maneuvered to improve their standing. As with theatre managers, the few who succeeded left behind more evidence than the majority who did not, and even successful stories of upward mobility highlight the persistent limits and liminality horsemen faced. John Craggs's career serves as an example. Craggs came from Yorkshire to work for Virginia planter-merchant John Tayloe II in the mid-1760s. Caring for and training horses, and even traveling back to England to identify new purchases for his employer, produced such a reputation that Tayloe's brother-in-law, Marylander Edward Lloyd III, "expressly wrote for Craggs" to help him develop his own racing stable. Tayloe sent his man to Lloyd for several months at a time, and Lloyd's horses did well.[76]

The success appears to have turned Lloyd into Craggs's primary patron. The groom soon relocated to Maryland, presumably after his contract with

Tayloe ended. He married there in 1775. However, by the end of the Revolution, Edward Lloyd III had died and his son was losing interest in racing. Craggs's response was to lease a tavern and ferry just outside of Annapolis from John H. Stone, a powerful Annapolis landowner who soon became governor of Maryland. From Stone's property, Craggs established one of the first independent racehorse training stables in America. A 1785 letter he wrote to John Cadwalader makes clear Craggs's setup. It mentions no employer and refers only to Craggs's authority, asking Cadwalader to send his own "boy" to work under Craggs's guidance. After telling Cadwalader how to prepare the horse for the trip with "Walking Exercises," and how much food he should send to feed both the horse and its groom, Craggs promised he could "Depend on me Doing Every thing in my power to make him Run." Craggs did not rent enough land from Stone to include a paddock, but he contracted with local planters to use their paddocks to host breeding sessions with other men's stud horses, so he probably did the same thing for his training stable. Though he never called himself a "gentleman" like Douglass, Craggs did buy a thoroughbred for himself on a trip to England in 1792, which constituted a step toward crossing the line between gentleman and pro.[77]

Yet Craggs did not mimic Douglass's rise in the end. He just moved from patron to patron. When Stone's fortunes turned sour in 1800, he sold the house Craggs rented. The pro relocated but no longer had his tavern or his equine business. Before the end of the year, he announced that his thoroughbred "horse will be sold cheap for cash." Whatever his gains in the 1780s and 1790s, Craggs never shed his need for a stable patron.[78]

Slave groom Austin Curtis experienced greater change by advancing from slavery to freedom. Curtis had won multiple purses and wagers for northern North Carolina planter Willie Jones, but Jones's petition to free Curtis cited "his attachment to his Country" and "his fidelity to his Master"—references to Curtis's defense of Jones's horses when other slaves ran away from a British cavalry raid during the Revolution. Again, faithful service to a stable master yielded opportunity. Yet a closer inspection of the evidence indicates the limits of Curtis's gains. For one thing, his master did not free him until 1791, almost ten years after the Revolution and after he was too old to hire himself out to ride horses. Curtis probably remained Jones's groom for the next ten years, since he had little money to go anywhere else and the rest of his family remained enslaved on Jones' plantation. The freed man slowly bought nine of his eleven children out of slavery over the ensuing years, presumably with wages and tips earned from his continued horse work. There is no suggestion that he may have left his job until Jones died in 1801 and again demonstrated his gratitude by leaving Curtis two hundred dollars, along with the use of fifty acres and a house. Whether Curtis then devoted himself to farming or kept on at the stable is unclear. He managed to accumulate at least $900 over the next eight years, which he used to buy three hundred acres before he died in 1809. He might have used that land to set up some of his freed children, or to augment the fifty acres Jones gave him to use for the rest of his life. Either way, while Jones gained his freedom and some assets in return for serving his master, it all came belatedly, kept him tied to the plantation, and thus limited his greatest gains to the final years of his life.[79]

Even white men who ran their own independent equine businesses had to know their boundaries if they wanted to thrive. Philadelphian Jacob Hiltzheimer was not a groom. The German immigrant started out as a small-time horse trader and stabler, basically running a parking lot for horses in town. Then, during the 1760s, he assumed responsibility for managing the Philadelphia Jockey Club's races. Hiltzheimer received no direct remuneration for this role. But by honestly registering and weighing participants, handling entrance fees, and maintaining the racetrack, he earned the trust of the club's members and developed a lucrative clientele. By the end of the decade, he had enlarged his urban stable. By 1780, he owned a country house, three lots in the city, and pasture along the Schuykill River. Hiltzheimer was invited to exclusive club dinners and social events, and he meticulously listed every gentleman present in his diary, surely in part to remind himself that he was no mere "jockey." However, he never applied for admission to the Jockey Club or any other genteel society. His social engagements with clients were almost always at all-male gatherings. Taken in context with daily entries describing family, infor-mal visits to close friends' houses, and leadership positions in the German community, his diary conveys his pride in attending genteel affairs with wealthy and powerful men while recognizing the limits of those friendships. Perhaps his ability to accumulate connections without presuming elite status helped lead to his eventual election as a state assemblyman.[80]

Hiltzheimer's rival, Alvero D'Ornellas, followed an opposite strategy. Ar-riving in Philadelphia with cash in hand in 1770, he immediately rented a sum-mer villa outside the city and acquired membership in local hunting and fishing clubs. D'Ornellas and Hiltzheimer both viewed sporting activities as routes to profit and status, but there was a significant difference between them. Hiltzheimer gained clients and respect by serving gentlemen. D'Ornellas tried to demonstrate his trustworthiness to clients by proving he was one of them. He fit the backhanded compliment of being a "gentleman horse jockey." He survived for only two years.[81]

Tavernkeepers, too, faced a precarious future if they did not stay on a sober middle path between roguish behavior and pretension, as the familiar cases of Robert Dillon and Benjamin Backhouse attest. Dillon entered the tavern trade after years as a successful ship captain, which allowed him to purchase his fine facility. He then solidified elite support by building on his establishment's reputation for business and genteel gatherings. Notably, he neither pressed nor defended against debt charges during his first three years in Charleston. After that, having established his reputation, he sued gentlemen for delinquent tavern bills more often than he faced charges from his own creditors, and any default charges against him came only after additional grace periods of at least a year. Early on, Dillon played the role of forgiving supplicant while he ran a genteel tavern and limited his own reputation for delinquency. Then, with his reputation in place and his business booming, he grew more aggressive and began to act like his patrons' equal. By the time the Revolution began, he had leased out his tavern, entered into a wine importing partnership, and acquired a plantation.[82]

Backhouse fared differently. First, locals knew he already had failed as a merchant in the Caribbean before immigrating to Charleston. Second, his tavern's raucous social mixing attracted some gentlemen but did nothing to improve his reputation. For these reasons, Backhouse found creditors unforgiving. He negotiated loans from gentlemen to pay for expanding the tavern after he took it over when his wife's father died in 1762, but those gentlemen, along with the craftsmen who actually did the work, brought suit as little as three days and never more than a year after Backhouse missed repayment deadlines. In contrast to Dillon, Backhouse was almost exclusively a defendant for his first four years in the tavern business. Fearing default on his loans, he and his wife kept the title to the building solely under her name to prevent it from being seized. Their fortunes only began to turn once the local Revolutionary movement created a new value for ungenteel venues in the late 1760s. This development receives more attention in the next chapter, but the Backhouses did not benefit much from it. Benjamin died just months after his first suit against a delinquent "gentleman" patron in 1767, and his wife Katherine passed away eight weeks later.[83]

As with other sporting professionals, only by facilitating gentility, pandering to elites, and seeming creditworthy could tavernkeepers get the financial and political support they needed to survive. Even then, significantly improving their circumstances generally required leaving their profession. As much as successful pros capitalized on reputations for being skilled and politic, they also needed time to plot and navigate their escape from the sporting industry. For every Douglass, Craggs, Curtis, and Dillon, dozens of fleeting references mention actors only by last name, erase the individual identity of slave jockey "boys," and advertise taverns run by men and women who, like the Backhouses, either never received the support they needed or did not live long enough to make the most of it.[84]

Nothing makes this point better than a letter from an Englishwoman named Mary Harriman to Virginia thoroughbred owner John Baylor. Baylor had brought Harriman's husband to America to be his groom, and he died less than a year later. Mary had remained in England and had since been "delivered of a Boy which is now living, with which I have struggld very much for support." She asked for her husband's back wages to help cover the costs of parenthood. Isaac Harriman's death offers a grim reminder that the rise of genteel sport in British America prompted pros and their families to take risks beyond the bets, investments, and claims to gentility that motivated the financiers of the movement.[85]

"A Public Cheat"

Not all pros aspired to gentility. Some, like Backhouse and Glenholme's groom, refused to play the role of a polite, obedient servant. Others were more conniving, achieving success while undermining gentility. Robert Gay belongs in this latter camp. Gay first appears in the *South Carolina Gazette*'s coverage of the 1769 Charleston races. He had arrived in Charleston a few months earlier to work as a groom and jockey for planter and merchant Morton Wilkinson, whose horse Noble was a heavy favorite in the premier event of the spring races. But Noble lost, apparently because Gay threw the race. "Every sportsman saw the cheat," the *Gazette* claimed. Confronted by officials immediately after the finish, Gay admitted to reining in his horse, holding it back to prevent its victory in return for a bribe of £500. Even in inflated South Carolina paper money, the bribe was worth more than a year's wages. Gay did not get to enjoy the payoff, though, as he was "committed to gaol, to take his trial at the next sessions as a public cheat."[86]

Before his trial even started, Gay told all in an effort to reduce his punishment. Authorities soon confirmed that the bribe came from Fenwicke Bull, Esq., a relative of both the acting governor and a leading local planter and racehorse owner. Bull's lineage had led to several small appointed offices in the colony and a position within its genteel elite, but for sapping the honesty from high-minded genteel sport, "this worthy Magistrate and Placeman" was stripped of his several appointments and received "the usual and proper discipline of the horse-whip," a demeaning and decidedly ungenteel punishment usually reserved for slaves.[87]

As for Gay, he was banned from racing in South Carolina. Yet a thin paper trail in records scattered along the east coast shows that he continued to conspire with gentlemen at the expense of thoroughbred racing's gentility. His first stop after leaving Charleston was none other than the Maryland farm John Cadwalader had acquired by marriage. Cadwalader's accounts show Gay employed there as a farrier, crafting horseshoes and bits, by the end of 1769. Many grooms in Britain acquired some smithing skills to make and mend basic horse equipment, and Gay must have turned to these abilities to get by. He probably eased back into jockeying by helping to train the riding horses raised on the farm, under the supervision of the aptly named head groom Oliver Gallup. Gay's skills undoubtedly impressed, for the records of his otherwise steady farrier work conspicuously vanish during the weeks of races in nearby Philadelphia, Annapolis, and Chestertown in the early 1770s.[88]

Then, in 1773, Gay's jockeying again made headlines. In the main event at Philadelphia that year, a rider named Metcalf was "deemed incapable to Ride any Horse &c over the Center Ground" racecourse ever again after he reined in his mount Nettle "within 100 yards of the Winning Post" when "he could have won the Jockey Club Purse Easy." Not only did Metcalf keep himself from winning, he slowed Nettle "directly in the way of Why Not," a hard-charging horse owned by Cadwalader's brother-in-law, Edward Lloyd IV. The congestion allowed King Herod, ridden by Robert Gay, to win. Fewer details illuminate this race than the one in South Carolina. It could be mere coincidence that Gay claimed victory in 1773 by the same method he had used to guarantee defeat in 1769. Or maybe Gay replicated the Carolina plot with the clever adjustment of having another rider commit the foul. He could have lured Metcalfe into the plan by splitting the bribe or the larger pay he received for winning. The alliance also might have drawn on racial antipathies, since Gay and Metcalf were white jockeys and a slave was aboard Why Not. One reason owners increasingly put slave jockeys on their horses was that they thought they could control slaves better than free white riders, and so reduce the likelihood of cheating. The *South Carolina Gazette* implied as much in the wake of Gay's scandal, claiming "there is great reason to suspect that the Race has not been to the Swift since white grooms have rode our horses."[89]

Whatever the origins of the scheme, Metcalf ended up banned for life from racing in Philadelphia, but Gay's victory stood. He then claimed contracts to ride James DeLancey's horses in the week's remaining featured races and won both those competitions, apparently cleanly. Having swept all three major events in Philadelphia, he then promptly disappears from John Cadwalader's farm records and reemerges on James DeLancey's payroll with a salary of more than fifty pounds a year.[90]

Robert Gay was less obedient than Craggs, Curtis, Hiltzheimer, Douglass, or Dillon. He shared their renown for outstanding ability, but also perpetrated outright fraud. Did DeLancey not know about his past? The New Yorker had close friends and family members in Charleston. He either ignored the reports or never bothered to ask.[91]

DeLancey's decision and Gay's success point to the dangers of genteel sport. Even as gentlemen intended the new sporting events of the mid-eighteenth century to craft a distinguished and unified elite, those activities inspired competition among them as well as among the pros straining to escape the limitations elites imposed on them. The potential prizes from this competition—economic, social, and political gain—led some gentlemen and pros to collaborate on bending and even breaking the rules of gentility. DeLancey's hiring of Gay prioritized victorious ends over genteel means. Such priorities contradicted the very rationale behind genteel sport, making gentility seem like a sham of conceit more than a show of substance. Invented to win deference, genteel sport turned out to have the potential to undermine it.

CHAPTER 2

A Revolution in Sporting Culture

Robert Gay was not alone in challenging genteel sport. While gentlemen were establishing new activities and venues in the 1760s, rising tensions with the British Empire led more and more colonists to question genteel sport's value as a tool for crafting social order. In Charleston, the connection between imperial concerns and genteel sport surfaced two weeks before the Stamp Act went into effect in the fall of 1765, when the town's Sons of Liberty hoisted an effigy of local stamp inspector George Saxby onto a gallows outside Dillon's tavern. The demonstrators tattooed their doll-like stamp man with a figure of the devil on his right hand and, in the spirit of a well-worn pun, they attached an impish representation of Prime Minister Lord Bute peeking out of his left boot. Notably, though, Saxby never saw the portentous display. He had anticipated intimidation and headed to the British military barracks outside of town. His absence led the Sons to conclude their demonstration by marching to Saxby's house and breaking some windows when nobody answered the door.[1]

Why did demonstrators raise the effigy at Dillon's, and not at Saxby's home or the waterfront where he eventually would debark? Because they wanted to influence everyone who frequented the high-end tavern, not just the stamp man. Far from preventing or containing dissent, the reputation of Dillon's tavern for genteel deliberation made it—or, more accurately, the street outside it—an ideal spot to merge a demonstration against imperial tax policy with a broader challenge to gentility as a means for building elite authority. True, Charleston's patriots communicated a tempered rage with their witty placement of Lord Bute, and the local patriot newspaper proudly remarked that "no outrages were committed during the whole procession, except the trifling damage done to Mr. Saxby's house." But the paper also noted that "it required great prudence, and no less exertion of influence in many to restrain them from leveling it to the ground." Leading merchant Henry Laurens, a less sympathetic reporter, described "unbounded acts of Licentiousness & at length Burglary and Robbery" committed by the demonstrators. Whatever the limits to their unruliness, the Sons clearly took elements of aggressive behavior from their base at The Bacchus and applied them to a gentlemen's home and the streets outside Dillon's polite tavern. By bringing rough sport to genteel venues, they declared their opposition both to the Stamp Act and to a genteel approach to politics that favored gentlemen.[2]

The Sons equally refused to concede authority to gentlemen who mingled with them in ungenteel haunts. Like James DeLancey in New York, Christopher Gadsden was well known in Charleston for pitching wild "Grand Barbecu" treats and associating with what another local politician called "the profanus vulgus" at bear baits and other blood sports. Yet, again like DeLancey, Gadsden was no radical. He supported the colony's first-ever slate of legislative assembly candidates from the ranks of artisans, but later opposed any violation or redistribution of loyalist property during the war and defended property requirements for voting. He liked to think that he steered the Sons toward his moderate positions by chairing their meetings at The Bacchus. However, his archrival Laurens gleefully noted his difficulty controlling the group. Its members periodically harassed people against his wishes and even mocked his leadership outright, as when Laurens reported that Gadsden once "grew very crabbed" after the rank and file called a meeting, offered no agenda for it, and then laughed at him when he "plumply took the Chair" and presumptuously tried to lead a meeting he knew nothing about.[3]

As patriots fueled resistance to British imperial authority with rhetoric encouraging free men of all ranks to be "tenacious of just liberty," affronts common at rougher taverns like The Bacchus spread to theatres, thoroughbred markets, and thoroughfares where participants could simultaneously contest British policy and the hauteur of gentlemen. Charleston was hardly the only city to witness this development. All along the Atlantic coast, demonstrators aimed partly to influence and partly to challenge the colonies' nascent genteel elite by confronting them at the sporting venues and events designed to distance them from reproach. Gentlemen only encouraged these efforts by regularly straying from the standards of gentility, making genteel status seem like a part-time construction conveniently employed to artificially elevate them. The result, as the rest of this chapter details, was that genteel sport either provoked resentment or lost its exclusivity. In reaction, patriot gentlemen in need of popular support to resist British policy retreated to the old tavern sporting culture. In 1774, Christopher Gadsden and his fellow representatives in the First Continental Congress actually banned genteel sport altogether, certifying its failure in Revolutionary America.[4]

"Turn'd Topsey-Turvey"

The steady growth of resistance to genteel sport in the 1760s and 1770s was punctuated by a handful of extreme acts. The most noted of these took place in New York in May 1766. A month earlier, a band of touring actors led by a defector from David Douglass's troupe had come to the city. The group immediately requested permission to perform from Governor Henry Moore and General Thomas Gage, who had arrived the previous November to quell local resistance to the Stamp Act. After receiving approval, they advertised their opening night in newspapers and broadside "playbills" posted around town. The company followed standard protocol, but the Stamp Act had created unusual circumstances. In a city so divided over the act as to warrant military occupation, the actors had only requested clearance from royal authorities, not resistance leaders, aggravating the local Sons of Liberty. The Sons quickly organized "a Grand meeting," where, according to British army Captain John Montresor, "some stamps as tis said found in the streets were publickly burned at the Coffeehouse together with some playbills." This description is unclear. The company may have printed their playbills on stamped paper, since they performed at the pleasure of the governor charged with upholding the Stamp Act. Or perhaps the Sons burned stamps and unstamped playbills together because both symbolized the actions of imperial officials who did not consult the general population. Either way, the bonfire outside the city's coffeehouse had the desired effect: the manager postponed the performance.[5]

The actors languished in New York for the next month, unable to make enough money to travel elsewhere. Then came news of the Stamp Act's repeal. Within forty-eight hours, the company posted fresh playbills announcing a show on May 5, carefully stating that with "the good News relative to the Repeal, it is hoped the Public has no objections to the above Performance." But the Sons of Liberty did object, for two reasons. First, initial reports of the repeal were unofficial, so the Stamp Act remained in force and the new playbills again may have been printed on the stamped paper the Sons still opposed.

Second, and perhaps more importantly, the Sons had a history of attacking exhibitions of genteel distinction. They had christened their resistance six months earlier by destroying the governor's fine carriage and a military officer's mansion. To them, premature reinstatement of the theatre was just another expression of the privileged elitism they blamed for blinding officials to the hardships caused by imperial policies.[6]

Opinions on those policies did not break cleanly along class lines anywhere in America. Nevertheless, New York's Sons of Liberty, like Charleston's, folded a reproof of gentility into their protests because it promised to help recruit patriots to the cause. By aligning Toryism with genteel aristocracy, the Sons aimed to attract not only men who were aggravated by trade or tax policy but also those angered by the steady concentration of wealth among a small cadre of New Yorkers over the previous twenty years—a cadre which then weathered the post–Seven Years' War recession better than average New Yorkers. Championing this concern also presented the Sons with a way to stay relevant even if the Stamp Act was repealed. As Montresor put it, opposition to the genteel theatre helped "prevent Their spirits to flag."[7]

Since theatre alienated rather than awed the Sons, they responded to the actors' latest announcement by spreading word "that if the play went on, the audience would meet with some disturbance from the multitude." They justified the warning by criticizing the wasteful expense of genteel sport, thinking "it highly improper that such entertainments should be exhibited at this time of public distress, when great numbers of poor people can scarce find means of subsistence, whereby many persons might be tempted to neglect their business and squander that money which is necessary to the payment of their debts and support of their families." The warning espoused protection of the poor, but implicitly cautioned the wealthy against flaunting gentility before what one gentleman called his "poor, cross, and desperate" neighbors still caught in the throes of the recession that heightened the traction of the Sons' class-based tactics.[8]

The actors apparently expected the Sons to have trouble mobilizing malcontents following the news of repeal. Perhaps at the insistence of their supporters, they ignored the threat and performed *The Twin-Rivals* as scheduled on May 5. Reports disagree about whether the Sons showed up during the opening scene of the first or second act, but when they did, "by the usual English Signal of one Candle and an Huzza on both sides, the Rivals began in earnest, and those were best off who got out first, either by jumping out of Windows or making their Way through the Doors." Montresor was not at the theatre, but he heard that the Sons threw "brick Bats, sticks, and bottles and glasses, crying out Liberty, Liberty" while they "began picking of pockets" and "stealing watches." Patriot newspapers mentioned no missiles or missing wallets, though they admitted that "a Boy unhappily had his Skull fractured, his Recovery doubtful." Their lists of the Sons' targets included "Caps, Hats, Wigs, Cardinals and Cloaks, Tails of Smocks" and "a certain He (who was to act the Part of Mrs. Mandrake) being caught in the She-Dress, was soon turn'd topsey-turvey and whipped for a considerable Distance." The evening ended with another bonfire, this time using the ransacked theatre for kindling.[9]

While opponents accused the Sons of indiscriminate theft and assault, the patriots themselves claimed to train their attack on markers of gentility: the clothes, buildings, and effeminacy they believed had seduced some local gentlemen into aloof elitism or elitist authoritarianism. By attacking the theatre and related genteel trappings, the Sons did not so much announce an intention to take power as demand that elites not allow gentility to divorce them from those of lesser means in their community.[10]

The 1766 New York theatre riot was extreme, but it was neither the first nor the last episode of dissent at colonial theatres. Four years earlier, David Douglass offered New Yorkers a small cash reward for information about "the Person who was so very rude to thro Eggs from the Gallery upon the Stage last Monday, by which the Cloaths of some Ladies and Gentlemen in the Boxes were spoiled, and the Performance, in some Measure interrupted." Such "repeated insults which some mischievous persons in the gallery have given not only to the stage but to the other parts of the audience" prompted similar complaints in Philadelphia. Just because "ruffians in the gallery . . . pay three shillings for their admittance into a public assembly," a plaintiff there wrote, "they are not, therefore, warranted to commit repeated outrages upon that part of the audience who go there really to see the play and be instructed and entertained." The new theatres were built to segregate and distinguish gentlefolk, but patrons sitting outside the boxes did not always accept that message. The Philadelphia editorialist knew why. Spectators in galleries felt entitled to express their resentment because they, too, had bought tickets. Differences in ticket price or seating section were immaterial to them. Commercial admission gave all paying customers the right to expect a good time, yet actors and theatre architecture pandered to the genteel. In response, neglected gallery-goers vented their frustration on the haughty, and did so with increasing frequency as the patriots continued to fold antielitism into their resistance rhetoric through the 1760s and 1770s. Just six weeks after the Philadelphian published his complaint in 1772, "a Number of evil disposed Persons burglariously and feloniously broke open the Gallery Door of the Theatre, tore off, and carried away the Iron Spikes which divide the Galleries from the upper Boxes." Incensed invaders completely removed the separation between the cheapest seats and the pricey boxes. Genteel elitism was under assault.[11]

Dissent in playhouses exemplified genteel sport's failure to cultivate the kind of deference its financiers desired. Such behavior did not attempt to over-throw elites' social or political power but refused to grant the distance and unquestioned authority genteel sport was designed to promote. In many ways, though, gentlemen invited this reaction. Their own behavior at genteel sporting events made gentility look like an artificial, arbitrary, and part-time distinction, rather than a natural and holistic one worthy of respect.

First, the genteel did not successfully police their distinction. Theatre man-agers tried to keep box seats exclusive by screening prospective purchasers, making them apply in person or in writing for tickets. Yet they could not prevent patrons who left the four-hour program early, or never went at all, from scalping their box seat. Stories circulated of box tickets sold for half-price, or even given "to a Negroe who attended me at Tea." Nor were theatres the only sites of this infiltration. Following the initial Philadelphia Jockey Club races, members felt compelled to employ a doorkeeper "to take Order that none but members and persons introduced by them be admitted to the Club Room." Just as theatre managers had no need to restrict box ticket sales but for unwanted purchasers, the Jockey Club would not have hired a bouncer if interlopers were not a problem.[12]

The keepers of genteel taverns and coffeehouses could not afford the en-try barriers raised at theatres and racecourses. Sailors, artisans, and merchants all met in the ground-floor public rooms of these upscale venues, along with seemingly genteel gamblers, called "sharps," who "watched for such as they apprehended might have money and had a thousand artfull ways to draw them into play." Meeting the genteel dress and etiquette requirements to get into exclusive card games, these "Gaping Pickpockets" prioritized win-ning over sociable interaction. They made play their work, becoming "Proficients so able in these illiberal Arts and Sciences as not to be out-done or over-matched." Critics thought their politeness was spurious and their approach undermined the genteel play designed to distinguish a class of superior men. Some called them "reasoning Savages" for their combi-nation of skillful calculation and uncivilized greed. The oxymoronic label underscored sharps' place as another breed of the liminal sporting pro. Like Robert Gay, they saw more opportunity in manipulating genteel play than in upholding its standards.[13]

Of course, as James DeLancey's employment of Robert Gay indicated, gen-tlemen themselves often failed to uphold the standards of genteel sport. For a more explicit example in a tavern setting, consider the dice game that took place at a Virginia public house between a scion of the prominent Carter family and the noted local gambler "Mr. Sharper, John Crain." When Crain won, Carter charged him with cheating. Professional gamblers were vulnerable to such allegations because they relied on winnings for survival. Their need for income allegedly made them risk-averse game-riggers. Meanwhile, the accusation implied Carter's honest play, which protected the young man's reputation, excused his loss, and stole a social victory from a gaming defeat. But Crain was not played so easily. He threw the charge back at Carter. Angered by an insult to his reputation from a sharp, Carter abandoned genteel decorum and leapt "to vindicate a Charackter and to do it by battle." He ended up in court on assault and battery charges.[14]

Few went as far as Carter, though plenty of gentlefolk—both men and women—transgressed the boundaries of gentility. Ladies had little choice but to visit and even stay over at taverns in places where they knew no one. George Washington and Thomas Jefferson both purchased pit tickets as often as box seats at the Williamsburg and Annapolis theatres in the early 1770s. Those theatres did not have galleries, so their pits were catchall alternatives to the genteel boxes. In fact, the decision to assert gentility through box seats appears to have had as much to do with a man's company as his desire to announce elite status. While in his twenties, Philadelphia printer Thomas Bradford sat in the pit and even the gallery so often that he felt obligated to explain a rare and expensive one-pound disbursement at the theatre in 1767, a cost almost impossible to tally without box seats. "Play cum puella," he noted in his memo book. He was on a date.[15]

Erstwhile gentlemen did not always keep themselves from behaving badly in the company of proper ladies, either. Drunkenness and fighting occurred at ostensibly polite dinners and balls just as they did at the ungenteel taverns gentlemen continued to frequent. Scottish merchant Nicholas Cresswell thought a Twelfth Night ball in Virginia "looks more like a Bacchanalian dance than one in a polite assembly." Cresswell "went home about two o'clock, but part of the company stayed, got drunk, and had a fight," he noted with disgust. After another such party, where young Virginia planter George Lee, "with great Rudeness as tho' half drunk, asked me why I would come to the Ball and neither dance nor play Cards," the ascetic and pious New Jersey–born tutor Philip Vickers Fithian linked Lee's drunken forwardness to a compromised gentility. "He was ill qualified to direct my Behaviour who made so indifferent a Figure himself," Fithian concluded. Even Massachusetts "Gentlemen" were accused by their fellow townspeople of wasting themselves "in Honour of Bacchus." Exhibitions of raw masculinity might impress the lower sorts, but not by proving gentility.[16]

Not all events invited the same likelihood of transgression or confrontation. Reports place more cross-class assaults in the North than in the South and more in taverns and theatres than at racecourses. Genteel elitism seemed more artificial in more commercial venues where access could simply be purchased, as well as in northern cities with a larger population of nouveau riche merchants as opposed to the third-generation planters who dominated the South. Still, although races were free to attend and open to the public, racing in both the North and the South did present opportunities for challenging presumption. Besides the need to block intruders from their exclusive space, the Philadelphia Jockey Club failed in its effort to raise a "Vintners Purse" funded by shopkeepers, artisans, and publicans whose businesses stood to benefit from the races. Only a handful of these middling men played their grateful role and subscribed. Club members had to complete the purse. As at theatres, the imperial crisis only multiplied such dissent. Amid the nonimportation movements of the 1760s, "the Mechanics of Charles Town" subverted the town's jockey club by organizing their own races altogether. The artisans even rigged the main event, eliminating handicaps so that a horse belonging to local tavern-keeper and saddler Thomas Nightengale easily bested a mare owned by established planter and Tory Edward Fenwick.[17]

The evolution of genteel sporting activities only abetted these challenges to gentility. The adoption of the billiard "Qu" over the old mace privileged skill over polite posture and invited players to lean on the table in ways previously called "slovenly." The crouching style of ridership developed by African American jockeys had a similar effect, introducing a more effective but less polite posture that signaled the priority of winning over manners. Many of the most commonly staged plays in the colonial theatre satirically debunked gentility as a fantasy of deceitful and foppish gentlemen who actually survived on the skills and knowledge provided by their coarse yet practical servants. Joseph Addison, one of the few popular playwrights who clung to a noble vision of gentility, bewailed these "loose Diversions of the Stage," which celebrated uncouth humor loaded with sexual innuendo. He thought it made the "mixt Crowd . . . Giddy, Lewd, and Vain." A "Gentleman contributor" in Philadelphia agreed, and urged David Douglass's company to be more "prudent in their Choice of Plays." Yet the writer then explained why his urging fell on deaf ears. Citing an example of a "prudent" play, he noted his wish "to see the House better filled whenever this justly applauded Entertainment is exhibited." Celebrations of gentility generally did not sell well. The pursuit of victory at the billiard table and the racetrack, and the need for paid attendance at the theatre, reduced the degree to which these activities could venerate gentility. Ends ultimately determined means.[18]

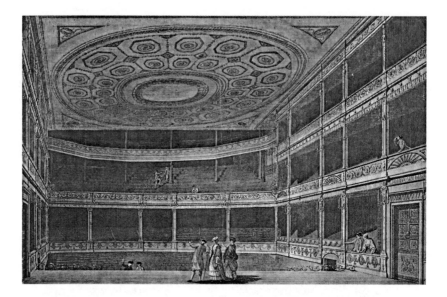

FIGURE 2.1. *Inside View of the Theatre Royal, Drury Lane*, Benedetto Pastorini (London, 1775), hand-colored etching on paper, © Victoria and Albert Museum, London.

The shortcomings of genteel sporting architecture further undercut genteel goals by failing to create an appropriate setting for refined behavior. Mid-eighteenth-century British Americans identified gentility with the Georgian style. As exemplified in mansions, churches, and government buildings, this manner featured symmetrical brick exteriors, large windows, and classically inspired ornamentation. Inside, paneled or painted walls physically excluded coarse visitors from the most genteel spaces, where fine furnishings bestowed more comfort than the back pews and entrance hall benches frequented by the ungenteel.[19]

In contrast to these standards, only the last two of the twelve known purpose-built theatres in colonial America featured a full brick exterior. Colonial playhouses were large, with later ones seating more than three hundred people, but they were not otherwise impressive. Most were more like enormous barns with clapboard siding, and, inside, the same plain hard benches with the same width and legroom in boxes, pits, and galleries. David Douglass trumpeted the installation of rough "board partitions" between boxes in his New York theatre because even this bare-bones version of a standard element in fine British theatres was rare in America. Only a row of (apparently removable) iron spikes separated the boxes from the gallery in Philadelphia, which was a far cry from the separation constructed in London theatres, as seen in figure 2.1 above.

Distinct seating sections meant less when there was little distance between them and when they were divided by an intimidating apparatus instead of refined, seemingly natural, barriers of elevated space.[20] Racecourses measured up similarly. Few included so much as a rope to mark off spectator space from the field of competition. Unlike sturdier brick "galleries" or "stands" in England, colonists called their elevated viewing spaces "scaffolds" in reference to their basic and exposed wooden frames (see figures 2.2 and 2.3). Only a few taverns, usually built to resemble or converted from mansions, met the mark. The vast majority of public houses in the colonies were common homes, with asymmetrical façades and floor plans, and rough accommodations inside (see figures 2.4 and 2.5).[21]

These architectural failings largely stemmed from the stinginess of subscribers. Several months passed between gathering subscriptions and collecting payments. By the time a deadline arrived, business failures, travel, a lack of ready cash, and plain neglect resulted in numerous defaults. Eight months into building a theatre in Annapolis, David Douglass had to ask "if the gentlemen who have neglected to pay their subscription money will be good enough to send it as soon as possible, as the sum collected is by no means sufficient to answer the necessary demands that will very soon be made." Similarly, the Philadelphia Jockey Club's officers annually issued a directive in the final weeks preceding the races, asking that "every Member shall use his utmost Endeavour to

FIGURE 2.2. *The Famous Race between Hambletonian and Diamond*, John Whessell (London, 1800), engraving on paper, courtesy British Museum.

Figure 2.3. Brick stands like the one pictured in Figure 2.2, which was built in the 1760s, did not exist in the colonies. Records of dimensions and building materials suggest that colonial "scaffolds" looked like the flimsy structure on the right in the background of Rowlandson's drawing. *York Race Ground*, Thomas Rowlandson (1816), ink and watercolor on paper, © 2017 Museum of Fine Arts, Boston.

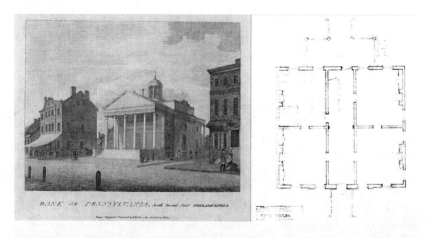

Figure 2.4. The City Tavern is located to the left of the Bank of Pennsylvania in the center of Birch's engraving. Exterior view and floor plan of City Tavern (1773), Philadelphia, hand-colored engraving by William Birch & Son (1800), and drafting by John M. Dickey (1975), courtesy Philadelphia Athenaeum.

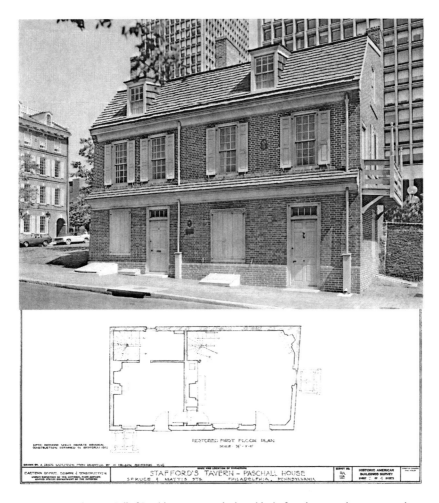

FIGURE 2.5.   The Man Full of Trouble tavern stands three blocks from its more elegant competitor in Figure 2.4, but its façade and floor plan reveal differences in scale and symmetry that allude to the less genteel tone of common taverns in the colonies. Inventories suggest that differences in furnishings reinforced these architectural discrepancies. Exterior view and floor plan of Stafford's Tavern (1759), courtesy Library of Congress, Prints & Photographs Division, Historic American Buildings Survey, PA, 51-Phila-276.

collect the annual Subscription." In the 1770s, acute delinquency from the established and aspirant ranks alike led the club to send its doorkeeper door-to-door to collect subscription fees from members. Efforts to collect pledges universally came up short, reducing the means for expressing gentility at any given event or venue.[22]

Finally, genteel sport also faced opposition from within elite ranks. Quaker leaders in Philadelphia regularly protested "horse races and other irreligious amusements" as "the most scandalous Profanation of both Sacred and Religious Obligations." Even in Charleston, austere wealthy men not unlike Henry Laurens opposed the city's succession of new theatres in language reminiscent of New Yorkers during the Stamp Act, thinking them "unfit for the present low estate of the Province," since "large sums are weekly laid out for amusements there by persons who cannot afford it." They also claimed that those who could afford attendance were bankrupted morally, inspired to "act as if religion and riches could not abide together." Debate among elites over the value of genteel sport further prevented these activities from forging a unified and respected cohort of leaders.[23]

"Not to Race It, but to Breed From"

Racing may have hosted less direct confrontation over gentility because middling and poorer spectators did not have to pay to attend races, but if racing remained relatively uncommercialized, the thoroughbred did not. Commercialization of the breed in the late 1760s and 1770s diluted the original distinction offered by thoroughbred ownership, and explains the rise in class tension at the track at least as well as the patriots' egalitarian rhetoric.

Just as importantly, the commercialization of the thoroughbred represents a shift in how gentlemen approached the economics of genteel sport, and this shift spread to other activities in later years. Initially, gentlemen had pursued profit from these events indirectly, through expanded social and business networking opportunities. The costs of staging genteel sport mattered, but the goal was to break even rather than to generate a direct profit from it. So theatre subscribers received free tickets up to the value of their subscription, which amounted to repayment of the principal without interest. Racehorse owners similarly aimed to recoup expenses, as the studbook for Samuel Galloway's champion horse Selim details. Selim cost the Maryland merchant £187 when he bought it as a yearling on three years' credit in 1761. Adding interest for those three years, plus an insurance policy on the horse, Galloway had to repay £276 in 1764. He paid this sum by charging for his stud's breeding services. Like other owners of successful racers, Galloway grossed roughly £100 per year from a select group of about twenty-five breeding clients, virtually all of whom were merchants, planters, and powerful government officials in Maryland. He used this limited breeding business to complete his payments on the horse, a year late, in 1765.[24]

Galloway could have cleared his debt sooner. Selim claimed £367 in prize money, not counting wagers, in 1762 and 1763. However, owners could never be certain of race winnings, so Galloway never planned on them and never used them to pay for the horse. Instead, winnings offset the costs of training, entering, and traveling to races, as well as entertaining in style while there. Virginian John Tayloe II followed the same strategy. When he wrote that "My chops water at the 100 G[uineas]" offered as a prize purse, and his brother-in-law Edward Lloyd III refused to race unless "you make the [handicap] weights as I have desired" and "you make the purse 100 Guineas," they were expressing their intent to treat friends at the races without draining their cash or adding to their debts. Whether they won or lost, they relied on their peers' dependable demand for exclusive breeding services to pay the fixed costs of horse purchases. Thoroughbred owners might charge a few percentage points of interest for credit on expensive equine purchases, but like other investors in colonial-era genteel sport, they basically aimed only to cover the expenses incurred in using racing to build their reputations for superiority and generosity—traits that helped them build social, business, and political networks.[25]

Although a few Long Island breeders began to alter this approach in the early 1760s, Virginian John Baylor best represents the shift toward a more commercial kind of thoroughbred ownership, because he stood at the apex of genteel society and the Chesapeake soon became the heartland of America's thoroughbred breeding industry. Baylor developed a passion for thoroughbreds while at school in England. When he returned to Virginia in 1726, he received a tobacco plantation from his father and named it Newmarket, after the English town where thoroughbred racing was invented. There he built a mansion with a floor plan unique in Virginia but common to the manor houses of England. Then he added a large stable and a private racetrack to the property. The estate consciously and obviously emulated those of England's aristocratic thoroughbred owners. Like James DeLancey, Baylor's racing may also have helped him consolidate political support. He repeatedly won election to the House of Burgesses while he raced horses in the 1740s.[26]

If racing advanced his political career, then at least Baylor got something out of it. His first known racehorse, Boro, won only one of six recorded races between 1739 and 1741. Later racers apparently fared no better, since Baylor stopped competing in the 1750s. Yet the master of Newmarket had grown disenchanted with racing, not racehorses. Baylor aimed to recoup his racing losses by breeding and selling thoroughbreds. As early as 1752, he ordered "a fine horse" from England, "not, I assure you to race it but to breed from, for our young Gentl[eme]n are grown so extravagant in the Prises of Horses that We have nothing more to doe than to show them a fine Horse & then sett our own Price on him." In switching from "the troublesome & expensive

Diversion of Raceing" to "the more certain & gainful one of breeding," Baylor took advantage of gentlemen's desire for the social rewards of thoroughbred ownership. By 1761, he claimed to "abound in fine horses" and had "sold within these two years £753 worth of horse flesh."[27]

Baylor's stables, built to reinforce aristocratic pretensions, soon turned into a commercial stud farm. Besides £753 in sales between 1759 and 1761, he collected £530 in 1763 and claimed he was owed over £3,000 at the end of 1764. These were enormous sums in an age when few Virginia planters made more than £300 a year.[28] Baylor built up his credits by selling foals born from crosses he engineered between recent imports and his own native-born descendants of earlier transatlantic purchases. When he felt he had saturated the market with a particular bloodline, he brought over a new one and bred his various mares to it. An English contact warned of the potential social repercussions from commercializing thoroughbreds, saying it "may be thought a little out of Character to have a good Horse & not try him." But Baylor had failed at racing and predicted that "the establishing of a good breed may not only prove extremely advantageous to me but to mine hereafter." For him, the economic opportunity of sales and breeding outweighed the social and political benefits of racing. Indeed, Baylor experienced his first electoral defeat in 1752, the very year he first mentioned his withdrawal from racing.[29]

In truth, Baylor's decision to maximize his stable's income potential might have sprung less from a change of heart than from his financial difficulties. By the end of the 1750s, Baylor admitted to a debt load that "frightens me." He owed thousands of pounds to British merchants who supplied fine goods for Newmarket, and his efforts to build local networks by cosigning loans for friends sank him further into debt when several of those friends failed. Baylor appears to have commercialized his equine interests as part of a broader effort to clear these obligations, an effort that also included forays into land speculation, iron production, and even wine-making.[30]

Yet his plan for a more robust thoroughbred business entailed its own risks. Baylor imported horses through the same British merchants he already owed, adding to his debt. Then he sold horses and breeding sessions on credit, so he needed his local clientele to enjoy strong harvests and good prices to ensure repayment. Moreover, paddocks, feed, and stables reduced Baylor's own tobacco acreage. He sent smaller and smaller shipments of the staple crop to his British creditors, usually in years when his horse customers did not pay well, "as every little helps," he wrote sheepishly in 1764. His creditors thought the help too little that year, and issued "a friendly admonition" asking him to reduce his requests for goods until they received more payment.[31]

In the end, Baylor's thoroughbred business did not overcome his "monstrous Debt." Tobacco and grain prices rose over the 1760s, but planters outspent their heightened income on a wide range of consumer goods. There simply was not enough tobacco or wheat to pay for it all, and there was even less cash once Parliament began to pass currency and trade restrictions in 1764. What payments were made tended to go to overseas British merchants who provided a broader range of expensive supplies than local men like Baylor who specialized in one-time purchases. Baylor's other ventures fared no better. He bequeathed a "somewhat injured" estate "burdened with encumbrances" when he died in 1772. His son liquidated the stables to satisfy his father's creditors.[32]

Despite his failure, Baylor opened up a whole new approach to thoroughbred ownership, and his peers forged ahead. Waves of nonimportation pacts in the mid-1760s, followed by the Revolution in the 1770s, diminished the number of new thoroughbred arrivals from almost ten per year between 1764 and 1766, to fewer than three each year from 1767 to 1776, and none once war broke out. By 1776, then, owners were stuck with an aging stock of thoroughbreds and a British blockade preventing new imports. Under these conditions, more and more of them took up Baylor's model and expanded on it. Advertisements and owners' studbooks chart a radical drop in thoroughbred stud fees starting in the mid-1760s. Stud fees typically had ranged from four to ten pounds before the Townshend Acts were passed in 1767. But that year, the moderately accomplished racer Partner bred for just a single pound, the imported Jolly Roger "covered" for two pounds, and John Tayloe II offered his champion, Yorick, at three and one-half pounds. These prices rose just slightly despite rampant inflation during the war years, dramatically lowering the real cost of accessing thoroughbred blood.[33]

More affordable breeding prices enlarged the breeders' clientele. Cross-referencing local tax records with breeding records indicates a swath of new customers beyond the exclusive circles of the early 1760s. In 1777, for instance, John Tayloe's Yorick served "common mares" belonging to a score of middling farmers such as William Barber, who owned a mere fifty-four acres, two slaves, two cows, one horse, and one mare, which he sent on a forty-mile trek from his home two counties away to breed to Tayloe's prized stud. Four noticeably poorer men also bred to Yorick, including Tayloe's tenant Robert Callis, an owner of two horses, but no land, no slaves, and no cows. Callis paid for the breeding session by calling in a debt owed to him by Tayloe's weaver. The weaver had no more ready cash than Callis, so he gave Tayloe a pair of wool cards. Wealthier men did not shy away from the old stud just because lower sorts gained access to him. Moore Fauntleroy, James Gordon, and

Samuel Kelsick—each a local grandee with more than thirty slaves, thirty head of cattle, and a posh carriage—had mares covered by Yorick in the same season.[34]

Yorick was not unique in serving a larger and more diverse clientele. Peyton Skipwith, one of the two richest men in Mecklenburg County, Virginia, just north of the North Carolina border, quintupled the number of normal breeding clients in the 1760s when he allowed his stud Figure to cover 156 mares at five pounds each in 1777, reaping a gross income of £535 from an assemblage of middling farmers as well as the local "storekeeper," blacksmith, and "cakeseller." Stephen Cocke of Amelia County, Virginia, surpassed Skipwith the following year, logging 180 different mare owners, and tallying £1,119 in gross proceeds. The real value of these incomes was far less due to wartime inflation, but they mark the expanded scale and customer base of an emerging thoroughbred breeding industry during the 1770s. By the 1780s, even Robert Gay, now too old to ride and working as a blacksmith in Piedmont North Carolina, brought his common mare to a thoroughbred near his home and soon owned a half-blooded horse.[35]

Sales prices dropped alongside breeding fees. For instance, John Tayloe's old stud Nonpareil sold for one hundred pounds Virginia currency in 1779, a price that would have amounted to roughly seventy-five pounds sterling—just below average—in the 1760s. Tayloe's account book reckoned the sum to be worth about five pounds sterling in the midst of the war. Poor men still could not afford this expense, but men on the fringe of planter society could. Piedmont planter Lewis Holladay typified the new cohort of owners. He stood one step down from the wealthiest men in his county, and bought his first thoroughbred horse, Liberty, from Tayloe's neighbor Robert Wormeley Carter during the war.[36]

Holladay then followed the new approach to ownership himself, attracting a breeding clientele of planters and lesser farmers, in part by specifically advertising to common husbandmen. He had his peers sign their names to "certify that the well known horse Liberty, the property of Lewis Holladay, has covered mares in our neighbourhood from the first of his [arrival], during which time he generally was approved of for geting foals well calculated for the farmer."[37] As Liberty's advertisement makes clear, thoroughbred studs no longer served only full-blooded mares or the wealthiest planters and merchants. Owners discovered they could profit by widely selling and breeding animals renowned for their endurance, which previously had marked exclusive status and wealth. But in their desire to make money off their thoroughbreds, owners reduced the breed's exclusivity, and thus its ability to distinguish an exclusive gentility.

"They Play Away and Play It All Away"

Gambling presented losers with a question not unlike the one faced by sub-scribers and thoroughbred owners: How much were they willing to pay to cre-ate exclusive gentility? The answer was uncertain because the law let bettors off the hook. Since the late seventeenth century, English common law had dis-tinguished "play debts" from other economic obligations, refusing to regard wagers as contracts and therefore denying winners the right to sue recalcitrant losers. A 1710 statute codified this practice, to the point of inviting losers to sue and recover any sums over ten pounds they already had paid. In the mid-eighteenth century, every American colony either followed this statute or com-pletely banned gambling on certain sporting activities.[38]

These regulations stemmed from anxieties seen in period newspaper re-ports, in which writers grew concerned that "gaming is now become rather the business than amusement of our persons of quality," and "that estates are now almost as frequently made over by whist and hazard as by deeds and set-tlements." High-stakes gambling threatened the elite by facilitating rapid and vast exchanges of wealth. Making wagers unrecoverable, and enabling losers to recover substantial lost bets, was intended to confine gambling to sums incapable of significantly moving a gambler up or down the economic ladder. Commentators subtly acknowledged the law's role in supporting a stable elite when they described it in genteel terms as part of a project to convert gambling from a vulgar "business" into a polite "amusement" for "persons of quality."[39]

Not all gentlemen agreed with this approach. Many men in elite circles val-ued gentility and gambling as related tools serving their business and political interests. Since "amusement" and "business" were not mutually exclusive to these men, they crafted a "gambler's code" to bypass the law. The code trans-formed gambling losses from immoral and illegal payments into "debts of honor" that were litmus tests of character. Under the code, failure to pay a lost wager became a breach of manners costing more in masculine reputation, or "honor," than it saved in money. A 1749 cockfighting manual explained how this price was paid when it ordered that "if any man lay more money than he hath, or cannot satisfy the party with whom he hath laid [it] . . . then he is to be put into a basket to be provided for that purpose and to be hanged up in that basket in some convenient place in the cockpit, that all men may know him." Throughout the eighteenth century, the decision to "plead the act" and use the law to avoid paying losses generated similar public embarrassment. It was "a plea very odious in the Eyes of Mankind," wrote one Virginia planter, whose son lost £1,893 to a sharp so well known for pillaging wealthy men that he was nicknamed "the Turk." "How to save his honour is the question," the father pondered. He concluded he "would have him by all means pay every shilling, even if it took the whole of his property, rather than forfeit his honour." His son ultimately mortgaged a plantation to pay off the debt. Refusing to conform to laws explicitly designed to turn gambling into a less threatening "amusement," gamblers preserved the wager as an exhibition of virile risk-taking by tying the esteem of "honor" to the principled payment of losses.[40]

Honor thus encompassed a blend of rough and genteel masculinity. To claim it, a man needed to prove superior manhood through bold but decorous competition. However, the two components of honor—striving for victory and orderly play—could run at crosscurrents against each other. When to abide by one element more than the other, and even whether to abide by the gambler's code at all, depended on a man's circumstances and who he was trying to impress. After all, honor, like gentility, was bestowed by observers. But because honor required the legal power to take economic risks with property, it was anchored in gender and race as much as class. As a result, middling and even poorer white men had a greater claim to it than to gentility. Elites who wanted to maximize their reputation for honor had to interact with a much wider array of white men than they did when asserting gentility, and they sometimes had to choose whether to prove honor through demonstrations of rough, results-oriented manhood or more genteel, means-oriented methods. The contrast between these two options, and gentlemen's inconsistent adherence to the latter, meant that gambling did little to help craft a coherent genteel elite.[41]

The value of honor and the range of methods for proving it explains why Robert Wormeley Carter took on a well-known sharp, and why an insult from that sharp moved him "to vindicate a Charackter and to do it by battle." Carter was a young heir who had not yet established himself. He sought to prove his standing by besting a pretentious sharp. When he lost, he first attempted to salvage his reputation by claiming he was more honest than his opponent. However, when the sharp threw his accusation of cheating back at him, Carter shelved his assertion of superior genteel character, embraced the permissive behavioral rules of common taverns, and defended his honor physically. In doing so, he illustrated how gambling, honor, and members of the colonial elite were not bound by gentility.

Even the gambler's code was not sacrosanct. Presumptive gentlemen such as William Byrd III and William Henry Drayton weighed the social penalties of violating it against the economic and political costs of sticking to it. Like John Baylor, Byrd was the scion of a leading Virginia planter family and he acquired a taste for "fashionable amusement" during his English schooling.

Also like Baylor, Byrd's sport cost him more than it won, though Byrd's various gambling losses far outweighed Baylor's racing expenses. To repay the thousands of pounds he owed on races and card and dice games during the 1740s and 1750s, Byrd milked his wife's dowry, speculated in land, and sold dozens of young slaves. Perhaps showing signs of addiction, he continued to gamble heavily despite this cost. Visitors noted he "is never happy but when he has the box and Dices in hand." Meanwhile, his losses continued to mount. By 1765, Byrd was in dire financial straits, and rumors suggested he had "reduced himself to that Degree by gameing, that few or nobody will Credit him for Ever so small a sum of money." He became a living example of the old gaming manual warning that "By the Disreputation of being a Gamester, if you lose not your Estate, you will certainly lose your Credit and good Name, than which there is nothing more valuable."[42]

As with most tales of fortunes lost by gambling, Byrd's attributes too much to his betting. He lost money on lots of risky ventures. After the death of a close friend and colonial official in 1766, estate documents disclosed that the powerful ally had loaned Byrd money from the colony's coffers to cover debts from land speculation and a failed lead mine, as well as wagers. Public outcry for immediate repayment forced Byrd to raffle off all his remaining property— valued at over £55,000—in a lottery. Fittingly, Byrd sold the lottery tickets on credit and the majority of purchasers never paid. He mortgaged his family silver and another 150 slaves to settle an account with a British merchant, though he never cleared his debts to the colony or several other traders. Paying his gaming losses contributed to his situation but was not solely responsible for it.[43]

Byrd's politics exacerbated his situation. Many patriots used their opposition to British policy as an excuse to avoid paying their British creditors. But Byrd was a stickler for "great politeness," and endeavored to pay all his debts. His submission to rules extended to his distaste for colonial dissent. He only joined the patriots in 1775, after Virginia's royal governor threatened the colony's racial order by inviting slaves to run away to the arriving British army. By then, having sided against the resistance movement for so long, Byrd found himself locked out of the patriots' leadership. Passed over for a military command in 1776, and admitting that his "own folly and inattention to accounts" left him "still greatly incumbered with Debts which imbitters every moment of my Life," Byrd committed suicide on New Year's Day 1777.[44]

William Henry Drayton mirrored Byrd's path for much of his life. He allegedly spent and lost more than £10,000 during his collegiate career at Oxford and continued prodigality after returning to Charleston without graduating in 1763. Elected to the colonial assembly two years later on the strength of his father's good name, he was unseated after just one term by opponents who pointed to his gambling losses and argued that "no parish in this province will ever think it prudent to trust their interests in such hands." The following year, 1769, saw Drayton attempt to right his finances by cheating. A few weeks before Fenwicke Bull and Robert Gay were caught rigging a horse race, Drayton conspired with them to throw a contest between his horse Adolphus and Gay's charge, the local favorite, Noble. Drayton laid large bets on his underdog, expecting to pay off his debts with the winnings. But on this occasion, Gay could not deliver "in such a manner as to lose without being discovered," so he bailed on the fix. Locals noted that Adolphus's defeat cost Drayton "great, very great sums." He borrowed against his inherited plantations and his wife's dowry to make good on his losses, even paying interest on his wagers despite claims from astonished winners who "never have thought of demanding Interest upon a Debt of this Nature."[45]

Drayton seems to have believed that paying his debts of honor (with interest) would secure his reputation, especially after his attempt to cheat. But, like Byrd, the Carolinian soon discovered that paying heavy gambling losses over and over again made him seem reckless rather than bold and so did nothing to protect his credit and standing. Also, like Byrd, Drayton's gambling defeats were compounded by other business losses. For instance, in 1767, a riverboat sank with a full load of his rice aboard, costing some £3,000, which could have saved him. Instead, his wife soon sued to recover her dowry and he was written out of his father's will.[46]

As his resources ran dry, concern for his honor motivated fewer of Drayton's actions on all sorts of debts. First, he was sued for welshing on a £95 raffle ticket bought on credit from well-known Tory Edward Fenwick. Since raffles involved tickets with fixed prices, and were seen as a charitable mode of raising money, they were not considered dangerous to the social order and were not included under the restrictive legislation of 1710. A court therefore found Drayton guilty of "fraudulently Intending Craftily and Subtilly to deceive and Defraud the said Edward." Then Drayton tried to cheat his uncle—the absentee Royal Governor James Glen—"by selling off all his negroes and runing away." In 1771, he failed to repay £5,000 in credit and loans for various goods and expenses, including wagers. His father thought him "lost," though his nearly cheated uncle procured him a seat on the colonial council and loaned him money, out of concern for Drayton's doting stepmother, who was Glen's sister.[47]

Drayton's drift away from the honorable payment of losses should have sealed his fate. Instead, it led to a new strategy for recovering his wealth and reputation. While he stuck to the code, Drayton remained a strident Tory. Like

Byrd, he opposed the resistance movement in the 1760s, aristocratically deriding the "profanum vulgus" associated with Christopher Gadsden. But after his stepmother died in 1773, Drayton's politics changed along with his approach to honor. He began to withhold the £1,300 annuity payments from her estate that were due to his generous uncle. Without his sister to think about, this latest indignity finally turned Glen against Drayton, and he threatened a lawsuit. But political opposition to the royal governor presented Drayton with a justification for withholding the annuity payments. By aligning the governor's suit with patriot cries against greedy royal officials, Drayton secured £1,300 a year and popularity among the patriots. Having opposed a boycott of British goods in 1769, he spoke in favor of reinstating nonimportation in 1774. He received "Public thanks" for his stance, and was elected to the Continental Congress.[48]

Drayton became a model of the reformed gentleman demonstrators wanted to cultivate, even though he never mingled with the populace as Gadsden did. He won popular support by issuing bold statements and challenges, folding public assertions of his gentility and honor into attacks on British prerogative in the same way New York's Sons of Liberty blended antielitism into their political agenda. The difference was that Drayton did not detest gentility or elitism. His tactic was to redefine honor and gentility, often conflating the two, in order to build a less alienating patriot elite whose sense of superiority was rooted in righteous opposition on behalf of common people but who nevertheless assumed their right to leadership and wealth. This approach required more than simply withholding gaming and other debts from Tory gentlemen. He challenged loyalist "upstarts" to duels, though he had fallen so far in their circles that they could afford to ignore his attempt to "settle the affair like a Gentleman," as he still thought he was. Drayton also stopped racing and supported more accessible "festivitie." At Congress in 1779, he cited "the Olympic Games" as a model for planning Independence Day celebrations "calculated for improving bodily strength—to make Men athletic and robust." This was no proposal for genteel sport. His fellow delegate from South Carolina, Henry Laurens, predictably sneered at Drayton's preference to mark independence with "joy & mirth" instead of "fasting & mourning." Yet those predilections fueled the "temper to persuade" and "superior vigour of soul" that made Drayton an influential speaker and writer for the patriot cause. They were the traits cited by his eulogists following his untimely death from typhus just a few months later. By then, his sporting reputation had cost him honor in one circle while helping him to recover it, some wealth, and positions of leadership in another.[49]

The paths taken by William Henry Drayton and William Byrd III illuminate how one man's honor could be another man's dishonor, because there was no single definition of gambling's relationship to gentility in Revolutionary America. While moralists considered gambling a genteel "amusement" only when wagers were small, William Byrd's friends described his play for high stakes "as a fashionable amusement merely—avarice being then and even after, a passion alien to his breast." For Byrd, Drayton, and other scions, big wagers were neither a means of income, as they were for sharps, nor a means of doing business and winning votes, as they were for established and aspiring gentlemen. Born to fathers who had built fortunes and proved themselves through risky enterprises, then urged greater caution to their heirs, these young men could not prove themselves through upward mobility or expanded networks. Instead, they expressed their superiority by taking a different kind of chance, coolly staking their inheritances and paying their debts of honor. They saw honorable gaming as one of the few metrics available to prove themselves worthy of their standing, which explains why Byrd's friends thought his death could have been prevented "if his country could have been prevailed upon to put as much confidence in him as to have given him as high a military command as his rank, his honor, and his high claims to preferment entitled him." At the end, Byrd clung only to the honorable status he had carefully tried to maintain at the expense of his fortune. Yet, contrary to the genteel values that privileged etiquette over base motives, his choice to preserve honor at all costs had actually reduced his reputation among creditors and patriots. When he realized this fact, it compounded his loss of wealth and drove him to suicide.[50]

In contrast, William Henry Drayton thrived once he abandoned the gambler's code. Gambling's mix of rough and genteel manhood made it a relative test of character and status. Behavior that certified standing with some men eroded it among others, and the imperial crisis only heightened the chances of such differing perspectives. Byrd failed to see the relativity of honor, but Drayton capitalized on it. He coupled his repudiation of debts owed to loyalists with broader shifts in politics and the kinds of sport he supported, successfully recapturing his standing and wealth by folding claims of gentlemanly status into claims of honor as patriots saw it—even to the point of having "held it as an honour" when he was removed from the Governor's Council.[51]

Historians have long considered honor and its expression through gambling a particularly southern phenomenon, born of the supposedly anticommercial ethos and emphasis on bravado inherent to the region's brutal regime of slavery. But while more Southerners openly wrote about their gambling practices than did Northerners, a parade of antigambling petitions and legislation in the North suggests that plenty of young men there used wagers much as Byrd and Drayton did.[52] Concerned citizens of northern cities specifically complained "that the practice of Gaming in Public Houses is now become very general, especially amongst the Apprentices and other young People of the said City," causing "the Corruption of Morals as in the Impoverishment and often total Ruin of those Frequenters of Public Gaming Houses." Their focus on the young echoed Southerners' concerns about the "debauching of many of the younger sort, both of the nobility and gentry, and others, to the loss of their precious time and the utter ruin of the estates and fortunes."[53]

In reality, few men gambled away their patrimonies. For every Byrd and Drayton, who lost in business as much as at wagers anyway, there were handfuls of men like George Washington, Thomas Jefferson, and Robert Wormeley Carter's cousin of the same name. Bets of five pounds or less dot their ledgers at the rate of two or three per week, with annual winnings or losses balancing out to less than ten pounds. This evidence suggests that the urge to prove honor through reckless high-stakes gambling was less particularly southern than particularly rooted among younger men who felt they had few alternatives for gaining respect. Fathers, like Robert Wormeley Carter's, complained that "they play away and play it all away," but "it" was not so much wealth as any universal standard for honor or gentility. In fact, despite the efforts to gentrify gambling by either limiting the size of wagers or making payment a test of status, many men periodically pursued respect by jettisoning gentility altogether. A distinct type of tavern even emerged to cater to erstwhile gentlemen interested in such options.[54]

The Rise of Sporting Taverns

Almost exactly one mile straight up High Street from Philadelphia's London Coffee House stood the Center House Tavern. On the site of today's City Hall and adjacent to the colonial-era racecourse, the Center House boasted a bowling green and one of the city's few billiard tables in the 1750s, making it an early example of a tavern specifically designed to attract patrons through its sporting offerings. Like other "sporting taverns," such as The Bacchus on the Bay in Charleston, the Center House welcomed gamesters from all corners of society. For instance, on a business trip in 1765, Virginia-based Scottish merchant William Gregory started a night out with his local hosts at the London Coffee House. There the gentlemen dined and "drank two bottles of wine a-piece, then went to the Billiard Table almost a mile out of Town—they are forbid being in the Town—& played till towards bed-time." Hannah Callender Sansom, a lady of Philadelphia's genteel circle, knew that Gregory and well-connected young men of her acquaintance enjoyed "pleasure and dissipation" with "no distinction of company" at the infamous venue on the edge of the city.[55]

Drunken mingling at the Center House often got out of hand. The *Pennsylvania Gazette* reported a number of thefts and assaults in and around the tavern, solidifying its notoriety as a haunt on the outskirts of town where absconded servants could hide away and highwaymen could lie in wait. Nicholas Scull met a more gruesome fate. The son of Pennsylvania's chief justice, he was murdered while playing billiards at the Center House in August 1760. After watching Scull's match for "a considerable time," convicted counterfeiter and decommissioned British army officer John Bruluman suddenly pulled out a gun, allegedly issued a melodramatic segue, "Gentlemen, I will shew you a fine stroke," and shot Scull "through the body." The suicidal Bruluman, who recently had failed at taking his own life, then explained his motive to his dying victim. "Sir, I had no malice nor ill will against you, for I never saw you before," he reportedly said, "but I was determined to kill somebody that I might be hanged and you happened to be the man; and as you are a very likely young man, I am sorry for your misfortune." No wonder scrupulous Philadelphians called the Center House Tavern the "ill red house."[56]

Benjamin Backhouse's tavern resembled the Center House in terms of both the activities it offered and its renown for violent confrontation. The reputation persisted under new management after Backhouse died in 1767. One summer night in 1771, doctor John Haly and Postmaster General Peter DeLancey left a large dinner at a private home in Charleston "heated with Liquor" and decided to settle a long-standing quarrel at the "Tavern on the Bay," the reference to Bacchus having been dropped from the name with Backhouse's passing. Other members of the party went to drink at Dillon's, but the two antagonists intentionally selected a more appropriate setting for their "Affair." They arrived "staggering drunk," entered a small back room, "called for a Bottle of Wine & shut the Door. Immediately afterwards, two Pistols were heard to go off." Only Haly exited the room. A ball to the chest from close range instantly killed DeLancey.[57]

Confrontation, violence, and cross-class mingling had a long history in colonial taverns. But at the same time a new set of genteel establishments emerged to counter this experience in the middle decades of the eighteenth century, the appearance of enormous "sporting taverns" indicates a persistent demand for it. Even in Boston, which boasted some of the strictest antigaming legislation in the colonies, elegant tavernkeepers such as the pseudonymous Bacchus Fairplay feared the competition presented by these renegade facilities. Fairplay complained that upstanding venues like his, "as free from gaming as any private house," had "customers of late not so many as formerly, owing, I am persuaded, to private houses of entertainment in the town . . . in which all sorts of liquors are sold, clubs entertained, billiard table kept, and all sorts of gaming allowed." Apparently, not all gentlemen shared Dr. Hamilton's opinions, at least not all the time. Milieus catering to rougher mingling multiplied alongside those encouraging gentility.[58]

When gentlemen entered a sporting tavern, they crossed a cultural threshold. All sporting venues brought diverse people together, but sporting taverns—unlike genteel ones—were not built to inspire politeness among their assorted patrons. Certainly, arguments erupted at coffeehouses. Though elegant, they retained the competitive air that pervaded all public houses. Yet reports rarely mention physical violence in the same breath with these venues. When merchant James Thomson challenged ship captain Jaspar Farmer to a duel in 1757, he called Farmer down from the porch of New York's Merchant Coffee House and into the street instead of heading to a back room inside. Physical violence that did occur in elegant taverns tended to be targeted and limited, not random or extreme. For instance, after Boston patriot James Otis was "very liberal in his abuse and scurrility" toward loyalist John Robinson in Boston's British Coffee House in 1769, Robinson "attempted to pull him by the nose" and then cane him. Nose-pulling and caning were traditional methods of declaring a presumptive foe's inferiority, communicating chastening through brief and controlled physical abuse. Although patriot writers tried to claim Robinson's "ungentleman-like and barbarous" assault "would have been fatal," Robinson found this assertion "really astonishing" and adamantly asserted that the attack was "a simple Assault and Battery," fitting within the confines of an established ritual. Notably, Otis originally proposed "to decide this controversy by themselves in a separate Room," but Robinson declined and the confrontation took place in the coffeehouse's downstairs public room, the least genteel and most public space in the establishment. Would removal to a private room have led to a more violent conclusion? Perhaps, but even though men considered duels a genteel way to defend honor, carrying one out under the roof of the British Coffee House would have been unprecedented.[59]

Differences in behavior resulted from material differences between genteel and sporting taverns, which surface in advertisements for their purchase or lease. Though sporting taverns were equal in "commodious" size to genteel public houses, ads for them tended to reference sporting equipment or gatherings of raucous societies like the Sons of Liberty, and never described the facility as "fit for a gentleman or a tavern" the way ads for refined taverns did. After all, sporting taverns did not occupy former private mansions or new buildings that looked like mansions. They were only "well situated for keeping a tavern," "convenient," or "neatly finished," almost never "genteel" or "elegant."[60]

Sporting taverns also boasted more accessible spaces. Whereas elegant taverns lured exclusive genteel functions with several rooms on upper floors and in the back of the structure, sealed off from public barrooms and dining rooms in the front of the house, sporting taverns boasted more large accessible rooms. For example, the London Coffee House in the heart of colonial Philadelphia had a public bar and dining room on the ground floor, much like the Center House, but its barkeeper screened access to its coffeehouse "exchange" upstairs. In comparison, the Center House featured a billiard table on its second floor. Billiard rooms in the back or upstairs, along with cockpits in the tavern yard, created more fluid and accessible complexes. Exclusive rooms were available, as Haly and DeLancey knew, but they did not take up as much space as at genteel taverns.[61]

In addition to differences in interior decor and floor plan, sporting taverns typically stood on the urban fringe, while genteel taverns occupied central city lots. New York newspapers advertised business meetings and genteel club gatherings at taverns on the Bowling Green or, later, on Broadway. Venues cited in reports of coarse social mingling tended to stand either in sight of the wharves or "in the fields" on the northern edge of the city. In Charleston, too, taverns known for cockfighting were situated "on the Green" or "on the Neck" at the city's outskirts.[62] In colonial Philadelphia, nine of twelve documented taverns with billiard tables were located outside the city, in the neighboring Northern Liberties, Southwark, or west of Seventh Street where urban density did not yet reach. Not one of these nine taverns was advertised as "genteel."[63]

Differences in architecture, furnishing, location, and the kinds of sports on offer all encouraged rougher behavior at sporting taverns than at finer public houses. Yet the line was not hard and fast. Benjamin Backhouse's tavern featured backgammon tables and some rooms "furnished in the elegant manner" with porcelain "China" teapots and mahogany chairs. Such spaces created some reprieve in a facility designed on the whole to foster rough rather than polite play. Indeed, in terms of size, operating costs, and tavernkeeper tenure, sporting taverns stood alongside genteel ones atop the tavern market in colonial British America. The Center House again provides an example. It stood on an enormous 35,000-square-foot lot, and publican Robert Dixon rented it for fourteen years until he died in 1761. His widow then ran it for the next eight years. In comparison, in the second half of the eighteenth century, less than half of all tavernkeepers in Boston, Philadelphia, and Baltimore stayed in the business at the same address for seven years. Less than a quarter stayed for more than ten years, and they tended to be either the most genteel taverns or the most sporting.[64]

Still, stability was not a given among sporting tavernkeepers. Most of them rented their establishments, like the overwhelming majority of publicans, and sporting equipment raised their operating costs above all but the most genteel taverns. A secondhand billiard table could cost up to thirty-five pounds, somewhere between one-half and one-third of the annual net profit from liquor sales at taverns with the largest sales volumes on record. Nor was ownership without risk, as demonstrated by Backhouse's decision to keep The Bacchus under his wife's name in case he defaulted on the loans he needed to turn it from a common into a sporting tavern.[65]

The politics of the Revolution added another source of instability. Edward Bardin hosted New York's Sons of Liberty, which explains how he got away with also staging an "innocent Amusement" of concerts for "Gentlemen and Ladies" just a month after the theatre was destroyed. Bardin's landlord, James DeLancey, no doubt helped him straddle the line between genteel and sporting taverns. But DeLancey drifted away from the patriots in 1769 and soon evicted his tavernkeeper, who apparently stuck with the cause. Bardin spent the next four years in five different taverns in New York, Boston, and the Caribbean island of St. Eustatius, before returning to manage a new sporting haunt, Hampden Hall, erected by patriots within sight of his old facility in the fields north of town. He left again when the British occupied the city, and only came back after the war, when his patriotic credentials earned him the lease on the subscription-built and genteel Tontine Coffee House, which he ran for the last twenty years of his life. If Bardin eventually enjoyed success, his path nevertheless illustrates the precariousness of sporting tavernkeeping, which required connections and credit beyond the common tavernkeeper's while not matching the prestige, stability, or income potential of the top genteel taverns.[66]

In promoting an accessible, unpredictable, and generally unrefined competitive experience for patrons as well as proprietors, sporting taverns differed from both the new elegant taverns and more typical ones which were smaller, provided fewer sporting options, and were driven by an overcrowded market toward narrower clienteles among particular ethnic or occupational groups.[67] In effect, sporting tavernkeepers carved out a niche by satisfying a steady demand for the rough mixing of the old traditional tavern. Men concerned with reinforcing genteel order should have avoided such venues, but many of them could not, because any man aspiring to prove himself could not resist going.

Young gentlemen did not have to gamble to exhibit their manhood at sporting taverns. Just mingling and competing granted a basic opportunity to project manly status. Alexander Graydon, who attended the best schools in Philadelphia, later admitted that he spent his teenage years "lost in idleness and amusement" at places like the Center House. A desire to prove his masculinity clearly pushed him there. He describes developing his "fascination with a billiard table" at sporting taverns only after giving up dancing lessons "from an idea of its being an effeminate and unmanly recreation." He claimed he never gambled, but again indicated how a gendered notion of status drove his participation at these venues when he described how they helped him become "acquainted with a set of young men whose education and habits had been wholly different from my own. They were chiefly designed for the sea, or engaged in the less humiliating mechanical employments, and were but the more to my taste for affecting a sort of rough independence of manners, which appeared to me manly."[68]

Sporting taverns also attracted older men, especially those with political ambitions who saw a chance to win supporters by engaging them there. In Williamsburg, Virginia, burgesses organizing colonial resistance met at the billiard table–boasting Raleigh Tavern, not the town's coffeehouse. The Raleigh also featured an assembly room like Dillon's, and in this regard merged genteel elements into a sporting tavern. James DeLancey "constantly attended" similar houses, like Bardin's, until his faction's dominance of the elected assembly and appointed offices led him to believe his power was secure. Then he moved his "open" meetings from his sporting tavern on the edge of the city to the Merchant's Coffee House in the center of town. The whole demeanor of the meetings changed with the location, as "only a small proportion of the citizens attended the meeting inside the coffee house," and the city's merchants used the polite, orderly setting to control the meetings and thereby temper the Sons' radical voices.[69]

A similar story unfolded in Philadelphia, where failed merchant Timothy Matlack engineered a Drayton-like redemption by supporting the resistance movement. Yet Matlack went further than Drayton, participating more fully in the rough-and-tumble world of sporting taverns. The popularity he won in these settings helped him get elected to militia offices in the 1760s and resistance committees in the 1770s, offsetting his previous business failures and excommunication from the Quaker meeting. He clung to his ungenteel sporting identity through the war years, leading his political foes to call him "Tim Gaff"—"gaff" being a colloquial term for a cockspur. Rising to political prominence on the shoulders of Philadelphia's radical militia, who knew him largely from his sporting habits, his former Quaker brethren marveled at how "Dear Tim" had "rose so great, from trimming cocks to trim the state." Once he achieved power, however, Matlack, like DeLancey, withdrew from rough sport and grew more moderate in his politics. As a powerful officeholder during the Revolution, he joined the city's elite cavalry unit in "cutting and slashing" and jailing the militiamen who once had supported him when they rioted in Philadelphia in 1779.[70]

Sporting taverns satisfied a demand for rough and competitive mingling that persisted despite the rise of genteel sport. Their very existence underscored gentility's inability to craft enough deference to render DeLancey's and Matlack's tactics unnecessary. If aspiring gentlemen tended to pull back from ungenteel sport once they felt they did not need the popularity it fostered, the spike in antielitism caused by the resistance movement limited the number of patriots who could copy Matlack. Indeed, by the mid-1770s, the patriot elite had begun to see genteel sport, not the stuff of the sporting tavern, as too incendiary to help them.

To "Discourage Every Species of Extravagance"

In October 1774, just six weeks after convening, the First Continental Congress adopted the "Continental Association," a set of regulations intended to guide American resistance to the Coercive Acts—the latest Parliamentary legislation aimed at the colonies—which had been passed a few months earlier in response to the Boston Tea Party. The eighth of the Association's fourteen articles pledged that patriots would

> in our several stations, encourage frugality, economy, and industry, and promote agriculture, arts and the manufactures of this country, especially that of wool; and will discountenance and discourage every species of extravagance and dissipation, especially all horse-racing, and all kinds of gaming, cock-fighting, exhibitions of shews, plays, and other expensive diversions and entertainments.[71]

The Association thus banned a wide range of sport, much of it explicitly associated with gentility. Congress passed this provision for two reasons. First, the Association coupled the proscription with a vast boycott aimed at hurting the British economy and persuading critics who questioned the patriots' claims of economic distress resulting from British policy. How bad could things be, skeptics in Britain wondered, if colonists had "ordered richer and richer goods of all sorts" during the 1760s, and had not even "given up concerts and plays and gambling and horse races?" The second purpose was domestic: to reduce mounting class tensions among the colonists by outlawing public displays of genteel elitism that frequently exacerbated those tensions. In sum, the Association tried to unite colonists and make them appear deserving of redress from Parliament.[72]

The decision to ban several forms of sport as part of these regulations was not a foregone conclusion. Up until 1774, gentlemen like those who dominated the seats in Congress had been divided about sport's role in the imperial crisis. Fervent religious dissenters had always opposed sport as an immoral waste of time and money. Their arguments gained greater traction as imperial critics began to argue that "it is ridiculous and absurd to pretend to curb the effects of luxury and corruption in one instance or in one spot without a general reformation of manners." Meanwhile, other gentlemen on both sides of the imperial issue saw sport as a means to rally support for their cause. Ever the shrewd professional, David Douglass played to this demand from across the political spectrum. True, he appealed more to patriots when he changed his troupe's name from the London Company of Comedians to the American Company after the Stamp Act controversy. But he also adjusted his content. Moderate critics soon noticed "a moral tendency" in "most of the new plays that have come under our observation." Douglass intentionally began to favor malleable material rooted in the peculiarly British language of liberty, sacrifice, and patriotism. Both patriots and Tories identified these ideals with their side, and the moral tone associated with them was calculated to defuse "the censure of the more rigid part of the world." Douglass essentially traded on the crisis, using moral themes to pacify his critics and invite audiences of all political persuasions to come to his theatres and interpret his shows in ways that would serve their ends.[73]

Organizers similarly presented horse races and cockfights as events where both sides could meet to express and compete for support. Several match races drew interest for pitting a British import against "a Native" or "the gallant American" horse. More subtle was the "great cockfight" between Timothy Matlack and James DeLancey held outside Philadelphia in 1770. Newspaper advertisements attracted perhaps hundreds of people to the host tavern, where they watched a contest loaded with regional and political overtones between the increasingly Tory New Yorker and the Philadelphia patriot.[74]

The politicization of sporting events fed a growing conception of politics as a type of sport. Patriot newspapers in particular began to describe political developments in sporting terms, as when the radical *Pennsylvania Chronicle* reported on the factional fight for control of Parliament in 1768 as if it were a horse race. Each faction's leader was represented as the owner of a horse whose name summarized the leader's political reputation in patriot eyes. William Pitt received the most stinging rebuke, for becoming more conservative in his view of the colonial crisis once he received a peerage as Lord Chatham. The article concludes by predicting that "the famous horse Liberty, formerly belonging to Lord Chatham, who has since sold him, will come to the post" and win the day. Despite Pitt's reversal, patriots in 1768 still believed the right parliamentary leadership would resolve tensions and secure their liberty.[75]

The patriot press portrayed more than elections in these sporting terms. They frequently characterized local rioters as "sportive," "playful," or out "to divert themselves," enjoying "anticks" or a hearty "frolic." These reports typically described sailors, laborers, and artisans, sometimes with "Gentlemen Actors disguised in Trawsers & Jackets," with "great numbers of Boys" among them, too. Here, sporting language downplayed any violence or threats doled out by the crowd. Likening these confrontations to the personal challenges for status and respect common among young men at sporting events disassociated them from charges of rebellion. The framing minimized the threat of "sporting" behavior to British sovereignty, but heightened the sense of overlap between sporting and political action. Where sporting venues were once merely sites for electioneering, by the late 1760s sport had become a discursive framework for expressing political opinions.[76]

The connection between sporting and political culture took material form when colonies opened their legislative assembly houses to the public, turning them into theatres of a kind. Virginia and Massachusetts did this first, though almost all the colonies had followed suit by 1773. State houses fulfilled the requirements of genteel architecture better than theatres. As a result, along with the time of day assemblies met and screening procedures for entry (both of which precluded many workingmen from attending), the initial public galleries featured more polite audiences than playhouses. They also represented how the "republican" values of the patriots' movement helped colonists conflate politics and sport: by empowering citizens to judge and challenge the performance of their politicians, just as they evaluated professionals and each other at sporting events. Of course, having made politics more like sport, representatives should not have been surprised when attendees based their evaluations as much on being "entertained" by a speaker as on agreeing or disagreeing with him.[77]

As this preference for "entertainment" suggests, politicians grafted sport onto politics in an attempt to engage the public and win support. But they had trouble controlling the outcome. The problem was worse at venues more accessible than legislative chambers. Theatre gallery dwellers increasingly lashed out at genteel elitism and commandeered politically neutral shows by trying to "interrupt the actors" and "call for a song or prologue" related to their cause. At cockfights and horse races, too, efforts to engage the community in a competitive but orderly expression of political sympathies devolved into outright riot. The DeLancey–Matlack cockfight ended early when a massive brawl erupted among the partisan spectators. South Carolina patriot Isaac

Harleston's match race against Tory Edward Fenwick never even got started. Fenwick canceled, saying he was "loth to incur the anger of the publick."[78]

Many of these outbursts reflected patriots' efforts to fold class tensions into the imperial debate. Patriots steadily outdid Tories in applying sport to win popular support because the class tension already present in colonial sporting culture served their tactics more than their foes'. Since colonists already went to sporting events to prove or confront class distinction, sporting activities and terminology provided effective tools for blaming the imperial conflict on the aristocratic conceit of British authorities and their sympathizers. Although wealthier patriots like Christopher Gadsden and Timothy Matlack initially encouraged linking class tension to imperial politics through sport, they lamented their inability to guide the way rank-and-file participants acted on it. Their "exertion of influence" during the earliest Stamp Act demonstrations could not prevent unplanned vandalism and assaults. Throughout the 1760s, gentlemen on both sides of the conflict worried that "the mob was its own master" and exhibited an "independence of action" suggestive of those "poor, cross, and desperate" men who "don't seem to care who are their masters, or indeed for any masters."[79]

As patriots applied sport to politics, average protesters increasingly delivered the kinds of personal affronts associated with sporting settings. Attacks on genteel houses, clothing, and the people who owned them expressed disrespect as much as political opposition, and were akin to lobbing rotten eggs at genteel theatregoers or whacking a gentleman with a billiard cue in a sporting tavern. By 1774, patriot leaders thought the imperial conflict was being lost in the class antipathy of personal assaults meted out by rank-and-file protestors. In Boston, John Adams complained that "this breaking open Houses by rude and insolent Rabbles in Resentment for private Wrongs or in pursuance of private Prejudices and Passions, must be discountenanced." Adams agreed with some loyalists that the "sportive cruelty" of these punishments, motivated by personal "Resentment for private Wrongs," was incompatible with the larger fight against British policies. For him, only the broader "public" cause of imperial dissent legitimated crowd action, and that action needed to be more orderly—and less "sportive"—than personal attacks designed to bring high men low.[80]

Patriot leaders had employed sport to bring class tension to bear on their side in the imperial conflict. In practice, though, bringing sporting culture into the crisis injected the personal status politics of colonial sporting settings into acts of resistance aimed at both the British and the internal dynamics of the patriot movement. Challenges soon targeted more than just pretentious Tories, as patriots from outside elite circles vied for political prominence against their presumptive leaders, many of whom had participated in the effort to construct gentility. In New York, a faction of "trades men" elected artisans to the committees in charge of organizing the resistance. Another "mechanic's interest" emerged in Charleston. These alternatives to the existing political leadership surfaced amid ever more independent and violent policing of resistance policies. "So exasperated are the People," wrote one patriot merchant in Philadelphia in 1774, "that to appease them and indeed for their own safety, the merchants are obliged to pawn their word and honour and give from under their hands that they will not import any more Goods." In the city where artisans lent Carpenters Hall to Congress, those craftsmen publicly pushed for nonimportation and organized their own ticket to enforce it less than a month after the passage of the Association. The ban on sport, then, must be seen as not only an effort to demonstrate solidarity but as an attempt to scale back a politicized sporting culture that, by 1774, had gotten away from the gentlemen in Congress and jeopardized their leadership of the patriot movement.[81]

The Association discouraged theatre, racing, cockfighting, and gaming because these activities promoted class antagonism by highlighting differences in rank and means. Notably, though, Congress left taverns out of the resolution despite their historic role as preeminent bases for cross-class confrontation. In part, this decision stemmed from the historic unpopularity and failure of previous attempts to limit the tavern trade. Candidates backing such agendas routinely lost in the mid-eighteenth century, when every colonial city saw its number of legally licensed public houses increase alongside its number of illegal unlicensed "dram shops" and "grog shops." So the Association's silence on taverns reflects the patriot leaders' desire to grow popular support, not alienate it.[82]

Additionally, taverns successfully served patriot leaders in two ways. First, genteel taverns were rare examples of genteel sporting spaces that worked. Theatres prompted anger for segregating the genteel from the ungenteel within sight of each other, but anyone could step inside a genteel tavern and participate in relatively decorous activity, if only in the limited number of ground-floor public rooms. When Charleston's taxman yielded to popular will and publicly declared that he would not enforce the Stamp Act, protestors took him to Dillon's and shared a drink with him, signaling their unity in accessible genteel space. True, these venues hosted exclusive balls and club meetings, but such seclusion typically took place in back and upstairs rooms rather than in front of everyone, as in theatres. Along with the relative inclusivity of their genteel public rooms, their concealment of exclusivity spared genteel taverns from the kinds of violence enacted at theatres. Protestors demonstrated outside them, instead of destroying them from the inside out. Their very effectiveness explains why the patriot elite in New York and Philadelphia both shifted "open" political meetings to them from sporting taverns. The accessible yet polite setting at genteel taverns helped elites keep control of meetings by limiting the form of dissent they would face and privileging them as gentlemen who best knew the rules there.[83]

At the other end of the scale, sporting and even common taverns avoided blacklisting because the social mingling at these venues remained essential to winning broad support for the resistance. Not only the Sons of Liberty, but, later, the Continental Army, too, enlisted many of its participants at such sites. Alexander Graydon relied on his experience at the Center House when, in his role as an army recruiter, he challenged men to enlist at taverns. He, and others, reported that signatures often came only after rounds of treats and competitive confrontations. Seeing value in taverns as popular venues for establishing order and recruiting supporters, Congress excused them from the Association's proscription and instead banned the specific sporting activities which they thought posed a greater danger to domestic unity and would not trigger popular outrage.[84]

For the most part, Congress gauged the law's impact correctly. The speed, uniformity, and degree of compliance with the Association were remarkable. The Continental Congress lacked the power to compel colonial assemblies, which typically ignored or only partly complied with its resolutions. Yet within weeks of the announcement of the Association, colonies began to pass their own versions of it as law. As a result, David Douglass had to set sail for the West Indies and jockey club–sponsored horse racing came to a complete stop. Smaller-scale and spontaneous events proved harder to eliminate, as suggested by a succession of laws passed in several colonies "for the Suppression of Vice and Immorality" because "sufficient provision hath not hitherto been made" or an earlier act "hath not been fully and duly executed and enforced." Still, the impact of the Association on major genteel sporting events stands out in comparison to the usual response to congressional decrees.[85]

In the end, the Association did more to achieve its domestic than its external goals. Parliament did not reverse its course, but the patriot elite did face fewer formal internal challenges after 1774. Of course, this decline is not wholly attributable to the ban on public sport. The onset of the war for independence did what sport had failed to do, emphasizing national political goals over social differences among colonists. The patriot elite amplified this emphasis by devising inclusive celebrations of nationalism and using a nationwide network of patriot printers to share the stories of these fetes, fostering an "imagined community" of shared national identity over class lines.[86]

Yet social friction never completely disappeared. When congressmen planned exclusive and ornate balls at Philadelphia's posh City Tavern in 1775 and 1778, they were disconcerted by "threats thrown out" against the building, and a crowd wearing mock genteel attire paraded by in disdain of the celebrants' blatant disregard for Article Eight. In 1779, rank-and-file members of Philadelphia's militia captured suspected price gougers at the height of wartime supply shortages, forced them to mingle and drink with them at a sporting tavern called Loud Hall in order to reduce their genteel distance from the population at large, then paraded the violators around town in degrading fashion, ultimately exchanging gunfire with other elites who feared the same treatment. Similar riots and assaults, sparked by similar concerns about prices, had cropped up in Boston in 1777.[87] In Charleston, a "Mere Mob" confronted their one-time leader Christopher Gadsden after he sponsored a proclamation of leniency toward loyalists. In all these cases, public demonstrations demeaned leaders who were perceived to have arrogantly ignored popular will. Such acts were inspired not only by the well-studied leveling rhetoric of Revolutionary republicanism and traditional English modes of popular dissent like riding skimmington and tarring-and-feathering, but by the recent and repeated experiences of social challenge at colonial sporting venues and the broader application of sporting culture to the patriot movement, which historians have largely missed.[88] Indeed, Gadsden called the Charleston demonstrations "insults on Government," much as Adams decried "sportive" crowds motivated by "private Wrongs." If political dissent had become inseparable from a personal "insult" issued in a sporting setting, the one-time rabble-rouser Gadsden wondered, "Where can this end?"[89]

PART TWO

The Early National Period

CHAPTER 3

Sport Reborn

Sporting investors shut down genteel sport on the eve of the Revolution because it fostered challenges to their authority. After the conflict, they reconsidered. Tweaking their approach, they reintroduced it in a renewed bid to craft power through sport in the young republic.

New York theatre trustee William Henderson was a leading implementer of the new strategy behind genteel sport's rebirth. Like past trustees of sporting projects, Henderson was an up-and-comer. Little is known about him until he joined established New York merchant William Denning's son on a tour of Europe in 1792. On his return, he was elected to join the city's Tontine, an exclusive investment club that owned the coffeehouse run by Edward Bardin. Two years later, Henderson joined the board of directors of the Society for the Establishment of Useful Manufactures, a high-profile corporation led by Secretary of the Treasury Alexander Hamilton. By 1798, he was about thirty years old, had married Denning's daughter, was trying his hand at land speculation, and had just been voted into the trusteeship of a subscription to erect a new theatre.[1]

Henderson's background suggests that the same kind of men who led sporting projects in the late colonial period led their reemergence in the 1790s. But the demands these men made, and the demands made of them, had changed. Subscribers now owned the venues they financed, so when construction costs for New York's new theatre careened some $150,000 beyond the subscription total, the trustees personally bore responsibility for the sum as the legal representatives of the subscribers. Henderson was in a particularly tight bind, since he already owed over $100,000 for land purchases and a fashionable new house on Broadway. Having "borrow'd from the Banks untill he is ashamed of asking," he proposed to spread the theatre's extra costs over the whole body of subscribers through a surcharge levied on each individual subscription. To his chagrin, however, the subscribers balked at this proposal. They told Henderson that they "do not chuse to become responsible for the engagements enter'd into by their Committee" of trustees.[2]

Panicked, Henderson quickly contrived a new scheme to put the subscribers "in good humour" and access the cash he needed. He offered subscribers free season tickets in lieu of the dividends promised in the original subscription plan. Most subscribers believed the theatrical money pit would never realize a profit anyway, so they agreed. Freed from paying dividends, Henderson could apply all revenue toward the trustees' debts. Better yet, from Henderson's perspective, he paid almost nothing for the season tickets. He passed on the bulk of their cost to the theatre's tenant, David Douglass's old acting company, now run by New York City hardware retailer and aspiring cultural impresario William Dunlap. Dunlap's lease required him to pay a percentage of each night's receipts as rent, but Henderson did not lower the percentage enough to make up for the income the manager lost by having to give free tickets every night to 130 of his most dedicated customers. The ticket scheme promised to eat Dunlap's profits.[3]

In addition, Dunlap had accumulated his own debts in order to buy into theatre management and maintain his company while the theatre was being built. Having "weakened my capital in trade and stretched my credit, undergoing fatigue and anxiety beyond calculation," he bristled at a plan calculated to save the trustees at his expense. But when he pressed Henderson to adjust the ticket deal, the trustee responded as coldly as his subscribers had when asked to pay more. "When people employed their money they expected something in return for it," he told Dunlap. If the subscribers would not receive dividends, they deserved tickets. Dunlap was astounded. He "thought few would think of speculating in such a case," and added, "if I had such a surplussage of money as would have justified me to myself for becoming a subscriber to such a build[in]g, I should never have looked for any profit from it." Henderson responded even more curtly to Dunlap's self-serving idealism. He said that "people who had the greatest surplus of money generally wished to encrease it."[4]

Henderson's profiteering maxim was hardly new, yet Dunlap was shocked by its application "in such a case." Colonial theatre managers had granted free tickets to subscribers, but those tickets had constituted mortgage payments. Managers owned their theatres once they repaid the principal of the subscription in free admission to subscribers. The Park Theatre's subscribers never planned to relinquish possession of the playhouse. Henderson simply rechanneled the manager's fees from the subscribers' pockets to those of the trustees' creditors, while shrinking Dunlap's pool of paying customers.

Dunlap had little recourse against this plan. As a tenant, his only alternative was to find another theatre, and the playhouses in the country's other major markets were occupied as acting companies multiplied in the 1790s. Trapped, Dunlap steadily lost money, then credit, then assets, until he declared bankruptcy in 1805. He later gained fame as a painter, but never recovered the wealth he lost as a theatre manager.[5]

The story behind the financing of New York's new theatre was repeated at sporting ventures across the newly United States. This chapter explores how and why investors increasingly sought greater and more direct economic returns from sporting events in the years after the Revolution. As Dunlap himself eventually discovered, elevating the importance of profit was not an end for investors, but a means for establishing more control over the reborn sporting industry and translating that control into broader claims of power and authority.

"Approved Guardians of Their Country"

Before investors could benefit from theatres, racetracks, and other sporting sites, they had to relegitimate sporting events. Virtually every state had passed stringent bans against theatre, racing, and gambling on the eve of the Revolution. Most of these bans remained untouched until after the Constitution went into effect in 1789. This timing was not coincidental. The same men who favored a stronger federal government drove the reemergence of sport because they saw both as vehicles for spreading a new economic culture—a system of values, beliefs, and institutions guiding economic behavior—that supported their vision for the nation and their quest for authority in it.

The Pennsylvania legislature's debate over legalizing theatre provides a closer look into how certain post-Revolutionary leaders molded and channeled sporting culture into a foundation of a broader economic culture. The debate erupted in 1785, ostensibly over a petition to repeal the state's existing ban on theatre. Theatre company managers had submitted similar petitions in each of the previous three years, and all had been dismissed with little ceremony as legislators clung to the moral terms of the Revolutionary proscription.

According to this argument, theatres provided "encouragement of licentiousness" and "luxury," traits that "might not be detrimental in a despotic or Monarchical Government, [but] would be wrong in a republic wherein the manners and morals of the people should be Strictly and Rigidly preserved."[6]

Patriots adopted these arguments in the 1770s, though their roots lay in an older political philosophy that theorized republics as fragile states dependent on a "virtuous" citizenry defined by vigilance and selflessness. Lazy or selfish citizens hastened a republic's disintegration through their negligence or greed, which invited elected officials to serve narrow interests at the expense of the greater good of the nation.[7] Zealous "republican" critics thus added a secular danger to long-standing complaints about sport based on religious doctrine. "Nothing facilitates the progress of luxury more than places of public amusement," wrote one such ascetic, "where the idle and lazy resort to waste their time and plan other schemes of dissipation." Self-indulgent theatre patrons portended nothing less than "the certain means of destruction to the state."[8]

Though it helped keep restrictive legislation on the books, the republican critique never fully eliminated sporting activities. Ad hoc races and brief theatre seasons took place throughout the country during the war and through the 1780s.[9] But in 1785, a quartet of well-known Philadelphia legislators who had served the Revolutionary cause decided to take up the actors' annual petition. Robert Morris, George Clymer, Thomas Fitzsimmons, and General Anthony Wayne made their case by borrowing from David Douglass and other apologists who claimed theatre supported morality rather than destroyed it. Phrasing their argument in equally republican parlance, they said theatre was "a School for Virtue" that "held up to ridicule Characters that were Ridiculous and likewise evil and immoral."[10]

These men suddenly spoke out on behalf of the theatre because they believed it would help support another institution they all backed: the Bank of North America. Morris had founded the bank, Fitzsimmons was a director, Clymer was a stockholder, and Wayne held substantial state securities which—under the rules of 1785—generated interest paid in the bank's notes. However, the future of those payments, and of the bank in general, was under assault at the precise moment the men launched their theatre initiative in the winter legislative sessions of 1785–86.[11]

Morris had formed the bank during the later years of the Revolutionary War to help stabilize currency values and purchase war matériel for the patriots. Capital came largely from private investors, though both the state of Pennsylvania and the Continental Congress held shares. After the war, Morris and his friends applied the bank's resources to fund myriad private ventures in trade, manufacturing, and western land, all in the hopes of simultaneously benefiting themselves and the government.[12]

Opposition soon mounted against the bank as a tool controlled by a small circle of elite Philadelphia merchants and landowners. Critics, led by representatives from the western part of the state where the bank was less active, worried that "the bank will be able to dictate to the legislature what laws to pass and what to forbear." In effect, they saw the bank as "an engine of power" capable of coercing representative government because of the state's vested interest in it. Citing Pennsylvania's 1776 state constitution, which specifically declared that "government is, or ought to be, instituted for the common benefit, protection and security of the people, nation, or community; and not for the particular emolument or advantage of any single man, family, or sett of men, who are a part only of that community," the bank's opponents first tried to charter a second bank. When Morris's cohort defeated that effort, his foes rallied enough allies to pass a law in early 1785 creating state-issued paper money. Both efforts aimed to reduce the bank's monopoly on cash and its resulting control over investment. Living up to their foes' fears, bank officials declared the alternatives "an act of state suicide" because they promised to diminish the value of the state's own shares in the Bank of North America. To protect that investment, the bank announced it would only accept the new currency at less than face value, diminishing its utility and leading opponents to pledge to repeal the bank's charter when it came up for renewal later in the year.[13]

Morris and his friends fought their challengers in part by calling for a sporting culture that would promote the same economic values and system as the bank. Morris's own description of a legal theatre resembled the most optimistic descriptions of the bank, which called the institution "salutary and beneficial to the community"—not just to its shareholders and loan recipients—because it circulated dependable money and thereby propelled economic opportunity for everyone. Similarly, when arguing for drama, Morris said that "a well-conducted theatre would mend the morals and improve the manners of the people." "It is under that belief," he said, "and not that I would gratify myself at the expense of the good of the community or to the injury of the morals and manners of the public, that I am an advocate for a theatre." Notably, Morris never disavowed personal political or economic gain from the theatre project or the bank. He simply claimed that any such "gratification" was secondary and would be in harmony with "the good of the community," not at its "expense."[14]

Morris's circle rejected classical republican theory by claiming that the pursuit of personal interest would bind and advance the republic, not split and destroy it. They also thought the theatre could help bring people around to their thinking. But in supporting the bank and the theatre, Morris's faction did not argue for unrestrained selfishness. Rather, in both cases, they advocated strong guidance from "the most respectable among us." They wanted the theatre to be censored by the state's Executive Council, in order "to discriminate between vicious and moral exhibitions." In the same vein, these men wanted the bank's directors to control fiscal policy and not be "restrained or embarrassed by an attempt to establish a new Bank" or state fiat money. Morris and his friends would have neither the theatre nor the bank governed by the state's full legislative assembly. They thought such important institutions ought to be led by smaller and more select groups who, as Morris put it, could "urge reasons and arguments which we, at least, think ought to have weight and to carry conviction."[15]

Morris envisioned a theatre that would reflect, support, and normalize the economic system constructed by the bank—a system that empowered private capital to guide the rest of society in the simultaneous pursuit of both personal gain and public good. Since the sixteenth century, critics had decried theatre for teaching audiences to emulate marketplace charlatans who adopted and abandoned different identities with ease. But Morris and his friends thought these lessons were more helpful than harmful. When Morris said that plays "held up to ridicule Characters that were Ridiculous and likewise evil and immoral," he was not just pandering to republican ideology. He thought the stage could stimulate and guide an economy of strivers, in which masses of aspiring men would need the cash and credit ultimately controlled by the bank. In such an economy, as one bank supporter put it, "Credit depends on opinion. Opinion, whether well or ill founded." To earn credit and make sound investments, men needed to identify and project trustworthiness and confidence. Morris's supervised theatre would perform a public service by teaching spectators to look out for false personas and to cultivate honorable ones. The Philadelphia faction envisioned the theatre inspiring economic growth by encouraging the traits that would facilitate borrowing and investment.[16]

The rub was that creditors wanted borrowers to pay their debts whether their ventures were successful or not. Morris turned to another sporting tool to teach this lesson about the sanctity of debt. When his opponents attached a rider to their antitheatre bill perpetuating a defeated gambler's right to sue and recover gaming losses, Morris lobbied to limit this right to a brief ten-day window. According to one newspaper report of the debate, Morris "added if he had ever lost money at it [gambling], he would never seek to recover it, and did not hesitate to say that he that would, under protection of the law, seek it, was *****."[17] Whatever the deleted remark, Morris clearly thought a man who refused to accept risk and pay his losses deserved to lose trust and reputation among his fellow men. In essence, he defended the old gambling code of honor, and tried to bring it closer to the law by shrinking the difference between wagers and any other kind of contract. Making lost wagers more like other debts turned sporting culture risk-taking into an object lesson in the rights of creditors. Taken together, a new theatre would create more credit-worthy citizens, while limiting the recovery of gaming losses would teach them to take calculated risks because they had to pay their debts. A reborn sporting culture would promote energetic striving from men of all ranks while encouraging investment by supporting creditors' rights and justifying elite investors' power at the helm of bank and theatre monopolies.

For their part, Morris's foes did not oppose entrepreneurialism or a culture of risk-taking. After all, they wanted to increase the amount of money in circulation. They just wanted money and culture governed more directly by the state's most representative body, not by a private clique of "the most respectable among" them. These critics trained their attacks on the "aristocratical idea" behind such a "highly dangerous" system, where "all is done by nine or ten men." Harkening back to the bank and theatre advocates' own words, they said that "if we enquire what constitutes the respectability meant in the report" urging for power to rest with "the most respectable among us . . . we shall very probably find it riches. They have more money than their neighbors, and are therefore more respectable." Claiming to expose the bank leaders' trope of community service as a charade, they continued to see drama as "a species of amusement Calculated only for men under despotic Government," and accused the bank men of using theatre to "draw the public attention to amusements in order to prevent it from being too much turned to politics."[18]

Newspapers recognized the importance of the bank and theatre debates when they noted that "among the various objects of discussion before" the state legislature in 1786, "none bid fair to create so warm debates as the motion relative to the bank . . . and the bill for regulation of the theatre." The votes on these issues confirmed the link between them. All but one out of seventy-three legislators either supported or rejected both institutions. Together, the bank and the theatre drew the battle lines in a political fight over the power of private capital, and the degree to which that power would be normalized through a sporting culture that espoused the values and structures of capitalism.[19]

Morris and his friends lost the first encounter in this fight. Both the bank and theatre votes went against them in late 1785 and early 1786. Over the next two years, though, the faction banded together with men of similar mind in other states and reversed their losses. Key to this reversal was their decision to drop the rhetoric of explicit censorship and guidance by a self-appointed elite, in favor of describing their proposals in terms of "freedom." It certainly helped to have Thomas Paine come out in favor of banks as "the offspring of free countries," in contrast to authoritarian ones where "the rich secret their money, or keep it locked up for their own use only; and the bulk of the people, from the want of its free and confidential circulation, are kept poor." Along with the devalued state money's failure to improve the economy, the rhetorical shift toward "freedom" helped sweep Morris's cohort back into power in the fall of 1786. They quickly reinstituted the bank in the spring of 1787, and then spent the summer leading Pennsylvania's delegation at the Constitutional Convention, where they became known as "Federalists" for their support of a new central government that could check the states through its economic powers to tax, coin hard currency, and govern interstate trade.[20]

In arguing for the Constitution's ratification, Federalists across the country rearticulated Morris's concept of virtuous self-interest by linking it to freedom. As James Madison famously argued, "faction," or the division of citizens "by some common impulse of passion or of interest," could be eliminated only "by destroying the liberty which is essential to its existence." If selfish interest was an expression of liberty, then constraining self-interest in the name of virtue was actually an act of tyrannical oppression. Reframing profit-seeking as a liberty common to rich and poor men alike emphasized a democratic sense of opportunity that helped defuse the explosive antipathy unleashed by foes who had labeled the bank, the theatre, and then Federalism as "aristocratic." Their new rhetoric helped Federalists win ratification in Pennsylvania, and they sealed their ascendance by legalizing theatre eighteen months later. The successful petition to sanction the stage, submitted not by actors but by prospective investors in a new playhouse, likewise made its case in terms of freedom. "Those who wish the prohibition of the Drama," it announced, "seek to deprive their opponents of what they consider as a rational enjoyment, and by their success will abridge the natural right of every freeman to dispose of his time and money according to this own taste and disposition." Opponents did not have to attend the theatre, but a ban infringed on the freedom of others.[21]

As with risk-taking, Federalist leaders did not believe in unlimited freedom. They wanted to govern it by hitching it to an economic system that inspired striving, and that they could control through private capital. The first Congress made this approach clear when it chartered a new and even more powerful national Bank of the United States, which would invest the federal government's money and have its directors elected by its private shareholders—not by citizens or their elected officials. Advocates rationalized such control by claiming that an economy based on opportunism and open competition

meant that wealth reflected the superior ability deserving of greater authority. "A country like this," wrote one Federalist, "knows no distinction but that
which arises from merit." So Americans "have nothing to fear from the profu-
sion of wealth which" in other countries "gives one class of men the advantage
above another." Under this logic, wealth was not indicative of inherited advantages. It reflected the virtue and merit of men who successfully served
their own interest and the community's at the same time, and thus deserved
the power to guide the country and its economy.[22]

Yet the new economic culture, and the sporting culture behind it, did not
grant wealthy investors unchecked authority any more than it granted citizens
unlimited freedom. By Morris's own logic, leadership belonged to men whose
pursuit of interest successfully benefited the whole community. Hence, the
subscribers across the country who incubated the new economic culture by
legalizing and then founding new versions of genteel sport in the 1790s all justified their endeavors the same way bank directors did: by citing how these
projects fostered business in general. Theatre advocates claimed that tailors,
rope-makers, and shoemakers all stood to benefit from contracts to raise the
building and outfit the company. The sale of refreshments inside the house
would support butchers, bakers, and local farmers. "All these trades and orders
of citizens, therefore, will undoubtedly be benefited by a Theatre," concluded
one Boston advocate. Of course, such stimulation of the local economy also
justified subscribers guaranteeing themselves a return of 6 to 10 percent.[23]

Indeed, every major city in the country built at least one new theatre between 1790 and 1820, and all of them promised investors an annual dividend.
Such income was not just a sign of greedier investors. The new sporting
culture did not support theatre as a product of elite beneficence, as in the
colonial period. That approach reeked of aristocratic hierarchy. The new republican elite was supposed to be rooted in commercial success, and dividends
indicated the transformation of theatres from sites of aristocratic patronage
to worthy republican businesses.[24]

Similar principles motivated jockey clubs as well. The breeding boom in
Virginia led owners elsewhere to clamor that "absurdly banishing horses from
the race ground" only led "the breed of our horses to degenerate," while "the
breeding of fine Horses in this state would be very advantageous to the farming interest." Massachusetts permitted racing in 1809, and its jockey club
avoided any reference to elitism or "fine" thoroughbreds, instead calling itself
an "Association for the Improvement of the Breed of Horses." Whether they
pandered through utilitarian phrasing or not, all the new jockey clubs legitimated their existence by claiming to help people vet bloodlines in the expanded
thoroughbred market.[25]

Clubs also commercialized the racetrack experience. As common land disappeared in the pursuit of growth and profit, clubs had to purchase tracts for their racecourses or pay rent to landlords.[26] Rather than cover these costs by raising subscription rates, members chose to erect fences, charge admission, and cull rent from concessionaires. Some even subleased the track to a "proprietor" who paid rent covering the club's ground lease and in return pocketed any additional income from concessions and admissions. By steadily raising rents and requiring proprietors to fund improvements to courses, such as new stands and taverns, clubs added infrastructure and expanded their budgets without raising annual subscriptions above ten or fifteen dollars. On the other side, however, less than a quarter of known track proprietors kept the same job for more than five years.[27]

In their quest for revenue, several clubs charged gentlemen for "showing" their studs to the widened market for thoroughbred breeding that gathered to evaluate horseflesh at races. At the Nashville course, run in part by Andrew Jackson, crowds at these shows blocked views of the track and choked pedestrian traffic, leading Jackson to push all stud horses "but such as contend on the Turf" outside the grounds in 1805. No jockey clubs paid dividends because owners were members and they competed for the direct income racing generated. Nevertheless, in their efforts to foster the equine economy while minimizing out-of-pocket costs, club members unleashed a commercial bonanza that risked overshadowing the races themselves.[28]

The drive to prove worthiness through a more commercial version of genteel sport did not mean that investors gave up on trying to impress the public in other ways. In fact, much of the money they put into sporting events went toward erecting spaces that marked their distinction as a meritocratic "Natural Aristocracy" by mingling old symbols of exclusive gentility with new symbols of republican virtue—materially folding superior refinement into superior worthiness in an effort earn deference.[29]

Sporting venues communicated this message in several ways. Perhaps most obvious was that investors announced theatres' newfound civic importance by building them within sight of a state house or city government headquarters, instead of on the edges of town. Theatre exteriors made the same point. Whereas colonial examples failed to meet the architectural standards established by churches and mansions, post-Revolutionary investors erected new facilities of unquestionable gentility. The new theatres in major cities cost at least ten times as much and accommodated at least three times as many spectators as their colonial predecessors. As the example in figure 3.1 attests, they featured brick exteriors instead of wood, and included Palladian windows, formal pediments, and ornamented cornices. All these elements

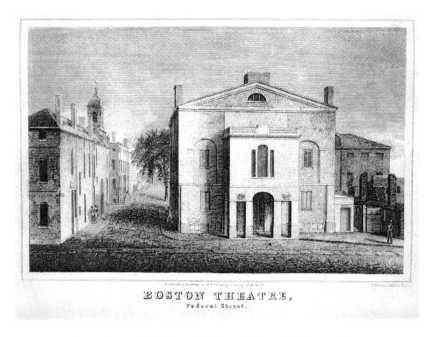

FIGURE 3.1. *Boston Theatre Federal Street*, Abel Bowen (Boston, 1825), engraving on paper, courtesy Massachusetts Historical Society.

were executed in a monumental neoclassical style reminiscent of ancient Greece and Rome, America's historic models of republican virtue.[30]

Every playgoer received the theatres' civic lessons, but interiors signaled the superiority of box seat patrons in ways that were unprecedented in America. Paneled woodwork, Greek columns, classically festooned drapery, and "Fancy painting" or gilded trim on the front of the boxes distinguished them from the simple turned balustrades and colorless decor of the gallery above and the pit below (see figure 3.2).[31] Playhouse architecture further declared the eminence of box patrons by separating them from the moment they approached the building. Box ticket holders climbed steps and walked through the elevated front doors of classically ornamented façades, while pit and gallery ticket holders came in through unadorned entrances, sometimes located off a side street. The managers of Philadelphia's new Chestnut Street Theatre even advertised that their "entrances are so well-contrived and the lobbies so spacious, that there can be no possibility of confusion among the audience going into the different parts of the house." Distinctive spaces, rich in classical overtones, simultaneously linked box patrons to the older distinction of refined gentility as well as the commercial republic's newer emphasis on virtuous wealth.[32]

FIGURE 3.2. *Inside View of the New Theatre, Philadelphia*, Ralph, *New York Magazine* (April 1794).

Like theatre investors, jockey club members advertised and demonstrated their deserved place in the natural aristocracy. Racecourse stands actually became more exclusive spaces in the early national period, despite becoming bigger. Club records even started to call these structures "club stands," denoting their exclusivity and permanence in comparison with the colonial-era "gallery" or "scaffold" intended "to accommodate Gentlemen and Ladies" regardless of their relationship to members. The Massachusetts Jockey Club instructed race attendees "to apply to a member" for stand tickets, and Charleston's club publicly stated that its stand was "built exclusively for the accommodation of the Club and their families and strangers that may be invited." Even the small Tappahannock Jockey Club in rural Virginia limited stand access to members and "any person who is a citizen of any State of the Union other than Virginia, on being invited by a member." The new version of genteel sport was more explicitly commercial than its predecessor, but investors still wanted it to produce the exclusivity and deference that had eluded colonial subscribers.[33]

For the second anniversary of Boston's jockey club, in October 1811, local poet Robert Treat Paine delivered a poem that articulated why members thought they deserved such distinction. His ode made horse racing into an allegory for American society as club men imagined it under the new economic culture. The poem began by claiming:

All ranks try the turf—'tis the contest of life
    By a heat to achieve a renown.
So throng'd are the lists in the full blown strife
    That but few know what steed is their own.

The opening lines picture society just as Federalists wanted it, with everyone competing for renown. Yet the accessibility of the competition does not mean that all contestants are equally likely to win. The throes of such a crowded field cause most people to misjudge themselves, to over- or underestimate their abilities. Only a "few know what steed is their own," and pursue realistic goals. But while the many

Loose their rein and their course as they go,
    The Rider, high train'd, knows each pace in his stud
And hark forward he flies, Tally ho!

The "high-train'd" rider not only knows his abilities but possesses many, and knows when to use each "pace," enabling him to navigate the crowd, get ahead of the pack, and win renown.

The remainder of the poem introduces the heroic soldier, the indecisive statesman, and the hard-working farmer as different equine breeds, each pulling Columbia—the nation itself—to victory. The poem grants value to all three groups, though the refrain constantly refers back to the "high-train'd" horseman, no doubt representing the club's members, whose skill and knowledge makes the others work together so that

Columbia is drawn by the Steeds of the Sky
    The long journey of Empire to run.

Club members appreciated Paine's paean so much that they submitted it to a local newspaper, which published it along with the members' toast to themselves. Drinking "To the smiles of the fair; the encouragement of talent; and the patronage of the public," members confirmed their intertwined pursuit of recognition, merit, and profit.[34]

Theatre subscribers did not present themselves any differently. The petition to legalize the stage that finally cleared the Pennsylvania legislature concluded by describing the investors who wrote it as "men of science, friends to virtue, and approved guardians of their country." Federalists had won the right to install their economic and sporting systems, but they knew their victory had come at the cost of acknowledging the need for popular approval. They endeavored to earn it by asserting their merit and by crafting economic growth and opportunity.[35]

Investors' rhetoric linking their leadership to superior ability was belied by the fact that more than three-fourths of identifiable sporting investors between 1789 and 1820 were born to families ranking in the upper 20 percent of wealth in their communities or had failed at least once in business. In truth, more than superior talent, investors benefited from inherited wealth and the superior connections required to rebound from failure.[36] Yet banks, theatres, and jockey clubs all espoused the rhetoric, shrouding the privilege of wealth and connections behind messages of merit, while opportunity came to outsiders largely through cultivating support from an elite investor. For instance, the percentage of bank loans to nonshareholders increased over time, but less wealthy borrowers still needed ample collateral or, more often, wealthy and connected friends willing to cosign their loan. In this system, even "new men" who rose from obscure origins did so through hierarchical networks of patronage that fed Federalist aspirations.[37]

Genteel sporting projects similarly revolved around tight mercantile networks. Trustees remained men on the make in their late twenties and early thirties, reliant on older, wealthier men to lure other subscribers and assist them in their rise. The only major change to the mechanics of sporting projects in the early national era was the sharp rise in the percentage of merchants and "merchant-planters" involved. In New York, 65 percent of theatre subscribers, and all of the trustees, belonged to the elite merchant investment club called the Tontine Association. Boston's Tontine claimed 90 percent of investors in the city's new Federal Street Theatre.[38] Philadelphia had no Tontine, but one-third of subscribers to the 1791 Chestnut Street Theatre and ten of its first twelve trustees were invested in other projects with Robert Morris. Full subscription lists are not available for Charleston's 1793 theatre, though the prologue spoken at its opening suggests the same mercantile dominance. It "compared the opening of a new theatre to the launching of a ship, and followed up the metaphor through all the vicissitudes of nautical hopes and fears" that merchants knew better than most.[39]

Jockey clubs followed roughly the same model. In smaller towns, clubs were led by established leading owners who possessed the best horses but also saw club management as part of their general role as hubs for business and investment in their communities. In bigger cities, clubs were led by aspiring young merchants and traders who owned no horses but saw the club as a networking tool or a complement to their primary business. For this reason, auctioneers and wine merchants dominate the trustee lists of major jockey clubs. Auctioneers hosted sales at tracks, and wine merchants sold their products to concessionaires.[40] Morris was not involved in any jockey club, though the clubs' reputations for facilitating selective networking and maximizing members' business profits led his foes to attack his circle with a satirical pamphlet titled *The Philadelphia Jockey Club, or Mercantile Influence Weighed*. Networking goals also explain why jockey club members spent almost half of their subscription funds on exclusive balls and dinners, as well as why they limited membership to the same demographics as theatre projects despite annual dues that held steady across the country at just ten to fifteen dollars while inflation made that sum more affordable than theatre subscriptions costing fifty dollars or hundreds more.[41] Finally, the goal of exclusive networking also explains why clubs restricted their new stands to out-of-town guests. Admitting local nonmembers, though they might prove useful associates, reduced the sense of a club's selectivity. Members could meet local nonmembers at any time. However, "strangers" expanded members' connections while embodying their vision of a national elite bound together by shared interests.

As in the colonial period, exclusive gentility did not just aim to distinguish an elite but to help forge one by deepening the economic connections among its members. Neither a new language of freedom and opportunity, nor new expectations of commercial success and productivity, changed this function. As a result, with the exception of even greater merchant dominance, the rosters of the early republic's meritocracy looked much like those of the colonial era's genteel elite. Sporting culture, like the larger economic culture it supported, endorsed an economic and political hierarchy even as it also espoused greater possibilities for every citizen. Indeed, investors wanted the latter to justify the former.

The Curious Case of Dr. John Stratton

The legalization of genteel sporting activities took longer in some places than in others. New Jersey was one of the last states to legalize racing, in 1835. Yet the attempted prosecution of New Jersey doctor John Stratton in 1803 reveals that the popularity of revitalized genteel sport helped it take root even when antisporting laws remained on the books.

New Jersey did not technically ban all racing in the wake of the Revolution. It only barred races "for money, goods, or chattels, or other valuable things." However, prizes and gambling proved difficult to prosecute because authorities needed proof of payment. The law prevented large advertised prize purses, but smaller events and personal wagers left no records, and convictions were hard to secure when all the evidence was hearsay. So, in an effort to better enforce its ban, the New Jersey legislature simply assumed gambling was present at every race with a crowd, and prohibited any equine "trial of speed" attended by more than ten people.[42]

State Circuit Court Judge Josiah Foster did not agree with this law. Early in 1803, Foster presided over a series of cases in which Evesham Township resident Samuel Matlack charged Dr. John Stratton, Dr. Benjamin Budd, and three "assistants" with organizing a race between the doctors' horses. Matlack headed the township's Committee for the Suppression of Immorality, a Quaker-dominated citizen vigilance organization formed "to see that the laws against Horse-racing, Sabbath-breaking, Prophane Swearing, &c. were carried into execution."[43]

There was little question of the defendants' guilt. There was no firm evidence of gambling, but numerous witnesses confirmed that "several times" the minimum number had gathered along an open roadside to watch the races. The event was so big that Matlack's committee members heard about it in advance. They arrived prior to the race and announced their intent to prosecute if the event went on. The warning irked one of the assistants organizing the event, Joseph Merit, who reportedly "swore by his Maker that they came there to run horses and would run them in spite of all the damned Quakers on this side of the Bottomless Pit." So they did, and the committee pressed charges.[44]

The defendants' alibis were so far-fetched as to imply extraordinary confidence in acquittal. Stratton, a twenty-five-year-old graduate of the University of Pennsylvania's medical school who had recently returned home to the area and acquired property through marriage, claimed "he was on a borrowed horse, which had run away with him several times that day; and could run away with him when he pleased." He produced a witness to testify to the animal's temper. Budd, Stratton's senior by nine years and a member of one of the township's most powerful families, used the exact same excuse, though he at least supplied a different witness. In effect, the doctors asked the court to believe their race was really the result of two men who just happened to be riding next to each other in front of a crowd on borrowed horses that spontaneously bolted at same time. Two of the assistants even vowed that they "did not assist in the race," thus conceding one had occurred. The third assistant offered no defense whatsoever.[45]

All five men were exonerated, which is not surprising given Foster's handling of the proceedings. Most notably, he issued special orders that allowed only the defendants to choose jurors. "The plaintiffs objected to most of them, alledging they were on the [race] ground; which was acknowledged by several of them," but none of these racing enthusiasts were removed from the jury. A juror in one case even testified on behalf of the defendant in another.[46]

The trials indicate more than the doctors' ability to evade the law. Foster could not have manipulated proceedings so baldly unless the general population treated antisporting laws less seriously than outspoken critics did. Tellingly, no newspapers mention the cases. The sole remonstrance against Foster was a pamphlet published by the defeated Quaker committeemen. Only religious zealots, austere republicans like the western Pennsylvania antitheatre bloc, and a cohort of elitist social conservatives—together constituting a smaller fraction of the population than their constant petitioning and publishing makes them seem—believed that gambling and its related activities threatened the social fabric of their communities. Legislators passed laws against these activities as symbolic nods to republican and religious ideals, and to the active minority who lobbied hard for them. "Indeed," Philadelphian Lynford Lardner wrote to a friend who recommended stricter gambling laws, "passing them seldom amounts to anything more than a legislative Testimony against the Evils they are intended to remedy." The statutes were poorly enforced everywhere, as evinced by the steady stream of petitions and laws drafted from Massachusetts to South Carolina because an existing act "hath not been fully and duly executed." In New Jersey, prosecution for racing was so unpopular that a new ban in 1811 included a provision to protect whatever self-righteous officer actually attempted to enforce it, specifically warning violators not to "assault, beat, or otherwise ill treat any officer designated in this act in the execution of his official duty."[47]

Why were local men of standing such as Foster, Stratton, and Budd not swayed by the critique of racing? Put simply, they thought that sport offered them opportunities that outweighed their fears of disorder. When opponents described "the *unbounded freedom*, the *manly* and *elegant* recreations of the Europeans—such *innocent* and *sentimental* amusements as *horse-racing*," they used italics to mock the characteristics commonly associated with racing. Yet the regular use of the terms they mocked indicated the uphill battle they faced. Like Robert Morris (and James DeLancey before him), Foster, Stratton, and Budd saw an opportunity to craft order from the alluring perception of unbounded freedom and competition at sporting events. On a road in Evesham, two well-connected doctors raced their horses, assisted by two "yeomen" and one tenant farmer whose only taxable property was a single cow.[48] No evidence suggests Stratton and Budd rode thoroughbreds, but their race functioned much like genteel thoroughbred races. The community gathered to watch a competition featuring its presumptive elite, though in this case the gentlemen jockeyed the horses themselves and so allowed their community to judge their sporting prowess. Just as Morris and his friends saw a chance to secure economic and political power by forging an alternative morality of freedom and self-interested ambition through sport, so the New Jersey gentlemen maintained their prominence by refuting the unpopular strictures of religious ascetics who wanted a social order built in opposition to risk-taking behavior. In the wake of a Revolution rooted in liberty and opportunity, well-to-do racers and theatre advocates figured their approach was more likely to yield deference.

"First on the Turf"

Of course, providing popular entertainment was only part of the equation. The new economic culture required aspiring elites to justify claims to leadership by securing profit for themselves and growth for their communities. Theatre investors did this by demanding commercially viable playhouses while touting how they benefited artisans and merchants. Jockey club subscribers did it by expanding their business networks while sponsoring races that helped identify superior bloodlines accessible to a widening swath of the population. The small percentage of club members who actually owned thoroughbreds added an additional layer of direct personal profit, since they were the ones doing the racing, breeding, and selling. During the early national period, a handful of these owners came to dominate the market, consolidating the economic and political rewards it offered by committing more resources to racing than anyone else. The story of such "leading owners" illustrates how the commercialization of racing abetted a centralization of profit and power not unlike what happened in the theatre.

John Tayloe III exemplified this process. Tayloe's affinity for racing started early. When he was just two years old, his father considered sending him away to be raised by family friend George William Fairfax, "lest he becomes a racer, for he is fond now of horses to distraction." The son had merely learned from his father. "Indeed," John Tayloe II admitted, "his father is foolishly so." Ultimately, the younger Tayloe was educated in England rather than the Fairfax household, a move that did nothing to quash his predilection for fast horses. Like John Baylor and William Byrd III before him, John Tayloe III came home in 1791 to manage his family estate smitten with thoroughbreds and equipped with the wealth and English connections to satisfy his taste.[49]

Upon his arrival, Tayloe discovered that Baylor and his father had revolutionized the thoroughbred market by lowering stud fees in order to attract a broader clientele. While colonial owners had hoped their thoroughbreds would generate just enough income to cover the costs of racing, the economic crisis of the Revolution jolted owners into angling for a clear profit from their thoroughbreds as much as any other commercial product. Breeding boomed as the economy recovered and new imports arrived from England after the war. Traveling through the Chesapeake in the 1790s, Polish émigré Julian Niemcewicz saw "in the inns the doors covered with two kinds of placards or notices. The first announce that such and such a stallion offers its services to mares at such and such a price. The others all begin with these words, Run away." Only escaped slaves were advertised as much as thoroughbred studs.[50]

Though a crowded market heightened the competition to profit from thoroughbreds, significant income remained possible. Niemcewicz marveled at the stud operation run by a former Revolutionary cavalry commander in New Jersey. "He paid 1,800 dollars for" his top stud, Niemcewicz reported. "He hires it out to cover and takes 10 dollars for each occasion. The stallion has served one hundred and more mares in a single summer; the income therefore is 1,000 dollars. He had another stallion which he sold for 2,000 dollars." The astonished Polish visitor could not believe the sums. "Can it be true that a single stallion that the General owns brings in perhaps more than his farm of 200 acres?" It could. Tayloe's operation yielded comparable returns by 1800. He grossed almost $2,500 off thoroughbred breeding and sales in banner years, a total equal to his annual land rents.[51]

Breeders chased these large profits through the regular importation of horses representing different bloodline combinations. The goal was to amass an assortment that would appeal to a wide cross section of society. Tayloe's 1801 order for "one capitol horse, the other tolerable" effectively summarized the strategy. But with dozens of horses arriving each year, and their offspring generating hundreds more, owners struggled to make their horses stand out. Tayloe's fellow Virginian John Hoomes recognized the solution to this dilemma. One of his purchases, Escape, had "head & ears bad, his rump strait as a goose's & about 7 inches lower than his withers or shoulders." Fearing the horse would "be thought nothing of & would not fetch 300$" when he had cost $750 to buy and transport across the Atlantic, Hoomes saw only one way to improve the value of such an eyesore. "What to do with him, I do not know," Hoomes wrote, "except he runs well, & I must, altho I can illy afford to train him, try by placing him well to win some of the purses & sell him." Racing victories negated a horse's aesthetic shortcomings by proving its physical superiority. The inverse was also true. "Let his beauty be what it may," Tayloe once wrote of a slow but comely stud, "his performances have been so indifferent, he will not sell." The growing number of stud horses, and the uncertain physical appearance of new arrivals and new foals, drew owners and their prospective clients to racing as an objective way to sort the superabundance of horseflesh and "improve the breed."[52]

As in the colonial period, thoroughbred races involved running multiple heats of two to four miles in a day, proving strength and endurance in addition to speed. As many thoroughbred stud advertisements stated, these qualities "bid fair for getting the best stock either for saddle or harness" and had been "approved of for geting foals well calculated for the farmer" since the war years.[53] Races also proved the value of more than just the entrants. Since British owners generally refused to ship successful racehorses during or immediately after their careers, many imported studs were too old to race and were judged on the performance of their progeny. Virginia planter Peyton Skipwith's horse Baspar acquired a "great Reputation, as many of his Colts prove Excellent Coursers. Some of his Colts of ¾ [thoroughbred] mares have beaten full Bloods." A fast racehorse elevated the value of its entire bloodline.[54]

Seeking to raise their breeding and sales income by winning races, a handful of men poured resources into breeding and training champions. These "leading owners" differed from others in several ways. Most obviously, they tended to buy, sell, and breed thoroughbreds on a larger scale. But also, like other active sporting investors, their thoroughbred business represented one part of an unusually diverse and aggressive investment portfolio. For example, besides his enormous thoroughbred operation, Tayloe converted his plantations from tobacco to grain, continued his family's investments in iron forges, and speculated in urban development (including Washington, DC's theatre), turnpikes, and stagecoach lines—the latter also benefiting from fast horses, of course.[55]

Men outside the ranks of the leading owners did not fit the same mold. Tayloe's cousin, Edward Lloyd IV, similarly grew up with a father deeply engaged in racing, planting, and shipping. But Lloyd scaled back the diversity of his investments during and after the Revolution, until he derived over 90 percent of his income from farm rents and crop sales in the 1790s. Accordingly, he stopped racing, did not replace his father's thoroughbred stock when it died, and slave grooms disappeared from his inventories in the 1770s. When he died in 1796, his son followed his program, rejecting the opportunism of the new economic culture and instead taking a more conservative approach to investment.[56]

Leading owners also invested more than others in racing infrastructure. This included founding local jockey clubs in order to facilitate regularly scheduled races. John Tayloe III organized the Tappahannock Jockey Club near his home in 1796. The club's members all bred to Tayloe's studs, had their horses shod by Tayloe's blacksmith, and traded plantation foodstuffs with him. Rather than pass along costs to spectators Tayloe wanted to cultivate as clients, he also covered annual expenses that exceeded the subscription total. Predictably,

Tayloe's horses won the two largest purses in each of the club's first four years. His streak only ended when the club moved to the larger town of Fredericksburg, where it attracted entrants from other leading owners. Similar stories of jockey club entrepreneurialism sprang up elsewhere. Leading owners went on to compete against each other at major regional events in Charleston, Richmond, Petersburg, and Baltimore, having created and monopolized local races in order to maintain superiority in their neighborhood markets.[57]

Tayloe and his ilk differed even more by committing significant portions of their landholdings to support racing. Tayloe converted some of his remaining tobacco fields to oats (to feed the horses) and erected an "Oakley Stables" complex that included expansive paddocks and a one-mile training track besides horse stables. He also acquired a staff of slave grooms, owning between three and six at any one time. Like other leading owners, Tayloe offset these costs by training lesser owners' horses. These clients paid a small daily fee that rarely covered Tayloe's stable expenses. But when one of his clients' horses proved promising, Tayloe negotiated for rights to organize its racing and breeding schedule, and took a share of any profits. He also bred these animals to his own stock at reduced rates. Racing and breeding were high-risk endeavors. Purses only went to winners in this era, and champions as well as quality sires often came from unexpected parentage. Leading owners used their superior facilities to lower the cost of accessing the widest possible range of potentially profitable horses.[58]

Tayloe's records also expose how leading owners took control of the equine labor market. Most leading owners were Southerners, a result of the breeding boom's origins in Virginia and the subsequent speedy reinstitution of racing in the region.[59] Ever since the shenanigans of Robert Gay, southern owners had begun to replace hired white horsemen with supposedly more tractable slave labor. This movement quickened in the 1780s and 1790s, as owners' concerns shifted from cheating to reducing competition and expenses. White grooms like Gay and John Craggs demanded high salaries and pursued other owners as clients, just as Tayloe did when he asked Maryland planter, forge owner, and local leading owner Charles Carnan Ridgely, "Will you be good enough to inform the Gentlemen Sportsmen in your State Where they may be furnished with some of the best stock in America?" Ridgely purchased horses jointly with his salaried trainer, who also facilitated sales of his accomplished racers, illustrating the competition Tayloe faced from free white trainers and grooms. Some of these horsemen, including Craggs, set up independent businesses, though leading owners grew perturbed at their presumption even when they were contracted. Both Tayloe and John Hoomes complained about their white "Groom having lately behaved much amiss" and "above the duties of his Stable," comments suggesting irritation at white stable chiefs who lorded over slave staffs and thoroughbred stock as if they themselves were genteel masters rather than hired labor. As proponents of the new economic culture, leading owners relished competition. Yet because they needed to finish on top to justify their power, they were unwilling to risk losing income or control of the system. So they increasingly turned to slave grooms whose unfreedom limited their ability to challenge their owners' position and profit.[60]

The development of slave stable staffs helped leading owners control and extract further profit from other owners. When Tayloe asked Ridgely to spread the word about his horses for sale, he also offered Ridgely a slave jockey on a ten-year loan for $800. South Carolinian William Alston similarly bought grooms as well as horses from Tayloe. By the 1810s, leading owners' slaves had acquired renown for managing their masters' fine horses. Many lesser owners hired them rather than buying and training a slave or sending a horse to a leading owner's stable. "Where is Dunwody?" asked a planter with a small stable seeking to hire Andrew Jackson's well-known slave groom in 1805. "He is the only man I wish to assist me in preparing the horses this next season." Not unlike the horses they cared for, slave grooms and jockeys traveled hundreds of miles, expanding their owners' influence and income. The value of this work explains why John Tayloe's first slave groom, Sam, was appraised in his fifties at the same amount as a field hand half his age. Grooms in their twenties and thirties were among the highest valued slaves Tayloe owned, worth about four hundred dollars, or 25 percent more than a prime field hand. Only domestic servants were reckoned at higher sums. Tayloe's inventories reveal how he developed this valuable labor pool by cycling into his stable young, sickly, cheap slave boys unsuited for field work, training them as lightweight jockeys or grooms through elders like Sam, and then hiring out or selling the ones he did not keep. A lesser South Carolina owner acknowledged the advantage gained from controlling this labor force when he concluded his request to hire Richard Singleton's slave groom by telling the leading owner, "I will do what I can to get him & will make reasonable compensation for his service."[61]

In all, Tayloe had more than $4,000 invested in his stable at any one time, including animals, feed, facilities, and slaves. This sum earned him a place alongside the biggest leading owners, such as Wade Hampton II, Richard Singleton, and J. B. Richardson from South Carolina, and fellow Virginians Miles Selden and John Hoomes.[62] These men already sat atop the thoroughbred market by 1798, when Tayloe's British supplier wrote, "I wish you Success with all your Stud, as you are first on the Turf there. I hope you will continue so."

Tayloe and a small group of owners realized the supplier's hope by competing further and further afield from their local bastions. Winning at the state and regional levels expanded their clientele, allowing owners to earn even more in breeding and sales. In turn, this income funded another round of imports, infrastructure improvements, and racing. Soon, the circle of leading owners able to compete beyond their locality shrank to the eight or ten men at the top of the pyramid. Tayloe made the cut. He and Selden won several more Richmond and Washington races than any other owners between 1800 and 1810. Singleton and Richardson similarly dominated Charleston between 1810 and 1820.[63] This small clique came to control not just the most valued thoroughbreds in their counties, but in the country. An average owner near Charleston told the tale in 1819, when he wrote to Singleton, "I learn that there will be no competition against you in this quarter." Later that year, a pair of Virginians wanted to consign their horses to Singleton after failing to get "the stock in to notice" under their own names. By the 1830s, Tayloe's sons and Singleton were sending studs and racers as far away as Tennessee, Alabama, and New York.[64]

Leading owners used their racing victories to convince lesser owners to buy and breed from them. With each new wave of imports, they sold older foreign stock and its lesser offspring to smaller owners. These men in turn sold their aged and poorer stock to men further down the pyramid. At the bottom of the hierarchy stood middling and even poor tenant farmers in possession of ill-shapen, slow, domestically bred, part-blooded horses.[65] Yet even these men could tie their misbegotten animals to the leading owners' champion racers, and advertisements for lesser horses encouraged this association. For example, breeding to the horse Orion cost six dollars in 1807, a steal—according the advertiser—because his sire was the "imported Stirling who covered at 30 dollars the season." Similarly, an 1808 ad lured customers to Virginia-bred Plough-Boy by claiming he cost just ten dollars while his brother Gallatin had just set the American sales record at $4,000 "and is now standing in S. Carolina at a higher Price than any Horse in the State." By the 1810s, leading owners had used racing to arrange a diffuse breeding market into an inclusive and national yet hierarchical arrangement of vertical networks, each made up of a wide range of owners with a shared interest in the same bloodline.[66]

The influence embedded in these vertical networks of ownership supported political as well as economic power. Tayloe, Singleton, and Hampton all followed in the footsteps of James DeLancey, turning their notoriety as successful owners into elected office. Indeed, almost all leading owners played active roles in state politics. These men stood on both sides of the partisan divide that emerged in the 1790s as Thomas Jefferson's Democratic-Republicans emerged to challenge the Federalists. Jeffersonian leading owners, though, tended to rank as moderates within their party because they remained proselytes of the new economic culture. They favored an energetic government that promised to create opportunity under the guidance of centralized private capital. What they opposed was their own personal exclusion from the empowered Federalist cohorts of Robert Morris and Alexander Hamilton, and the degree to which those cohorts thought the creation of opportunity required tariffs on imported goods. These Jeffersonians were, as one recent biographer wrote of Wade Hampton II, "officially Republican, but often sympathetic to policies that were Federalist." They were locked out of Federalist leadership, but their opposition was not rooted in a different economic culture, and they were as prepared as any Federalist to use sporting culture to prove their merit and gain public support.[67]

"A Sensible Man but He Is Very Weak"

Theatre investors resembled leading owners in applying their financial control over playhouses and managers to serve political and social—not just strictly economic—ends. Although the independent mobility of actors and the requirement that they take on multiple personas minimized support for a turn to black labor onstage, the story of William Dunlap's predecessor (and David Douglass's stepson), Lewis Hallam Jr., details how politics and reputation conspired with concerns over profitability to drive investors' decisions and prevent early national performers from replicating Douglass's success.

Hallam inherited the leadership of Douglass's troupe while it performed on Jamaica during the Revolution. After the war, assisted by his stepfather's old lieutenant John Henry, Hallam pushed to repeal theatre bans in the new United States so he could bring the company back to the mainland. In fact, it was his petition that sparked the Pennsylvania legislature's theatre debate in 1785. The company had arrived in town earlier that year at the behest of theatre advocates convinced of impending victory. Hallam covered the moving costs by mortgaging Douglass's Philadelphia theatre to the troupe's longtime friend and creditor, printer William Bradford's son, Thomas. The mortgage contract granted Bradford a seventy-year lease on the theatre in return for five hundred pounds.[68]

At first glance, the deal did not seem to work out in Bradford's favor. He could not make the most of the facility until theatre was legalized in 1789. After that, his income never added up to his costs, which included an additional five hundred pounds loaned to Hallam over the next ten years. Correspondence and accounts suggest Bradford received next to nothing in repayment, despite Hallam's constant promises. When the company reaped nightly grosses of one hundred pounds during successive seasons in New York in 1785 and 1786, less-forgiving creditors received all the attention. Bradford delivered Hallam's payments to these men, and the manager even asked him to help cover for delays, such as when Hallam claimed he was "mistaken" on the due date for repaying a loan from a Philadelphia broker. "It should not have run [over the deadline] a moment," Hallam wrote. "I'll have it the instant I arrive, and the Difference occasiond by the Delay, so pray tell him."[69] Paying these debts never left enough for Bradford, who only received a series of notices telling him that "Disappointment of every sort have for some time been a Constant Companion," and "a Train of Cross Accidents and Misfortunes" led to "seeming neglect" of the printer's requests for remuneration.[70]

Why did Bradford accept a loss from his association with Hallam? Maybe his deep investment in the company and the playhouse reflected a sincere affinity for the stage, but it also helped declare him a political moderate in a time of polarized extremes. In the 1780s, the printer backed the theatre while he supported the western representatives against Morris's cohort on the bank issue. Whatever his personal proclivities and social goals, his relationship with Hallam and the playhouse helped keep Bradford connected to both sides in a political firestorm, a helpful position considering Bradford's newspaper was not a one-party mouthpiece.[71]

Things changed in the 1790s, as Bradford drifted more fully into the Federalist camp. Then, in accord with the emerging economic culture, concerns about profit and genteel distinction affected his lenience toward Hallam. At the same time, Hallam began to jeopardize Bradford's return on both these fronts. The manager's troubles multiplied in 1789, when he hired a beautiful eighteen-year-old actress named Elizabeth Tuke. Long separated from his wife, the forty-seven-year-old Hallam started an affair with Tuke shortly after her arrival. The young woman seems to have had a serious drinking problem. As the years passed, she often took the stage "in too degraded a State to be seen." Her alcoholism also contributed to frequent illness. Once, on the road from Philadelphia to Baltimore, she spasmed into "A Difficulty of Breathing attended with Spitting of Blood with an ardent and Nervous Fever." Fearing the worst, Hallam feverishly wrote to Bradford, wishing "to God you coud take a Ride as far as here." He enclosed a plea for medical assistance addressed to the famous Philadelphia physician Benjamin Rush. As the letter to Rush remains folded and tucked inside the letter to Bradford, the printer apparently believed the situation was not as dire as Hallam portrayed it. The theatre manager had a stereotypical tendency to overdramatize events. Tuke recovered. Hallam, however, slipped into depression. He told Bradford that "the Millancholly

Impression left on my Mind by that Event" left "my own Situation Truly Distressing."[72]

The manager soon began to complain regularly about his own health. Perhaps his rising debts caused his bout with "a kind of Vertigo of that most Alarming Sort." He was also stressed by competition from Thomas Wignell, one of his actors who had developed a fan base and used it to push for lead roles Hallam usually played. When Hallam refused to relinquish the roles or promote Wignell into management, Wignell split from the troupe in 1791 and drew on his wealthy supporters to raise a new company as well as the Chestnut Street Theatre to house it. Abandoned by most of his Philadelphia investors, Hallam kept his company in New York.[73]

Thomas Bradford did not subscribe to Wignell's projects. His investments kept him tied to Hallam's company. Yet Wignell's ability to attract attention and funding reflected Hallam's declining reputation. "O Ye Gods & Goddesses what a feast the dry-boned Devil must have had," remarked one critic when Hallam married his mistress a month after his estranged wife died in 1793. "The old wretch has long been under restraint by reason of a wife," but "I'll bet he's had many a tiss of the woman before he was married." Additional criticism of the marriage came from Hallam's oldest and most faithful company members, who questioned the woman's character more than her age. Emboldened by wedding the manager, Tuke allegedly compounded her onstage inebriation with offstage bullying. She spoke to performers, backstage personnel, and even her husband's co-managers in "ill language" and "true billingsgate tone." Supporting actor Joseph Jefferson thought the new Mrs. Hallam "the worst woman that ever lived." Veteran company member Joseph Tyler blamed Hallam, who he thought was "certainly a sensible man but he is very weak." "Sooner than be concerned any longer where Mrs. Hallam was," John Henry allegedly commented that "he would transport himself to Botany Bay," the new British penal colony in Australia. After thirty years as second in command of the company, Henry sold his shares and departed (though not for Australia).[74]

These grumblings might just reflect the opinions of older men opposed to taking orders from a younger woman whose marriage had given her some authority. Nevertheless, Hallam's censure had far-reaching consequences. The next year, a bid to gather subscribers for a new theatre in New York failed. Two years after that, in 1796, another rising star named John Hodgkinson gathered enough backers to buy Hallam out of his management role. Hodgkinson then partnered with William Dunlap and found enough subscribers to build a new theatre—the one William Henderson oversaw. Hallam tried to protest. He told Dunlap he was "out of money," so he "went around to his old supporters and complained loudly," but they would not give him enough to prevent the buy-out. Still, he insisted on giving directions to the new managers and clearly itched to reassert himself.[75]

His opportunity finally came in 1801, when Wignell's Philadelphia troupe signed a contract with Bradford to perform off-season sideshows in Hallam's old theatre. Hallam wrongly believed that the 1785 mortgage contract reserved him the right to accept or reject other performers' use of the facility. He had explicitly transferred this right to Hodgkinson and Dunlap as part of his buy-out in 1796. As a result, in 1801, the new managers decided to try to make extra money by helping Bradford rent out the theatre, and had already booked the place when they learned that their old patron had leased it to their archrivals. Enter Hallam. In a scathing letter to Bradford, he threatened "to seek legal redress" and demanded to know "by what right, or under what pretext that property is made use of without our Sanction or knowledge." Hallam's tone presumed equality with Bradford, and it reflected both his sense of betrayal and a desperate effort to retain influence by securing the playhouse.[76]

But Hallam was not Bradford's equal. The printer controlled the theatre and Hallam's credit, and the manager's personal life exposed his supporters both financially and socially. So the investor used his legal control of the old theatre to align himself with the more reputable and creditworthy local troupe. In response to Hallam's letter, he wondered how the actor could presume to direct him when "he has received no pay for taking care of the house for 13 years past." Bradford concluded by declaring "that he had full powers to rent the house in such manner as he thot proper . . . till he was paid what they owed him." The New York managers were barely solvent themselves, facing rapacious investors and debts accrued to maintain their company while the new theatre was being built. Since nobody could pay Bradford, Hallam's power play failed. The onetime manager was forced into smaller and smaller roles. Only an appreciation for his work in reestablishing theatre after the Revolution kept him from being kicked out of the company altogether. His second wife received no such mercy.[77]

Lewis Hallam Jr. kept control over his company, and friends covered his constant losses, only as long as he served a political purpose and maintained his reputation. As several period observers noted, "all the American managers are losers." Every man who amassed a small fortune as a star actor "began now bitterly to reproach myself for having meddled with management," as their losses forced them to sell genteel trappings such as carriages, when David Douglass had used management to periodically acquire them. Those who tried to diversify their investments while they had money could not break free of their investors' grasp either. Actor James Fennell opened two salt refineries with thousands of dollars of loans from wealthy fans. When the refineries required repairs that prevented Fennell from repaying his creditors on time, they seized the facilities. Fellow thespians joked that Fennell's salt schemes doomed him to "always be in a pickle," but Fennell did not laugh about his time in debtor's prison or his inability to escape the acting profession.[78]

Performers' financial straits reflected investors' new strategies and goals. Their ownership of playhouses and demand for dividends were symptomatic of both the new economic culture and their growing economic control within it. Down years saw subscribers everywhere vote to pay themselves, or at least limit their losses, by selling theatre chandeliers, seizing bar receipts contractually promised to managers, and refusing to make repairs. Powerless managers and actors had to bear these decisions and serve investors' social and political ends in order to receive the leniency they needed to avoid failure and default. Even William Dunlap, whose assets in New York City were worth just one hundred dollars less than trustee William Henderson's in 1789, was constantly insulted by the trustee's refusal to accept his visit while "the great man was at table" with friends he considered to be peers. Dunlap's estate mattered less to Henderson than the inherent subservience of his position as a sporting pro. Under such conditions, performers who lost public favor, were insubordinate to financial backers, or pressed for equality by trying to escape the confines of their sporting profession found investors less friendly than when they remained dutiful and popular vassals, vessels of the virtue and gentility investors wanted to reap from theatre along with their profits. This less forgiving reality meant even fewer pros realized social and economic advancement than in the colonial period.[79]

"The Room Where Formerly a Billiard Table Stood"

Tavern gaming did not follow the pattern of racing or theatre because it was harder to justify. Unrelated to the productivity associated with better horses or more work for artisans and retailers, strict republicans and religious moralists argued that gambling did not create wealth but only circulated it. Moving money based on games involving chance rather than based on rewarding those who ably generated growth for the whole community defied the new economic culture as well, so tavern gambling remained illegal in every state. Robert Morris tried to reduce the window for recovering gambling losses but did not try to legalize wagering. His limited goal was not the result of living in a state associated with Quakers. South Carolina levied a heavier fine than New Jersey for playing cards, dice, and period versions of roulette. Meanwhile,

Massachusetts, Pennsylvania, North Carolina, and Virginia all declared tavern billiard tables "liable to be seized and publicly burnt or destroyed."[80]

Everywhere, the strict laws first enacted on the eve of the Revolution particularly targeted tavernkeepers for their alleged "hoary duplicity" in entrapping "incautious youth," the "industrious mechanic," and the "wealthy farmer" through the "taverns, billiard tables, and different games" they "daily set up."[81] Lawmakers punished sporting professionals more than the gamblers they hosted because they were easier targets. Players had to be caught in the act of a proscribed game, but tavernkeepers could be prosecuted merely for possessing the equipment. Still, gaming persisted. After one citizen cheered South Carolina's latest "energetic law passed for the suppression of Gambling," he wisely added that "there remains nothing but the will of the virtuous part of the community to be exerted to crush the hydra Monster and prevent him in future from corrupting the rising generation." That will was missing all across the country. Richmond visitor Isaac Weld "had scarcely alighted from my horse at the tavern when the landlord came to ask what game I was most partial to, as in such a room there was a faro table, in another a hazzard table, in a third a billiard table, to any of which he was ready to conduct me. Not the smallest secrecy is employed in keeping these tables," he reported, despite their illegality. Philadelphians admitted the same "easy Evasion." In Connecticut, too, outraged commentators noted how often they saw "a billiard table kept in open defiance of the laws of the state."[82] Periodic raids nabbed a few violators, usually those with the fewest connections to authorities, but did not diminish the prevalence of gaming.[83]

Yet despite minimal variation in gambling legislation and enforcement, regional differences did influence the evolution of sporting taverns. As a comparison of architectural evidence and business records makes clear, the new sporting culture crafted by investors during the early republic was not immune to the emerging sectional differences over slavery.

Philadelphia's venerable Center House Tavern epitomized the sporting tavern's post-Revolutionary development in the North. Changes to the "ill red house" were apparent by 1788, when the venue hosted a sermon by the famous radical Quaker evangelist, Jemima Wilkinson. Wilkinson's preaching defied accepted gender roles, and she underscored that defiance by wearing a long black gown like a male Puritan minister, as well as by advocating celibacy and abolition. Jacob Hiltzheimer, the city's aging don of horse sales, attended the sermon and noted the irony of having Wilkinson preach "in the room where formerly a billiard table stood." The Center House was still a tavern, and the audience probably went as much for the spectacle of Wilkinson's performance as to seriously consider her message, but Hiltzheimer's description suggests that the venue was not the same place where Alexander Graydon went slumming and John Bruluman shot Nicholas Scull.[84]

The ensuing years brought a complete overhaul of the facility. In 1798, the city erected a market adjacent to the tavern, bringing regulated commerce to the site and thereby reducing its image as a shady meeting place on the outskirts of city authority. The next year, hairdresser John Mearns bought the lease and transformed the rear yard into a pleasure garden "arranged as to present a most picturesque variety and rural retirement." Additional outlays for fireworks, ice cream, and an "elegant Organ" transformed the one-time bawdy tavern into an "agreeable and pleasant Evening Lounge" for "Ladies and Gentlemen . . . combining at once all the recommendations of the city with the peaceful simplicity of a village." The tavern structure became merely the façade for the garden rather than the site's primary attraction.[85]

The Center House might have been the only sporting tavern converted into a pleasure garden, but every northern city saw its number of sporting taverns shrink and its number of pleasure gardens rise between 1790 and 1820. New York's row of sporting taverns facing the field that became City Hall Park came down in favor of fine townhouses, and a row of pleasure gardens went up further north along Broadway, culminating with the most famous American example of the genre, Niblo's, which opened in 1828. In Boston, too, a theatre replaced the sporting tavern at the south end of the Common in 1796, and the Washington Gardens opened nearby in 1814.[86]

Patterned after British models, pleasure gardens offered romantic settings complete with landscaped spaces, music, fine food, and alcoholic beverages. In effect, they were genteel outdoor taverns. American examples were more accessible than British ones. Admission cost between eighteen and fifty cents, the same amount as gallery or pit seats in theatres. So, while advertisements announced separate spaces available for private parties, higher entrance fees for special events, and portrayed a select clientele, eyewitness reports blandly depicted attendees as "an immense concourse" or simply "the public," and described Irish tailors bickering in brogue with their self-proclaimed superiors over who really deserved the title of "gemmen" (gentleman). Conspicuously absent from such observations were references to "ladies and gentlemen," "the respectable crowd," or other terms that denoted exclusivity. In sum, pleasure gardens featured social mixing not unlike sporting taverns, only they framed the mingling in genteel terms. Pleasure gardens invited all comers to assert their gentility, just as sporting taverns had invited all men to prove rough virility. Demand for such venues rose in part because the new economic culture led to the removal of tavern price regulations. As upscale taverns and new hotels grew more expensive, pleasure gardens provided more accessible places for a wide range of people to perform gentility.[87]

Meanwhile, the demise of sporting taverns in the urban North did not mean the experiences they offered disappeared. Aggressive masculine competition remained available at new and more specialized venues such as gambling houses and billiard halls. These facilities were smaller than the sporting taverns they replaced, occupying "apartments" or townhomes instead of sprawling complexes. Proprietors of these venues also specialized in a particular brand of sporting experience, not just in a single kind of activity. Fine gambling houses endeavored to replicate the renowned clubs of London. "An elegant house furnished after a superior manner" cloaked aggressive competition in genteel accoutrements well enough to make reporters think the clientele was "respectable." At the other end of the spectrum stood small tavern-groceries, where "a horde of profligate companions" might "play for three cents or a glass of liquor" while using "violent and reproachful language," and the proprietor was less likely to have the connections needed to keep him out of criminal court or debtor's prison.[88]

The rise of pleasure gardens and the shift away from sporting taverns in northern cities reflected the rise of the new economic culture. Laws and enforcement did not change much, but the invitation to achieve upward mobility created a growing demand for accessible genteel sporting venues at the same time upscale taverns became more exclusive. The advertisements for pleasure gardens make clear that many operators wanted to cater to a select clientele. However, like the tavernkeepers before them, the cost of establishing and running their venues meant they could not sustain their business on elites alone. For half the cost of theatre box seats, or the price of the "fashionable cloths" required to access a high-end public gaming house, aspiring patrons could lay their claim to refinement.[89]

The proprietors' broad clientele was largely the product of elite investors themselves, who owned the land and buildings that housed the new facilities. These investors persistently pushed for maximum returns rather than scaling back rent in order to permit less profitable exclusivity. The Center House's John Mearns knew the problems created by this choice. Hairdressers, confectioners, musicians, and actors were typical pleasure garden managers because they came from crafts already connected to gentility and elite investors. They sank themselves into debt to produce polite settings, a range of food options, nightly "illuminations," and other performances. But multiplying competitors and short summer seasons made profits difficult to realize, and the few proprietors who had purchased their properties quickly lost them, while renters rarely survived for more than two or three seasons. Even William Niblo lasted largely by subletting his place to a train of actors. Astonishingly, as in the theatre, new managers were never in short supply. Despite high failure rates, another high-end tradesman or actor always thought their ability and connections could turn a profit. Only in smaller southern cities with longer summers and less competition did pleasure gardens witness stable and profitable management.[90]

Gaming hall proprietors fared no better. Their costs were lower, but keepers of upscale examples still went into debt for furnishings and gaming equipment. Records of those who were prosecuted suggest that many were foreigners who received little protection from creditors when they failed to pay or were charged during a periodic crackdown. In New York, men like cornet player Augustus Gautier and former sugar planter Aaron Soria—both of whom had fled the slave revolt on St. Domingue—tried to rebuild their capital by running gambling establishments but did not last long enough to succeed. Others, often native born, skipped town as soon as they made money, jilting creditors and leading peripatetic lives. Only a select few were decorous, well connected, and profitable enough to run stable and successful gaming establishments.[91]

Gaming houses and pleasure gardens opened in the South, too. But sporting taverns also survived there, albeit with a slightly altered management model. Robert Armistead was among the new mode's pioneers. The son of a small planter outside Norfolk, Armistead first arrived in Petersburg on the eve of the Revolution. His training as a carpenter was valuable in a boomtown just taking off as the port city for a rapidly growing expanse of south-central Virginia known as Southside. Armistead made the most of his skills, buying a lot in town after the Revolution. He built and ran a tavern on that lot, joined the town's nascent jockey club, and made his public house the premier stop for sportsmen heading to the races. Upwards of seventy guests resided there during the spring 1796 event, including Benjamin Henry Latrobe, who reported "a number of Gentlemen, professed Gamblers," running roulette and faro tables. In contrast to gaming hall proprietors like Soria, Armistead's standing and his tavern license shielded him from prosecution for these activities. After all, he was a church vestryman, and his tavern hosted the local hustings court. It was also the site of the town's exclusive ball during George Washington's presidential tour. By the time he died in 1802, Armistead had held several town offices and had branched out into retail sales, leaving his wife to manage day-to-day operations at a sporting tavern that also hosted genteel events.[92]

Other southern sporting tavern proprietors blazed even grander trails, having come to the business with greater resources. English immigrant John

Wise amassed capital through successful real estate speculation, then built a tavern in Alexandria in 1785 that featured both fashionable architecture and a billiard table. By 1792, he owned three other taverns and added a "hotel" next to his first one, replete with an exquisitely finished "assembly room" for exclusive balls. Since southern newspapers still described tavern billiard rooms as places where "the sot, merchant, cobbler, captiain, blacksmith, spruce gallant, pick-pocket, and jockey are all, 'hail-fellows, well met," Wise's facility—like Armistead's—was home to both exclusive genteel events and nonexclusive gaming.[93]

The cost of building these all-inclusive facilities was staggering. Armistead's tavern was insured for $5,100, Wise's for $3,100, and Connecticut merchant Edward Hallam insured the Eagle in Richmond for $51,000 after he married into a Virginia planter family and poured all of his own resources as well as his wife's dowry into renovating and running that complex in the 1810s.[94]

These sporting tavernkeepers survived better than their colonial predecessors. But they also defied colonial precedent as tavern owners who operated their facilities instead of leasing them. The model lured tavernkeepers of lesser wealth to try to replicate it, though their lack of capital tended to yield different results. For instance, Esme Smock left his tavern in northern Virginia in 1802, in an effort to monopolize central Virginia's sporting taverns. After one year, he had leased both Armistead's and the Eagle. He probably relied on Masonic connections to finance his fledgling empire, but doubling his costs stretched his credit. He abandoned both taverns by 1806. Undaunted, he tried again the next year, leasing a racetrack and its on-site tavern north of Richmond. His performance must have cultivated trust from jockey club members, since several soon loaned him money to re-lease the Eagle. Again, however, his vision exceeded his means. When he was unable to repay over six thousand dollars in loans, Smock's creditors seized his lease on the racecourse in 1809 and he died in debt several years later.[95]

John Gadsby was the exception that proves the rule. He arrived from England and rented Wise's tavern in Alexandria for eight years, then leased Baltimore's Indian Queen hotel from 1804 to 1819. After fifteen years, he held city lots and shares in bank stock, turnpikes, and mail coaches. He also was Baltimore's largest slaveowner. Still, he was a renter. Gadsby finally opened his own hotel in Washington in 1827, after thirty years of successfully renting and steadily building his assets. Most tavernkeepers simply did not enjoy the combination of management skill, longevity, and good luck required to follow Gadsby's long road to ownership and fortune.[96]

The relationship between tavern ownership and long-term success was not new or unique to southern tavernkeepers. Pleasure garden proprietors, gaming hall operators, and every other kind of sporting pro had a better chance of surviving if they owned their sporting facility. What was new was the sudden appearance of wealthy owner-operators hosting both exclusive and genteel, as well as accessible and raw, events at sporting tavern venues that were disappearing from the urban North at the same time. A few sporting taverns, such as Williamsburg's Raleigh Tavern and the one owned by James DeLancey on the edge of New York City, had hosted this range of events in the colonial period. However, Wise and Armistead represented a growing number of southern proprietors who did so in the post-Revolutionary years. McCrady's Tavern in Charleston was another example, mingling a public billiard room with polite parties and bridging the colonial-period division between Dillon's and Backhouse's facilities.[97] The trend was a southern phenomenon. As genteel taverns morphed into hotels in the North, examples such as Oeller's in Philadelphia and New York's City Hotel did not possess billiard tables. An exception, stashed in the attic of Boston's high-end Exchange Coffee House, was highly controversial (as well as the starting place of a fire that burned down the whole building). Neither did northern gaming halls host publicized genteel gatherings. Only in the South did men of wealth enter into tavernkeeping and then cater to both rough and polite crowds.[98]

This regional difference cannot be explained without discussing how the evolution of slavery influenced early national sporting venues as much as the new economic culture did. The value of urban land rose in both the North and the South during this period. Immigration did not become a significant difference until the 1830s. Of all the possible explanations, none accounts for the regional differences in sporting taverns better than the evolution of slavery. Although the Revolutionary movement had called slavery into question and triggered a brief increase in manumission in much of the South, the institution's persistence and its subsequent expansion as part of the cotton boom maintained the value of rough manhood as evidence of the physical prowess necessary to exercise mastery over slaves who might violently rebel.[99] At the same time, as we have seen, southern sporting investors also embraced genteel sport as Northerners did, hoping it would help them create both an empowered elite and settings in which everyone could improve themselves. Together, the emergence of the new economic culture and the persistence of slavery permitted a concoction of gentility and raw virility in the South that required less spatial separation between the two. In contrast, the drift away from slavery in the North during this period helped delegitimize displays of rougher brawn and led to a greater emphasis on the pursuit of gentility and its tempered offshoot, "respectability." Hence, new types of accessible refined sporting venues multiplied there, and rougher sporting spaces grew more marginalized. Pleasure gardens and gaming halls opened across the country, but the cultural impact of slavery's decline pushed the North's sporting taverns to fracture, while slavery's persistence in the South—along with the renewed push for gentility—prompted sporting taverns to grow more prominent by encompassing both genteel and rough sport. Slavery was crucially linked to the mainstream acceptability of rougher sport.[100]

Across the country, the evolution of sporting taverns, like that of theatres and racecourses, reflects how a connected cohort of aggressive investors attempted to inculcate a new economic culture of risk-taking and opportunity within the confines of a genteel hierarchy. Regional distinctions in the tavern market emerged from diverging approaches to slavery that produced different relationships between rough and genteel sport, but the importance of facility ownership to long-term success in both regions alludes to the overarching goal behind sport's return: the construction of economic and political systems that espoused competitive opportunism while rooting power among the few men with the assets and connections to control capital flows. The only question was whether the revamped sporting sites would fulfill their purpose any better than did their colonial predecessors.

CHAPTER 4

Prestige or Profit

When William Henderson told William Dunlap
in 1798 that New York's theatre investors wanted a financial return on their
subscription to a new playhouse, the manager was astonished at the investors'
greed "in such a case." After all, their colonial predecessors had not looked
for direct returns from theatre subscriptions. But investors in the early republic differed. Because they saw sporting events as incubators of the broader economic culture of capitalism that they wanted to oversee, they approached
genteel sport more like the other business ventures they hoped it would
foster.[1]

The investors' goals were ambitious. They wanted sporting events to turn
a profit while simultaneously generating both an inclusive sense of opportunity and a reverence for themselves as the "Natural Aristocracy" who merito-
riously provided that opportunity. Dunlap quickly perceived the incompatibility
of these objectives. If sporting event managers were forced, in his words, "only
to fill the treasury or pay hungry creditors," they would have to pander to the
masses to maximize ticket sales, and that goal would necessitate more democratic content than shows enshrining a natural aristocracy of elite "friends of
virtue and good order." Indeed, Dunlap spent most of his life bewailing
the "mercenary managers" and greedy investors whom he blamed for "the
corruption of the theatre." He believed that a less commercial, even a less
sporting, culture would have "let us give to theatres that purity, as well as

power, which shall produce the high moral purpose here aimed at." The tension Dunlap saw, between culling profit from sporting events and crafting prestige from them, animated the evolution of sporting culture in the early republic. Investors, professionals, and participants of all types wrestled with the issue and ultimately leaned in one direction or the other. This chapter explores their decisions.[2]

Dunlap knew which side he preferred. "I have been myself a shopkeeper," he once wrote in his diary, "but I was never a thorough bred one." While many Federalists justified their roles as "approved guardians of their country" by trumpeting themselves as purveyors of economic opportunity, Dunlap clung to the classical vision of a less profit-oriented republican elite that merited its position simply by being "the wise and the good." As their cultural representative, he aimed to "set proper exhibitions before a free and well-ordered people," as he put it in an effort to fit the new rhetoric of freedom within the older one of hierarchy. He wanted to help build an ideal republic that was both free and orderly by ignoring the issues created by commerce and wealth and focusing instead on "communicating that knowledge which leads to virtue, of exercising Justice or benevolence, and bestowing happiness."[3]

To Dunlap's unending consternation, however, he repeatedly discovered that the majority of theatregoers disagreed with him. Even nonelites in the audience embraced the new economic culture, seeing it as a vehicle for opposing any aristocracy, "natural" or otherwise. Dunlap recognized the reality of public opinion early on. In 1794, before he had formally entered the theatre business, he implored his peers to "go to the Theatre" and "support by your applause every chaste and moral production"—implying that he already saw unvirtuous content as ascendant. Four years later, audiences rejected Dunlap's vision more directly by deriding his play *André*. The drama tells the tale of British Major John André's capture and execution by American forces during the Revolution. But rather than offer a nationalistic celebration of the event, Dunlap complicated the story by foregrounding André's well-documented rectitude. His character had moved Alexander Hamilton so much that he entreated George Washington to alter his death sentence from a common spy's hanging to an officer's execution by firing squad. Essentially, the play asked American audiences to consider whether an enemy spy might have possessed virtue, and whether Washington was right to reject Hamilton's plea and hang him.[4]

The play answers both questions with a "yes," applauding Washington's cold but rational fidelity to military law as well as André's equally noble acceptance of his fate. It thus exemplified Dunlap's "high moral purpose" by appreciating all men of upstanding character regardless of which side they were on. But his point was lost among critics and audiences unable to shelve their nationalism. Newspaper reviews complained that the decision to hang André portrayed the soon-to-retire president as "an unfeeling, obdurate monster!" Critics and audiences also decried a scene in which the Hamiltonesque character Captain Bland learns he cannot save André, plucks the American cockade from his officer's hat, and "tramples it underfoot, vehemently cursing his country." Further criticism targeted the play's focus on officers at the expense of "the brave and heroic veterans" of the common soldiery. While the play grossed an impressive $817 on opening night, the fifth-largest gate of the New York theatre's inaugural season, attendance subsequently fizzled as word of the unpatriotic message spread. Despite altering the script to have Bland apologize for his anti-American tirade, a second showing on a rainy night failed to meet expenses, and the piece was staged just once more.[5]

Still more frustrating for Dunlap was the profitability of extravagant patriotic spectacles boasting, as he saw it, "execrable" substance. John Daly Burk's *Bunker Hill* typified this genre in Dunlap's mind, and he alternated between calling it an "utter disgrace" and "vile trash." The tragedy portrays British warmongers laying waste to virtuous self-sacrificing Americans. The protagonist is Boston patriot Dr. Joseph Warren, whose famous erudition and ties to elite colonial circles receive little treatment in a script that portrays him as an uncompromising agent of democracy willing to fight "as private or as leader."[6] Staging the heroic death of an antielitist patriot amid fellow martyrs who slaughtered more than their number of British soldiers appealed to American audiences. The play "brought them full houses" in Boston, making a cash-strapped Dunlap "sorry to say" that he had to stage it as well. The egalitarian patriotism of *Bunker Hill* trumped *André*'s elitist lesson in cosmopolitan conciliation.[7]

More concessions lay in Dunlap's future. By 1803, he had completely rewritten *André* to emphasize the roles of the farmer-militiamen who captured him. He appropriately retitled the piece *The Glory of Columbia, Her Yeomanry!* The revised script matched his company's increasing reliance on German playwright August von Kotzebue's melodramas, which highlighted man's natural inclinations to virtue rather than making it a product of learning and rational thought, as implied in *André*. Dunlap's original vision was defeated. He had to present plays like Kotzebue's *The Stranger* because, as he later put it in his memoirs, "the success of this piece alone enabled the author to open the theatre."[8]

Dunlap was hardly unusual in making this kind of decision. Other sporting events' investors and managers also chose to pursue profit at the expense of rules and content that might have engineered greater exclusivity and exhibited higher moral standards. However, their choice was not fully their own. It was at least partly driven by audiences who saw the same contradiction Dunlap did, and who refused to accept an elite unless it appeared to be forged in democratic environments where they felt they could engage and influence it. The resulting negotiations between participants, investors, and professionals explains why profit ultimately won out over prestige and how sporting venues ended up building a white male republic instead of a republican elite.

"A Consequential Air"

In the spring of 1810, a Philadelphia literary magazine detailed how nonelite audiences drove this negotiation when one of its correspondents described a recent visit to the Baltimore theatre. "I should have been high gratified," wrote the author after he reviewed the performance, "had the performers not been interrupted by several quarrels which took place in the upper lobby, which destroyed the effects of many of the best parts of the play." One of these distractions merited a full recounting. "A certain Cock Ram, who I suppose of the age of 18 or 19, and who has not long since been transplanted from a board-yard to the U.S. Navy," wanted "to display his elegant person as well as his uniform suit to the greatest advantage." So, "when the first act was nearly over, he strutted into the house and ascended as high as was practicable, with as consequential an air as though he had the command of a fleet." The writer watched with contempt as the bold sailor first "visited nearly all of the boxes in the gallery, mounting himself on the benches that he might be sure of being taken notice of," and then "majesticly descended to the boxes to try what effect his suit would have on the young ladies" in the highest-priced seats. After "not meeting with many tokens of their admiration, he concluded to visit the pit. There he posted himself with his back against the orchestra, that he might display himself before those who were in the boxes, pit, and gallery all at once."

Soon, though, "some of the young bucks began (as they call it) to quiz him." Their jeers led the sailor to climb back up to the gallery, where he sat "between two Cyprian goddesses," a period euphemism for prostitutes. At the next intermission, the sailor "went to the bar for the purpose of whetting his whistle," and was confronted by another audience member irritated by his parade through the house. "They were about proceeding to try each other's strength when [the sailor's] fair protectress rushed out of one of the [gallery] boxes and, throwing her arms around his neck, swore 'no one should strike her Cock Ram.'" Though she was a prostitute, being draped in her arms saved the sailor from a fight, "lest some of the men should whip him," the author thought.

The tale then concluded by warning "this knight of lumber that he had better keep cool, as I have heard some of our bloods say if he does not, they will very probably cool him."[9]

The sailor's adventure illustrates an expansion of accessibility and mobility inside the playhouses of the early republic, as well as the new battles for status triggered by this expansion. Importantly, the agents responsible for pushing this change were men like the sailor himself, who asserted his right to access every seating section. That this assertion was not yet fully acceptable is clear from the reaction of the "bloods" and "bucks," terms for fashionable but raucous young men who took offense at the sailor's "consequential air" and meant to put him in his place. Such confrontation was not new to theatres, of course. Insouciant gallery denizens had resisted claims of superiority from genteel box seat patrons in the colonial period. But the opportunities for conflict multiplied when men once relegated to the gallery started to move throughout the house.

Managers and their investors did not set out to invite this movement. They built post-Revolutionary theatres with separate entrances and pathways for gallery, pit, and box ticket holders, intending to segregate attendees according to social rank. A combination of profit motives and antiaristocratic sentiment undermined this design. The profits investors demanded were difficult to generate in the competitive early national theatre market. While colonial British America had hosted at most two or three touring companies at one time, six of the young republic's seven largest cities boasted at least one permanent theatre with its own resident troupe by 1800. Boston and Charleston possessed two of each, and New York and Philadelphia matched them by 1820. All these companies competed for talent, driving up salaries for top performers and forcing trustees to accept that "pecuniary advances will, under the existing opposition, be necessary." Such labor costs came on top of those for building playhouses, which, as at the Park Theatre in New York, almost universally ran over budget by thousands of dollars.[10]

The economic culture investors crafted did not allow them to respond to these costs by accepting a loss. Indeed, despite managers' difficulties, investors steadily escalated rent while seizing income they originally had granted to managers (from licensing refreshment vendors, for instance).[11] Managers reacted by making tickets more affordable, seeking to grow their income by expanding their audience. Across the country, managers abandoned the old requirement for patrons to apply in advance for box seats, and the price of box seat tickets remained steady at one dollar from 1790 to 1820. Although wages fluctuated widely according to local conditions, inflation reduced that dollar's real value by up to 12 percent, so the steady price and the greater accessibility of box seats admitted a broader range of citizens. A self-titled "aristocrat" at the New York theatre in 1794 described the new mélange when he noted that in "several of the Boxes I saw a considerable proportion of respectable mechanics and other industrious members of society."[12]

As important as commercial pressure was to democratizing box seats, demand for access to those seats predated the new theatres of the 1790s. Philadelphia lawyer John Lardner already complained about "boxes indeed rather shabily fill'd" at an illicit performance two years before theatre was legalized in Pennsylvania. "But this you'll say is quite natural," Lardner wrote. "As our government is become more republican, the Minds of the People of course become more so, & every body aspires to the fire place."[13] Lardner believed the Revolution had unleashed egalitarian expectations among "shabby" people, who began to push into the boxes. Nonelite theatregoers then relied on antiaristocratic sentiments to defend their places in those seats. When the manager of Philadelphia's Chestnut Street Theatre altered the new protocol of waiting in line for box seats on the day of the show, allowing guests to secure an entire box in advance if they paid for all eight seats, one prospective patron accused him of creating "Aristocratic Distinctions" that discriminated against "us humble folks who can only from our circumstances form small parties." The same outcry greeted the next Chestnut Street manager in 1811, when he decided to sell box seats for multiple nights if parties of four or more paid in advance. Offended locals deplored that "people in general have not an equal chance for a seat" in a plan they thought "encouraged an attempt at invidious distinction." Fearing public protests that might reduce attendance, both managers swiftly rescinded their proposals.[14]

Greater access to the boxes spurred social contest. Elitist writers suddenly began to complain about "sluyed victuallers, union-fed footmen, or jolly jacktars," like the Cock Ram, squatting in their box seats. Should a ticket holder arrive and "ask him to move," these commentators groused, "a challenge ensues necessarily." The initial occupant perceived his requested removal as a snobbish accusation of inferiority, and he typically defended himself vigorously against any assumption that he did not belong. "Insolent" retorts were, reportedly, "no uncommon case."[15]

Less social distance between spectators did not preclude conflict. The *South Carolina State Gazette* published affidavits pursuant to a case of assault among gentlemen in the boxes of Philadelphia's Chestnut Street Theatre in 1800. The episode began when three Marine officers realized Virginia Congressman John Randolph of Roanoke was in the box next to them. Aggrieved by Randolph's recent proposals to cut federal military spending, the officers first called him and his friends "black Virginia ragamuffins," then entered Randolph's box and "did jostle Mr. Randolph on his seat," finally pulling at his coat as if "determined to provoke him to a quarrel." Randolph reacted by calling the leading antagonist "a puppy," a term implying youthful immaturity and inferiority, but he did not respond physically. Others had no problem with fighting. William Dunlap's friend, Dr. Elihu Hubbard Smith, recorded "a fracas" or "a riot in one of the boxes" in New York's theatre five times in 1796 alone. Such "unpleasant altercations" in box seats had been virtually unknown in the colonial period. A seating section invented to enshrine gentility had become less predictably polite.[16]

Confrontation peaked in other parts of theatres, too. Pits continued to host gentlemen like Englishman Charles Janson, who preferred to venture there from the boxes "when I go for the purpose of giving my whole attention to the performance." In contrast, boxes were filled with "fashionables who think there is nothing so genteel as to disturb the performance by whispering as loud as most people speak." Yet gentlemen were not the only ones who went to the pit to focus on the play. While in the pit of the same Baltimore theatre graced by the Cock Ram, Janson met a "vulgar, noisy, squat figure" sitting on the bench behind him. The man critiqued the show in "the most coarse and vulgar phrases." In response, "often did I turn and in vain intreat his silence," Janson wrote. He wanted to forcibly quiet the man, but knew that if "I had seized the noisy intruder, instead of finding support, I might have had the whole pit upon me." Pit crowds were notorious for defending their right to judge performers. They destroyed most of the interior of the Charleston Theatre in 1817 when the manager refused to rehire a popular actor and pompously told dissenters in the pit "that any dispute between an Actor and himself was a private matter in which the audience had no right to interfere." Any hint of elitism—whether from a gentleman or a manager—was anathema in the new theatres of the republic, where spectators had long opposed privilege and now could do so face to face in more seating sections.[17]

This sense of empowerment also kept gallery patrons as active as they had been in the colonial period. The upper tier remained a stronghold of sailors, African Americans, and young men from reputable families who noted when "the theatre was so full that I had to go into the gallery." Published accounts portrayed these marginalized patrons shouting orders to performers just like pit occupants, as well as continuing to pelt pretentious playgoers beneath them with organic refuse. Washington Irving, writing in the guise of cynical elitist Jonathan Oldstyle, joined Janson in seeing no escape from the onslaught. He counseled his peers to "sit down quietly, and bend your back to it." A Charleston newspaper explained the motives for these bombardments when it reported in 1794 that a group of French sailors justified a "furious and indiscriminate attack on the audience" on the grounds of having "been grossly insulted."[18]

In sum, instead of helping a prospective elite earn deference, theatres became places where men of all ranks contested social hierarchy. Yet class distinctions were challenged, not blurred, by the greater accessibility of box seats and movement throughout the house. The wealthy and elite were not confused with the middling or the poor. They simply faced more direct and personal affronts from both supposed inferiors and peers who wanted to prove their equality even if they could not move up into more powerful circles. Philadelphia printer Matthew Carey summarized the resulting milieu when he wrote that

> the play-house, like the grave, brings friends and enemies together, and both are, as in the grave, promiscuously placed by the side of one another: yet, unlike the tomb in one respect, they assembled in the theatre not to lose the passions of nature, not to drop the asperities of the heart or forget they ever had a foe, nor yet 'to cease from troubling and be at peace'; but every man comes armed, either with the terrors of prejudice or the less hostile (though frequently not less dangerous) weapons of prepossession."[19]

Theatres across the country hosted nightly battles for status and respect, in which a cross section of (as we will see) mostly white men asserted their right to compete by asserting their opinions about performers, performances, and each other.

In limiting his description to "every man," Carey implicitly recognized that women faced stiffening constraints on their engagement in this environment. Most notable was the firm line drawn between box seats on the one hand and the pit and gallery on the other. Although box seats were recognized as the most genteel spaces in colonial theatres, little had been said about women of any rank who sat elsewhere. In contrast, illustrations such as figures 4.1 and 4.2 reveal the absence of ladies from pits in the United States, even though British examples showed them sitting there. English travelers corroborated the difference in the visual evidence, specifically noting on their American travels that "women never go to the pit."[20]

Women avoided pit-sitting out of fear for their reputations. As one Philadelphia newspaper conceded, even if ladies from a respected family "ventured into the pit, after finding it impossible to get seats in the boxes," they soon found "their reputation was entirely lacerated" for "their indiscretion, or what was called their boldness." This punishment came despite the reality of increasingly accessible box seats, which meant that "if she goes into the boxes, she is

FIGURE 4.1. Charleston Theatre Interior, Charles Fraser, Sketchbook, 1793–96, p. 51, ink and watercolor on paper, courtesy South Carolina Historical Society.

INTERIOR OF THE REGENCY THEATRE, TOTTENHAM STREET, TOTTENHAM COURT ROAD.
BUILT ON THE SITE OF THE KINGS CONCERT ROOMS.

FIGURE 4.2. *Interior of the Regency Theatre*, Robert B. Schnebbelie (London, 1817), etching on paper, © Victoria and Albert Museum, London.

subject to be squeezed in the same method and to meet with the same promiscuous assemblage formerly to be met in the pit." Genteel behavior had become less certain in the boxes, but it remained altogether uncommon in
other sections of playhouses. This difference justified labeling any woman in
the gallery a prostitute, and dismissing those in the pit as "not women of any
social standing," even though white men moved with increasing ease between
sections.[21]

White women faced firmer class lines at the theatre precisely because white
men found it easier to challenge them. Under an economic culture demanding that white men act boldly when opportunity beckoned and with restrained
etiquette when recklessness would alienate friends, they had to prove themselves refined and polite or coarse and aggressive, as the moment demanded.
The confrontation and confusion caused by this range of behavior led men to
limit women's ability to copy it, lest gender hierarchies become subject to the
same challenges as class. Men increasingly expected women to avoid sites of
rougher sport in order to prevent them from competing for social gain. The
republic's leaders helped shape these developments by predicating their notions of citizenship on masculine rights of property ownership and traits of
"energy," "vigour," and "reason," all defined explicitly in contrast to women
as economic dependents inherently endowed with "irrational passion." According to this logic, men possessed full economic and political rights because
they had the mental capacity, physical fortitude, and economic responsibility
to negotiate, challenge, and maneuver. Women were naturally unsuited to
brash environments, and so had no need for the behavior there unless immoral
disposition or dire economic circumstances drove them to it, and both these
realities indicated ungenteel standing. Proper ladies had the responsibility of
fostering gentility through conversation with men that would "mutually polish and improve one another," and so they were supposed to remain in the
boxes—the only theatre seating space where gentility was possible.[22]

Constructions of class among white women thus restricted their mobility
in order to prioritize their function as signifiers in a world where white men
could perform multiple brands of masculinity. A man surrounded by polite
ladies was evidently genteel. A man surrounded by women from whom he
might purchase sex was expressing his raw, virile economic power. If women
could move through theatres like men, their ability to designate a particular
brand of masculinity would be diminished because they themselves would not
be rooted. These gendered limits to movement only grew more important as
white men defied the behavioral rules formerly established by sporting space.
As the latest round of sporting architecture failed to order men's behavior, constructing and isolating different types of women became an alternative way

to signal genteel or rough sporting space. The residue of theatre's overall reputation as a site for genteel sport left minimal tolerance for any physical violence around women—as the Cock Ram's "Cyprian goddess" knew—but the presence of reputable ladies in the boxes even ruled out aggressive arguments and uncouth language men might otherwise now use to prove themselves in those seats.

Although the behavior of white men of all ranks established and enforced these gendered restrictions, gentlewomen actively policed them as well. The newspaper article bemoaning women's exclusion from the pit described how transgressors' "lacerated" reputations came from their tale being "bandied about from tea-table to breakfast and from the breakfast to the tea-table." Both settings were famous spots for women's gossip. Such treatment awaited women whether they sat beneath or above their supposed station. When some New York gentlemen showed up to an exclusive theatre event in New York with "women gandily dressed who appeared to belong to a low grade of society," other ladies present called them "publick females" but hardly criticized the men. Of course, this kind of criticism only identified women who were caught defying the rules. Whether others succeeded or not, the presence of these critiques demonstrates that some women resisted the tightening constraints even as others defended their social rank by enforcing them.[23]

Racial lines reinforced these class distinctions among white women. Gallery seats lowered the status of the white women there not only because men assumed they were prostitutes but because those seats put spectators on more equal terms with "colored people who can't sit anywhere else." Some southern theatres divided the gallery to preserve racial distinction for the whites sitting there. Charleston's city council went further in 1818, completely "prohibiting the admission of negroes or persons of colour, whether bond or free." Even in the North, the fleeting colonial-era references to blacks in box seats disappeared in the early national period.[24]

By 1820, increasing segregation and exclusion led African Americans to respond by opening their own theatres. Several scholars have studied the African Grove in New York, the most famous black playhouse of the period, but Charleston, too, was home to a "sable corps of players." In both places, however, the African American challenge to white men's control of formal theatre lasted only a few years. At the Grove, black performers and interracial mingling all over the house only intensified the behavioral confusion seen in white-run playhouses. Without race complementing gender as a marker of behavioral norms, boxes and galleries were even less differentiated. The chaos allegedly led the Grove's manager to complain that "White People Do Not Know How to Behave at Entertainments Designed for Ladies and Gentlemen of Colour." Rival white theatre managers and city magistrates used the chaos (and may have encouraged it) to justify shutting down the venue. Charleston's company disbanded after a leading actor was convicted of theft.[25]

Investors and other authorities permitted striving white men to behave roughly or genteelly, but tried to restrict black men to rough settings because leading thinkers, including Thomas Jefferson, disqualified them from gentility due to "a want of forethought" and an "existence [that] appears to participate more of sensation than reflection." So theatres did not become sites of class-based deference as investors originally planned, but they did help reify the gender and racial boundaries of a broader white male republic in which all white men—but only white men—could assert both the genteel and physical masculinity necessary to compete for opportunity, wealth, and power.[26]

The Banditti of Commercialization

Like other participants in sporting culture, investors, too, battled each other for profit and influence. Some of Boston's most successful artisans and aspiring merchants financed a rival theatre in 1796 after their proposal to incorporate a second Tontine was blocked by the wealthier members of the original one, who also had funded the city's first playhouse. Denied their own investment club, the subscribers saw a new theatre as their next best alternative to challenge the influence and power of better-established merchants. Similar events unfolded in Charleston, where investors in the city's first theatre lobbied authorities to license only one after a second had opened and the threat of competition meant that "their shares, which cost 50l. each, [and] sold for 60l. or 70l. each," suddenly "might be purchased for 40l."[27]

Competing interests similarly pulled at the seams of the racing elite, as the history of John Tayloe's Tappahannock Jockey Club illustrates. The club was named for the hamlet where it operated, directly across the Rappahannock River from Tayloe's home. Tayloe's closest friends filled club offices, and he won almost 90 percent of the club's races before 1800. He also personally covered shortfalls in club purses and expenses to ensure that the organization survived. But in 1801, club members voted to pursue larger crowds and a broader pool of members by relocating to the growing city of Fredericksburg, about forty-five miles upriver.[28]

More members and more distance from Tayloe inspired bolder efforts to reduce his control. Shortly after moving, the club met without its founder and decided to shift its 1801 fall races from October to September. "Who can train Horses in July and August to be in order to run in Sept?" Tayloe asked when he heard about the change. He also wondered "where is yr. company at the races to come from when at that sickly Season—everybody will be at the Springs." The club's new members probably did not overlook these points. They aimed to reduce Tayloe's stranglehold by making the event something he could not fully prepare for, and something other than a confirmation of the power held by his small circle of spa-going friends.[29]

Sensing this subterfuge, Tayloe protested "the proceedings of the late self-created meeting of our Jockey Club" in a letter to new club official William Herndon. The club's by-laws mandated racing on the second Tuesday in October, and Tayloe informed Herndon that the date was "never to be altered or amended during the Existence of the Club." "I therefore consider their proceedings a complete Nullity," Tayloe wrote. He told Herndon he would show up on the appointed day in October. If nobody was there, his horses would walk over the course alone, and "if the money is not at the Poles—I shall sue for it." He then concluded his tirade with an explicit statement of his influence and power: "We will see what member can refuse paing to me their Subscription."[30]

Tayloe wanted more members, more spectators, and larger purses. He just did not want more competition. But he could not get the one without the other. So, in the end, he compromised. The races were held in late October, not in the middle of the month as he wanted, or in late September as the new club members wished. The change still yielded the effect club members desired. The new date was at the end of the racing season, and Tayloe's prized champion Leviathan "had lost his spirits" from a hard race one week earlier in Richmond. Fatigued, he suffered his first-ever defeat. The Jockey Club's records, previously kept by Tayloe and preserved in his papers, disappear starting with this race, affirming his loss of control over the organization.[31]

The Tappahannock club's evolution suggests that its new members wanted to follow the model established in Petersburg, where leading owners had little to do with organizing one of the biggest race meetings in the country. In fact, no leading owner lived in Petersburg when its jockey club started in 1785. The town was growing quickly then, as the chief port for a region of southern Virginia with some of the best available land in the state. This growth lured several merchants from Britain. Two of them, John Bannister and William Haxall, presided over the formation of the Petersburg Jockey Club. Club records indicate the pair was joined by other local merchants and a few nearby farmers of note, such as Robert Bolling and Averill Cocke, who owned significant estates by local standards, though not in comparison to the enormous and varied holdings of leading owners like John Tayloe III. The membership was young, except for old Erasmus Gill, who owned the land on which the Newmarket course was laid out. In stark deviation from colonial practice, the club also accepted tavernkeepers James Bromley and Thomas Armistead into the fold. Not a single leading owner appeared on the subscription roster.[32]

It was a commercially minded group. Bromley and Armistead may have accrued social status from membership, but they also saw the potential to profit from a monopoly stating that "none but those who are now subscribers to this Jocky Club shall be at Liberty to Vend liquors on the ground."[33] Indeed, the motives for starting the club all seem to have sprung from racing's potential to help sell everything but thoroughbreds. A shockingly low number of the club's early members owned any racehorses at all. Young mercantile jockey club officers typically owned no racers, but even the Petersburg club's local planters only dallied in the breed. The club had to recruit owners to race at their events. Fortunately, its mercantile membership and location in a burgeoning entrepôt gave the club greater access to cash than most small jockey clubs. By 1800, only Charleston's races offered prize money on par with Petersburg's.[34]

Large purses attracted the best horses in Virginia and the Carolinas, and quality racers drew enormous crowds. Benjamin Henry Latrobe estimated that 1,500 watched on one day in 1796, and he complained about the accompanying spectacle of packed taverns, "sharpers," and "whores all agog." That crowd facilitated business for club members beyond the tavernkeepers. Postmaster John Grammer delivered and received packages. Haxall staged auctions in conjunction with the races. What Charles Fraser later recalled about Charleston's race week also described Petersburg's. It was a time when "the planter came to settle accounts with his factor, or to receive the proceeds of his crops, as well as to pay off the annual bills of the merchant who had supplied him with groceries and other articles throughout the year." Attendees mixed work and play, noting it was both "a dissipated week, and [one] when I was throng'd with business."[35]

In many ways, the jockey club not only capitalized on Petersburg's growth but fed it. "Southside" Virginia, the region serviced by Petersburg's port, became known as America's "horse racing region," and the Petersburg racecourse grew into Virginia's primary horse market. The track itself hosted major equine stock sales, many orchestrated by Haxall. By 1820, full-time stables lined the road leading east out of town toward the racecourse, preparing horses for races and the sales block.[36]

Yet the success of the Petersburg Jockey Club also defied logic. Nearby Richmond was a larger city and the capital. Norfolk was an Atlantic port. In those places, as in most cities, most jockey club members were local merchants, but clubs and races were dominated by regional leading owners who used them to highlight their own stock.[37] The secret of the Petersburg club's success lay in the absence of leading owners from its early membership. With no dominant local owners to serve, members concerned themselves less with the profitability of particular horses than the profitability of a general marketplace built around them.

By the 1810s, clubs everywhere were following Petersburg's lead. They contracted proprietors to manage their races and commercialized their courses in order to limit their costs and focus their spending on exclusive new stands, balls, and dinners that were calculated to increase their business connections.[38] Meanwhile, as leading owners lost their grip on jockey clubs, competition among them for profit from a widening range of breeding clients drove them into a host of compromising interactions that weakened their claims to exclusive distinction. Trackside "shows" of thoroughbred horseflesh, staged to win breeding clients, permitted social inferiors to paw and judge leading owners' stock. More importantly, this access became requisite because the owners' grooms became infamous for sneaky dealing. The "great variety of professional manoevers in the art of horse dealing" meant that a "purchaser must be in possession of a great share of good fortune or sound judgement to elude the ill effects of deception and imposition." Horse ownership manuals told potential clients that their only defense lay in executing their own careful check-up. "Deal with an honest man as you would with a rogue," they warned, for

> it is to be much lamented that men who entertain a proper idea of honour in all the common affairs of life, so soon as they become the owner of a horse, feel at liberty, without being sensible of doing violence to their morals, to knock off two or three years from his real age and express themselves with apparent delight, of services, gaits, and qualities to which he never had any sort of claim or pretensions; carefully keeping a secret every vice and defect to which he is subject.

Gentility and honor apparently had little purchase when a horse sale was at stake.[39]

A writer from New York's *National Advocate* recounted how the newly commercialized racetracks produced an experience not unlike that of the early national theatre. "Bless me! What a crowd!" the author exclaimed as he opened his story with a panoramic view of the Long Island race field. "Booths with cold ham and blind fiddlers—stage, with puppet shows—punch and judy." The reporter jettisoned complete sentences in favor of brief phrases calculated to capture the cacophony of activity. "Roly poly tables, EO—black and white, and vingt un—sweeps tossing coppers—sailors and their doxies from Corlaer's Hook—bucks in berlins." The field was awash in gambling games and a variety of patrons, from African American chimney sweeps to sailors and their supposedly promiscuous girlfriends to modish young men costumed in Berlin wool. The panorama ended with a glance to the grandstand, that "elevated situation, comfortable to run off with a young lady out of the second story window." In contrast to the ground level "concourse," the exclusivity and "elevated situation" of the stand was seemly enough to host a reputable "young lady" and was likened to fine townhouses with genteel parlors on the second floor overlooking the street. As at the theatre, class distinctions among women helped distinguish genteel from ungenteel space.[40]

If the *Advocate* seemed to mock the carnivalesque feel of the concourse, others feared it. Just a year earlier, the *Alexandria Gazette* questioned whether the Washington, DC, racetrack was no longer "what its name intimated—a course where horses ran races" but had become "a field for the banditti of the dice box and EO table to congregate upon like locusts for the purposes of plundering the inconsiderate, poisoning the morals of our youth, and preparing them for the gallows." The *Gazette* report spoke for a vocal minority opposed to racing, but English traveler Charles William Janson supported the sport and still found the scene distasteful. On a visit to the Washington track in 1808, he "saw on the race-ground, as in other countries, people of every description, sharpers in abundance, and grog, the joy of Americans, in oceans." Janson aimed to keep his distance, staying aboard his horse on the concourse. However, being "well mounted and a stranger" attracted rather than repelled gamblers. His fine steed marked his wealth, so he "was constantly pestered by these sharks."[41]

As the gamblers' attraction to Janson indicates, the concourse—like the theatre—did not blur class lines. Distinctions were apparent but challengeable in an environment flush with opportunities to assert individual status and compete for profit. Contention only increased over the next decade. According to the pseudonymous Simon Snipe, whose satirical *Sports of New York* described an ingenue's trip to the races in 1823, the confrontations started en route to the track. Aboard a ferry crossing the East River, a drunk dandy bumped into "an old fat black woman" and she reproached him for it. "Wat de debbil you mean by dat, hey," said the woman, called "sooty Dinah." "Why'nt you knock agin you own color, hey? Musn't tink to bang gin me wen you like. I'll give you a jab side de head nex time you doo't," she threatened. Since the 1770s, newspapers had described ferries sinking and stages breaking down on their way to the races, overloaded with assorted arrays of passengers. The black woman's aggressive response represented a new twist on this old story,

FIGURE 4.3. Close-up of commemorative scarf from 1823 Great Match Race, roller-printed cotton, courtesy American Antiquarian Society.

underscoring how the sporting milieu encouraged self-assertion even beyond the ranks of the white men it privileged. Yet a scarf commemorating the famous race Snipe attended in 1823, seen above in figure 4.3, restates the expectation that gender, class, and race would largely determine women's engagement once they entered a venue. It entirely erases African Americans' presence and shows just a few white women amid the throng of white men on the concourse, including one on the right who dons less genteel attire and appears to be neglecting her maternal duties.[42]

Whether at theatres or racecourses, ladies were supposed to avoid the most accessible ground-floor space because of the unrestrained cross-class contest there. The gentlemanly Snipe confirmed the inescapability of disagreeable mingling on the concourse in his report on the 1823 race, which he claimed to have watched while standing next to "a butcher boy" along the outer boundary of the racetrack. Snipe "desired that he would turn his head another way when he wished to shout again," but the youngster "bluntly assured me that he would hollow where he chose to." As in playhouse pits, common folk rejected any attempt to limit their self-assertion on the concourse. Yet, also like pits, concourses continued to attract gentlemen who went, as one put it, "in order to obtain a more distinct view of the struggle" than they could get from the polite and exclusive but distant and distracting experience of watching from stands and carriages.[43]

Sometimes the jumble turned violent. When the stabler at the Washington racecourse took his time bringing out Janson's horse at the end of his visit, Janson called him a "servant" and "spoke in a more angry tone, conceiving myself insulted by neglect." The stabler, who doubled as the local jockey club's secretary and no doubt equally felt insulted, "sourly replied, 'I must wait upon the gentlemen.'" Janson roiled at being excluded from the category, and claimed the response prompted him "to knock the varlet to the ground." He reacted much as Robert Wormeley Carter had when accused of cheating fifty years earlier, intending to prove his superiority by force when he could not do it through uncontested insult. Such pummeling was uncommon among gentlemen at tracks, though several duels arose from "the unjust and unprovockd attack you made on my feelings and reputation publickly on the race field."[44]

These confrontations over masculine status do not appear to have reached the stands, which clubs succeeded in keeping polite and exclusive to their members. No club records describe policemen like the one hired by the Philadelphia Jockey Club in the 1760s, nor do surviving reports cite infiltration. So, although owners and members created a more commercial and competitive concourse atmosphere in which their pursuit of profit and performance of masculinity contradicted their claims to gentility, they managed to balance profit and prestige better than theatre investors. They were able to preserve an exclusive space by bringing a wide range of white male patrons into equine families that remained headed by elite leading owners. Nobody demanded commercialization of the stands because everyone at the track had bought into the hierarchy of horse ownership and club membership. Nevertheless, commercialization bred a host of new challenges to owners, and not just from non-owning club members or crowds on the concourse.

"I Refer You to Cornelius"

The thoroughbred industry's black workers lived at the intersection of racing's social hierarchy and commercial chaos. Owners turned to black labor because most of it was enslaved and owners thought slaves would be easier to control than free white men in an expanding market. In fact, slave horsemen did help leading owners increase their income, but the realities of the thoroughbred business also created opportunities for bondsmen to defy the kind of dependence typically associated with slavery.

Cornelious Johnston seized these opportunities. Johnston originally belonged to Henry Garrett, a small planter in northern North Carolina who hired him out to other owners for twenty-five dollars per month, just less than those owners paid for white overseers. The months added up to a tidy sum. Records from South Carolina leading owner Richard Singleton show Johnston in his employ almost constantly between 1809 and 1819, after which the payments to Garrett cease, though Johnston's continued work for Singleton and a half-dozen of his friends suggests Singleton purchased him.[45]

"Hiring out," as Johnston's contracted work was called, was a common practice among slaveowners. Many sent their slave artisans and laborers to work for long spells on other plantations or in nearby cities. The slaves often found their own work, settled their own lodgings, and managed their own expenses while away. Johnston and other grooms differed only in degree, working in more places and traveling further than most slaves over the course of their careers. In 1833 alone, Johnston spent the spring breeding season in southwestern Virginia, then traveled over two hundred miles to the central South Carolina plantation of Singleton's racing rival and importing partner Wade Hampton II, then headed to Charleston in the fall to care for newly arrived imports from England.[46]

Notably, owners did not always determine Johnston's peregrinations. The slave himself orchestrated a remarkable trip in 1819 after he got sick while attending mares on loan in North Carolina. Johnston's local host sent Singleton a forty-dollar doctor's bill, along with a letter explaining that Johnston had asked him to write Singleton "and beg the favor of you to send him $150, as the Doctors have given it as their opinion that as soon as he is able to travel he should go to some of the Springs to relieve him of his Liver complaint." Virginia's spa towns hosted a lively black community, but most slaves traveled there with their masters. Singleton nevertheless complied with his slave groom's request to head there alone. The local owner fronted $150 to Johnston and Singleton reimbursed the owner in full.[47]

Carrying such a sum was not unusual for Johnston. Singleton frequently sent him out with notes totaling one hundred dollars or more in order to settle accounts, purchase animals, and arrange long-term accommodations for himself and his equine charges. These notes, like those given to him to visit the spa, probably referenced what the owner wanted them spent on, limiting Johnston's autonomy. However, Singleton often directed "the ballance" of remaining cash, "if any, to be given to Cornelius," and he "Paid Cornelious on his own Act. at different times for Services rendered." Other owners tried to lure Johnston to short-term work for them with the promise of additional personal income. As Wade Hampton once put it in a letter to Singleton, "he would be very useful to us & might be advantageously employed for himself."[48]

Such requests reflected esteem for Johnston's skills. Wherever he worked, the slave was responsible for deciding when to pull mares from their breeding seasons, how many mares a stud would service, what kind of treatment to give an ailing animal, and how to train for an upcoming race. Hosts frequently wrote back to Singleton to confirm that they had followed Johnston's instructions, and further recognized the slave's superior knowledge by letting him convey details to Singleton without screening the information. "For particulars, I refer you to Cornelius," they often wrote.[49]

When he stayed with a local owner, Johnston followed protocol and communicated to Singleton through the planter. But an extraordinary letter he sent directly to Singleton from the Petersburg races in 1810 illustrates Johnston's ability to act with even greater authority. The letter opens with an update on Singleton's mare Lottery, whose "leges is some better than when she left Richmond." The slight improvement was not enough to convince Johnston to gallop her in training, let alone run her as scheduled in a race at Petersburg. Johnston informed Singleton that he chose to withdraw the horse, ruining a chance to impress the public. "Sir," Johnston continued, "[should] not [that] unfortunate surcumstance of happened, I would preform wonderful on the turf and [she] would of gave me a great deal of satisfaction and [we] shuld [have] gaind a great applause with her." Besides deciding whether Singleton's horse raced, Johnston also was charged with scouting out potential purchases. "I do not no What horse to tell you sir," the groom concluded on this count, "for I am afraid Wee might make a mistak and get holt of some, sir, that might [not] be any acount to you, for I have not seen any that [are] Worth your purchis." Given Lottery's injury and the lack of quality horses for sale, Johnston thought "it unesserary for my mar to stay in Pettersbourgh." Besides, he wrote, "if [I am] to stay [and] see the Raises, you Depend it Will be moor expence, and as for the Rases I dont car to see them." He intended to return to Richmond, where Singleton had contracted an illness that kept him from coming to Petersburg. But first, Johnston explained, "I have not let my famoley get word agreeabl to my Wishs, and as such I will Come in five or six day." After boldly referring to Lottery as his possession, then obsequiously expressing concern for his master's money and his dutiful distaste for the carnival of racing, Johnston finished by telling his master he would take a week off to visit his family, presumably at Garrett's plantation. Given slave literacy rates, Johnston probably dictated rather than wrote the letter. Yet the message is his, right up to his conclusion with a polite valediction common among white men that obscured his enslaved status: "Your most Honorable Servant, Cornelious Johnston."[50]

Three years later, Johnston underscored his influence and ability to negotiate with white men in another remarkable transaction. In February of 1813, Richard Wall bought "in Trust for Cornelius Johnson a Negro wench named Charlotte and her future issues." Wall was a white grocer in Charleston, a well-known veteran of the Revolution, and his marriage to a free black woman made him the perfect intermediary to purchase a slave woman on behalf of an enslaved man. Presumably, Johnston intended to marry Charlotte and wanted her with him. But tight restrictions on manumission and slaves' lack of formal property rights meant he could not purchase her, let alone free her.

In response to these restrictions, free blacks and some slaves purchased other slaves' freedom through third parties. The purchaser nominally owned the slave, but did so "in trust" for the black kin behind the sale. In practice, then, the slave was free. Johnston no doubt paid Charlotte's $280 sale price, and the low sum as well as Wall's willingness to act as intermediary probably had something to do with the horseman's reputation in white circles. Both the financial and social capital he had accumulated as a slave groom helped him purchase his wife's freedom.[51]

Cornelious Johnston was unusual but not unique. Other top slave grooms shared many of his experiences. John Tayloe's head groom, Sam, covered the same circuits and pocketed equal sums. Often, Tayloe even chose to reimburse Sam for costs he covered with his own cash while traveling, instead of giving him money up front. Andrew Jackson's trainer, Dunwoody, fielded as many demands from his owner's friends as Johnston did. By the 1830s, leading owner Miles Selden even advertised for white apprentices interested in being trained under his enslaved stable boss, William Alexander. Noting that horse work was "a profitable trade; few others adding as much to the value of a slave, or to the productive capacity of a free labouring man," Selden's call alluded to the integrated workplace his slave groom led. Richard Singleton was not the only master permitting slave horsemen a degree of authority in order to profit from their reputations.[52]

In fact, racing remained a rare spectator sport in which whites and blacks competed against each other. In both the North and the South, it was not uncommon to see races featuring slave jockeys alongside Irish immigrant professionals and free, native-born, white farm laborers and artisans who rode part-time. In contrast to the uneasiness sparked by interracial competition in racing and boxing later in the century, or even in theatres during the early national period, racehorse owners in the early nineteenth century seem not to have worried about the implications of such commingling. One reason is that, for all the mayhem on the concourse, racing maintained a hierarchy of ownership that positioned leading owners as ruling equally—if in different ways—over poorer whites as well as blacks. Leading owners did not fret about interracial racing because they used their control over racing to showcase their abilities to lead slaves and free men, white and black alike, in competitions designed to benefit the nation by improving its horse stock.[53]

Another reason for the lack of concern about interracial competition was that almost all black horsemen were slaves, and this reality limited the danger masters saw in granting them some authority and autonomy even in interracial settings. Masters retained the power to take this latitude away, and that possibility constrained what most slave stable staff could do with it. As one recent historian of slave riders and grooms put it, "what horsemen had was not freedom, but it was closer to it than any other life they could see readily available to them." Indeed, Johnston, Alexander, and Sam all resembled Austin Curtis by working within the system, yet none of the renowned early national slave horsemen were manumitted. Granting liberty to these men would have made them a real threat to the order owners wanted to construct. That order granted sporting investors the power to make the country's different populations work together, but it also relied on a racial alliance with white workingmen in order to minimize class tensions. As long as black horsemen remained slaves, their legal status limited the threat a winner might pose to ordinary white spectators.[54]

Nor did masters shy away from exercising their power. A groom or rider with a prosperous owner and an established reputation for skill and success, like Johnston or Sam or Thomas Turner, who belonged to South Carolinian William Alston, "was a great favourite and was indulged and respected." But owners in tightened straits were not averse to having a horseman "hired in the Gold Mines."[55] Losses or mistakes could bring similar repercussions. Andrew Jackson constantly demoted and repromoted Dunwoody between 1805 and 1835 based on his horses' success or failure. The slave was a skilled trainer "of account" one year, then put under white men after his "neglect destroyed" or "ruined" horses the very next season. Owners blamed losses on a "supposed mistake by rider" and publicly punished grooms rather than let defeat injure their reputations or the value of their racehorses.[56]

Whether as part of a demotion or a transfer, few slave horsemen did not experience the trial of sale either firsthand or through the departure of a work mate. Inventories and accounts indicate that owners typically purchased horsemen rather than select them from among their own slaves. The youth of these workers when they first appear in records means they could not have mastered much horse knowledge at the time they were first bought into the business. But as one of them later recounted to his biographer, "I was monst'ous lean an peart fur twelve year ole." A perfect body type for a jockey. Nothing demonstrates the limits of slave horsemen's opportunities better than the steady traffic in young, "lean" potential jockeys and future grooms. John Tayloe III's inventories, the era's most complete annual stable rosters, show an almost yearly turnover. For every Sam on the lists for decades, there was a Joe, Peter, and Ruffin whose stay was short.[57]

With so much at stake, it is no wonder young jockeys rode with a reckless abandon that risked their health as well as the horses'. Some kicked and whipped opponents as well as their steeds. One jockey was pried off his mount at Lancaster, Pennsylvania, in 1806 when his horse ran too close to a thick wooden pole marking the inside boundary of the course. In a single race at Pineville, South Carolina, in 1819, one rider "fractured his scull very much" in the first heat, and another horse "fully threw the Rider" in the second.[58] Even if some successful slave "hostlers" survived the dangers of the job and enjoyed enough success to defy the presumed parameters of slave life, they still faced the vagaries of living as someone else's property. Sam's replacement at Tayloe's stables, Ralph, illustrated this point in several missives sent from local owners, which communicated that he "is well and wishes to be remembered to his family." Success, along with degrees of authority and even autonomy, came at the price of being sent away for months at a time at his master's will.[59]

The uncertainty of the job led many slave horsemen to make the most of their autonomy when they had it. Running away was rarely an option, because they were well known. Yet even Cornelious Johnston did not keep Singleton informed of his progress at the spa while recovering in 1819. The master was uneasy enough to ask a local friend to look around; the friend reported back that he "made every inquirey after Cornelious boath on the road & here but can hear nothing of him." Who knows where the esteemed trainer may really have gone with that $150? Singleton's top rider, Levin, who also drove his carriage, once was found "Rapt up in a Drab Cloak or Big Coat deadly Drunk" inside the coach on the side of a road outside Charleston, with "the Horses therein exposed" and "the Articles in the Carriage liable to be Stole." Levin was a prized jockey, so he kept his position. But Adam, a jockey for a small-time western Virginia breeder, disappears from the historical record after he got into a fight over a card game and his opponent stabbed the thoroughbred he was transporting.[60]

Other slaves besides horsemen made the most of racing, too. When George Washington "rid to all the Plantations" on a seasonable day in October 1786, he "found most of my people had gone to the races." The next day provided an explanation for the slaves' unannounced holiday, as Washington again discovered "people all gone to the race and those at Dogue run all idle—Overseer being gone to the Race." The commercial circus of racing attracted overseers and slaves alike as everyone sought to momentarily escape the toil of everyday life. No wonder reporters from New York to Savannah commented on "the whole covey, 'black spirits and white,'" mixed together on the concourse.[61] Certainly, races could have unwanted repercussions for slaves, as some owners staked them in wagers, but the concourse also provided ideal cover for runaways seeking support from friends and family. As Charlestonian William Reed wrote to his brother in Congress in 1800, "Cousin Pinckney is with us & must see the Races. I have got some persons looking out for your Hercules, as I think him in or about this city & that would be a very probable place to meet with such villains."[62]

Thoroughbred owners built an equine industry that provided uncommon opportunities to slaves while never threatening the institution of slavery or the nationwide racial hierarchy it supported. If the opportunities did not often afford legal freedom, they nevertheless did offer the chance to assert manhood on the track and concourse by competing for acclaim, aggregating wealth, and resorting to bravado and drink just like white men. Even slaves who appear just once in the historical record, in reference to bad behavior, testify to the fact that the owners' drive to maximize profit from thoroughbreds invited slaves to take liberties and join the sporting fray.

"We All Have Equal Rights and Privileges"

The opportunity slaves and free blacks saw in sporting culture was nothing compared to the greater freedom middling and poorer white men enjoyed to challenge class lines and assert their equal standing as fully empowered members of the sporting fraternity. Because taverns and gaming venues had always been more accessible than any other type of sporting facility, they hosted this kind of assertion even more frequently than theatres and racecourses. No one person documented the centrality of white male self-assertion at gaming venues better than professional gambler Robert Bailey. Bailey's autobiography belongs to a genre of moral literature ostensibly written to warn readers away from gambling. But while he dutifully wrote about the benefits of "a steadfast adherence to the principles of morality and religion," and closed his tale with claims to "fear greatly the wrath of divine justice" for his misdeeds, the bulk of Bailey's self-portrait defends his unabashed effort to claim status through successful participation in sporting culture.[63]

A deep-seated desire to prove his standing in society drives Bailey's narrative. As a young apprentice, he "recoiled at being bound" to his master's authority and swore such legal power was "of no consequence" in keeping him from leaving. At a local ball in his teenage years, his blood boiled when he was paired with "the daughter of a very rich gentleman" and she "refused me her arm." As he recalled, "my resentment soon got the better of my mortification," and when the pairing was repeated later in the evening he rejected the woman before she could repeat her refusal. "Thus I thought I had restored myself to an equalization," he explained.[64]

In his twenties, Bailey discovered that accessible sporting activities provided ample opportunities to prove the "equalization" he so wanted. His descriptions of his sporting experiences make this attraction clear. "To my surprise, I saw gentlemen of the first characters and of all professions," he noted on one of his first visits to a gambling house. Thereafter, he always pointed out when he played "with gentlemen of the first respectability." Bailey's attention to elite company deflected criticism of his gambling toward those leaders whose example he claimed to follow, but it also showed how he thought moralists were wrong when they said gaming was unrespectable.[65] Bailey underscored this point by carefully calling himself a "sportsman" rather than a "gambler." "The line of distinction, which I deem a very broad one, between a gambler and a sportsman," Bailey wrote, was that "a gambler is defined by Johnson's dictionary to be a cheating gamester," while "on the other hand, a sportsman may be defined to be a high-minded liberal gentleman, attached to amusements regardless of loss or gain; his motto is honor, his shield is judgment; no insidious tricks does he practice to vanquish his adversary." So when Bailey declared, "a gambler I never was," he staked a claim to genteel status by virtue of embracing the honest risk-taking long central to sporting culture and more recently installed at the heart of the republic's broader economic culture. In effect, Bailey aimed to realize the new economic culture's promise of opportunity for bold, successful risk-takers, and he aimed to do it in the flourishing sporting marketplace at the epicenter of that culture.[66]

Bailey pursued his vision by following the model set by William Dunlap, sapping his modestly profitable tavern, mercantile, and livestock businesses in Staunton, Virginia, to provide capital for his new sporting trade. Dunlap would have cringed at Bailey's effort, based as it was on selfish greed without concern for civic virtue or moral instruction. Bailey relocated frequently, leaving his wife and living with mistresses as he chased sporting crowds and evaded periodic crackdowns by authorities. Yet both men were active Federalists who attempted to make a living from sporting businesses.[67]

Bailey's career choice may have embraced the country's emergent economic culture, but, like Dunlap's, it put him on the defensive as a sporting pro trying to claim gentility. He tried to reduce doubt by attracting elite patrons, writing that "my orders to my dealers always was to suffer no person to bet but gentlemen, and to exclude all common persons." He also cultivated his own gentility, even being tapped to manage the exclusive dancing balls at Sweet Springs, Virginia, while he ran a gaming hall in the courthouse. Although he claimed this post was "evidence that I was at all times competent to be a gentleman," his status remained insecure. When he refused to close down his gaming business one night in favor of an impromptu ball, the ladies of the Springs labeled him a "gambler," "excommunicated" him from the dance, and forced him to leave town. He set up in nearby Winchester, but was denied access to the dancing ball there, too. Considering himself wronged, he challenged the ball's manager to a duel. The manager refused, then offered a telling explanation. "Major Bailey, your deportment is that of a gentleman, and I had no objections myself, nor no one else of the male side," the manager said. "But I believe some of the ladies had." Circles of genteel women had more power to vet gentility than established gentlemen, since white men could not easily reject each other for honest sport without risking their own honor by refuting the accessible contest on which the new republic was based. The open competition that bound white men together in the public spaces of economic and sporting culture made elite women the ultimate arbiters of claims to genteel status beyond those public domains.[68]

Shunned men had limited recourse against ladies' opinions, though Bailey claimed to have exacted revenge by exercising his manly economic wherewithal to purchase the slave fiddler at the ball and depart with him, ending the event. In contrast, male censors were vulnerable to violent public reprisals if they denied another white man's assertion of gentility. Like Charles Janson on the Washington racecourse, Bailey claimed he found a man in a tavern who supported his ban, "took him by the nose," and "knocked him over and put him through a window into the street." A few years later, he roughed up Thomas Jefferson's personal secretary after the man ordered his removal from a White House levee. Bailey defended these assaults by declaring, "I would whip any man that would insult and burr my feelings," even "the President himself; in this country we all have equal rights and privileges." According to Bailey, those rights included claiming gentlemanly status through honorable participation in the republic's accessible sporting culture, as well as the right to physically prove his worthiness when unmanly snobs rejected his self-assertion.[69]

In defending his assertions of gentility with his fists, Bailey often conflated honor and gentility in ways that reflected the confusion of behavioral norms in early national sporting spaces. In fact, honor did incorporate elements of both genteel and rough manliness. This compound made the concept supple, as men such as William Henry Drayton and William Byrd III had learned during the Revolutionary era. But gentility's relationship to honor grew more unstable in the ensuing decades, when heightened accessibility to genteel sport collapsed the spatial distinctions that previously had helped determine behavioral norms in any given sporting setting. As physical violence surfaced in genteel venues and rougher settings witnessed claims to gentility, it became easier to confuse honor with gentility and vice versa.

The rise of fighting in theatre boxes exemplified this trend. So did several altercations in southern sporting taverns that hosted both genteel and rougher sport. British officer and prisoner of war Thomas Anburey described one that erupted over a billiard match in Richmond in 1780. The contest pitted doctor and soon-to-be Mayor William Foushee against a "low fellow" unknown to the gentlemen in the room. The game crossed class lines, resembling the one Benjamin Henry Latrobe sketched some fifteen years later (see Figure I.1). But on this occasion, the gentleman did not know his socially inferior opponent, so there was no personal relationship to mediate class tensions. "In the course of play," Anburey recalled, a dispute emerged and "some words arose, in which he [the low fellow] first wantonly abused and afterward would insist on fighting Mr. Fauchee." As the trouble began "in the course of play," it probably related to a disagreement over scoring or a foul. Either the low fellow felt slighted or Foushee accused him of cheating. Whatever the cause, the low fellow leapt to prove himself and immediately desired "to know upon what terms he [Foushee] would fight," but "Mr. Fauchee declined any, saying that he was totally ignorant as to boxing." Then Foushee made an important concession. He told "the other, calling himself a gentleman, he would meet him in a gentleman-like manner." The low fellow had asserted his gentility and Foushee accepted it by offering a duel, the polite mode of proving honor through violence. But the doctor mistakenly thought that the low fellow's use of the term "gentleman" aligned with his own. Foushee "had scarcely uttered these words before the other flew at him and in an instant turned his eye of the socket." "Gouging," as this form of attack was known, was hardly a genteel mode of settling differences. Whether the low fellow was a lousy shot, detested the duel's haughty protocol, or intended to insult Foushee by treating him as more worthy of raw abuse than polite settlement, he surprised the doctor by refusing to see the duel as commensurate with his use of the term "gentleman."[70]

Robert Bailey's frequent resort to his fists sprang from the same refusal to recognize gentility's traditional opposition to brute physicality. Once asked to settle a dispute between "two gentlemen" in the billiard room at John Gadsby's Baltimore hotel, Bailey "gave my opinion unfavorable to Mr. Hammon, who was one of the gentlemen at play. He said it was a damn'd lie, let who might say so; I told him he was not a gentleman, or he would not ask a man for his opinion and then give him the damned lie; he said I was a damned liar if I said he was no gentleman." Bailey then claimed to have "knocked him down and drubbed him severely." In this case, Bailey fought to defend his honor as an honest man, and to treat his opponent as the ungenteel fraud Bailey had just said he was. But, as with Foushee and Janson, Bailey saw gentility at stake in places where it had not been during the colonial era—places where raw honor also remained salient, and so disputes over either form of status could now trigger physical violence.[71]

Just before he told this story, Bailey explained why he often resorted to corporal combat. "The reason is to be found in the mixed crowds and variety of scenes through which I have passed, and not from my bad nature," he wrote. He had to fight to defend his status claims because the broad mélange in accessible sporting venues led to so many challenges, and his own gentility was too insecure to allow him to ignore an insult.[72]

Bailey spent most of his time in the South. But in the North, too, the press circulated stories about gamblers who conflated the "lines to be observed which mark the gentleman and the man of honour." One such character claimed gentility because "I dress like a gentleman," "dukes and lords are my intimates and friends," and, above all, he was no cheating "pilferer, a despicable picker of pockets." Like Bailey's, this pseudonymous (and probably fictional) gambler's claim to genteel status was questionable, so he was always ready to defend it physically. Yet to justify physical violence, he had to shift quickly from claims of gentility to those of honor. "Who shall dare call my honour in question?" he asked just one sentence after announcing his genteel qualifications. "No man shall dare do it while this weapon graces my thigh and I have an arm to wield it," he concluded. At the same time, established sporting gentlemen in the North advocated "the dissemination of the pugilistic art" specifically to help "the aristocracy of fashion and gentility" provide "the lower orders of society" with "manual examples" that would literally fight their "low-bred insolence and disposition to insult and abuse those who are their superiors." As sporting sites subsumed emerging class distinctions and refracted them into thousands of individual confrontations, challenges from all quarters drove many men to defend gentility roughly. The behavioral rules and exclusivity originally embedded in genteel sport only remained in force in the company of polite ladies.[73]

The urge to compete and prove manly status even extended to interracial play. Despite the segregation of black patrons from reputedly genteel spaces, southern states continued to pass laws into the 1830s to "prevent free persons from gambling with slaves," indicating the persistent ubiquity of the practice.[74] Observers noticed it in the "noisy sporting associations of white and black boys," or the "mixt multitude" at "Holly-day" festivities where "drinking, gambling, swearing & fighting ensue."[75] Northern states did not forbid interracial gambling once they outlawed slavery, though a growing tide of white and black writers declaimed "the low gambling house kept by blacks," where "cards, gambling, and dicing of all kinds," along with "the deadly snares of prostitution," lured "sailors and idle young men" of all races.[76]

Most commentaries describe interracial play as limited to unrefined settings and poor whites. Some of these games may well have reflected genuine friendships among men who worked together as sailors and laborers in some of the republic's harshest jobs. But whether the contests sprang from affability or rivalry, white men never described them in terms of honor because they kept that concept to themselves. Since only white men could compete for honor or gentility, doing so bound them together, if uncomfortably, and limited what black men could gain from a fluid moment in sporting culture's evolution that appealed to men of all races. As Robert Bailey reminded readers in his autobiography, "this vice finds votaries and patrons among all grades and conditions, from the most exalted to the most humble slave."[77]

The popularity, disorder, and violence of increasingly accessible sporting venues only amplified the voices of sporting culture's critics. Once focused on the immoral waste of genteel excess, critics after 1800 increasingly trained their sights on the obsession with honor that confounded the promise of a genteel hierarchy. One tongue-in-cheek guide to Saratoga, New York's rising spa town, reminded visitors to "never pay any debts if you can help it, but debts of honor" because "by the law of nature, man has a claim on society for the necessaries of life," while manly status was not guaranteed and so needed to be protected. "If the tailor trusts you," the guidebook concluded, "good—it is at his own risk." More serious and direct assaults on honor also appeared. "Indeed, is it honour," asked a correspondent to the Albany literary magazine *The Stranger*, "to sacrifice all that is estimable to the villanous designs of sharpers" in a place where "all distinctions are lost in that strange bewitching infatuation, which places stupidity and wit, beggary and wealth, the bosom friend and the profligate sharper, upon a level." Some writers tried to channel honor away from sporting culture, claiming, for instance, that it pertained only to business contexts. "It will be for your honor," they wrote, to pay debts and "conform to what you suppose to be the will of those whom you serve." Other critics replaced honor altogether with an emerging language of "respectability" that tempered genteel performance with a layer of modesty and morality at odds with risk-taking or violence. "Education is always respectable," wrote one of these advocates, promising that "the gambling table will not be resorted to . . . when the library offers a more attractive resource."[78]

Historians have tended to see these attacks on honor as a particularly northern phenomenon, but they surfaced in the South as well. For example, consider what happened to George Carter's plantation two decades after his father forced him to mortgage it to settle an enormous gaming debt, "rather than forfeit his honor." By 1810, "the Turk" who had received that mortgage, John Cooper, had accumulated debts of his own. In an effort to get payment, one of Cooper's creditors, Thomas Ludwell Lee, sued to seize the Carter mortgage. George Carter had died in 1802, but his family mobilized in response to

Lee's suit, arguing that a third party could not sue the winner of a bet for his winnings because the winner had no legal right to the winnings in the first place. As the Carters' lawyer John Brown Cutting reminded the court, the law did not require losers to pay. They chose to do so, following the "code of honor" rather than the law. Cutting then indicted honor as a backward, extra-legal concept. "Perhaps it may be alleged that this sort of family honor is so dear to equity," he argued, "that the infant appellees, although already steeped to the lips in privation because of their parent's delirious worship of this false idol, ought to acquiesce in being further stripped of nineteen hundred pounds current money." Cutting's argument asserted that the protection of the estate on behalf of Carter's children outweighed whatever credit or "equity" the family might lose by refusing to pay a debt of honor. In the American republic, Cutting said, "statutes declare open war against the wretched idolatry of the duelist and the false honor of the gamester."[79]

The court sided with the Carters, but in an important corollary on the continuing value of gambling and honor, Cutting himself loaned $450 to George's youngest brother, Landon N. Carter, "for gaming purposes" while he prepared the family's defense. Carter soon lost the sum. His father gave him money to repay Cutting, but the young man gambled that away, too. As in the eighteenth century, young gentlemen from wealthy families remained committed to proving themselves through honorable gambling. The new economic culture of capitalism only spurred more men like Robert Bailey to join them in the early national period.[80]

In the end, in the North and the South alike, the various renewals of a century-old effort to separate honor and business from gambling and sport all failed. The members of the Massachusetts Jockey Club explained this failure in the concluding toast at their second anniversary celebration. To "The Race of Life," they cheered. "Heels at starting; bottom at winning; but to honorable competition no distance post." The mantra illuminates the attraction to sporting contexts where striving was key and defeat could be more acceptable than in reform circles. While those peddling "respectability" treated losses as signs of poor character, sportsmen celebrated "the handsome and honourable manner with which" losers who competed well and paid up "sustained their defeat and their losses."[81] Sporting investors helped propagate an economic system and culture that welcomed honest competition among all white men, but privileged their own superior access to private capital, granting them a better "heeled" start and reserves more likely to endure over the course of a lifetime. Part of crafting this economy involved rebuilding sporting culture into practices that would support it by portending opportunity while celebrating wealth as honorable proof of success and superiority. Yet this legitimation came at a price. Sporting culture's popularity rested on a sense of opportunity that, though fleeting, still generated as much confrontation and confusion as deference. Elites continually had to prove themselves worthy of leadership by engaging supposed inferiors and pursuing commercial success amid challenges that easily bled from sporting into the business and political settings sport increasingly resembled.

Political Theatre

The popularity of sporting culture led early national politicians to borrow more heavily from it than ever before. Despite complaints that elected officials who knew "grog or beer the voters best inspire" also knew they could later "never mind the men that put [them] there" in office, men like Meriwether Jones demonstrated the persistent value of tavern electioneering when he "adapted his manners and conversation to the understanding, habits, and tempers of the company" in the Hanover Town billiard room in 1797.[82] Thoroughbred owners similarly continued the Revolutionary-era practice of expressing political allegiances through their horses' names. "Anti-Democrat" and "Little Democrat" were unambiguous examples at the Lancaster, Pennsylvania, racecourse. South Carolinian William Alston named his champion Gallatin, after Thomas Jefferson's treasury secretary. Later, when South Carolinians threatened to nullify the federal tariff signed by Andrew Jackson in 1832, the president's supporters celebrated his equine namesake's victory in the four-mile race at Richmond while a horse named Nullifier lost the two-mile event.[83]

Jackson himself shrewdly used sport to remain in the public eye after financial difficulties forced him to resign his seat on Tennessee's Supreme Court in 1804. He helped open Nashville's first purpose-built racecourse, then harkened back to the politicized cockfight between James DeLancey and Timothy Matlack by staging a Fourth of July main in 1809 that pitted his political faction against rivals from the eastern part of the state. He also dueled to publicly defend his sporting honor. He was hardly alone in using sport to fuel political ambitions. Most leading owners and dozens of theatre trustees held elected office. Even Robert Bailey ran for office seven times, carrying the spa towns in the 1805 congressional election before he fell out of favor there.[84]

More than just copying older uses of sport, early national politicians also brought sporting culture into politics in new ways. The most prominent of the new practices was betting on elections. "This electioneering wager is a new species of gambling," newspapers reported around the turn of the century. If the species was new, the genus was not. Wagerers "paraded the election ground offering to bet from 100 to 500 dollars in favor of" their candidate, applying the gambling method first developed by racehorse owners such as Petersburg Jockey Club founder William Haxall, who "paced about the field proclaiming in his firm manly voice and rapid articulation . . . 'One hundred guineas upon the Sir Harry against the field.'" Haxall hoped heavy bets on his horses in public would draw attention to them in a crowded equine marketplace. As one of the Tayloes later explained, "I am glad that you have gone into large stakes, as it shows confidence in our stock." Such bets were the latest versions of the same kind of "public wager" laid by Thomas Glenholme's acquaintance in 1767. Early national politicians adopted this form of betting for its power to attract attention, express confidence, and tie men together into networks of support.[85]

The changing structure of electoral politics in the early republic prompted politicians to look for ways to build that support. The federal Constitution created enormous electoral districts in many states. Then, between 1790 and 1830, partisan conflict and competition for population among states led to the reduction or elimination of property requirements on white men's suffrage, as well as the direct election of more offices. In 1789, only half of all states elected their governors or their presidential electors by popular vote. By 1832, 80 percent elected their governors by popular vote, and only South Carolina did not do so for president.[86] Seeking to reach voters they did not know, and largely prevented from campaigning for themselves by a widespread belief that such behavior signaled greed and overambition, candidates had their supporters turn to the same form of gambling that brought attention and clients to horses. "I have offered to bet more pounds than I am worth pence that you have [a] 1000 majority," wrote upstate New Yorker Joab Griswold to incumbent Congressman William Cooper in 1796. Local "friends" like Griswold placed wagers on candidates they knew, or at least ones tied to factions they supported, in an effort to persuade their neighbors. Voters then decided between candidates in part by evaluating who in their neighborhood bet on each one, and how much they were willing to risk on their conviction in the man.[87]

Of course, friends wanted something in return for their efforts. Cooper lost his reelection bid in 1796, but his connections still helped Griswold get appointed as his county's clerk in 1798. Repayment did not always take the form of political office. One Philadelphia newspaper accused Governor Thomas McKean of paying "a pauper . . . sustained by public bounty" to offer bets on him in the streets of Philadelphia before the 1805 gubernatorial election. According to the exposé, "numerous persons were employed to make bets, whose risks were covered by persons who did not appear." McKean's backers allegedly paid poorer men to announce bets on their candidate's behalf in hopes of encouraging support for their man among the "lower sort." Tangible benefits like jobs, money, and preferential legislation motivated bettors to support a candidate at least as much as any ideological agreement, making election wagers networking opportunities just like racing bets.[88]

The new practice appalled moral critics as much as tavern treating had. Some mocked the thought of likening politics to sport through the "charming, conciliating invention—this gambling at elections," which "makes us believe that we are only at a horse race, bull-baiting or cock-fighting." Others saw sporting elements as threatening, not minimizing, the importance of political processes. "Is the Representatives' chamber to become like the turf for gamblers and jockeys to sport on!!!" exclaimed one Boston newspaper when it suggested that odds could lead politicians to win bets by throwing elections. Once again, however, these critics ran afoul of popular beliefs by considering sport as beneath other categories of activity—this time politics instead of business. Most white men experienced sporting culture as an integral component of both in a republic of competitive risk-takers. For them, as for the sporting investors and politicians who encouraged this vision (who were sometimes one and the same), sport was a cornerstone of the country's broader culture of opportunity, and so wagering on politics was a natural byproduct of sport's centrality to the polity.[89]

White men constructed gendered and racial limits to that opportunity through sporting culture as much as through law, as further analysis of the public wager demonstrates. For instance, records suggest that proper ladies almost never staked cash amounts in public wagers as men did. Reputable women bet money in polite domestic card games, but at the races in Charleston, Richmond, and New York their stakes involved goods such as bon-bons, "gloves, watch guards, and keep sakes." Just as importantly, these bets were laid with friends and acquaintances in the stands or in the privacy of a carriage rather than with strangers after open negotiation on the concourse. The difference is significant. Although married women's property rights expanded in the first half of the nineteenth century, sporting culture reified an older model of gendered economic power that supported the white male republic. Ladies' racing wagers kept them from unseemly competition with strangers and remained within the limited confines of their traditional economic purview under laws of coverture.[90]

It is no coincidence that by the time these reports of gendered wagering appeared in the 1820s and 1830s, a window of greater political participation among women during the nation's initial decades was closing in favor of constructing "separate spheres" that aimed to constrict women's political activity. Much as women were welcome at sporting events but were limited to specific roles serving men's needs, they became banner-makers and parade-watchers when they had been speechmakers, marchers, and, in some places, even voters.[91]

More than just a vehicle for rallying political support, sport helped define the emerging white male polity because it was a locus for the manly risk-taking that had become central to political and economic life in the republic. As one New York magazine described "betting at elections" at end of the period, "an opinion was rarely hazarded without an instanter challenge to back it with a bet, and a refusal to do so subjects you to the taunts and jeers of those around." In the colonial era, "great monied men" had to bet or risk losing their networks of patronage. In the early republic, publicly negotiated wagers became a de-fining practice for all white men, lest they lose the manly reputation that sig-nified empowered citizenship.[92]

Not surprisingly, then, black men faced barriers similar to women. No evi-dence refers to African Americans making public wagers, despite plenty of de-scriptions of interracial gambling. If it happened, no white man wanted to record the fact. After all, publicly negotiated wagers announced a man's mem-bership in networks of shared risk, interest, and mutual obligation. They were an economic statement of civic inclusion at a time when most white men sought to exclude black men from full economic and civic participation. As with women, restrictions on black men's gambling reflected prejudices based on an allegedly "degraded condition" that left them devoid of the "active and enterprising spirit" required to weigh risks rationally. Hardening restrictions on African American males' ability to participate like full-fledged men in all sporting forms and spaces corresponded with their disenfranchisement. While just two of the thirteen original states denied black men the vote in 1789, and just five of sixteen states did so in 1800, all but four of twenty-six did by 1840. To be sure, sporting practices alone did not precipitate this development. But sport's place as a venue for electioneering and exhibiting masculinity made it a key locus where the boundaries of the white male republic were drawn, dis-played, and reified.[93]

The public wager thus functioned as a mode of "status politics," an effort to mobilize political action by connecting it to a reward of prestige. Today we tend to think of parties and issues producing status politics, but in an era when voting rights were in flux and less than 40 percent of eligible voters typically participated, the practice of betting became a bipartisan way to lure voters by making voting an announcement of membership in the empowered commu-nity of manly risk-takers. Whether a white man was a bettor or merely a voter who could determine the outcome of a bet, his participation expressed his standing as an engaged sporting man in contrast to those who faced humiliating "taunts and jeers" for not engaging.[94]

The public wager was not the only mode of status politics to draw from sporting culture in the early republic. If public bets underscored racial and gender lines, the Democratic-Republican party, formed in opposition to the Federalists in the 1790s, both attracted and mobilized nonelite white men by urging them to challenge their supposed betters' superiority at the theatre. The Democratic-Republicans attracted a range of supporters, from Anti-Federalists who had opposed legalizing theatre to disaffected Federalists who defended the Constitution and its concomitant economic culture but disapproved of the extent to which the federal government acted on it. A third group overlapped with the first two but was primarily concerned with supporting the antiaristocratic French Revolution, in opposition to Federalists, who favored a close relationship with royalist Britain. In the early 1790s, Thomas Jefferson used his national network of friends to establish a string of newspapers designed to unite these groups into one opposition voice. The new partisan periodicals depicted Federalists as aspiring aristocrats out to betray the egalitarian promise of the Revolution, famously limning Jefferson's Federalist rival John Adams as the "Duke of Braintree," committed to "changing a limited Republican government into an unlimited hereditary one."[95]

Borrowing from their Anti-Federalist wing, the Democratic-Republican press cited the theatres Federalists created as evidence of their aristocratic intentions. Overwhelmingly British material and performers, along with seating areas built to reflect social rank, supported the accusation. In Boston, attacks from the opposition press hammered the appropriately named Federal Street Theatre enough to allow its fired manager to parlay the criticism into funding for a rival house, which the Democratic-Republican papers endorsed. Yet the commercial realities of the period meant that the new theatre staged the same material and with just as many British actors. By the time the Englishman William Priest visited Boston in 1797, he estimated that "one third of the public papers are crammed with what is called Theatrical Critique, but it is in fact either the barefaced puff direct in favour of one theatre or a string of abusive epithets against the other, equally void of truth and decency."[96]

In Boston and Philadelphia alike, Jeffersonian editors ignored the similarities between the theatres they backed and the ones they claimed were Federalist, in order to mobilize political supporters. They seized on any difference they could find, usually interlude music or methods of ticket sales, to blame theatre managers for being "affraid of giving offence to their opulent friends"—the partisan financiers allegedly behind the scheme to foist an aristocracy on the republic through theatre. Yet, in truth, every theatre had investors from both parties. Known Democratic-Republicans actually outnumbered known Federalists among the subscribers to the Chestnut Street Theatre in Philadelphia, and their numbers were roughly even among the founders of Boston's Federal Street Theatre. More importantly, investors tended to be wealthy no matter which party they belonged to. While 90 percent of identifiable Federal Street investors in the 1790s held taxable assets valued at more than $1,000, the same was true for 66 percent of investors behind the supposedly Jeffersonian Haymarket Theatre. None of the latter owned estates worth more than ten thousand dollars, as did half the Federal Street shareholders, but this is only a distinction between the top 0.5 percent of the population and the next 6.5 percent. Men from the bottom 93 percent of Boston were a distinct minority among theatre investors. Priest was right: partisan bombast proclaimed false distinctions, in terms of both the content on stage and the investors behind it.[97]

Charges of aristocratic hierarchy among spectators were no better founded. Except at the Haymarket, the Democratic-Republican press presented galleries as home to "the democracy," and referred to boxes as bastions of "the aristocracy," as if the investors' intended class distinctions actually had taken root. In practice, as we already have seen, "the unruly could stealthily mingle themselves with the respectable," as theatre manager William Wood put it in his memoir of the period.[98]

The depiction worked despite its inaccuracy. Newspapers and diarists reported theatres erupting with partisan conflict couched in class antagonism. The press often spurred as much as recorded this behavior. For instance, on the opening night of *Tammany*, a play about New York's largest Democratic-Republican club, one of the party's papers feared Federalist dissent against the piece and issued "the hue and cry of aristocratic opposition" in order to "collect a vast number of people" able to counter the "aristocratic junto who were determined at all hazards to damn poor Tammany." By packing the house with partisans eager to confront the play's opponents, Democratic-Republicans ensured "the Junto were kept aloof," and the play came off. Likewise, Boston's Jeffersonian *Independent Chronicle* urged attendees to demand the Federal Street orchestra play "Ça Ira" instead of "God Save the King" before shows in January 1794. When it turned out that "some persons object to the playing of this Republican tune," the paper only repeated its recommendation. Most protests started in the galleries, but cross-class partisan alliances could span the entire house in order to express dissent. One night, Sarah Flucker, from a Federalist-leaning Boston family, saw "a large Party forming in the Galleries to Govern the Music," and then reported "words of command" coming from Democratic-

Republican leaders seated elsewhere in the house, which triggered an "alarming opposition between the ragamuffins, Loyalists, and Orchestra."[99]

Flucker's labeling of the different combatants reveals that Federalists embraced rather than combatted Democratic-Republican accusations of their elitism and Anglophilism. They counterattacked by claiming Jeffersonians were demagogues out to subvert the government and bring French-style revolutionary mob rule to America. In their own newspapers and correspondence, they delegitimized Democratic-Republican playhouse agitators by calling them "ragamuffins," "myrmidons," or a "mob." They defied those who claimed such terms only bolstered the case against them. "These remarks, I am aware, will be termed aristocratic—be it so," wrote one resolute Federalist critic of accessible box seats. "They are truths which will flash conviction in the faces of those to whom they are principally addressed, and which they will feel too, when not inebriated at a porter house or with the noise and support of their associates at a theatre." Federalist newspapers refuted claims about the party's unpopularity by citing gallery patrons who shouted down "Ça Ira" and by noting the popularity of plays that urged peace and order over the fight to create a classless democracy. By the late 1790s, then, both parties encouraged their partisans to claim superior status at the theatre. Jeffersonians considered themselves truer republicans than Federalist "aristocrats," while Federalists believed their rivals were lawless guttersnipes.[100]

Actors and managers appreciated partisan drama because the potential for discord attracted audiences from both sides. A Federalist describing the *Tammany* incident suggested that the theatre's managers actually provoked it by advertising the "objections which might possibly arise" at the show. "It served their purpose extremely well," the reporter concluded. "The house overflowed at an early hour." Characteristically, William Dunlap disapproved of such base marketing. He complained in his diary when one of his actresses chose for her season-ending benefit production *The Federal Oath*, which Dunlap thought was written "to inculcate some grand and novel political truths, Such as that we ought to damn all Frenchmen."[101]

The popularity of the theatrical frame led politicians to apply it beyond the walls of playhouses. They soon offered general political commentary in theatrical terms. The Federalist print *A Peep into the Anti-Federalist Club* (see figure 4.4) epitomizes this theatricalization of party politics, showing leading Democratic-Republicans in stylized dramatic poses. The image calls these men "Anti-Federalist" in order to accuse them of grave designs on the Constitution, and spotlights a melodramatic Jefferson paraphrasing Hamlet as he stands above the motley crew. "To be or not to be, a Broker, is the question," he asks. "Whether tis nobler in the mind to knock down dry goods with this hammer;

FIGURE 4.4. *A Peep into the Anti-Federal Club,* unknown artist (New York, 1793), etching on paper, courtesy Historical Society of Pennsylvania.

or with this head Contrive some means of knocking down a Government and in its ruins raise myself to Eminence and Fortune." Federalists maintained the theatrical metaphor in later pamphlets such as "a New Play called 'Republican Governments Ought to Have no Secrets,'" and "A New Farce" called "Pandemonium in Dishabille, or, Pretended Republicanism put in Practice." The theatrical format of these attacks insinuated that Jeffersonian policies and strategies were actually tyrannical, but their authoritarian ends were hidden beneath layers of stagecraft and performance espousing democracy. Democratic-Republicans replied in kind. In Connecticut, they blasted the Federalist majority for spending state turnpike money on party expenses in a pamphlet titled "The Turnpike Road to Fortune, A Comic Opera or Political Farce in Six Acts," which was "performed at the Theatres Royal and Aristocratic at Hartford." In Kentucky, Jeffersonians even named one of their newspapers *Political Theatre.*[102]

Although both parties used theatre to rally support, Jeffersonians swept into the presidency as well as majorities in Congress and most state legislatures in 1800, and they remained in control of government into the 1820s. Their assault on class distinction contributed to their success, as the party generally embraced broader suffrage for white men and firmer exclusion of women and black men from the polity. Given the theatre's long history as a place where poorer white men had asserted their place in society, Jeffersonians were wise to use playhouses as staging grounds for party action framed in class terms. However, Jeffersonian leaders did not score a total victory. After all, many of them had joined Federalists in funding playhouses originally designed to craft class distinction. Federalist and Democratic-Republican leaders alike possessed extraordinary wealth, and both believed it entitled them to political leadership. Jefferson himself believed in natural aristocracy as much as any Federalist. By encouraging opposition to class hierarchy in theatres, Jeffersonian leaders undermined the order that they, too, had once sought. Their language of democracy won them political power but required conceding their own desire for deference.[103]

The success of political theatre soon rendered other political events more like sporting ones. Debates became known as "spouting matches," pitting each candidate's "friend to his election" in a contest of oratory before "Cursing, Fighting, &c closed the whole scene."[104] If election debates resembled athletic sports, Americans came to think of the ones in legislative halls as akin to theatre. The analogy began with publicly accessible seating areas in the Revolutionary period. By the 1810s, politicians played to spectators there much as actors did, directing comments to observation balconies as if they were tiers of box seats. A South Carolina senator even spoke of the Senate chamber "as a theatre upon which members acted for public applause." Visitors thought the sight "was as good as going to a play, but here all the characters are real instead of fictitious." No wonder 1790s speculator William Duer placed a chapter on theatre immediately after a chapter on politics in his memoirs. "The transition seems natural from the scenes enacted on the floor of Congress to those exhibited on the dramatic stage," Duer wrote.[105]

But the transition was not natural. Politicians had consciously tightened the ties between sport and politics over the course of the republic's early decades in an effort to win votes, even if that effort also threatened to bring the disorder of sporting culture back into politics. In both settings, the popularity of egalitarian experiences drove elite leaders to chase profit and power at the expense of order and prestige. In response to incessant confrontation in the resulting white male republic, the men behind the sporting industry turned it into the font of mass culture.

PART THREE

The Antebellum Period

CHAPTER 5

A Mass Sporting Industry

On July 11, 1836, eighteen thoroughbred owners signed a charter creating a jockey club in Camden, New Jersey. After fifteen years of on-and-off debate, the state legislature had finally legalized thoroughbred racing the previous year, and the owners saw a ready audience across the Delaware River from Philadelphia, where it remained illegal. Not one of the Camden club's eighteen charter members, though, hailed from New Jersey.[1]

It was not that there were no thoroughbred owners in the state. As soon as New York legalized racing on Long Island in 1821, Jersey owners and breeders tried to copy the well-worn economic argument used to win legalization in several states. They complained "that ever since the prohibition of trials of speed and bottom in New Jersey, the stock of Horses has deteriorated and there is scarcely a fine blooded Horse to be found in the state." Only "by trials of speed and bottom" could owners improve their stock, "prevail on southern and eastern gentlemen to give large prices," and find that their "chance of profit is greatly enhanced." Hence, they concluded, "in the opinion of your petitioners, a properly regulated Race-Course would be of great advantage to the State."[2]

These calls went unanswered until the value of thoroughbreds reached new heights in the 1830s. The record sale price of $4,000 in 1808 had doubled by 1832, despite general deflation. In real terms, the value of top thoroughbreds had more than tripled. By 1837, these figures had almost doubled again, with top sales prices nearing $15,000 and top breeding seasons exceeding $1,500.[3] The rapid acceleration in value finally won over New Jersey's legislators in 1835, after evidence showed that "in districts where the sports of the turf have for some years been abandoned, we have known well bred horses sell for less than one fourth of what the same horses would command in a racing country." Jockey clubs quickly formed, and major racetracks opened in Camden and across the Hudson River from New York.[4]

Yet New Jersey owners had little control over these new venues. The course outside Hoboken was leased to a Virginian who also managed the track on Long Island. In Camden, the entire jockey club came from Virginia. Every member belonged to a Virginia jockey club, ten managed or invested in other racetracks, and all but one of them owned Virginia stud farms inventoried in the *American Turf Register and Sporting Magazine*, the trade periodical of the thoroughbred industry.[5]

Indeed, in the 1830s, a small cohort of Virginians dominated racing and the thoroughbred market across the country. They maneuvered into other states because theirs boasted the highest concentration of bloodstock in the country. As early as 1819, Virginian Harry Heth, brother of Camden club member John Heth, sent his horses to South Carolina, explaining that his "main object is to get this superior stock of Horses into notice, which it is impossible to do in this State." Opening and managing racetracks nationwide helped them showcase their horses outside their home state's overstocked market.[6]

The "Turf Gentlemen," as these aggressive owners called themselves, or "turfmen" for short, were not leading owners. In fact, they replaced leading owners at the top of the thoroughbred industry by crafting a new business model for racehorse management. Building on the drive for profit that sporting investors had articulated in the early national period, these men escalated their potential income from racing in the 1830s by making it their primary business. They blurred the line between investor and professional by centralizing control of day-to-day racetrack management, standardizing the length of courses and race reporting, and expanding access to stands in order to generate more revenue for enlarged purses. In effect, they turned racing into something more like mass entertainment than it had been when it featured exclusive seating sections, jockey clubs serving the business interests of elite nonowners, and no *Turf Register* existed to "rigidly enforce some system" of racing out of fear that "the public will lose all confidence in their vague statements and their horses will lose their reputation."[7]

The process of reshaping racing actually took place in two stages. The first came in the early and mid-1830s as turfmen took over the thoroughbred market from leading owners by managing racetracks, standardizing racing, and inflating sales prices. The second followed the Panic of 1837, which popped the bubble the turfmen had blown. They recovered only by instituting new reforms that further democratized and depersonalized the racetrack experience.

As in other periods, the structural changes seen in one corner of sporting culture appeared elsewhere as well. Theatre, which already possessed several qualities of mass entertainment by the 1820s, also saw its investors centralize and step into management during this period. Few gaming establishment proprietors could also claim to be investors, though both gaming hall and theatre managers responded to the panic by specializing and standardizing their venues in order to re-create distinctively genteel and rough experiences that reduced competition in their sectors of the sporting market. By 1860, investors and managers had reorganized the chaotic sporting culture of the early national period into an early version of mass entertainment, defined by heightened and impersonal accessibility, standardized variations of content and experience, and more centralized control over the industry. The maintenance of racial and gender lines precluded full-blown mass culture until the twentieth century, but the rest of this chapter traces how competition among investors and managers gave birth to its initial form in a sporting industry designed to limit producers' financial risks while promoting a white male democracy of risk-taking consumers.[8]

Napoleons of the Turf

The rise of the turfmen reveals more than the process of turning sporting culture into a foundation of mass culture. It also illustrates the persistent tensions and divisions among wealthy sporting investors, and these differences drove much of sport's development in the antebellum period. Henry Augustine Tayloe knew this fractious reality better than most. Henry was the youngest son of John Tayloe III; his brothers were leading owners as his father had been, and they constantly criticized his decision to turn turfman. The brothers' rancorous relationship reveals how turfmen differed from leading owners, as well as how turfmen took over and transformed the thoroughbred market.

Henry's brothers unwittingly planted the seeds of his career. As the youngest son, he received little land from his father, so his elder brothers made up for his small inheritance by putting Henry in charge of the family's lucrative thoroughbreds. Henry threw himself into the business, planning racing and breeding seasons for the Tayloe horses, as well as those of paying customers. By all accounts, the family's Oakley Stables flourished under his guidance.

Then, in 1834, the brothers purchased land in Alabama together. Henry had a share in the new property and was slated to graduate from stable management in Virginia to plantation management in the Southwest.[9]

However, the young man soon made clear his disinterest in the new assignment. "Races and racecourses seemed to employ all his time & the overseers had full sway" over the plantation, his brother George rued after a visit. Henry's cotton suffered, while his horses reigned supreme. In 1837, "he won every day at Tuscaloosa without running. No stable would contend with him." He bought six thousand dollars' worth of horses and opened a racetrack with a consortium of other turfmen. "I think our Greensboro track will prove more profitable than cotton planting," he confidently predicted to his oldest brother William Henry. The senior Tayloes were not impressed. Their concern about the time and money Henry spent on racing identified a key boundary between leading owners and turfmen. When George complained about his priorities, "spoke to him of the bad management here & our heavy expences & the odious credit system he has given into, he got mad & said he wished I would buy his interest out in these two places to attend to them myself."[10]

Henry preferred the thoroughbred business to cotton planting, and the travel and expense of his racing commitments prevented the careful farm management leading owners valued from their perspective as planters. It was not that leading owners were averse to heavy investment in horses— they had set new standards for equine infrastructure earlier in the century. But they thought thoroughbreds should compose just one element of a robust investment portfolio including manufacturing, transportation, banks, and farming.[11]

Turfmen did not take such a balanced approach, and particularly rejected the usual commercial staple crops such as cotton, wheat, tobacco, and rice. The youngest Tayloe had little experience with these commodities. Others, like the country's foremost turfman, William Ransom Johnson, similarly avoided planting. Johnson had dabbled in land speculation but sold out. Like Tayloe, he began his horse business by taking over his father's stable. When he purchased a Virginia-bred horse named Sir Archy for $1,500 in 1807, trained him, won several races, and then resold him for $5,000 in 1809, Johnson saw a new way to make his fortune. He repeated the process with dozens of horses. Acquiring the nickname "the Napoleon of the Turf," Johnson went on to conquer the racing world by pouring all his resources into thoroughbreds. He moved to Petersburg, ostensibly to join a mercantile firm, though he eventually sold his share of the business to concentrate on his horses. He bought slave grooms and jockeys. He acquired a plantation by marriage, and turned it into a horse farm and training facility that would have made John Baylor blush.

Johnson knew what he was doing. He reportedly lost just two of his first sixty races. Later in life, once he had amassed capital from selling racehorses, he invested in banks, steamboats, and iron forges, acquiring the diversified interests of better-established leading owners. But he was never a planter. After he won election to the Virginia legislature as an advocate of internal development and a supporter of Henry Clay, the *Turf Register* introduced a profile of him by reminding readers of his racing success and also that "you have heard of him as a successful merchant and a sagacious politician." Nobody had heard of Johnson as a planter. He possessed the trappings of planter life, but he made his money by racing and selling horses.[12]

Turfmen built their business model on the one pioneered by John Baylor. Yet they went further, prioritizing short-term profit potential by emphasizing selling over breeding. Since the colonial period, owners had used breeding to pay off their thoroughbred purchases and pursue long-term returns from their horses. Sales largely focused on foals representing new crosses of bloodlines. Leading owners had rarely sold mature racehorses unless they had to pay off debts.[13] If leading owners took a long view and "invested" in thoroughbreds, turfmen "speculated" in them by prioritizing a quick turnover of stock. They raced their animals hard in an effort to quickly grow the horse's reputation, sell it at a profit, and use the income to purchase another top-tier horse in order to start the cycle all over again. Johnson's ownership of the racing mare Ariel illustrates the strategy. He bought half of the mare for $1,200 from fellow turfman William Wynn's estate sale, held during the 1827 Tree Hill races outside Richmond. The following day, Johnson "won with her the Jocky Club Purse of $1000 & that day week [one week later] entered her for & won the . . . purse & sweepstakes at Tree Hill, so that in about a week after the purchase, they won with her $1000 more than her cost!" Having demonstrated the mare's value, Johnson then resold his share back to Wynn's nephew, heir, and namesake for $1,600. In one month, the purses and resale netted Johnson $1,500, about equal to what an average cotton planter with thirty slaves made in a year.[14]

Winning races to advertise and increase the value of thoroughbred horses was not new. Selling winners in their prime was, and so was approaching purses as a source of income for purchasing racehorses. The importance of prize money in the turfmen's new calculus of thoroughbred ownership explains why so many of them entered racecourse management. As proprietors, they worked to enlarge purses in three ways. First, they raised jockey club dues. Members who owned no horses always made up the majority of the clubs, and they accepted higher fees reluctantly and only because turfmen managers partly reimbursed them through rent. So club members paid more up front in dues, but then received annual rent payments that reduced their out-of-pocket costs for the club's private dinners and balls.[15]

Second, turfmen expanded sweepstakes racing. Sweepstakes amassed purse money entirely from entrance fees, creating purses not funded from admission or club dues. Originally, the format was used to fund races the clubs had no interest in supporting: short undercard events for young horses that whittled down which colts and fillies could compete at top levels when they got older. But in the 1830s, turfmen raised sweepstakes entrance fees to create new headline races. Standard purses for major four-mile races stood between $1,000 and $2,000, but major sweepstakes exceeded $5,000 and sometimes $10,000. In 1843, the Peyton Stakes in New Orleans cost $5,000 to enter and awarded the winner $40,000. Enormous purses attracted media attention and large crowds, making it worthwhile for owners to enter as long as their horse could avoid being distanced. *Turf Register* reports show losing horses sold for $1,000 or more than their previous purchase price after such events, provided "you don't get him beat too far."[16]

The crowds drawn to these spectacles elevated gate receipts, which constituted the turfmen's third way to enlarge purses (and their primary method for paying rent). In New York, Richmond, and Charleston, advertising and race-day transportation deals allowed courses to regularly gross $1,200 to $1,500 in gate receipts, plus another $100 to $200 in refreshment licenses. Henry Augustine Tayloe's records reveal a $400 annual net profit from the small course he partly owned in Alabama, and a later one he helped fund in New Orleans netted a total of more than $10,000 at its peak in 1838.[17]

Through income from race winnings, sales, and track management, turfmen gradually drove the prices for top racehorses beyond anyone else's reach. The only way to outbid them was to beat them for lucrative purses or apply other assets to horse purchases. Leading owners were unwilling to do the latter, and, increasingly, they could not win the biggest races. In 1822, an observer at the Charleston races noted that William Wynn had won "as usual." Ten years later, the same two dozen turfmen swept virtually all the major races in the country. The *Turf Register*'s monthly roster of race winners listed fewer and fewer names as a small cadre of successful turfmen inflated and then cornered the high-end thoroughbred market. In 1831, the president of the Maryland Jockey Club was so overmatched at his club's Baltimore races that he settled for racing at small tracks in a rural county nearby. At the Fairfield Course outside Richmond, proprietor John S. Corbin instituted a race specifically for "Honest Countrymen who are 'kept out of play' generally by the 'high trump.' "[18]

A few outsiders managed to keep up. The enormous wealth of South Carolina's leading owners, and their refusal to lease out their tracks' management to proprietors, allowed men like Richard Singleton and Wade Hampton II to continue to compete.[19] At the same time, a handful of northern scions joined the turfmen's ranks. Cadwallader R. Colden, named for his great-uncle who was the governor of New York at the time of the Stamp Act, lost his share of the family land in speculative ventures and turned to breeding as part of his plan for a large farm he purchased with a $10,000 loan in 1820. He used his family name to get into New York's jockey club and pursued track management after he defaulted on the loan and lost the farm.[20] Richard Ten Broeck followed in Colden's footsteps. Excommunicated from his prominent New York family after he was dismissed from West Point in 1830, his name still gave him access to turfmen like William Ransom Johnson. He served as a middleman between Napoleon and owners in the North, then later managed a popular racetrack in New Orleans. In the 1850s, he owned the most lucrative racer of the era, Lexington, who tallied $56,000 in winnings.[21]

The capital turfmen poured into thoroughbreds, and their subsequent command of racing, relegated the vast majority of leading owners to a subsidiary role in the thoroughbred market. They became known as "breeders," in contrast to the "racers" who made their money through purses and sales. The *Turf Register* explained the difference in "a candid answer to the thousand inquiries made of the racers by the breeders. 'Why is not my colt as well bred, as stylish, and worth as much as my neighbour's?' Because, sir, your colt, though well bred and stylish, is engaged in no stakes."[22]

As most breeders learned, mere entrance was not enough. An animal did not have to win, but it had to show well to raise its value. The Tayloe brothers discovered this fact when their horse "Robin Brown, having been beaten by Brooks' horse," which itself was not well respected, "could do nothing here for want of reputation."[23] The widening gap between the breeders' and the racers' horses steadily pushed leading owners-turned-breeders to focus their stables on second-tier horses that could not compete at the highest levels. Some of these animals had top racing blood but failed to win when young, and so turfmen sold them for about $1,000 to breeders who could still profit off them by offering them at stud and by crossing them with other middling stock to produce foals they sold for a few hundred dollars each. Owners had proclaimed the utilitarian qualities of part-blooded and full-blooded stock since the late eighteenth century, and they continued to spread this message in the 1820s and 1830s through agricultural periodicals focused on disseminating the latest farming techniques. These magazines instructed small and middling husbandmen to breed their "common stock" or "the common cart breed" to thoroughbreds for "both power and action." "For almost every purpose," they declared, "a large proportion of the pure blood is attended with striking advantages—for the saddle, especially, and for every kind of harness, not excepting the wagon and the plough."[24]

Of course, most farmers could not afford to breed to champion thoroughbreds. By 1830, access to a competitive racer cost forty dollars or more, while the average farmer did well to net two hundred dollars a year. Most had trouble affording even the breeders' second-tier horses, so they focused on breeding to third-tier foals whose parents were no better than second-tier, and which were often sold by breeders to men still lower down the ownership ladder. Access to these animals cost between five and twenty dollars.[25]

The key element in this hierarchical pyramid of ownership was the connection between turfmen and breeders. Despite the tension between them, they needed each other. Turfmen sold their cast-offs to breeders, and breeders needed turfmen to insert the latest champion bloodlines into their own breeding and sales operations. Henry Tayloe's brother George referenced this dependence when he directed his brothers to sell their horses bred from William Ransom Johnson's stud Monsieur Tonson. The elder Tayloes had become breeders, and knew that rather than due to the Tayloe name, "the Tonson stock will sell well as long as William Ransom Johnson owns Tonson." Any offspring from a horse belonging to Napoleon had marketable cachet.[26]

Vertical networks of thoroughbred bloodlines continued to tie owners together, though the depth of the connection grew weaker over time. Whereas colonial men bet on and bred to each other's horses as an expression of friendship rooted in multiple business, political, and kinship networks, the horse was often the only node linking men who were otherwise perfect strangers in the 1830s. When aspiring turfman Callendar Irvine saw his horse Mingo looking weak on a race day in 1839, and said he would have withdrawn it "but for the bets made on Mingo" by Johnson and his friends, his reprisal of Thomas Glenholme's decision in 1767 did not stem from a business connection any deeper than the one the racehorse embodied. In fact, Irvine later complained that the men for whom he raced his horse "have not condescended even to acknowledge the rec[eip]t of my letters." Similarly, Richard Singleton ignored a spirited request from a group of former breeding customers in Tennessee who wanted him to contribute to the purse for a produce stakes—a race of young colts from different studs that evaluated the parentage more than the offspring. "It will not do for the friends of Crusader to flinch," they wrote, when rival "friends of a distinguished Stallion" challenged them. Singleton's stud Crusader stood to gain from the race, but was unlikely to visit Tennessee again, so Singleton demurred. As the lesser owners' own letter stated, they were friends of the horse, not Singleton. In the new mass market controlled by a small cohort of owners, Singleton owed them nothing more than the breeding session they paid for. Turfmen changed not just the structure of the thoroughbred market but the nature of engaging in it.[27]

"The Starring System, Now So Greatly Reprobated"

By the 1820s, theatres already had seen an expansion of mobility that led to more challenges between spectators. They also already featured standardized content, as the same Shakespearean plays and formulaic melodrama dominated stages across the country. In the antebellum period, standardization extended from content to performers. Moreover, like turfmen, theatre investors engineered a boom and then heightened their control over the industry by stepping into management in an effort to preserve it.

Stephen Price did more than anyone else to drive these developments. Like William Dunlap, who preceded him as manager of New York's Park Theatre, Price came to the theatre from outside the acting profession. Price's father, too, was a loyalist, and Price had graduated from Columbia and passed the bar before he indulged his dramatic inclinations by purchasing the bankrupt Dunlap's portion of New York's resident theatre company and its playhouse lease in 1808. He fulfilled his predecessor's role as financial manager while actor Thomas Abthorpe Cooper handled stage direction. But Price and Dunlap had little in common other than their backgrounds and responsibilities. Price harbored no reservations about "pecuniary values," and never expressed concern about the theatre's "power to do much good." He came of age as the tension between profit and prestige was being settled, and he ran his theatres to make money.[28]

In 1810, Price discovered a new way to do that. The plan started when Cooper convinced one of London's biggest stars, George Frederick Cooke, to come to America. Instead of contracting Cooke to their company, the Park managers booked him for short stops at all the major American theatres. Piecemeal records suggest each manager netted about $10,000 over two years, while the alcoholic Cooke made almost $15,000 before he died of cirrhosis in New York in 1812. These staggering sums led Cooper to leave management and adopt the strategy himself. Other leading actors soon followed. Price began to orchestrate an annual parade of English stars, bringing them over so often as to earn the title "Star Giver General to the United States." After the headaches of trying to keep the erratic Cooke on schedule, though, Price only contracted stars for a year or two at the Park before letting them loose to book their own tours through other cities.[29]

At first, the new so-called "star system" yielded unprecedented profits. Stars stopping briefly in dozens of cities "preserved a freshness which rendered them welcome." Average nightly grosses at the Chestnut Street Theatre, the only playhouse for which complete annual receipts survive, rose from $400 in the early years of the century to over $800 in the 1810s. Cooper and other household names regularly attracted houses over $1,000, a sum seen just once or twice a year before starring began. In return, stars received generous contracts, often amounting to half of the evening's net profits. As one star explained, "I engage with the managers on a regular salary for the season of eight months and I earn about fifteen hundred dollars independent of my benefit; I engage with them for a few nights, and I gain as much or more." No wonder so many performers joined the circuit. With nightly expenses hovering around $350, managers, too, made more out of half the net receipts from a star's performance than they made keeping all of the gate on an average evening with the stock company.[30]

But managers gradually overextended the system. Instead of interspersing visits from stars with standard stock company productions, they booked a constant parade of guests, even though there were not enough big-name attractions to fill a season. By the mid-1820s, supporting actors from London theatres and leads from provincial British companies came to America billed as "stars." The presence of such underlings on the star circuit motivated local stock actors to "commence the business of starring merely to escape utter obscurity."[31] After all, as one actor noted, "the favor of the public is lavished on stars while the deserving but less aspiring performer is neglected and disregarded." When "restless, discontented, and indifferent" stock actors took up starring tours, their departures depleted stock companies and forced managers to book multiple stars to fill out casts. As "the combination of 'two stars in one sphere'" became commonplace, shows struggled to meet expenses with such a large portion of receipts due to the leads.[32]

Overexpansion of the star system was exacerbated by a new wave of theatre building, triggered by the boom years of the 1810s and early 1820s. Fearing their desired stars would play one of the growing number of rival houses, managers conceded an ever-larger percentage of ticket sales to stars' wages. They drew up the first guaranteed contracts, promising a flat nightly salary regardless of how many people showed up. Edwin Forrest, the earliest native-born American star, refused to act for less than $200 a night after 1829. By 1840, top wages approached $500. Other stars gulled managers into promising half the night's gross income, instead of half the net profits. "The starring system, now so greatly reprobated, was in full effect and daily gaining ground," William Wood recalled in his memoirs. Even "small stars asked half gross receipts instead of half net ones or profits. If, therefore, on any night the gross receipts failed to be double the expenses of the house, the theatre lost, while the actor got his half share."[33] Monstrous star salaries were not the only problems generated by competition. Having at least two theatres in every major northeastern city led to a series of prolonged ticket price wars. For the first time in thirty years, the cost of a box seat changed, dropping from one dollar to seventy-five cents in many of the newer theatres. Wood, who retired from management after suffering multiple losing seasons, later looked back and denounced "the increase of theatres and their foolish rivalry." Star Louis Tasistro blamed the managers themselves, who "started it with a view to cut each other's throats, and they are now reaping the fruit of their own folly."[34]

Managers crumbled faster than ever under the combined pressure of higher salaries and lower ticket prices. One season at the head of Cincinnati's theatre in 1822 put Sol Smith $1,100 into debt. Moneyless, he fled to Pittsburgh, where he ran the theatre on credit and repaid backers with free tickets, further hurting his income. Eventually, the shareholders wanted more than tickets. When they came to confront Smith, he hid under the stage's trap door until they left and he could skip town. Charles Gilfert lived beyond his means in New York before he took over the Charleston and Richmond theatres in 1817. In his first five years at the helm in those southern cities, the balmy early days of the star system allowed him to prosper and stay out of equity courts for the longest stretch of his life. After that, rising costs hampered his ability to repay debts accrued from refurbishing the Charleston playhouse as well as his "well-appointed" townhouse there. Mired in lawsuits by 1825, "the improvident Gilfert" lost his lease and returned to New York.[35]

Systemic failure affected investors as well as managers. After share prices and dividends rose between 8 and 30 percent from 1810 to 1820, they fell anywhere from 25 to more than 50 percent during the late 1820s and 1830s.[36] The drop led many shareholders to bail. Every major theatre on the East Coast saw its number of investors shrink. In most cases, a few deep-pocketed individuals remained and bought up the stock, consolidating financial control of playhouses in fewer and richer hands than ever before. In some places, however, investors gave up entirely. Charleston's shareholders sold their playhouse to the state, which turned it into a medical school.[37]

The remaining investors maintained an emphasis on profit that only added to managers' troubles. Such behavior was not entirely new. Since the 1790s, investors had sometimes chosen to neglect maintenance or deny managers income in order to preserve dividends. But in the past, failing managers tended to remain in their posts as long as they maintained a genteel reputation among the theatre investors who also were their creditors. Some managers decided to depart on their own because they feared falling ever deeper into debt, but few were pushed out. However, as gentility became less exclusive, it no longer protected managers. Financial losses became enough reason to remove them. After seeing his rent triple from $3,000 to $9,000 between 1822 and 1840, when inflation warranted a $600 increase and annual gross income had declined, Chestnut Street manager William Warren "found that his recent friends, who had got possession of everything he had, were now his insatiable and remorseless creditors." As another manager put it, "his friends, in the hour of his utmost need, entirely deserted him." Warren had offended no one. Presiding over declining returns cost him his house, extensive library, and his shares in the Baltimore, Washington, and Chestnut Street theatres.[38] On the other hand, as long as investors believed a manager could earn them money, they remained willing creditors. Charles Gilfert returned to New York after having failed in Charleston and was welcomed as "a very enterprising, talented man with some powerful friends." Those friends financed a new theatre for him, the Bowery, in 1826. They built a second one to replace the first when it burned down after just two years, because Gilfert had not yet cost them enough money to reduce their confidence in him as the best possible challenger to Stephen Price. Gilfert died in 1830, still deep in debt, before he found out whether his New York friends' patience would last longer than his Charleston investors'.[39]

Stephen Price defied the failures that engulfed most of his colleagues by minimizing competition in two ways. First, he tried to ban his rivals. He lobbied to outlaw combustible canvas from theatres because such ordinances prevented pleasure gardens from staging plays under tented awnings. Once he lost his monopoly to calls for greater competition in the 1820s, he blacklisted actors who performed on rival stages by using his nationwide connections to impair their starring tours. At his death, even his friends described him as "an arrogant, bullying, envious, and dishonest man" with a "temper not of the sweetest kind."[40] Second, "King Stephen," as avid New York playgoer Washington Irving called him, expanded his control by buying into the management of other companies and theatres. When threatened by a circus, he rounded up loans from silent partners "who then objected to be known to be interested" and purchased all of the company's effects from its investors. He then installed one of his actors to manage the troupe and sent it on tour away from New York. In 1826, he reduced the cost of hiring new English stars by purchasing the lease of London's famed Drury Lane Theatre. He shuttled actors back and

forth across the Atlantic, preserving their freshness in each locale by periodically removing them to the other. After four years, the Drury's exorbitant
$50,000 annual rent left him almost $20,000 in debt, so he declared bankruptcy
in England and gave up the grand scheme, only to later implement a similar
but cheaper one connecting the Park to Philadelphia's Chestnut Street
Theatre.[41]

King Stephen did not ascend to the throne based only on superior strate-
gizing. He also enjoyed the enormously good fortune of having just two
investors, John Jacob Astor and James Beekman, own the Park Theatre he
rented. Because these two men owned the theatre for more than forty years,
New York had fewer theatre shareholders than its size would have predicted.
Price tapped the surplus of prospective theatre investors for the credit he
needed to fund his aggressive tactics. He also used these friends as leverage
against his landlords. Whenever Astor and Beekman tried to escalate rent too
steeply, Price and his assistant Edmund Simpson threatened to leave or have
their friends build another theatre. These episodes always concluded with the
Park's owners tempering their terms, realizing the danger of more competition or the chance of ending up with a less profitable manager. Price's rent
started off higher than most because he was in New York, where a larger population promised larger regular audiences. Still, what he owed did not even
double, while others saw their rent triple over the same period. Having a pair
of stable owners who preferred steady long-term gains to chasing maximum
profit in the short term allowed Price to amass capital in ways other managers could not.[42]

For those other managers, losses brought greater pressure to listen to investors who could help them keep their jobs. The 1799 articles of agreement
defining investors' responsibilities to the Chestnut Street Theatre stated they
could "not reserve or exercise any controul in the Theatrical management of
dramatic entertainments or in the employment of performers." But by the late
1820s, Chestnut Street trustee Richard Peters Jr. personally funded his managers' trips to recruit new English stars, and thought this funding entitled him
to direct which actors to hire and to review the manager's program for the
season. Manager Francis Wemyss was offended by this and other impositions
by investors, later writing in his autobiography that "I was compelled to yield
my judgment to the dictation of gentlemen who, understanding their own
business, might at least have given me credit for understanding mine."[43] The
remaining theatre investors gave no such credit, surrounded as they were by
playhouses failing under actor-managers. Charlestonians erected a new theatre in 1837 and hired a manager "very much under the influence of Dr. John B.
Irving, one of our citizens," who was also a theatre trustee and an officer in

the local jockey club. Trustees elsewhere dictated ticket prices and renovations to the house. Some took more direct control. After forcing one manager to retire from the Tremont Theatre, a shareholders' "Committee of Arrangements" hired his replacement rather than leasing out the theatre. Salaried by the shareholders, the manager had little control over the acting company, and the investors issued him instructions "for the sake of seeing a play acted as they would like to see it."[44]

Unlike past generations of trustees, the ones who became involved in management during the antebellum era were wealthier and more established. Richard Peters Jr. was a seventy-five-year-old prominent Philadelphia lawyer. His opposite at the rival Walnut Street Theatre was fellow attorney Henry Freeman, who was in his mid-forties when he started to make demands of managers. In Boston, Charles Bradbury and Joseph Coolidge called the shots at the Federal Street playhouse. Bradbury presided over a large insurance company, and Coolidge was among the one hundred wealthiest Bostonians in 1830. The Cohen brothers who dictated terms in Baltimore sat on the boards of local insurance and railroad companies. The days of esteemed gentlemen simply serving as a nexus for the recruitment of shareholders were over. The elevation of profit over prestige made theatres just like any other large business, and so a city's top investors and businessmen sought more active roles in steering them back toward profitability.[45]

In the 1830s, these men started to lease theatres to younger fellow investors, probably out of a belief that their backgrounds would make them more profitable and pliable than actor-managers. The new investor-managers typically came from established families but had checkered business careers that left them reliant on the credit and reputation of older and more successful trustees. Actors called them "dilletanti" managers, and Louis Tasistro saw them everywhere, noting that "nothing is more common in this country than to see a vendor of lottery tickets or a broken down stock-jobber, fresh from the baleful atmosphere of their respective vocations, suddenly stepping into the management of a theatre."[46] His comment may have been aimed at Lewis T. Pratt, who belonged to one of Philadelphia's most powerful families and ran a local lottery house before taking over the Chestnut Street Theatre in 1830. Likewise, failed Boston broker Francis W. Dana hailed from one of his city's leading families and had amassed a five-figure personal debt by the time he assumed the Tremont's management in 1829. In Annapolis, a hardware supplier, a construction contractor, and the subscribers' treasurer used their own personal credit to finish building the new Hallam Theatre after subscribers reneged on their pledges to pay for it. The triumvirate then waived lawsuits to recover their expenses in return for a controlling share in the playhouse and the "right to present theatre in the building."[47]

In the end, the investor-managers changed very little on stage. They may have selected different stock company members or even minor stars, but they did nothing to change the standardization of content wrought by major stars, who continued to perform the Shakespeare and melodrama which had changed only slightly since the early 1800s. Indeed, although stars varied in their acting style, material was so universal that even Stephen Price shared it, once writing to another manager to explain "my wish to be on reciprocal terms" with scripts, music, and sometimes scenery.[48]

Predictably, given how little they changed, the investor-managers did not revive the market. Dana's connection to shareholders at both the Federal Street and Tremont Street houses convinced them to combine forces, but less competition could not bring profit as long as the star system held sway. "They paid enormous sums to monopolise the erratic talent of the country," reported one local newspaper. Having "blowed up a great bubble" with the loans required to pay these salaries, "it burst in the eyes of the Stockholders, who had in a measure to pay for it" when Dana did not make enough to cover their contracts and loans. Pratt fared no better. By adjusting ticket prices based on the magnitude of the star in residence, he taught audiences that cheap seats meant inferior performances. Empty houses for lesser shows robbed him of the income he needed to cover large star contracts and the expensive operas he liked to stage.[49]

Yet investor-managers survived longer than actor-managers. Pratt remained in management at the Chestnut Street house for almost fifteen years in spite of consistent deficits. Dana lasted five years, while none of the three actor-managers preceding him in Boston had survived more than two. Domineering investors who did not formally enter management lasted even longer. Charles Gilfert accrued heavy debts to the friends who rebuilt his Bowery Theatre, but Charleston's theatre investors defaulted on their new playhouse and still retained their shares after it burned in 1837. The Cohen brothers suffered annual losses because they refused to fund a stock company at their Baltimore theatre, and so it stood dark for several stretches every season. They nevertheless retained controlling shares for thirteen years. These men enjoyed deeper kin and social networks among investors than most actors, besides having deeper pockets themselves. They levied assessments on shares to raise fresh capital as needed, and their prominence made it harder for the other remaining stockholders to refuse them. They absorbed losses rather than fleeing them, either because they had few alternatives (in the case of

Pratt and Dana) or because they possessed enough wealth and reputation to declare themselves successful in spite of the state of their theatres. None of these men left behind evidence explaining their motives, but the tone of their directives suggests that, having made the decision to sacrifice exclusive gentility for profit in the early national period, investor-managers and controlling trustees saw a chance to reclaim some degree of prestige as cultural arbiters by stepping into theatre management. This lure might explain why a lack of financial success did not prevent them from remaining for as long as they could hold out.[50]

In sum, theatre witnessed a movement of investors into management that paralleled developments in racing. Although this movement did not yield the same return as the one the turfmen enjoyed, it did tighten investors' control over theatres just as the star system heightened the standardization of content by giving audiences nationwide the same performers as well as the same plays. By the mid-1830s, both racing and theatre had become much more like mass entertainment than either had been in 1820.

"In the Dearth of Everything Else"

Then came the Panic of 1837. The panic was a complicated economic crash produced by government policies favoring gold and silver coins over paper bank notes at the same time global flows and reserves of silver were shifting. People reacted to these changes nervously, either by calling on their debtors to pay up or by trying to convert their paper money to hard currency. The resulting run on cash and credit constricted the American economy for the better part of the next decade. Unemployment and bankruptcy filings rose while incomes fell.[51] By the time a recovery started in the mid-1840s, the slump had forced turfmen and theatre investors to alter their management systems yet again. Both groups turned to standardizing not just the content and presentation of their events, but the architectural space and social experience of their venues. By pushing investors and managers to redevelop generic categories of genteel and rough sporting space, the panic furthered sporting culture's evolution into an early form of mass culture.

Changes to sporting culture inspired by the panic took place in the 1840s because it took time for the crash to affect the sporting industry. In fact, at first, the panic seemed like a good thing for both theatres and racetracks. "If an exception to the influence of that mighty incubus which has borne so heavily upon all trades, business, corporations, and professions were demanded, the Park Theatre, in its undisturbed prosperity, would be selected most prominent," stated the *New York Monthly Magazine* in September 1837. It was not just King Stephen earning the returns. From New York to Mobile, theatres enjoyed such a boom that "some folks think the managers of the theatres here are making all the money that is made"—except perhaps for racetracks. "In the dearth of everything," the *Turf Register* noted, "a race is no bad article of excitement." Attendance, purses, and sales prices all defied the crash during the fall 1837 season.[52]

The boom did not last, however. As in the 1810s and early 1820s, a brief window of profitability prompted a headlong rush into the market that soon overcrowded it. Between 1837 and 1840, four new theatres opened in New York, which already had five. Philadelphia, Boston, and Baltimore all saw new theatres go up when they already featured at least two. Southern cities such as Richmond, Norfolk, and Charleston replaced their old playhouses.[53] Melodramas evolved, taking on an "apocalyptic" theme befitting the economic climate, but they differed little from theatre to theatre. Managers even routinized the newly imported genre of opera, stirring one New York reviewer to grumble about having "no novelties in the character of the entertainments," just "humdrum melo-dramas at the Park and opera at the National." With theatres offering similar content and social experiences, the lack of distinction soon spread audiences too thinly across them. "Two and sometimes three theatres contended for an audience which could at no time could have supported very profitably more than one," surmised Philadelphia manager William Wood.[54] In southern cities where competition was not an issue, repetitive content still reduced the repeat attendance necessary for survival. A new tide of losses and failures rolled in during the early 1840s.[55]

Turfmen failed at the same time, but for a different reason. Broad popular interest in the thoroughbred market had been the foundation of the turfmen's financial success. Attachment to thoroughbred blood had motivated both attendance at the races and the secondary sales and breeding markets that allowed turfmen to still turn a profit from underperforming racers. However, the new business model grounded in successful racing pushed turfmen to run their animals at ever-younger ages. Races for two- and three-year-olds were shorter and worth less money than those for mature horses that began at age four, but owners needed their colts and fillies to compete well as youngsters if they were to gain the value that legitimated larger entrance fees for major races later. Because young horses needed to show well in shorter races that privileged speed over endurance, turfmen responded by prioritizing speed in their breeding. The result was "fleet but leggy," svelte horses that attracted concern even before the panic hit, as mare owners reminded turfmen that they "like large horses" and "want, he says, a large, well formed, strong constitutioned horse, thorough bred, as a getter of harness, carriage & saddle horses." Turf-men grew alarmed a few years later. "The times this Spring throughout the country is unprecedented," Henry Augustine Tayloe told his brothers in 1838. "I fear we are breeding too much for speed." Without endurance when they matured, these horses' four-mile races turned into sprints from the start. As one British observer dryly rhymed, "the Winner comes in decidedly blown, Tho 'ere two miles were done the race was her own." The problem was clear even to the relatively untrained eyes of British actor Tyrone Power, who wrote after watching races in several American cities that "a larger sort of brood-mare would, I think, be of more service to them."[56]

Breeding for speed cut the delicate legs out from beneath the spiraling thor-oughbred market. Breeders and other lesser owners were attracted to thor-oughbred blood for utilitarian purposes served by a combination of both speed and endurance. As panic gave way to lethargic depression, less functional thor-oughbreds were one of the first expenses that breeders and lesser owners cut from their budgets. Breeders publicly complained that turfmen, the "sporting gentlemen, are too often inclined to consult their individual interest or con-venience rather than the general prosperity of the Turf." Combined with the "distress in our city," the changes to the breed made Baltimorean Emory Stew-art "anxious to dispose of all this unprofitable perplexing property and quit the turf forever." He was not alone. By 1850, dozens of former leading owners had divested themselves of their thoroughbreds, including the Tayloes, who had been in the business for three generations.[57] Those who remained offered older thoroughbred bloodlines reputed for producing stouter animals, such as Virginian John Hartwell Cocke's aptly named Utilitarian, a thoroughbred wisely advertised as "possessing the essential qualities for the purposes of com-mon and practical life." Others shifted to new hybrids, crossing pure-blooded with half-thoroughbred horses to create pacers and Morgan horses. A new set of leading owners in the Northeast supported the nascent sport of harness racing as a way to test these bloodlines for quotidian use.[58]

Bailing breeders robbed turfmen of fresh capital. After all, without the breeders buying their underperformers, the turfmen could not keep elevat-ing purses, prices, and profits. They could only circulate the same money among themselves, buying each other's horses, applying the money toward new purchases or purses, and reselling the winners to each other again. To make matters worse, the disaffection spread further down the ownership hi-erarchy. Average race-goers had little reason to spend what cash they had on a trip to the track when they had no connection to the horses there. Just six months after issuing reports of solid attendance, the *Register* relayed observa-tions in the spring of 1838 that "the attendance was quite thin, notwithstanding the fine purses." A few years later, top purses plummeted from a high of $3,000 in the late 1830s to just $400 or $600. Tracks closed. Sales prices stalled. The *Turf Register* ceased publication in 1844.[59]

Turfmen, once the defiant conquerors of leading owners, now discovered the true power of breeders who maintained more diverse investments. "I am exceedingly poor, my Dear Col & I humbly crave your charity in the adjustment of this Matter," turfman and racetrack proprietor John Sawbridge Corbin wrote to planter and breeder Robert Wormeley Carter in an attempt to claim unpaid sweepstakes entrance fees in 1842. "While so small a sum as the am[oun]t of the forfeit would not be probably felt by yourself," Corbin pleaded, "I do assure you it would relieve me from a vast deal of wretchedness." Henry Augustine Tayloe compounded his thoroughbred losses with failed speculations in paper money. He owed over $167,000 to various creditors in 1840—a sum worth about $4.7 million in 2014. "I never would have wanted a dollar if I had not have gone on the turf," he admitted to his family just before he was forced to sell virtually everything he owned, from his horses to his silver and furniture. Even the Napoleon of the Turf met defeat. William Ransom Johnson endured the "great mortification" of a "Public Sale of Negroes, Stock &c " in the spring of 1845, in order to repay debts totaling $20,000.[60]

Yet 1845 was not Johnson's Waterloo. Nor was it the end of commercial theatre. In the mid-1840s, turfmen and theatre managers both orchestrated rebounds by adjusting their business models. Theatre managers instituted changes aimed at reducing competition, while turfmen reoriented racing to appeal to spectators without an interest in thoroughbred bloodlines.

Theatre managers minimized competition in three ways. First, the failures of the early 1840s left the surviving managers with enough clout to attract the additional support they needed to copy Stephen Price's strategy of managing multiple houses at once. While Price managed in Philadelphia and New York, James Caldwell operated theatres in New Orleans and Mobile, rising impresario John T. Ford took over in Baltimore and Richmond before adding his soon-to-be-infamous theatre in Washington, and Francis Wemyss operated Price's rival house in Philadelphia as well as the one in Pittsburgh. Unlike colonial and early national predecessors who operated multiple theatres as circuits, these men and others like them ran separate companies at each playhouse. Managing multiple houses allowed them to survive losses at one. Indeed, Wemyss demonstrated the importance of that safety net by failing the year after he abandoned Pittsburgh and managed only the theatre in competitive Philadelphia, which he called "the sink that swallowed up all the gains of Pittsburgh."[61]

Managers without the capital or connections necessary for running more than one playhouse could still improve their chances of survival by forsaking expensive touring stars in favor of stock companies engaged for an entire season. Stars still visited, but the post-panic bust finally propelled managers to scale back the system.[62] Managers made up for losing the allure of a star every night by selling cheaper tickets, something they could afford once they were no longer hamstrung by exorbitant star contracts and could squeeze company actors who could no longer react by heading out on their own tours. Box seats dropped to fifty cents in most theatres, with pit tickets falling to twenty-five cents and the gallery accessible for as little as twelve pennies. The best seats in the house had cost half a week's wages for a laborer in the colonial period. They cost less than a day's pay for the same group in the 1840s.[63]

The final change implemented to reduce competition involved heightening the distinction among theatres. Initially the differences were more advertised than real, as Stephen Price's rivalry with Bowery Theatre manager Thomas Hamblin demonstrates. The Bowery was the first theatre Price could not cow in New York. It was built by men convinced of Charles Gilfert's profitability despite his bankruptcy in Charleston, and Hamblin took it over after Gilfert died in 1830. The two playhouses actually featured the same types of seating sections and material, and both were cited for hosting riots and an "indiscriminate mass" of patrons "from all classes."[64] Yet visitors and the popular press frequently painted the two theatres as mirror opposites, with the "democratic" Bowery set in contrast to the "aristocratic" Park. The distinction was reinforced when the Bowery lowered ticket prices well before the Park did.[65] Then, in the midst of the depression, Hamblin stopped giving free tickets to the press. Out of "poor spite," critics and editors began to repeatedly depict his house as the sole site of "oaths, shouts, [and] shrieks from the throats of drunken outcast bands." They publicized Hamblin's adulterous private life and berated the playhouse as a reflection of the "practised rake and seducer" who managed it. The papers unwittingly played straight into Hamblin's hands, helping him attract patrons interested in a wild night out despite offering the same range of seats and experiences as Price.[66] In the final analysis, then, the Bowery was not less respectable than the Park. It just had the reputation of being less respectable. All kinds of white men looking for a raucous time—or just to witness one from the boxes—went there because it was reputed to provide that kind of experience. Indeed, the real difference between the two houses was the constant crowd drawn to the Bowery by its seamy reputation. As early as the spring of 1839, "that most positive and valuable superiority which the Park once enjoyed" had, according to the new sporting weekly

The Spirit of the Times, "been given up." Price died in 1840 and Hamblin took over the struggling Park in 1847, further underscoring their similarity.[67]

By the mid-1840s, not all distinctions between theatres were artificial. New managers came to the field from other arenas of entertainment, endowed with enough support to craft niches by raising new kinds of playhouses where architecture reinstated the distinctive behavioral rules blurred by the accessibility of gentility in traditional theatres. One set of new playhouses were the "lecture halls" attached to existing venues such as museums and pleasure gardens. They differed from traditional theatres by supplanting rows of pit benches with individual seats. They also forbade entry to unescorted women at night, in an attempt to lock out prostitutes from galleries, which were shrewdly renamed "the family circle." In effect, these theatres contained only one or two seating sections. Those opened by Moses Kimball in Boston and P. T. Barnum and William Niblo in New York sold every seat for the same low price of either twenty-five or fifty cents. In the words of one sporting magazine, the new seating arrangement was "conducted on the pure principle of democracy. Everybody is as good as anybody else there."[68]

Traditional theatres had invited male patrons to enjoy a range of distinct social experiences under one roof, though the distinctions grew less clear over time. In the new lecture hall theatres, rules of admittance, fewer pricing levels, and individual seating urged genteel refinement on the entire audience. Historians have often credited these changes and the impresarios who instituted them with democratizing American entertainment, but the adjustments drew heavily from steady changes over the preceding forty years. In many ways, the lecture halls were nothing more than entire theatres consisting of already accessible box seats. By eliminating other seating sections, and movement between them, the impresarios crafted a more reputable air. Aspiring gentlefolk of all ranks loved it, leading the managers of several traditional theatres to convert their houses to this plan in the late 1840s and 1850s. By then, many of these theatres specialized in a new brand of moral melodrama that fit the experience by exposing the dangers of drinking, gambling, and, occasionally, even slavery. The combination of content and seating plan explains why no reports ever mention verbal or physical ferocity among spectators in these buildings. The venues combatted traditional theatres' reputations for physical masculinity, going so far as to—in one historian's words—"effeminize" the theatre experience by discouraging brash confrontation.[69]

The other new type of theatre venue was the opera house. English opera had been a part of seasons at traditional theatres since the colonial era, and translated versions of foreign operas grew more common in the 1820s. Before the end of the decade, Italian and French troupes toured like stars and subleased playhouses from managers during traditional companies' summer off-seasons. The foreigners enjoyed enough support that when managers raised their rent in the mid-1830s, they collected their wealthiest backers and built their own opera houses.[70] Yet the first opera houses were not the exclusive bastions of high society that later ones became. Before the 1870s, these venues closed whenever they put opera "beyond the reach of the great body of the people," because, as a range of commentators recognized, "that class from whom support was mainly expected are not yet sufficiently numerous to be the exclusive supporters."[71]

Instead of being exclusive, early opera houses survived by reproducing the old behavioral divisions between the boxes and the gallery while eliminating the pit in favor of individual "arm chairs," which cost more than one dollar to sit in. Along with the cost and the formal attire required in such "parquettes" or "parterres," critics remarked that "the carpeted floor and mahogany-backed seats affect the spectator in a singular manner," producing a much less contentious atmosphere than at traditional theatres. But while the pit and boxes merged into one costly and exclusive seating section, the gallery remained for the hoi polloi. Gallery seats in the Astor Place Opera House in New York cost a mere fifty cents, the same as the box seats filled with all sorts of people at the Park and Bowery. Not surprisingly, then, newspapers described "vulgar wretches" and "low creatures" in the cheap seats at opera houses.[72]

Perhaps more significant than any of these changes to the theatre business was the fact that managers, not investors, executed them. The mid-1840s saw professional managers trained in the entertainment world reclaim oversight of theatre operations. If not all the new managers came from acting backgrounds, men like Kimball, Niblo, and Barnum at least had staged various kinds of commercial amusements before opening their lecture halls. Investors increasingly returned to men with this kind of experience as the losses under managers from their own ranks finally reached unsustainable levels in the 1840s. Just a few years later, flush with profits from having turned around the market, traditional managers strengthened their grasp by purchasing significant shares in their theatres, or even becoming outright owners. Hamblin and the lecture hall impresarios led the way, but by the 1860s others, including James Wallack in New York and John T. Ford in Washington, held the title to their venues. These managers kept their names on their mortgages by refusing to offer any dividend other than free tickets. Investors accepted this reversion to colonial practice because years of losses and the evolution of playhouses led them to view some theatres as standing outside the competitive sporting culture that required them to seek profit. The theatre market began to split, with some venues and versions separating from sporting culture and drifting toward a category of philanthropically funded "high culture" that crystallized in the 1870s and 1880s with symphonies, opera, and "formal" theatre.[73]

Whatever type of theatre a manager ran, few made enough gains to completely eliminate investors' influence. After all, managers still needed loans to open and operate their playhouses. Creditors gave up an explicit and vocal place in theatre management, but "the powerful influence of the proprietors incognito" remained unparalleled in picking which managers received the financial wherewithal and leeway to rise to prominence, and which ones never got the chance or sank under unforgiving loans as soon as their playhouses began to fail. As investors receded into the shadows following heavy losses after the panic, they remained influential—if quieter—kingmakers who channeled their investments into recoverable personal loans rather than risky shares.[74]

Turfmen did not face the same problem as theatre managers. They needed to reinvigorate racing's popularity, not reconsolidate control over its market. They pursued their goal by implementing three changes to the racetrack experience. First, they expanded stands and reduced the prices and social restrictions for sitting in them. Public stands had opened at courses across the country in the 1820s and 1830s, but only New York's seated over one thousand people, and admission to any of them cost an additional dollar above general admission fees. Following the panic, the construction of new stands capable of holding one thousand to three thousand people gave rise to the term "grandstand." Track managers also reduced the price of stand tickets from one dollar to fifty or twenty-five cents, and many eliminated general admission fees by 1845. After adding the cost of transportation to racetracks, which were typically located outside urban centers, spectators could enjoy stand seating for a total cost of about a dollar. By extending the privilege of stand seating to "aspiring loafers," "daring urchins," and "a heterogeneous crowd of persons"— all descriptions of people found there in the late 1840s—managers brought racetracks closer into line with traditional theatres. Mobility at the track was no longer the restricted purview of wealthy men coming down from the stands onto the concourse. Now aspiring men ascended the stands and claimed respectability, just as they did in traditional boxes and new lecture halls.[75]

Second, managers sought to replace the disappearing personal attachment to horses and bloodlines with interregional races that played on spectators' geographic identities. Periodically through the 1820s and 1830s, managers had organized special "match races"—one-on-one contests—billed as "North-South" events. Stakeholders chose representative horses from among the stock owned in their region, despite the fact that all American racers shared the same Virginia-based and imported bloodlines. After the panic, managers staged more of these contests. Besides North-South races, there were "East-West" affairs and state-level contests "between the champions of Louisiana and Kentucky," or Kentucky and Virginia, or Virginia and South Carolina, or Tennessee and Louisiana. Such events aimed to connect spectators to racehorses through geographic affiliations because fewer people were invested in thoroughbred bloodlines.[76]

Finally, turfmen implemented a gambling innovation to further attract race-goers because the public wager was losing its appeal. The whole purpose of public bets had been to inflate a horse's value by fostering confidence in it, but confidence mattered little and value could not be affected when a shrinking percentage of people invested in thoroughbred blood. So track managers turned gambling into an attraction in its own right by introducing pool-selling, or "auction pool" wagering, the forerunner of today's pari-mutuel system. Instead of direct betting between two or more parties, auction pools inserted a licensed bookmaker as an intermediary. The new method transformed wagering from a public declaration of affiliation into a private attempt to pick a winner and make money. The pool system operated on simple greed, and its fast, easy betting with immediate payouts for small bets worked with the accessible grandstand and regional races to rejuvenate thoroughbred racing. Besides attracting spectators, bookmakers also paid jockey clubs license fees to operate at their tracks, and this income was what allowed the elimination of general admission. By the 1850s, revenue from pool betting and grandstands had lifted prize money above its pre-panic peak. The continued success of the new business model, prioritizing anonymous and individual risk-taking over the old hierarchical networks of ownership, led to the racetracks of the 1870s that still anchor the sport today at Saratoga, Pimlico, and Churchill Downs, as well as the modern "dash system" built around more numerous shorter races.[77]

The changes made to racing in the wake of the panic depersonalized and democratized the experience of race-going. The handful of turfmen who masterminded these changes now recognized their dependence on breeders and spectators. They shifted their focus to managing tracks and stables for a small circle of new breeders in Louisiana, Mississippi, Tennessee, and Kentucky who viewed racing as a pastime rather than a business but were lured by the potential for large purses and popular acclaim. Relying on loans from these western breeders and some bankers who saw the renewed profitability of racing, William Ransom Johnson recovered and held credits worth twice as much as his debts by the time he died in 1849—just four years after he had to auction off slaves and other property to pay his debts. His protégé, Richard Ten

Broeck, similarly found enough backing to take a team of thoroughbreds to England in 1856, though he finished his career not as an independent owner like turfmen before him, but as an employee of English-born investor and breeder James Keene. So, in many ways, turfmen ended up with less autonomy than theatre managers, though neither could finance their work on their own. For their part, investors continued to fund sporting activities rife with opportunities for self-assertion and risk-taking, but withdrew from management in order to reduce their exposure to financial risk. As a result, investors became a smaller, more exclusive, and less publicized club, less concerned than their early national predecessors about building the broader economy through sport.[78]

Structuring "Indiscriminate Gaming"

The panic was not a bellwether moment for gaming venues. In that sector of the sporting industry, the key change of the period was a gradual shift in gambling legislation. Starting in the 1820s and picking up speed through the 1830s and 1840s, state legislators eliminated the proscription on specific activities in antigambling laws. In theory, this change widened the potential for prosecution. Any betting at all was now banned, not just wagers laid on enumerated sports. But the new laws were even more difficult to enforce than previous ones, since conviction required proof of gambling, not evidence of playing a banned game. Such proof was elusive because the only material involved in acts of wagering or paying were money, notes, and goods that defendants could claim were being paid for other, legal, purposes. By eliminating gaming equipment as evidence of illegal behavior, the new laws paid lip service to moral propriety while actually widening opportunities for wagering and thus confirming the centrality of risk-taking to participation in the sporting republic.[79]

The legalization of billiards, cards, and other games inspired a host of new gambling establishments. Although southern sporting taverns went the way of northern ones as wealthy proprietors passed away and rising urban land values lured descendants to partition and sell their lots, taverns everywhere (some now called "saloons") continued to host a variety of gambling games.[80] Yet it was the specialized gaming halls, first seen in the early republic, that became the venues most associated with gambling in antebellum cities. Of these operations, billiard halls charged up front for play, while those peddling card and dice games made money from customers' still-illicit gambling losses. So billiard halls gained greater legitimacy and became systematically traceable in city directories and advertisements, while other types of venues remained shadowy and surface only haphazardly in exposés and court records.

The data for billiard halls illustrates their proliferation. The number of documented halls in New York quintupled between 1820 and 1860, from twelve to sixty, while Philadelphia and New Orleans saw only slightly less growth.[81] Persistent published complaints and petitions expressing concern about "the mania for gaming" that was "increasing in many parts of our country to an alarming degree" suggest the boom was not limited to billiards. In South Carolina, the number of grand jury presentments and petitions remonstrating against gambling tripled from the years between 1790 and 1820 to the years between 1820 and 1850. By the end of the later period, New York's reform-minded citizens gave up on law enforcement and formed the Association for the Suppression of Gambling to make their own effort at dissuasion. This evidence suggests a wide range of gaming venues enjoyed growth during the antebellum years.[82]

As in other sectors of the sporting industry, stiff competition produced instability. Of twenty-five known billiard hall managers in New York, Philadelphia, and New Orleans between 1847 and 1850, only three still ran one in 1860. Out of forty-nine managers named in directories or advertisements over the entire period from 1847 to 1860, five significantly improved their circumstances over those ten years, either through their billiard halls or by moving from billiard hall management to more lucrative stations as hotelkeepers or restaurateurs. These five men possessed estates worth more than $1,000 in 1860. So did two others who appear to have entered the market with wealth and connections. Nine possessed property valued at $200 or less. Apparently, there was no upper middle class among billiard hall proprietors, as none of them had property assessed between $200 and $1,000. Beyond these sixteen men, the remaining 65 percent of the known managers had no estate of value attached to their name. Fourteen never even appeared in a census in the city where they had been listed, suggesting that they were never heads of households or that they relocated after just a few years.[83]

Two strategies helped some billiard hall proprietors survive and even succeed where many failed. First, particularly because fully a third of them were immigrants, they sought friends to invest in their business and protect it. The size of their estates suggests that very few proprietors could have afforded multiple billiard tables when they opened. Technology and the game's expanding popularity led some cabinetmakers to specialize in billiard tables by the 1840s, but their cheapest products did not cost less than $150 each until after the Civil War. Since billiard halls offered more than the one or two tables found in taverns and saloons—up to fifteen or twenty in larger establishments—the entry barriers to billiard hall proprietorship required outside investment for the majority of aspiring beginners.[84] Many rented their tables from their landlords. Others skirted rental costs by tying themselves to table manufacturers. Like the common tavern market, in which brewers increasingly financed neighborhood saloons in order to expand into the retailing of their beer, early New York and New Orleans table makers sponsored billiard halls as showrooms for their wares. At first, the manufacturers supplied tables and paid proprietors a sales commission. Later proprietors simply rented their facilities from manufacturers at a discount for promoting their tables.[85]

Michael Phelan was one of the rare success stories in the billiard hall market. He came to New York from Ireland as a child with his father. In fact, his father briefly ran a billiard hall in the early 1820s shortly after arriving. The elder Phelan did well enough to apprentice his son to a jeweler, but the boy ultimately preferred the craft on napped wool to the one in precious stones. He began as a "roper" or "whipper-in," luring strangers to play at halls near the theatres on Park Row and the Bowery. His skill allegedly caught the eye of well-known player and proprietor Joseph White, who introduced Phelan to his contacts. Soon, Phelan had his own hall populated with tables from local manufacturer D. D. Winant.[86]

This model of patronage was not unique to billiard hall or saloon proprietors. Entrepreneurs both inside and outside the sporting industry needed friends. Those running card and dice houses particularly sought prominent supporters in order to avoid being caught up in periodic waves of antigambling law enforcement. Veteran gambler John O'Connor recalled his first mentor investing only one-third of the $3,000 required to open a gaming house in Richmond. In New Orleans, where French and Spanish roots led to licensing gaming houses much earlier in the century than elsewhere in the republic, visitors reported that "establishing one of these banks is effected much as that of any other. Shares are sold, and many respectable moneyed men, I am informed, become stockholders; though not ambitious, I believe, to have their names made public. It is some of the best stock in the city, often returning an enormous dividend."[87] As in all businesses, dividends took away from the proprietor's income. But gaming houses without backers could only be fly-by-night ventures that ended at a moment's notice when the proprietor was chased out of town, arrested, or worse, as when the citizens of Vicksburg, Mississippi, lynched five gamblers in 1835.[88]

How could a prospective proprietor win the friends he needed? Twenty years earlier, Robert Bailey knew that genteel dress and etiquette helped. So did the timeless assets of profitability and knowing one's place. For billiard players, though, there was another way. Since playing billiard games did not involve wagering as a matter of course, like so many card games, public demonstrations of skilled play did not attract authorities and proffered renown that made the player look like a good bet to attract a steady clientele. Michael Phelan again presents a case in point. Though he had worked in billiard halls since he was a teenager, Phelan continued to be listed in city directories as a jeweler until 1850. Not coincidentally, Phelan advertised his first public match and published his first playing manual that same year. Both these moves were designed to win him a following. The match was proposed to reigning English champion John Roberts, with a prize purse of $500 and an international title going to the winner. Phelan most likely did not put up any of the money, as reports of similar matches throughout the era describe "a number of his friends" fronting purse sums for their favorite players. Roberts, however, never responded. The Englishman had little to gain by coming to America, and the proposal specifically stated that the match would be in New York. Phelan may have expected the challenge to land flat. Merely making the offer rendered him the "American champion," a player "for the honor of Yankee Land."[89]

Yet, as all managers learned, friends could be fickle. After Phelan's next major match, in Boston in 1852, his career seems to have taken a hit. No result from the match survives, but Phelan never overlooked an opportunity to trumpet his victories. His sudden silence after having expanded his presence with a book and newspaper columns following the 1850 "victory" hints at a defeat. The next year, newspapers reported that he had left to take his chances in the gold rush boomtown of San Francisco. He returned in 1855, only after winning a well-publicized match against the local champion there. The victory was just what he needed to round up a fresh batch of friends.[90]

In 1857, Phelan wrote a new manual, emphasizing the "civilities" and "scientific principles" of the game in an effort to further appeal to reputable men of means. He succeeded, opening a billiard hall on Broadway as well as a fledgling table-making business in 1858. He also scheduled more competitive matches to boost the visibility of those enterprises, though competition proved risky once again. Despite calling himself "The Invincible," he only won two of five matches in a round-robin between prominent players from New York and Philadelphia in 1858.[91] With support for his businesses perhaps hanging in the balance, Phelan quickly responded to his defeat by orchestrating "The Great Billiard Match," the largest stakes game of the era. With the help of "a number of gentlemen, amateurs of the game," he amassed a $5,000 purse and pitted himself against relatively unknown Detroit player John Seereiter. Phelan wrote weekly columns for *The Spirit of the Times* and *Frank Leslie's Illustrated* to drum up excitement, announcing an illness just weeks before the event to cast some doubt over his likely victory, though he ended up winning handily. Seereiter was never heard from again, while Phelan promptly announced his retirement from competition and stated that "his position is henceforth un-questionable not as Champion (for he very properly repudiates that impossi-ble title), but as the Representative Man of billiard science in America." He leased out his billiard hall, managed and then sold his manufacturing business, and published more manuals. He bought a summer estate on Long Island and died in 1871 as one of the few billiard men who had struck it rich. Central to his success was winning friends, less through a remarkable playing ability than a remarkable skill at publicizing his play.[92]

Whether a proprietor attracted wealthy backers by playing well or adver-tising himself better, and whether he operated a billiard hall or another kind of gaming enterprise, there was one other strategy for surviving the perilous market. Proprietors joined theatre managers in reducing competition by con-structing distinct types of venues that each promoted a different kind of sport-ing experience. One form of distinction, involving specialization in particular games, first appeared in the early national period when billiard halls and proto-casinos became separate from the sporting taverns that had predated them. Examples of this specialization multiplied in the 1840s and 1850s with the introduction of bowling alleys and even faro houses that offered just one kind of card game.[93]

Gaming halls also coalesced into clearer categories of architectural space regardless of the games they offered. At the high end of the scale stood ven-ues like the Café des Milles Collonnes on Broadway, a gaming hall featuring billiards, dice, and cards that was larger and boasted more elaborate classical architectural elements, as well as a richer décor, than its predecessors in the early national era. Named after a famous Parisian coffeehouse and operated by a series of foreigners including one-time opera company manager Ferdi-nand Palmo, New York's version was well known enough to appear as a set-ting in period novels. In the 1840s, an emergent genre of "sensational" literature espoused moral rectitude while titillating readers with portrayals of real sport-ing dens and references to their actual patrons and managers. More than one of these stories described the Café's "brilliant saloon," which radiated "daz-zling light, multiplied a thousand times by mirrors which formed the wall on each side," illuminating marble tables and "pictures in warm coloring of clas-sic nudity."[94] Inventories and fire insurance records describe other upscale bil-liard halls in like terms. The inventory for New Orleans billiard hall proprietor M. M. Miller cites mahogany furniture and three "French-plate looking glasses"

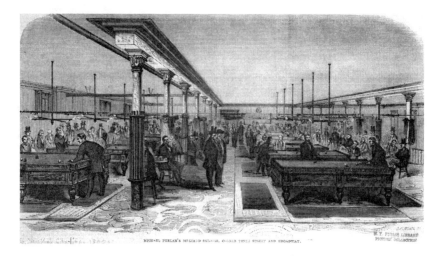

FIGURE 5.1. *Michael Phelan's Billiard Saloons, Corner Tenth Street and Broadway*, C.Edmons, *Frank Leslie's Illustrated Weekly*, January 1, 1859, courtesy Art and Picture Collection, The New York Public Library.

on each floor to reflect the blaze issued from gaslight fixtures. An 1846 fire insurance policy for a high-end "billiard saloon and reading room" in Philadelphia references a similar level of grandeur, though it only annotates architectural features, not the rich furnishings that probably accompanied them. The facility occupied the second floor of a five-story brick building just down the block from the Chestnut Street playhouse, filling a cavernous 2,800-square-foot room capable of holding up to ten tables. Visitors grasped a mahogany rail and climbed a flight of Carolina pine stairs to reach the room. Once there, they saw "plain pilasters with ornamental caps" between the room's twenty-seven windows. Six iron columns supported the eleven-foot ceiling, where a stucco cornice bridged the top and the wall. Altogether, the space looked much like Michael Phelan's posh hall at Tenth and Broadway, pictured above in figure 5.1, but with larger windows.[95]

Fine gaming venues compared favorably to upscale hotels and even the private clubhouses that multiplied in major cities during the antebellum period. For example, the American Hotel in Philadelphia occupied prime real estate directly across the street from the State House (Independence Hall), just one block east of the refined billiard hall. Its entrance vestibule had the same Carolina pine flooring and "plain pilasters" as the billiard hall one block away, and the formal hall into which the vestibule led contained a comparable stucco cornice. Other public rooms in the hotel went beyond the gaming room with an elaborate architrave frieze including molded cast iron ornaments as well as molded caps and bases for the pilasters. Billiard rooms in elite clubhouses also exceeded public billiard halls with paneling and classically inspired statuary, but similarly featured mahogany furniture and "pillars and pilasters . . . of the Corinthian order."[96]

Like hotels, clubs, and post-Revolutionary theatres, the antebellum era's most fashionable gaming houses evoked gentility by borrowing classical referents rooted in civic architecture. These material paeans to virtue laid a veneer of civility over whatever space they graced, fostering trust among players who were strangers by masking self-interest behind the manners they encouraged. But unlike the theatres and Southern sporting taverns of the preceding period, these gaming halls did not include both rough and genteel spaces. By building spaces entirely without features that promoted raw aggression and animosity, proprietors of classically inspired gaming halls created a decidedly decorous gaming experience calculated to attract patrons seeking polite play, much like lecture hall theatres (which were not as ornate but accomplished the same goal by eliminating the old galleries, favoring individual seating, and presenting moral content).[97] Of course, refined gaming venues were not entirely new. Robert Bailey ran several in the 1810s. But previous upscale gambling businesses were confined to small townhouses. They were limited in size and accessibility by their (often undercover) location in a residence. Changes to legislation in the antebellum years emboldened well-connected proprietors to open much larger, more visible, and more accessible venues full of more lavish classical referents.[98]

The aggrandizement of high-end venues helped distinguish them more clearly from others because little had changed at the other end of the spectrum. Dive taverns had hosted cheap games such as cards, dice, and ninepins since the colonial period. Billiard tables filtered down to these sites by the 1830s, but their presence did nothing to alter the environment. The billiard hall at Savin Hill, outside Boston, exemplified this type of venue. John Adams's grandson, Charles Francis Adams, complained that it "was a perfect oven, being built of thick wood without plastering, the sun came directly through and made it quite unpleasant." Adams's description equally applies to James McCehen's bowling alley on South Street near the Philadelphia waterfront. The fire insurance policy for McCehen's place notes bare lath with some plastered walls, none of which included moldings, baseboards, or cornices. Cheap yellow pine floors were another downgrade from the more expensive Carolina pine at finer venues. The suffocating heat inside these facilities pairs them alongside the newest low-end sporting venues, tucked into basements in cities all across the country. Such "cellars," including one three floors below the upscale billiard saloon in Philadelphia, often sold oysters with their games and were described as "infernal abodes, the heat of which was at least that of a hot-house." The heat, as much as the raw environment, prompted contemporaries to call them "gambling hells."[99]

Such "meanly furnished" establishments dispensed with veneers of propriety and promoted "right down gambling." Sensational guidebook author George G. Foster noted that "in the lower varieties" of billiard halls and bowling saloons, "it would be difficult to find anything else" besides players who "swear more, drink more, chew more tobacco, are more apt to quarrel, and not less intent upon winning." John O'Connor's gambling hall on the Bowery, "of the most ordinary description," witnessed all-out brawls. A Washington, DC, cellar known as The Epicure House welcomed urban dandies along with rougher sorts. Everyone "spit promiscuously round the room" while being "vulgar and uproarious" and cursing "in a stentorian voice." The "itinerant hells" on the Natchez waterfront were "obscene in their appointments," leaving a visitor only mildly relieved to find out that "murder is not nigh so common here as it was a few seasons back." Such incidents simply were not reported at classically ornamented gaming houses. A wider gap between the appearance of high-end and low-end gaming venues restored the differences between rough and genteel experiences that had been eroded by the accessibility of gentility in the early national period.[100]

To be sure, not every sporting venue fit neatly at one pole or the other. Minimally finished plain spaces filled the gap between the hells and the high end. Richard Nelms's Philadelphia billiard hall was one such site. Located two blocks uptown from where the State House, theatre, fine billiard saloon, and American Hotel all stood, it was half the size of its upscale cousin, with a ceiling three feet lower and "washboard" walls. Just six small windows lit the room, though they nodded to refinement with "Grecian mouldings" on the surrounds. The room was about equal to the one pictured in a broadside advertisement for Jeater's Subscription Room (see figure 5.2).

Subscription rooms were cheaper and more accessible versions of private clubs. Patrons paid a set membership fee to access the room. However, only the proprietor—not the members—had the power to accept or deny applicants. Fittingly, then, their appearance ranked below elite clubs and above the hells, perhaps a shade above Nelms's public facility. In accordance with this ranking, the ad illustrates a room with basic moldings and paneled doors accompanied by similarly refined yet sparse furnishings.[101]

Charles Francis Adams's diary records the impact of middling spaces on participants' behavior. He thought the billiard tables and environment at the high-end resort hotel in nearby Nahant were "remarkably fine," while those at the second-tier Franklin House in town were only "pretty good." Accordingly, Adams never notes indecorous behavior at Nahant, and does not present the

FIGURE 5.2.   *Billiards: J. Jeater's Subscription Room*, D. G. Childs, lithograph on paper (Philadelphia, ca. 1835), courtesy Historical Society of Pennsylvania. Childs copied this image from an advertisement for a London billiard room, printed in a well-known British playing manual. Significantly, he cut off almost a third of the image and removed several furnishings, so that this ad presents a more cramped and Spartan playing space, befitting a subscription room rather than a high-end commercial or club facility. For the original, see "John Thurston's Billiard Room, Catherine Street, London," the frontispiece to John Thurston's edited version of *Mingaud on Billiards* (London, 1835).

Franklin as an "uproarious" venue like the Epicure House or Savin Hill, though its mediocre rating did not prevent his friends from "abusing the table and everything else about it" after being beaten "considerably out of patience." As a middle-tier venue, the Franklin permitted verbal tantrums and even violence directed at the table, just not at people. A sensational critique of lawyers seconds this analysis by describing a law student who observed etiquette at his club but "though a gentleman, swore horribly at billiards" in a nondescript commercial hall.[102]

The paucity of data about gaming venues before 1830 makes it impossible to evaluate whether clearer categories of sporting space affected proprietors' stability. Still, the records after 1830 do make clear that proprietors from each tier stood among the gaming market's rare survivors. Those who accumulated wealth all operated luxury venues, but the rent and other costs of running those facilities could prompt failures just as at dives. The billiard hall in Philadelphia's high-end Arcade went through three managers in the 1840s, with one moving up to hotel management and two others disappearing from the historical record. Meanwhile, a long-running gambling house in Louisville occupied a cellar and "accommodated both black and white," hardly a trademark of fancier establishments nestled in the upper stories, where the only "colored gentleman will open the door." In addition, the sole documented billiard hall manager to span the entire period from 1845 to 1860 in the same facility ran a small middle-tier operation in New Orleans. The proprietor, J. Jalbert, never owned his hall and never was listed as a head of household in the census.[103]

Crucially, the differences between high and low commercial gambling establishments did not extend to their accessibility. Except for subscription rooms and clubs, none of these venues charged admission. Billiard halls charged fees only for playing, and they held steady at twenty-five cents per game throughout the period in cities across the country. With good players taking thirty minutes to play a game, and evenly matched players splitting costs, two hours' entertainment might cost fifty cents. The cost of playing cards or other table games was the price of the player's bet.[104] More luxurious venues made up their higher operating costs on pricier food and drink, but of course players did not have to select expensive refreshments. Unwritten standards for dress and appearance also applied at upscale places, though a wider range of men than ever before passed muster thanks to the explosion of ready-made clothing in the 1830s and 1840s. By the 1850s, accessibility to the full range of standardized types of gaming venues generated reams of complaints about "indiscriminate gaming" that mirrored developments at theatres and racetracks. Any given white male patron could choose to experience a wide variety of sporting milieus that were differentiated by specialized and standardized types of space, confirming the accessibility, anonymity, and uniformity that made sport into an early form of mass culture.[105]

This initial version of mass culture was not like the one that emerged in the twentieth century. Antebellum mass culture was based on active participants who took risks and challenged each other face to face, rather than the more passive experience created by mass media a century later. Just as importantly, as the reference above to racial lines at refined gambling houses suggests, limitations remained in place that permitted only white men to participate fully. Nevertheless, greater degrees of standardization and centralized control, as well as access and anonymity for white men of all classes in both genteel and rough sporting spaces, reduced the confusion and disorder that had surfaced during the early republic. In addition, the inclusivity and structure of the new mass sporting culture functioned much like its twentieth-century descendant's by selling a sense of democratic access and opportunity while limiting investors' risk and obscuring as well as cementing their power. In this sense, the shift toward mass culture was the final step in the century-long negotiation that made sport a cornerstone of both American democracy and inequality. But to see how the changes of the 1830s, 1840s, and 1850s helped broker this result, we must move from the business records that detail the strategies of investors and managers to exploring the sources that describe how participants experienced mass sporting culture.

CHAPTER 6

Sporting Cultures

In 1838, an ambitious group of teenage boys in Camden, New Jersey, tackled a burning question in their community: "Should Horse Racing be abolished?" The young men had organized a debating society to discuss the issues of the day, and Camden's racecourse was controversial. Local Quakers remained the most vocal opponents, petitioning the state legislature for a new ban on racing because, they claimed, the course was a magnet for "throngs of the dissolute and abandoned from the cities of other states, the most disgusting scenes of gambling, drunkenness, and other vices publicly enacted in utter disregard of all law." Legislators responded with typical superficial sympathy. "All parties admit you're right," they told the petitioners, "but we're watching each other now, and neither will do any thing out of which political capital may be made at the approaching campaign—it is not right; we regret it is so—party spirit is too high, but you must wait another year." Neither the state's Democrats nor their rivals in America's second party system, the Whigs, could afford to indulge a strident minority at the expense of racing supporters, who still outnumbered their opponents in the years immediately after the Panic of 1837. As in the past, moralizing petitioners got lip service. But now they no longer warranted new, if unenforced, legislation. The competitive opportunism of the mass sporting industry was too popular.[1]

The seeming paradox at the heart of this chapter is that despite sporting culture's popularity, the young debaters almost had to cancel their event because none of them wanted to publicly defend the racecourse. Apprenticed lawyer Isaac Mickle, who recorded the debaters' deliberations his diary, had railed against the venue in an entry just a few weeks earlier. "I cannot say much in favour of the moral character of Camden," he had written. The city's "lads from 12 to 20" spent so much time "swearing, cursing at each other, lying, insulting females," and "tippling and loafing at taverns" that "at 25 they are worn down by debauchery and disease." The only place Mickle specifically blamed for abetting this life cycle was "the Race Course situated near Camden," which he thought "aids greatly in their downward course."[2]

Mickle and his friends opposed the racecourse because it violated the rules of "respectability," the latest and most powerful reform attack on sport since the Revolution. Reformers first deployed the concept of respectability against sport as a disciplined alternative to the disorder created by the confusion of gentility and honor in the early national period. By the 1840s, a cohort of evangelical clergymen and secular advocates had built a new reform culture around the term, moored in self-control and domestic sociability. Reform culture peddlers of "respectability" scorned sporting vices such as gambling and drinking as part of a broader moral critique of risk-taking and competition. Instead of chasing large profits and recognition in confrontational and speculative public environments, they advocated steady work habits, incremental gains, and a social life of modest refinement centered in private homes. The message was not completely new, though its newest purveyors spread it in original ways, with everything from savings banks to restrained diets touted as paths to security and righteousness. A wide range of Americans worried about upheavals caused by immigration, westward expansion, a boom-and-bust economy, and universal white male suffrage all found comfort in respectability because it portended a social hierarchy based on morality, which seemed more accessible and yet also more orderly than the one based on striving for victory and wealth that was established by economic and sporting culture in the early national period.[3]

Reformers spread the tenets of respectability through the press. Cheaper printing technology and energized activists flooded the country with a wave of reform-minded periodicals, novels, and broadsides. The movement even seeped into the South, despite the fact that slavery preserved the need for all sorts of white men to display gentility and bravado. "Young man stop!" read the headline of an 1852 article in the *Southern Sentinel*. "You young man, on the way to the ball alley or billiard-room. . . . Are you not in a dangerous way?

Will those places or your habits lead you to respectability or usefulness in society?" The unpredictability enshrined at sporting sites clearly disconcerted the author. "Where is it leading?" he wondered.[4]

The order respectability promised made the term popular and ubiquitous—so much so that it was soon adopted by people and applied to settings the original reformers opposed. Isaac Mickle demonstrated the slipperiness of the concept when he ultimately agreed to defend the racecourse lest his society's debate be canceled for lack of opposition. Meetings of citizens protesting the racetrack were described as "large and respectable," Mickle noted, but "not one tenth of the voters of Gloucester [Camden's county] were there to raise their voices against the Course." Moreover, he concluded, "I doubt not that if a meeting of the friends of the turf were called, it would be as numerously and as 'respectably' attended." The closing retort shows how reformers had lost control of the term. Even turfmen and their supporters called themselves "respectable," and Mickle implied that, in other settings, they might have been deemed "respectable" by people outside sporting circles.[5]

Mickle himself knew how to move between reform respectability and other forms of status. Besides "jaunting and picnicking" on daytrips with friends "of the better sort," he spent time at the opera, theatres, billiard halls, and "a low rum hole & gambling shop" with "the dissipated junto," whom he further described as "a junto of young men more respectable for their birth than their lives—a bevy who move at once in the highest and lowest circles of society." Every New Year's Day, Mickle swore he would "humiliate myself no more by mingling" with these "rogues" and "rowdies." But a few weeks or months later, he would complain about the "dissipation to which I was forced," as he returned to patterns of behavior that violated rather than fulfilled his resolutions.[6]

He continued to pursue unrespectable avocations as he matured, even as he cited "the evils that flow from the race course" in his effort to prosecute the proprietors for erecting a cheap grandstand that collapsed in 1845. His efforts, along with the departure of profitable thoroughbred breeding to the West, led the state legislature to reinstitute its ban on racing later that year. Yet lawyering on behalf of reform respectability did nothing to change his worries that "one more year of idleness in Philadelphia would not only bankrupt me in pocket but in morals, too." He kept carousing after he was elected to the board of a temperance reform society, after his marriage in 1847, after he assumed the editorship of Camden's Democratic Party newspaper, and right up to his death in 1855 at age thirty-three from tuberculosis, partly brought on by his drinking.[7]

This chapter examines the experiences of men like Isaac Mickle. For while a handful of zealots in the cockpit of the reform movement may have held fast to its asceticism, hordes of less orthodox followers embraced the opportunity presented by mass sporting culture to assert "respectability" whenever it suited them—usually when they wanted to claim an advantage or deny it to others. So, in the end, the apparent paradox of a mass sporting culture emerging at the same time as a mainstream reform culture opposed to it is no paradox at all. Those who could participated in both, because both presented strategies for claiming privileged or empowered status in an era when a boom-and-bust economy threatened everyone with failure. The real tension sporting enthusiasts encountered came not from reform culture but from the continued negotiation of democracy and power at the heart of the new forms of mass sport. Indeed, Mickle's own attack on the racecourse had as much to do with the fact that "the whole concern" was "owned, located, and kept up by citizens of another and distinct state" as it did with any moral reservations. Their control over racing was what allowed greedy turfmen to aim "for the bankruptcy of men in character and purse," just as Mickle later joked that his pursuit of "Democracy" and "the equality of Man" through sport and politics had not given him tuberculosis but another "chronic disease—want of funds." The following pages detail how mass sporting culture, and the mass political culture it helped spawn, built on the egalitarian sporting experiences of the past while fostering and legitimating ever-greater inequalities of power and wealth.[8]

Cultural Mobility

The opportunities offered by mass sport were not new. Reputable men had long defied sanctimonious peers by visiting sporting spaces of both genteel and rough varieties. The antebellum years saw them continue to relish race-track concourses, raucous theatres, and gambling "hells" along with more refined grandstands, opera house parquettes, and fine billiard parlors where luxurious furnishings still generated descriptions of "gentility" that belied claims to the reformers' more restrained definition of "respectability."[9] The anonymity of mass sport only encouraged this range of activity, though any vocal reformer who participated "in the fond but delusive hope that he was unobserved" risked being outed by a new set of racy sporting publications eager to expose hypocrisy whenever they found a "certain ultra-moral friend of ours who never seems to have anything to do but rail at the theatres, seated in an obscure corner of the pit."[10]

If reputable men saw few changes to their opportunities in the 1830s, 1840s, and 1850s, those without much standing continued to gain greater access to refined arenas. Dozens of reform culture organizations invited workingmen to join and claim respectability, while sport's evolution into a form of mass entertainment opened up more genteel sporting spaces. At one extreme, lecture halls crafted a brand of theatregoing that was so devoid of risk and confrontation as to steer mainstream theatre toward reform respectability and away from sporting culture. Meanwhile, the new racecourse grandstands opened up a classic genteel sporting experience to the cross section of society identified by the three casualties in the Camden stand collapse: a bank clerk, a tailor, and a cartman. A reputable lady at a course outside New Orleans was consternated by the same hodgepodge when she found "two Irish cab-drivers" sitting near her. Similarly, sensational guidebooks told readers that access to any "first-rate gambling house" only required them to look the part and "proceed as if you know what you are about," an infinitely more possible ruse amid the ready-to-wear clothing revolution.[11]

The increased accessibility of genteel sporting venues combined with the renewed distinction of behavioral norms in different types of sporting spaces to produce more opportunities for all white men to claim both raw and refined manhood. The first increase in accessibility, in the early national period, had caused a breakdown of the differences between rough and genteel sporting experiences. In contrast, the antebellum period witnessed the construction of unprecedentedly specialized and standardized spaces that distinguished rough from refined sport while expanding access to even more white men.[12]

Conformity to the behavioral standards of both rough and refined establishments is a theme in a variety of records. For instance, recall Charles Francis Adams's diary entries noting verbal abuse at the middling Franklin House Hotel in comparison to polite play at the more upscale Nahant resort. Of course, Adams also visited the dive at Savin Hill, which attracted slumming poets who described themselves as "menne of hie or lowe degree, Whychever sort ye chuse," capable of being "fancy free . . . Bye [the] bramble boske" or "Ynn lady love" near the "greenwode tree." The poets referred to distinct experiences in different spaces through metaphorical references to nature, but Isaac Mickle's diary more literally confirms white men's ability to adjust their behavior to fit different sporting venues. Mickle described billiards on "fashionable excursions" to the resort town of Cape May without any of the tawdriness in his reports on nights spent with "a wild set of boys" at rougher billiard halls, which often left him pledging to "humiliate myself no more." Older men's diaries show the same divergence. Benjamin Brown French, a married congressional clerk in his mid-thirties, defended himself in his diary against criticism for playing billiards during working hours in an upscale

Washington saloon by—like Robert Bailey before him—citing the gentility if not respectability of the members of Congress he played with. At other times, in the same company, he attended gaming venues attached to cockpits and brothels. But after attending those sites, he offered no defense, and instead confessed to "feel[ing] ashamed of myself" for being "vulgar among gentlemen who ought not to be vulgar." Similarly, the "officer of the town of Brooklyn" caught "hovering over gallery chickens at the Park Theatre" presumably did not pursue women so baldly at refined venues, or else he would not have had the reputation of being "an honour to the town," a status his exposé suggested was now at risk.[13]

Published literature underscores white men's ability to conform to different behavioral standards by describing a broader range of participants than diary-keepers, who tended to be at least of middling rank. Newspapers compared racetrack concourses filled with "fighting and the usual number of bloody noses, black eyes, and cracked crowns" to grandstands where the various spectators experienced "delirium and excitement" but no violence and "the gaming going on there was much more orderly than that pursued elsewhere."[14] Reported fights were equally rare at "fashionable skinning-houses," where diverse patrons met dress requirements and tacitly agreed to demonstrate "polished manners with a social and genial disposition." In reputable theatre spaces, too, it was no longer just the company of women that kept an antagonist from physical confrontation. Either "fine clothes or the presence of Ladies" could "skreen him from the punishment his insolence deserves." Unlike during the confusion of the early national period, behavior now submitted to genteel appearance in refined sporting spaces.[15]

In unrefined sporting spaces, men might look genteel or not and still yell out to women passing by, "Damn fine piece! I should like bloody well to take her—." They could even take preliminary steps toward fulfilling that desire. A sporting paper once "noticed two Gentlemen (we call them so now) making themselves familiarly acquainted with the ankle and foot of one of Mrs. Franklin's Ladies" in the gallery of New York's Olympic Theatre. Ms. Franklin was a well-known brothel madam in the city, and traditional theatres remained sites where a variety of men met prostitutes. At The Epicure House, the "vulgar and uproarious" gaming and oyster cellar in Washington noted in the previous chapter, men "dressed in the latest New York Fashion" gathered alongside "young bucks dressed in the latest London fashions" and a "less original set of men, such as a person might see in any of the larger gin-shops of London." The groups did not mix, though everyone was "singing and swaggering" and spitting so that German visitor Francis Grund saw it as one congruent "little pandemonium." Grund saw no fighting on his visit to The

Epicure, though at sporting sites "of the most ordinary description" it was not unusual to witness "a square knock-down."[16]

The ability of a wide range of white men to move between distinct sets of sporting spaces, and conform to different behavioral expectations in each, suggests that the mass sporting industry had formalized a kind of "cultural mobility." In comparison to economic and social mobility, better-known concepts that involve long-term movement up or down in hierarchies of wealth and status, "cultural mobility" refers to frequent movement between different sets of values. We will explore the reasons why white men embraced cultural mobility in a moment, but we cannot explain its popularity without first recognizing how it worked. In a mass sporting culture comprised of distinct types of standardized and accessible spaces, each type of space promoted a certain kind of social experience that could be shared by white men from different social backgrounds.[17]

The evidence of cultural mobility revises long-standing arguments about the antebellum era as a period when cross-class "public culture," including sporting events, allegedly fractured into separate class cultures (such as a middle-class culture of "respectability"). But this argument has largely relied on reports from reformers and travelers who assumed that behavior indicated class.[18] The various descriptions of cross-class interaction and cultural mobility paint a picture of all sorts of white men acting similarly in a given space, rather than similar behavior signaling that only men from the same background were present. Past experience, reports of events, and the spread of etiquette manuals granted many sporting patrons enough cultural knowledge to "read" architecture and furnishings and adjust their behavior accordingly.[19]

The development of cultural mobility was fueled by both supply and demand. On the supply side, as we saw in the previous chapter, investors and managers strove to reduce competition by differentiating their venues. On the demand side, white men of all ranks had greater need than ever to claim the full range of masculine status because hardening class lines and economic instability combined to limit opportunities for real economic gains and jeopardized whatever position a man already had. The economic and political culture of the early republic had opened the door to cultural mobility by inviting men to disregard the distinction between genteel and rough sport, but the antebellum economy gave them a specific need for each type of experience and so led them to conform to the reconstructed distinction between them.

The situation was particularly pressing for poorer men. In the major northeastern cities, the wealthiest 5 percent of the population increased its share of the community's total assets from about 50 percent in the 1820s to almost 70 percent by 1850. In the South, the rising value of slaves produced a similar concentration of wealth. More importantly, the chances of rising from lower into higher economic strata were declining. Scholars of mobility in the South have noted that "opportunities were shrinking" there, while between one-half and two-thirds of the poorest workers in the urban North did not escape the position they were born into. Those who did move up did not make great gains, as America's biggest cities saw less than 2 percent of people leap from lower strata into the top 5 or 10 percent of wealth. Even middling New Yorkers and Bostonians had a less than one-in-ten chance of moving up into the top 5 percent, because roughly 80 to 90 percent of the wealthiest cohort stayed there through the period's booms and busts. In the rural North, where family farms predominated, economic mobility increasingly tended to be generational rather than achieved within a person's lifetime. Just as the early national elite had designed it, an economic culture inviting everyone to take a chance had produced a handful of singular examples of success but generally entrenched the few at the top with the assets and connections to survive a crash. Class lines were becoming firmer.[20]

Amid such an erosion of opportunity, genteel sporting events became rare venues where aspiring working-class men and newly minted clerks could stake their claims to respectability and gentility. For sure, refined sport still imposed a financial burden on those near the bottom of antebellum society. A dollar for transportation, food, and admission might equal a day's pay for an unskilled laborer, but it was manageable for almost any employed man above that bottom tier of workers. In fact, poorer men and women may well have skimped elsewhere in order to attend, given the well-documented "leisure preference" among workers who combatted occupational relegation by prioritizing the opportunity to assert themselves at leisure activities. Several commentators noted that "however poor may be the condition of an American family, or however inadequate the reward its members receive for their labor, they manage to be regular visitants two or three times every week to some place of public amusement." With opportunities for real social and economic mobility contracting, the cultural mobility afforded by relatively affordable mass genteel sport provided a key avenue for workingmen and their families to assert their standing and equality.[21]

Reports of encounters at genteel venues involving men of less reputable standing leave little doubt that asserting status remained a core motive for their visits. As in the early national period, suspected posers typically responded to accusations of interloping by returning the favor and attacking their accuser, "one of the Gentlemen, with the epithet of 'no Gentleman.'" Elite devotees of genteel sport continued to complain about such confrontations, which now occurred in upscale gaming houses as often as in theatres. They blamed these episodes on the low cost of admission and appropriate clothes, which allowed "any wretch, however base . . . if attired in the order of a gentleman," to "go forth with a malicious and poisonous tale and stain the character of his fellow man."[22]

If poorer men saw genteel sport as a vehicle for claiming refined status despite crystallizing class lines, richer men visited rough sporting spaces to disprove concerns about their enervated manhood. Young scions had attended these venues for just such a purpose since the colonial period, because they had few other ways to display their manly willingness to compete and take risks. Older politicians had visited to rally supporters. Yet a growing anxiety about effeminacy among middling and wealthy men in the antebellum period drove more members of these groups to join the fray at rougher sporting spaces than ever before. In the South, the martial patriarchy based on slavery still spurred white men of all ranks to exhibit their boldness and economic power by gambling together on concourses and at a range of blood sports that were staged much more openly than in the North, where reform culture was stronger.[23] Meanwhile, some reformers actually pushed respectable Northerners toward rough sport by ridiculing businessmen and other white-collar workers for the "slender" bodies created by their sedentary labor and overly refined leisure practices. Their targets responded by taking sparring lessons, attending gymnasiums, and, by the 1840s, playing baseball, activities by which their "narrow and contracted chests are soon turned into broad and expansive ones." But gyms were restricted to members and ballfields filtered individual striving into a team sport. Otherwise respectable men also sought to prove themselves in one-on-one competitions against working-class opponents whose strenuous labor gave them a reputation for physical prowess. So, just as refined sporting spaces granted poorer men the chance to prove their gentility in front of their supposed betters, rubbing shoulders with or competing against disreputable men in theatres, hells, and concourses granted gentlemen the opportunity to prove that their refinement had not sapped their manly strength. The lure was strong enough to pull one of Philadelphia's wealthiest men, Sidney George Fisher, to see the "violent" Edwin Forrest and the "intoxicating" dancer Fanny Ellsler at traditional theatres, and explains why he thought the concourse "the best place" at a racetrack: Because despite the "very few gentlemen there, but rowdies, loafers & blacklegs in abundance," men "are more independent in your movements" there than in the genteel grandstand. The *Turf Register* recommended more direct confrontation, instructing wealthy men to play billiards in public against all comers if they wanted to beat their peers at private clubs. "Few members will arrive at any degree of proficiency," the author wrote, "without, at times, playing on public tables and consequently mixing with characters the most question-able." Establishing true physical superiority still required mingling with the masses.[24]

The price of admission to a sporting space was the ante in a social gamble for masculine status. But, true to the nature of sport, the game was risky. Success depended on a convincing performance, and plenty of aspirants failed to meet expectations. The upwardly mobile "thought it a gross mistake not to have been taken for gentlemen" in refined sporting venues, where some of them (and their wives) were called out for being "over-dressed and genuine shop-keeper looking." Reputable men's failures to impress in rougher settings tended to go unreported, though at least one racy sporting paper provided a fictional stereotypical example. In the story, two young merchants head to the Bowery Theatre and buy tickets for the pit, only to be "lugged from the place" by butchers who thought the duo had stolen their seats. Proven to be the physically weaker men, one of them lamented, "I wish I could fight," as he and his companion slinked up to the "third tier saloon" in the gallery to reclaim their masculinity by commanding the affections of gallery prostitutes. If the propriety of refined sporting spaces favored those with the time and money to cultivate proper appearances and manners, the aggression in physical sporting spaces tilted the balance against white-collar workers. Clearly, then, the mixed company at sporting events did not erase class distinctions. Rather, sporting events invited all kinds of white men to challenge the stereotypes and alleged inferiorities attributed to their class, and to lay claim to the legitimizing power of both refinement and raw manly might.[25]

The motives for pursuing this kind of opportunity only grew stronger in the wake of the Panic of 1837. The losses and unemployment that followed the crash threatened men's traditional patriarchal roles as providers at home. White-collar and blue-collar workers, as well as farmers, reacted to this threat by lobbying for more generous pay and bankruptcy laws, but also by fueling the development of mass sporting events where they could defend and reassert their jeopardized manhood.[26]

Asserting their manhood did not always require men to compete against each other directly. They could also prove themselves against the deception, or "humbug," which lay behind many public commercial sporting presentations. Catching a jockey who won by whipping his rival instead of his horse, identifying how characters were fooled in plays, or how a gambler cheated, all evinced an astuteness that displayed a man's powers of perception—a crucial skill set in an economy still grounded in confidence and credit. As in competition, success or failure in unveiling a ruse did not always matter more than whether a man engaged in the effort to discover it. Isaac Mickle described

this "operational aesthetic" when he walked away from one suspect performance thinking, "sure, the pleasure is as great of being cheated as to cheat."[27]

As in the early republic, race and gender lines restricted the full enjoyment
of sporting culture's opportunities to white men. These boundaries encouraged white men's participation by making their engagement alone a mark of
their superiority, regardless of whether their sporting efforts were successful.
Nevertheless, the transition to mass sporting entertainment did open up some
new opportunities for white women and African American men. For instance,
the eradication of prostitution from lecture hall theatres, originally carried out
by preventing women from entering the theatre alone, eventually led to matinee shows that targeted an audience of unescorted reputable ladies. This gain
was a small one, circumscribed by the class lines that had inhibited women's
cultural mobility for decades. After all, only women with no job could attend
daytime performances on weekdays. So the reintroduction of distinct genteel
and rough sporting settings granted middling and wealthier women a bit more
freedom in refined venues, but did little to alter the class-based distinctions that
continued to make women accessories to men's claims of masculinity in any
given sporting space.[28]

Mass sport afforded black men new opportunities white women did not see,
providing further evidence of masculinity's centrality to sporting culture. "The
gambling-houses of various ranks and grades" in New York included, according to one sensational New York guidebook, both the working-class white
venue of "the low three-cent drinking and raffling den in the Bowery, and the
negro dance house, brothel, and groggery combined in the Five Points." But
the guide went on to describe how similarly "in these places, the various classes
of persons" gambled together, from "merchants, financiers, brokers, speculators, bank-clerks, &c., down to poor desperadoes who live on almost nothing." The author concluded by noting that "it is difficult to draw the line of
distinction very closely between rogues and honest men" in places where race
and class were not forgotten but rough sport pulled everyone into unrespectable behavior together. Charlestonians were shocked that their own racetrack's
concourse promoted a similar assumption of fraternity among the "most aw-
ful phalanx of every shade of colour who are your attendants at the table or
the bar." Although the relationship followed the acceptable form of blacks
serving whites, "the freedom taken, the coarse joke, are what we complain
of," the writer noted. The concourse was so rife with challenge that the African American wait staff refused to follow social conventions demanding less
familiar interaction with whites.[29]

While white women's gains were limited to refined spaces, blacks' gains
were restricted to rough ones. When theatre managers in Charleston and

Washington expanded their potential audience by successfully lobbying to overturn their cities' bans on "the admission of negroes or persons of colour, whether bond or free," they copied northern theatres by installing dividers in their galleries and restricting black patrons to segregated areas. Still, access to the event was granted. The same might be said of the rise of minstrelsy in the period, which welcomed more African American men onstage but confined them to roles that mocked them. Black men did not attempt to circumvent this treatment with black-run theatres, as they briefly did in the early national period. The public backlash had been too strong, and some cities now pro-hibited it. However, black entrepreneurs in New York responded to being segregated out of genteel gaming halls by opening their own "black Broad-way" on Church Street, a line of establishments with "Billiard tables, Pianos, [and] Sporting-Rings" furnished with "Rosewood and marble tables, spring sofas, and wilton covers" that inspired "easy negligence, careless abandon, and refined freedom." While the whites who patronized these venues did not consider them genteel, they were not mentioned as dives in the guidebooks either. Racial animus alone downgraded these facilities at least one notch. Genteel sport remained for whites only.[30]

Protected by racial and gender lines that preserved the fullest experience of cultural mobility for white men, their engagement in mass sporting spaces continued to diffuse class tensions among their own ranks into individual contests for masculine status. While this function was not new, its persistence amid shrinking chances for socioeconomic mobility helped temper rising class animosity. Unsurprisingly, then, clashes between class blocs at sporting ven-ues remained rare and brief. The most famous one, at New York's Astor Place Opera House in 1849, will be explored at the end of this chapter. As we will see, even in that example, the conflict did not trace class lines as closely as it may seem. Despite economic conditions that fomented separate class identi-ties, many different groups of white men appreciated cultural mobility in sporting contexts because it helped them defend and assert their individual membership in a democracy of white men that increasingly felt less demo-cratic and less manly.

"I Was de 'Boss'"

Only white men could earn the full rewards of sporting manhood, but the value of claiming as much of it as possible did not escape black men. Slave horsemen, who competed against and worked with white jockeys and grooms, had more opportunities than most African Americans to translate manly sporting success into real social gains. Charles Stewart certainly tried to take advantage of them. Stewart was a groom and jockey trained by Arthur Taylor, the white man who headed William Ransom Johnson's stables. Later, he belonged to Louisiana planter, judge, and breeder Alexander Porter. In 1884, Porter's daughter published an interview with Stewart in *Harper's New Monthly Magazine*, providing one of the most detailed surviving descriptions of a slave horseman's career.

The article must be considered carefully, since Annie Porter's editing reflects her interests as a white woman in the post-Reconstruction South. She put Stewart's words in a dialect calculated to make him sound uneducated, and she affirmed white rule by emphasizing his fidelity to his master's family. "During the war, he never left his mistress for a single day," Porter reported in her introduction, "and since its close he has been the constant never-failing factotum, adherent, and, as he calls it, ''pendence' of the whole family." Stewart, too, probably shaped his story to fit what his white interviewer wanted to hear. If he had any problems with his masters, he did not share them with Porter. Given the author's agenda and Stewart's self-consciousness, his prideful comments about the masculine autonomy he achieved through sporting success stand out. Period fears of black male prowess gave his editor little reason to aggrandize his account in this regard. On the other hand, Stewart had plenty of reason to exaggerate, since doing so underscored his grasp of how sporting success generated and justified masculine power, and helped him lay his claim to that power as best he could.[31]

Stewart began by recounting his family life before Johnson bought him. Claiming a freeborn, multiracial, seafaring father and an enslaved mother, he said that spending most of his time with his father's family made him an independent and cocky "rascal" despite a "lean" frame and technically belonging to his mother's owner. The skinny boy's confidence only grew when Johnson bought him at age twelve and had him trained as a rider and groom. Soon traveling with his famous master's horses from New York to North Carolina, Stewart regularly received a "new suit o' store clo's, wid ten dollars in my pocket an' more to come." Several years later, a portrait of one of Johnson's horses at stud in Pennsylvania showed Stewart wearing a collared shirt, neat waistcoat, and trousers (see figure 6.1). Recalling his resplendence, he told Porter, "I was 'high come up,' I tell you."[32]

Stewart's travels and clothes reflected his skill. He was good enough to ride an undercard event before a major North-South match race on Long Island in 1823. He later moved into training and managed one of Napoleon's many stables. "I went to de stable outside o' New Market," the Petersburg racecourse, he told Porter, "an' dar I was de 'boss' ober nine little niggers an' four

FIGURE 6.1.   *Medley and Groom*, Edward Troye (1832), oil on canvas, courtesy Catherine Clay. Photograph by Mary Rezny (2014).

big ones, 'sides two white trash dey called 'helpers.'" Throughout the interview, every time Stewart mentioned a new appointment, he pointed out that "I had my helpers an' jockeys, grooms, an' stablemen under me, nobody was ober me." His presentation of his standing stretches credulity at times, such as when he described conversations with planters and turfmen who called him "Colonel Stewart" because "I had done tuk my marster's title" and the slaveowners allegedly accepted his appropriation.[33]

Presenting himself like any respected and empowered man, Stewart next described his control over his own household. Porter quoted him saying he "neber had no notion o' wastin victuals on a woman I didn't love, or pomperin' up one wid love an' victuals bofe what didn't belong to me, hide an' hyar." So, once he became a stable manager, he looked "all roun' Chesterfield County all ready to pick up de fust dat 'peared like she would suit." Stewart described himself literally shopping for a wife, and he concluded the search by negotiating with a local planter to pay $350 for the woman he wanted. He cites no intermediary like the one Cornelious Johnston needed two decades earlier. Within a few years, however, Stewart fell out with his wife. Believing she lied to him regularly, and failing to "cure her" through "suasion an' finery, birch rods split fine, an' a light hickory stick," he ultimately claimed the mantle of master and purported the unthinkable—he said he sold the woman and his three sons by her back into slavery.[34]

Shortly thereafter, Johnson sent Stewart to Kentucky to manage his operations there. Under the nominal oversight of a local owner who was Johnson's business partner, Stewart's profitable work "had a heap of people after me," but his distant master would not sell. Meanwhile, Stewart married again. He was deeply enamored of his second wife, and was so distraught by her death two years later that he wanted to leave Kentucky. Although Johnson had refused all direct offers from white men, Stewart said "he writ back dat 'ef I could find *a owner to suit me, dat would pay his price fur me,* I could go." It is impossible to know if the italics, which appeared in the article, represented Stewart's emphasis, Porter's surprise, or both. The timing of Stewart's sale, about 1840, aligns with Johnson's financial trouble after the panic, and there is no firm proof to dispel Stewart's assertion. In his narrative, success brought control over "little niggers," "white trash," and black women, and culminated in a degree of self-determination by executing his own sale to Porter's father. Stewart then moved to the Porter estate, where "I had a mighty good large house at the top of de stable yard, an' my bell rung en de oberseer's house." Even the white overseer was beholden to a champion like Stewart.[35]

Whatever Annie Porter's control over the final product, Charles Stewart clearly wanted to describe how he translated his sporting success into manly power. In this regard, Stewart fits neatly alongside other men, black and white, who saw victorious and profitable sporting engagements as preludes to claiming masculine economic and social authority. Yet Stewart's goal differed from that of his predecessor, Cornelious Johnston, because Stewart hewed closer to a particularly white version of sporting culture masculinity. In describing his control over lesser workers of both races, and his sale of his first wife as well as himself, Stewart suggests that he used sport to become as much a master as he could within the existing system. Perhaps he only presented himself this way to Porter. Or maybe it was the only path open to him as mass sport made him too famous to get away for short periods as Johnston did, and steadily tightening regulations made manumission (for oneself or a spouse) less and less likely. In any case, comparing Stewart with Johnston demonstrates not only how mass sporting culture further enhanced black horsemen's opportunities, but how it invited them to pursue masculinity on white men's terms despite the fact that owners continued to permit slave horsemen an unusual degree of authority and autonomy precisely because their status as bondsmen limited their threat to the racial order. In fact, after the Civil War, twenty years of success as free men only resulted in black jockeys being barred from racing and relegated to menial roles as stable boys for the better part of the next century.[36]

The careers of female professionals in antebellum America further emphasize how the masculine framework of mass sporting culture created opportunities for men—even enslaved ones, to some extent—without changing much for white women. Certainly, white women still acquired wealth and celebrity as actresses and as proprietors of gaming houses, saloons, and brothels. However, while pros of both sexes sacrificed reform culture respectability for these prospects, women had far more trouble translating them into autonomy or influence beyond their sporting arena. Stewart claimed ownership of his wife. White racetrack, saloon, and even gaming house proprietors won elected offices in local militias. Top white performers such as actor Edwin Forrest, jockey Samuel Purdy, and boxer John Morrissey all received nominations for political office from major political parties. In contrast, restrictions on women's participation in formal politics and taboos on the public nature of their work left female pros with fewer paths for exercising the influence their careers might have afforded them.[37]

As a result, actresses, who were the most famous female pros, often chose to marry wealthy gentlemen and leave the profession. Well-known actor Joseph Jefferson's daughter Elizabeth married Baltimore merchant Augustus Richardson and promptly retired. Her return to the stage after his death signifies the pressure she faced to become a suitably respectable wife by leaving her profession. Indeed, when one actress refused to leave the profession after marrying respectably, she "resumed her own name of Pritchard in the playbills," withholding her married name "by the desire of his family." Actors, striving to prove their own reputations, reacted to these social rules by trying to retire their wives from performance. The unpredictable fortunes of the stage did not always make it possible, though actor Sol Smith was at pains to defend his head-of-household status by noting that only "in this emergency, my wife consented to go on the stage." While men enjoyed alternative forms of respectability, the lack of opportunities for female pros to craft reputation and influence led many of them to trade their profitable careers for conventionally respectable marriages.[38]

On closer inspection, even actresses who seem like exceptions to the rule conformed to notions of femininity that devalued them for working in the hypermasculine sporting industry. The most frequently cited anomalies are Fanny Kemble, Jenny Lind, and Charlotte Cushman. Yet Kemble only returned to the stage after her marriage to planter Pierce Butler failed, and then she performed "readings" rather than costumed performances in a cast with sets.

Lind similarly sang rather than acted, and presented herself as a simple domestic woman with a natural gift instead of a professional performer seeking
to maximize her income. Cushman countered her "unfeminine" appearance
and, often, manner of performance with a careful cultivation of purity and
"regal" womanliness in her public life offstage. These women's uncommon
wealth and good reputations did not free them from the expectations of reform respectability, which male pros also had trouble meeting but which did
not inhibit them from becoming empowered heads of households with public influence thanks to the popularity of mass sport.[39]

The Constriction of Honor

The opportunities presented by the mass sporting industry to an array of white
male pros and patrons were countered in part by an increasingly entrenched
elite's containment of honor. In the past, honor had referenced a white man's
individual masculine status based on respect earned through competitive
engagement with a broad range of fellow white men. Differences in wealth
or class inflected but did not determine one man's honor in the eyes of another. Moreover, gentlemen had cared about their inferiors' opinions, and
fought over them at card tables, in billiard rooms, and on racetrack concourses.
But in the 1830s and 1840s, firmer class lines and the anonymity of mass sport
began to excuse elite men from considering honor outside their own circle.
The change registered most tellingly in their ignorance of the old gamblers'
code that had led their predecessors to mortgage homes in order to pay losses
owed to lesser men. As elites' wealth and power expanded, movement in and
out of their circles became more difficult, and they were less likely to personally know their opponents, elite men limited the salience of honor. Doing so
allowed them to engage in the manly cross-class competition at the heart of
sporting culture while denying outsiders the social and financial gains of
sporting victory. In effect, sporting experiences remained accessible and full
of risk-taking and confrontation, but elite men minimized the consequences
of defeat for themselves.

Rich and powerful men justified their circumscription of honor through
arguments that merged reform culture with the economic culture of capitalism. Although early peddlers of respectability conceived of it as a moral code
at odds with the reigning economic culture's demand for risk-taking and profit,
a range of businessmen, intellectuals, and religious leaders soon wove risk and
profit into the concept by claiming that wealth reflected superior character.
Tension remained over "speculators" who got rich quick, but by the 1840s, re-

form literature aired little debate about the morality of men who presided over lasting fortunes, or whether reform respectability implied a certain amount of wealth (enough for a man to keep his wife and daughters out of labor markets, for instance). Preaching that "what is gained by hard digging is usually retained and what is gained easily usually goes quickly," synthesizers of respectability and capitalism attributed stable wealth to work ethic and intelligence rather than inheritance from successful risk-taking forebears and the ongoing centralization of capital in the antebellum period. Such logic built on early national investors' efforts to encourage respect for those who grew their wealth, but dropped the earlier concern about simultaneously needing to grow their local economies. As investors withdrew from public roles in sport management (and, as we will soon see, politics), and reformers focused on individual self-discipline as the road to order and success, the emphasis on individual striving diminished the directive to judge elites by their ability to create a rising economic tide that lifted all boats. Instead, the purveyors of the new argument blamed the poor for their plight. If they had worked more diligently and rationally instead of trying to get rich quick by gambling or speculating, the logic went, they surely would have succeeded in a country where an economic culture of "go-aheadism" made Americans "all to a greater, or less extent, men of business" and geographic expansion meant that men need only "ask of Commerce what she needs" and they would profitably discover that "her path lies among our own people."[40]

So, increasingly, reform voices folded respectability into the economic culture of striving. Indeed, even more ascetic versions of respectability recommended a lifestyle that required a certain degree of wealth, which only further pushed nonelite men to take risks in order to try to reach or remain at that level. In addition, because some men who were not aggressive failed during credit contractions and some speculators gained, the reality of who accumulated or lost money often defied the moralists' lectures. As a result, those lectures ended up legitimating rather than accurately explaining wealth. As one period commentator observed, "When speculation proves successful, however wild it may have appeared in the beginning, it is looked upon as an excellent thing, and is commended as enterprise; it is only when unsuccessful that it furnishes occasion for ridicule and complaint." Of course, successful speculation only became legitimate wealth if it lasted. In a country rocked by three major panics between 1819 and 1857, it was not uncommon for men who seemed ascendant one day to later fall back to their place. Even intellectuals such as Ralph Waldo Emerson refused to grant chance or inheritance a role in these outcomes, arguing instead that "nobody fails who ought not to fail. There is always a reason in the man for his good or bad fortune, and so in making money." The grafting of reform culture self-discipline onto the economic culture of capitalism thus lauded the wealthiest Americans for a morality rooted in their wealth.[41]

Their claim to superior morality was what excused established rich men from the protocol of honor when interacting with those they did not recognize as peers. After all, honor was rooted in honesty. If an opponent's poverty or greater financial insecurity rendered him less moral, the moral man was not bound to trust him and so was not bound to follow the rules of honor when interacting with him. The convenience of this logic becomes clear amid the evidence that honor remained valid among men of the same class, and that erstwhile respectable men did not stop mingling with those they thought were dishonorable. But because respectable men now grounded their moral authority in their wealth and not in their popular reputation, they did not need the badge of honor bestowed by perceived inferiors, and so they could disregard the precepts of honor when dealing with those men.[42]

Gambler John O'Connor experienced this new sporting "snobocracy" at first hand. In his memoirs, he recalled how his gaming house in Richmond in the 1840s catered largely to planters and slave traders, with the former playing against but avoiding "social contact" with the latter. O'Connor himself claimed he "would have felt myself lowered even if seen in conversation with" a slave trader, though he also acknowledged that "with all their bad qualities, I never knew a negro-trader to sue for money lost at gambling." By implication, his other clients, the planters, were prone to "plead the act" to recover lost bets—something they had been unwilling to do a generation earlier. The Turf Register also alluded to the rise of reneging, with more reports of punishing nonpayers and celebrating lawyers who refused to take their cases and recover their losses.[43]

Elite gentlemen not only bilked gaming house operators whose businesses were nominally illegal; they treated turfmen similarly, even though most turfmen operated legitimately and possessed family connections as well as wealth that were more like elites' than O'Connor's. Yet the turfmen's social and economic capital were not as secure as that of former leading owners and other jockey club members, who also bristled at how turfmen managed tracks, clubs, and horses. As a result, club members increasingly excluded turfmen from considerations of honor as if they were like any other gambler.

Cadwallader Colden experienced a classic example of this treatment in his dealings with New York City's jockey club. Having lost his patrimony, Colden's respected last name was his only asset when he gained admission to a club filled with large landholders and prominent lawyers, doctors, and merchants.

He failed to recognize how he differed, so he misread the club's subsequent vote to accept his management of its Long Island racecourse as a sign of social acceptance and leadership. He began to see that it was not when club officers repeatedly denied his authority to raise subscription fees and collect money from them. The club then added injury to insult by taking advantage of Colden's willingness to accept a verbal agreement instead of a written contract outlining how the existing subscription funds would be used. Club officers ignored their pledge to support Colden's plan for infrastructure improvements and larger purses, and instead spent the money paying off the club's back debts. With his name on the contracts for the expenses he had prioritized, Colden was stuck with an $11,700 bill. "Prudence would ask what security I had for laying out so much money," Colden admitted in a pamphlet intended to guilt the club into paying. "My reply is the plighted faith of the Jockey Club, an institution grounded upon the laws of Honor," he wrote. Colden thought the rules of racing and wagering that bound other jockey club members together also applied to their dealings with him. But the other club members thought of him as a hired hand under their direction, not as an equal with whom honor was at stake. When a "thunderstruck and indignant" Colden realized his position, he remonstrated in the press and in personal letters to club officers, asserting that they had "rested upon my word and my honour; I upon theirs; mine has been redeemed, theirs has been forfeited."[44]

Colden's assault did little to injure the club's members or earn him restitution. Club officials demonstrated their superiority by withholding funds, knowing the manager could "be ruined in a pecuniary sense" and did not wield enough social clout to force payment or cost them honor. Such treatment became common for Colden, who later lost the management of a racecourse in northern New Jersey after spearheading its construction, and then started a new racing periodical only to see it fail after three years due to unpaid subscriptions.[45]

Southern turfmen occupied an equally precarious position, which allowed Robert Wormeley Carter to flatly deny Richmond racetrack proprietor John Sawbridge Corbin his one-hundred-dollar portion of a sweepstakes victory in 1840. Carter had tried to get the date of the race moved, learned his petition had failed just four days before the event, then claimed he could not transport his racer the sixty miles to the race in time. Corbin rejected this excuse. Standard jockey club procedures only excused payment if the horse died before the race. When Corbin formally requested the money, Carter asked his neighbor, friend, and more experienced owner William Henry Tayloe how he should respond. Tayloe told him not to pay. He said Corbin only wanted the money to pay a debt owed to him, which Tayloe claimed he would not accept if the money came from his friend Carter. Tayloe's response revealed the social division between turfmen and leading owners as well as the economic weakness of the turfmen's position. Tayloe's standing as Corbin's creditor and Carter's friend supported the latter's refusal to pay.[46]

Corbin did not accept the refusal. Over the next two years, he badgered Carter with statements from other turfmen and breeders affirming the debt's validity under the gamblers' code of honor. The reputation of some of the letter writers drove Carter to agree to have the matter arbitrated by a neutral "sporting court." The two men then squabbled over who should sit in judgment. Corbin proposed turfmen. Carter demurred, citing their "fuzziness of mind." Insulted, Corbin argued that "their competency to judge of matters connected with their very livelihood" made them expert authorities and not "fuzzy" at all. For his part, he opposed any candidate with only "a sort of spectator knowledge of Turf Matters instead of that practical information derived from actual participation in the pursuits of 'the Sport.'" This exchange unveils the crux of the antipathy between turfmen and planters. Carter thought Corbin a base racketeer out to squeeze every planter for every penny he could. Corbin thought Carter an amateur ill versed in the rules of the game, trying to use his status to avoid payment.[47]

Ultimately, the sporting court ruled in Corbin's favor. But in yet another statement of the turfmen's weakness in the post-panic years, Carter simply ignored the decision. As a final gesture of contempt, Corbin threatened to "reduce the matter 'desuite' to a personal affair & expose in every public Place & Print within a hundred miles of his Residence his shameless indifference to the obligations of Honor." Colden had tried this tactic, too, and Corbin's proclamations similarly fell on deaf ears. Gentlemen had long been able to refuse inferiors who challenged them to a duel (as Corbin did by referencing a "personal affair"), but they now evaded a wider range of men on a wider range of questions about their honor.[48]

The constriction of honor did not prevent supposed inferiors from challenging gentlemen verbally or to sporting contests, nor did it reduce gentlemen's willingness to engage. Indeed, not having to compete for honor may actually have encouraged wider participation among respectable men. They could now assert their manhood without worrying about economic costs or the opinions of men outside their peer circles.

Yet honor still mattered within those circles. In the South, where reform culture was weaker, the planters' *Southern Quarterly Review* reiterated in 1853 the same dictum as the guide to Saratoga in 1828: "A gambling debt is a debt of honour, but a debt due a tradesman is not." The difference now was that a gaming debt due to a tradesman was no longer a debt of honor. In the North, respectability helped minimize honor's importance across class lines and pushed reputable men to shroud rather than celebrate their sporting participation. Underground sporting publications emerged to expose hypocritical participants. These periodicals and guidebooks appealed to a broad range of men, and by continuing to frame sporting endeavors in terms of honor—even though reputable patrons did not use the term when they chastised themselves in their diaries for participating—they suggest the resilience of masculine honor as a motive behind reputable sporting men's engagement.[49]

For men on the edges of respectability or even clearly below its threshold, honor's reduced valence did not push them to conceal their sporting inclinations as much as it exposed the limits of sporting culture's egalitarian promise. For them, the constriction of honor was another brick in the hardening wall of class distinction that reduced their chances for real economic and social gain. Still, they clung to the term, desperately deploying it to assert status when economic gain was elusive. After Isaac Mickle lost his newspaper editorship and ran out of money, he reassured himself and his wife by ignoring the mass of reform literature declaring their poverty to be the result of his shortcomings, and instead told his wife that "honest poverty is awfully uncomfortable but, thank God! No dishonor." The only non-elite sporting men who could afford to part with the concept were the few who were rich and still excluded. When star actor Edwin Forrest abandoned his nomination for political office, a theatre manager "asked him why the honor conferred on his profession by his election was not sufficient inducement" to continue. Forrest replied bluntly, "I want no further honor, and can't afford to give my time for eight dollars a day when I can make two hundred out of it."[50]

Forrest gave up on trying to acquire honor in elite circles, but the concept remained important to him. He made his living portraying rough masculine heroes who justified violence in terms of honor, and he once defended his own claims to it by physically beating a man he thought had seduced his wife. As was true of elites and respectable men, those outside their ranks continued to judge each other in terms of honor even if they did not always use the word. The sporting paper *Ely's Hawk and Buzzard* demonstrated this fact when it told the tale of Snuff, a man who "was rather lame / His mind to win was fully bent / Though in his pockets not a cent." He

Lost many a game, car'd not a pin
Till he was called to pay the chalk

Or consign his body to the *Hawk*
Snuff got mad—and in a fury
Soon summon'd up a gambler's jury
They decided against poor old Snuff
Who was handled rather rough.

No reader of this poem would have missed its support for the gambler's code of honor and the physical punishment of the welsher, despite the actual term's absence.[51]

Honor's persistence among men, if limited in cross-class settings, nevertheless protected its value as a framework for discussing politics. Formal statements as varied as Andrew Jackson's proclamation against nullification and Daniel Webster's defense of his treaty settling the northern boundary with Canada appealed to the white male polity by claiming to preserve "national honor." As the sectional crisis deepened in the 1850s, each side declared that the other had perverted the term. Just such a statement from Massachusetts senator Charles Sumner, accusing a South Carolina colleague of misplacing "sentiments of honor and courage" in his proslavery arguments, earned Sumner a caning in defense of southern honor on the floor of the Senate chamber in 1856. Honor was still not to be trifled by legitimate rivals, though it could now be disregarded more often by superiors when they interacted with men they considered beneath them.[52]

"Sport for Grown Children"

Another reason honor remained relevant in political rhetoric was that the ties between political and sporting culture only grew stronger in the antebellum period. Just as elites invested in mass sport and then contained its democratic dangers by adjusting the concept of honor, they also financed a new form of "mass politics" that borrowed from sporting culture's egalitarian experiences while copying its inegalitarian structure.

Politicians had long used sport to rally voters, but mass politics went further by applying the democratic feel of sporting events to make the whole system of electoral politics seem more democratic than it was. The era's newest electoral discourse reflected this expanded approach to the integration of sporting and political culture by popularizing elections as "races" featuring candidates who "ran" for office. An examination of this sporting metaphor provides some insight into how sport helped build a sense of democracy that ultimately supported elite power.

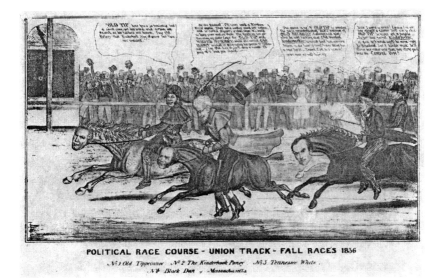

POLITICAL RACE COURSE - UNION TRACK - FALL RACES 1836

N⁰ 1 Old Tippecanoe   N⁰ 2 The Kinderhook Pony   N⁰ 3 Tennessee White .
N⁰ 4 Black Dan .   Massachusetts

FIGURE 6.2. *Political Race Course—Union Track—Fall Races 1836*, Edward Williams Clay
(New York, 1836), lithograph on paper, courtesy Library of Congress, Prints & Photographs
Division, LC-DIG-ds-00848.

Lithographer Edward Williams Clay illustrated the metaphor as well as anyone in his 1836 caricature, *Political Race Course—Union Track—Fall Races 1836*
(see figure 6.2 above). The print depicts a racehorse with the head of William
Henry Harrison leading a dash to the finish line against competitors bearing
the likenesses of his rival candidates for the presidency: Martin Van Buren, Hugh
Lawson White, and Daniel Webster. A crowd of white men wearing a range of
outfits cheers them on, representing the breadth of the electorate as universal
white male suffrage became law in most states. The jockeys are just as important
as the horses and the crowd. A frontiersman resembling Davy Crockett rides
Harrison, who was nicknamed "Old Tippecanoe" after the frontier battle site
where he defeated a coalition of Native Americans led by Tecumseh in 1811.
Meanwhile, his competitors are steered by allegedly less popular men. Sitting
President Andrew Jackson drives his Vice President Van Buren while complaining that his party has lost its popularity and "the People, too, are all throwing
up their caps for Old Tip." Hugh Lawson White carries a southern dandy, and
Webster is piloted by a prim jockey with the face of fictional character Major
Jack Downing—a New Englander who blamed democracy for debasing American politics. The image favors Harrison by putting him in front and showing
the other candidates as the creatures of party leaders, regional elites, or critics of democracy. In fact, Harrison ended up losing by a landslide in 1836, but
Clay's portrayal of the white male crowd, candidates competing before them,

and select supporters driving the candidates accurately rendered antebellum elections.[53]

The metaphor behind the cartoon was not new. Americans had described all sorts of political events in sporting terms since the eighteenth century. Specifically calling elections "races" was a practice inherited from the British, who used it to denounce factionalism and ribald campaigning. Americans drifted away from this negative connotation in the 1810s, as campaign reports began to refer to candidates who had *"run* a pretty even *race"* without mocking them for doing so. However, as the italicized words in this early example signify, the allusion to elections as sport remained a stilted artificial construction until the 1820s. By then, newspapers were dropping the italics when they reported that a candidate's "race is run." The metaphor had become everyday language because campaigns were no longer seen as being *like* races. They *were* races. As a result, visual representations of the metaphor soon multiplied, with examples picturing elections as boxing and cockfighting matches, or billiard and card games, in addition to horseraces and footraces. Virtually unknown before 1820, sporting-themed images became one of the most common genres of political cartoons between 1820 and 1860, accounting for 10 to 15 percent of the known published corpus.[54]

The timing of the sporting metaphor's florescence corresponds with the rise of candidates campaigning for themselves. After opposition to the War of 1812 triggered the demise of the Federalist Party, and the subsequent Democratic-Republican majority fractured during the 1820s, party caucuses lost the power to limit candidacy and election fields became crowded. While "friends" and bets continued to be necessary "for the purpose of making some little show and noise in the state," heightened competition pushed candidates to campaign for themselves in order to seem more engaged and approachable than rivals who followed tradition and refused to appeal directly to voters. Western voters in particular demanded such appearances. By 1834, the *Western Monthly* noted "that candidates are obliged to be constantly among the people, delivering stump speeches, harangues &c. Indeed, a candidate would be politically damned if he did not mingle with the people from the time he offers until the close of the polls." A few years later, southern candidates also had to "canvass," "expect a call for a speech," and travel to give it lest "the People . . . be much disappointed." Campaigning for themselves enhanced the sense of competition among candidates, fostering a metaphor about actively pursuing votes that stood in contrast to the passive British parlance of "standing" for election.[55]

The atmosphere produced by self-campaigning explains the initial growth of references to elections as races, fights, or contests. But these metaphors lasted because they also reflected the emergence of "mass politics," an approach to campaigning that offered the white male electorate the same kind of access and opportunity for self-assertion found at mass sporting events. The continued expansion of universal white male suffrage was only the most obvious parallel, opening full political participation to all adult white men just as mass sport opened all kinds of sporting spaces to them. By the 1840s, new political parties and campaign events made elections feel so much like sport that picturing them as such became commonplace. Indeed, sporting-themed political cartoons proliferated as both reactions to and advertisements of the relationship between mass sport and mass politics.

At the core of representing that relationship was the cartoons' conflation of sporting and political superiority. Because every cartoon was a campaign advertisement, each one pictured its favored politician winning. The images thus presented the best candidates as sporting champions, appealing to voters who associated masculine sporting prowess with leadership. This message particularly played into the hands of candidates such as Henry Clay, Andrew Jackson, and William Henry Harrison, who all campaigned on their status as bold westerners with renowned physical capacities. More than 50 percent of the period's sporting-themed electoral cartoons supported these men. Few prints depicted state or local elections, yet candidates at those levels also cultivated recognition through sporting endeavors. As in the early national period, at least a dozen turfmen and breeders served in their state legislatures, including William Ransom Johnson in Virginia and Richard Singleton in South Carolina. As we have seen, too, the 1830s and 1840s witnessed the first nominations of celebrity sporting pros. Even when Andrew Jackson and John Quincy Adams sparred over which was more unbecoming a president—Jackson's racehorses or Adams's billiard table—the debate was held to pacify reformers while advertising both men's sporting interests. In sum, then, the cartoons' equation of sporting success with suitability for office mirrored the way sporting renown really was a political asset.[56]

But the cartoons did not just advertise a candidate. They encouraged voters to cast ballots for that candidate. After all, until the mid-1820s, congressional and presidential elections had almost always turned out less than 50 percent of eligible voters.[57] One way the cartoons urged viewers to vote was by picturing a favored candidate in the lead but not yet having won. Portraying the race as over would have suggested that the result was a foregone conclusion and that voting was unnecessary. So the cartoons asked viewers to vote by granting them the agency to read the picture, get the message, and take action.

The images communicated party platforms similarly, by embedding policy positions within sporting situations that most men knew. For example, a

FIGURE 6.3. *A Political Game of Brag*, William R. Browne (New York, 1831), hand-colored lithograph on paper, courtesy American Antiquarian Society.

caricature of the 1832 presidential campaign, seen above, shows Henry Clay about to beat Andrew Jackson in a game of brag (the forerunner of poker). Clay's three aces are labeled with his policies in order to convince viewers that the "U.S. Bank," "Internal Improvement," and "Domestic Manufactures" were unbeatably strong positions. Jackson has three of a kind, too, though in a cutting jab at the president, he holds three knaves: "Intrigue," "Corruption," and "Imbecility." This example compares Clay's agenda to Jackson's character, but a depiction of the 1838 New York mayoral race (see figure 6.4) attributes the last-place horse's finish to the "burden" of its radical rider, identified by the quick-burning "loco-foco" matches that fall from his pocket and supplied the nickname for his faction. In both these cases, the images sought support by linking policies and parties to voters' existing knowledge of sporting activities. Clay's initiatives were aces, and radical politics unsettled horses. Winners were not just superior men physically. Their sporting superiority was rooted in better policy.

By couching evaluations of policy within sporting contexts, the cartoons deployed the same "operational aesthetic" that challenged participants at mass sporting events to examine the mechanics behind any given performance.

FIGURE 6.4. *The Three Mares, New York Course, Spring 1838*, Edward Williams Clay
(New York, 1838), lithograph on paper, courtesy Library of Congress, Prints & Photographs
Division, LC-USZ62-23786.

Whereas Federalists and Jeffersonians had referred to theatre to expose each
other as shady demagogues in the early national period, sporting-themed political cartoons reflected antebellum Americans' acceptance of grandstanding
and chicanery. They tended to portray the best candidate as capable of winning regardless of his opponents' obfuscations. In an 1836 example (see figure
6.5), Andrew Jackson's effort to signal William Henry Harrison's cards to his
friend, Martin Van Buren, cannot overcome Harrison's good play. Another
cartoon, depicting the 1844 presidential election as a footrace (see figure 6.6),
actually puts saboteurs on the side of the cartoon's champion, Henry Clay.
The victim, James Polk, gets mocked for not avoiding the "tariff grease" laid
down by Clay's friends, which indicates Polk's allegedly weak position in opposing import duties. These images argued that men who could not overcome traps and cheats deserved to lose. Such logic reflected the experiences
of a mass sporting culture rife with deceptive "humbug," and challenged
voters to evaluate politicians as they would any sporting impresario.[58]

The sporting context and voter agency suggested by these images reflected
actual campaign events, which mixed the humbuggery of "oily eloquence from
partisan demagogues" with opportunities for voters to express their own opinions amid an environment thick with competition and performance. To be
sure, candidates had thrown celebrations and treats since the colonial period,

FIGURE 6.5. *All Fours: Important State of the Game—The Knave About to Be Lost*, Edward Williams Clay (New York, 1836), hand-colored lithograph on paper, courtesy Library of Congress, Prints & Photographs Division, LC-USZ62-1579.

FIGURE 6.6. *Foot Race, Pennsylvania Avenue: Stakes, $25,000*, N. Bucholzer (New York, 1844), hand-colored lithograph on paper, courtesy American Antiquarian Society.

and complaints about "the noise & confusion which these Elections create" only grew after the Revolution, when gambling and political theatre combined with the Revolution's legacy of street demonstrations to draw a "lively picture" of "a Rabble Government in which the Vulgar dictate and where Licentiousness, the characteristic of these, is not limited."[59] The sense of social inversion that rendered some election fetes akin to rough sport remained in the antebellum years, and was augmented by a wider range of more polite gatherings that gave citizens the same options as sporting culture for more or less genteel experiences. "Everything is done to keep up the excitement," Philadelphian Sidney George Fisher remarked during the 1840 campaign, which launched the expanded approach. "Meetings, speeches, processions are daily & hourly held & made & marched throughout the country." Party newspapers described bets and fights between partisans, orderly parades enlisting thousands of marchers shipped in from long distances, as well as more refined hot air balloon ascensions, musical performances, and celebrity appearances. These sporting elements were not just window dressing. As in other sporting settings, they granted entertainers and partisans the opportunity to take center stage and steal their investors' thunder, or divert the gathering from its intended political purpose. For instance, when Chicago Whigs trotted out star tragedian James Murdock to speak at a rally, the audience cut short the politicians' introductory speeches and demanded Murdock perform Shakespeare. "The people had come to see a show," lamented the abbreviated politician, "and evidently did not care to hear speeches."[60]

Like mass sporting events, political spectacles were thoroughly accessible. Commentators noted that "the delicate and filthy mingle in one concourse" at rougher gatherings, where proceedings often concluded with "one or two fights." Meanwhile, even more orderly events led to claims that "I never saw so many folks. . . . Ladies and gentlemen, town folks, country folks, Hosiers, Country crackers, muster negroes, and all with all sorts of banners." The banners often expressed participants' policy demands on their political leaders, as when a group of Massachusetts workers marched with one that read: "We need relief—We demand reform—No reduction of wages." Just as common were partisans challenging each other, as when Indiana Whigs "brayed" at Democrats as if they were Irish mules, or Massachusetts Whigs declared Democratic marchers "a shabbier set of fellows." At parades, conventions, and other genteel mass political gatherings in the antebellum era, however, mocking and name-calling rarely devolved into physical altercations.[61]

Even the partisan press recognized that "it is not very agreeable to be compelled to wallow in politics day and night, for months together." Yet what one pair of scholars call the "politically harassed majority" was nevertheless lured into action by a "politically eager minority" who deployed sporting spectacle and discourse to enliven the longer campaign seasons they engineered. In the end, few reputable diarists could avoid spending a day every now and again reveling in the accessible egalitarian "circus," the "splendid humbug," and "the joy, the excitement, the vim and go of it all." The mixture of engagement and spectatorship had, as one cartoon put it, turned politics into "Sport for Grown Children." The popularity of that sport served at least one of its goals. Turnout for federal elections jumped to between 60 and 80 percent of the eligible population in the 1840s and remained at that level until the turn of the twentieth century.[62]

Besides the thrill of participating, the cartoons present at least one other reason why mass politics raised participation levels: because its relationship to mass sport transformed voting into a statement of inclusion in the empowered white male community much like participation in mass sport. Political rights had always been the bedrock of white men's empowered status, but voting's "sportification" expanded it from a citizen's right into an assertion of

A FOOT-RACE

FIGURE 6.7. *A Foot Race*, David Claypool Johnson (Boston, 1824), etching on paper, courtesy Library of Congress, Prints & Photographs Division, LC-DIG-ds-05217. In this early version of a sporting political cartoon, notice the two African American boys in the center who both cuttingly mock white men. Meanwhile, one woman is passing by in the background and Abigail Adams supports her son John Quincy. A range of white male ethnic, occupational, and status groups are also present.

manhood at a time when many men felt their masculinity was in question. The cartoons allude to this function by presenting electoral politics as a sport closed to women and African Americans. Early examples from the 1820s had included white women and black men (see figure 6.7), and written reports routinely noted their presence at sporting and political events throughout the period, but both groups disappeared entirely in later images as first sporting culture and then law solidified the boundaries of the white male polity. Erasing others, while carefully keeping a range of hats, coats, and dialects to identify the full range of white men, helped the cartoons imagine the merger of sporting and political culture as the white male electorate wished it would have been: a domain belonging exclusively to a brotherhood of equal white men who built and maintained their privileged power through open competition among themselves—or, as one foreign traveler described it, by "promoting the social relations of his vicinage by whipping his neighbor and then pledging him in a friendly glass of grog." The cartoons and the sporting metaphor they represented made political participation a statement of white sporting manhood, and the status politics of this statement implied that nonvoters risked being considered outside the fraternity of legitimate men.[63]

Yet the empowering and democratic opportunities that mass politics presented to white men also functioned to preserve elites' power. Edward Williams Clay referenced this fact in his 1836 cartoon, which pictured most candidates being guided by men who represented parties, wealth, and antidemocratic sentiments. The structure of the antebellum era's new parties provided the greatest check on the democratic potential of mass politics. Democrats and Whigs emerged from the organizational void of the 1820s with greater resources and more robust infrastructures than previous parties. They developed these assets by taxing the pay of men who received appointments from their victorious candidates and by soliciting prominent names for "subscriptions for defraying the expenses" of campaigns. Because wealthy donors contributed at local, state, and federal levels in return for insider information and influence over contracts, candidates, appointments, and legislation, and because party leaders at each level kept firm control over the positions at their disposal, the antebellum parties were far more hierarchical than their predecessors.[64]

As Clay and other cartoon artists illustrated, one result of this hierarchy was that politicians began to resemble sporting professionals, partly because they participated in and borrowed from sporting culture, and partly because they became reliant on key investors just like any other pro. Some of this reliance was rooted in party leaders' decisions to appeal to voters' democratic sensibilities with candidates who stood further down the social hierarchy than had previously been the case. While most presidential and gubernatorial candidates continued to come from distinguished families, each party began to help "party men" from modest backgrounds run for municipal councils, state legislatures, and even the House of Representatives. As one period exposé explained, "nearly every alderman has in some degree owed his success to the personal efforts and influence of 'backers' who must be recompensed for their services." So the new parties brought a broader range of white men into more powerful offices, but this change came at the expense of converting the old mutual relationship between a candidate and his peer "friends" into a dependence of candidates on powerful "backers."[65]

The new relationship, along with the generally sporting feel of electoral politics, led reformers to consider politicians much as they considered other sporting men. Novels and mainstream periodicals with a moral bent, such as *Gleason's Drawing Room* and *Frank Leslie's Illustrated Newspaper*, increasingly bemoaned "how volubly the lie is given and returned" at political gatherings, and "the froth and scum which rise upon the surface of our society" there. Politicians themselves joined in the refrain, declaiming "the mere chicanery of politics," which led to "a degradation of character and sacrifice of principle." They mimicked Isaac Mickle and Benjamin Brown French in lamenting "the vicious life of a politician" even as they continued to pursue it.[66]

Party systems of dependence and hierarchy penetrated beyond candidates to the armies of "strikers" and "shoulder-tappers" who brought rougher sport to politics by intimidating voters and fighting rivals representing the other party. Testimonies in contested election cases reference how these men generally claimed they "don't care who they get in" to office as long as they "have four or five hundred dollars to get them over." Gambler John O'Connor explained how boxing stars could progress from this role to candidacy. Their performance on behalf of the party led top punchers to prize fights, after which the winners "were usually presented by their admirers with a gorgeous drinking saloon, which became the general resort of all rowdies of whichever faction was so fortunate as to enroll them under its banner. In this manner did the prize-fighter find 'greatness thrust upon him,'" O'Connor wrote, "and became prominent as a ward politician" before moving on to citywide politics and sometimes beyond.[67]

Even the introduction of seemingly democratic processes only shrouded the power of party leaders and backers. For instance, the emergence of conventions in the 1840s gave rank-and-file members a greater say in party organization and nominations, though wealthy donors and party leaders typically arranged the slate of options in meetings behind closed doors. Infighting over these decisions sometimes spawned breakaway factions, but these were not without their backers, either. Like mass sport, mass politics presented a democratic experience, while elites increasingly withdrew from more visible management roles to preserve their power from behind the scenes.[68]

Voters' increased opportunities to participate in parties and campaigns, along with partisan bombast, obscured the "brotherhood of politicians" at the top of both parties' hierarchies, who were all tied to wealthy party elites favoring class cohesion over partisan dissension. As other historians have recognized, these men increasingly "treated it more as a game" than their predecessors. Reform-minded writer and ladies magazine editor Sarah Hale described the shift in a story she wrote comparing the 1830s to the 1790s. "Strange as it may seem to you—strange as it now seems to me," she wrote in 1835, "I did then believe that if the democratic party succeeded in electing their candidate, our liberty, laws, and religion would all be sacrificed and that we should experience all the horrors here, which we read were perpetrated in France." From the vantage point of an influential woman in the 1830s, the partisanship of the 1790s was more deeply rooted in ideological differences, and that seemed "strange" to her in an era when class unity outweighed party affiliation among her peers. A mass politics built around the white male sporting democracy had obscured the power of class for most nonelites by emphasizing racial and gender lines. Meanwhile, elites tightened their circles, grew more unified, and strengthened their power by focusing on their roles as backers and party leaders.[69]

To better control their application of sport, party leaders and backers actually reduced its presence in areas of political culture outside the election process. Most notably, by the 1840s, partisan uses of theatre had declined, as did rallying political support at the racetrack by naming horses for politicians and political causes. The potential for partisan action to spin out of control into class action was too great at sporting events where cultural mobility expanded cross-class confrontation. To better channel sporting experience toward party ends, politicians and their backers applied sporting elements at explicitly political events away from theatres and racecourses, though they continued to offer tavern treats that fostered personal but hierarchical relationships grounded in elites' generosity.[70]

The increasingly united elite that stood behind both major parties also agreed on defeating radical alternatives. A number of third parties had surfaced before the panic in the 1830s and then after the recovery started in the 1840s, and the application of mass sport to electoral politics helped Whigs and Democrats fend off these challenges. By picturing their own candidates as sporting champions, by likening radicals to incapable sportsmen, and by imagining electoral politics as a sporting democracy, the mainstream parties' use of sport countered radical opponents like Mike Walsh. Walsh led a faction of anticapitalist workingmen in New York City in the 1840s. He was tied to Irish gangs and clubs with sporting reputations, and his faction's newspaper reported on sporting events and even referred to upcoming elections as "sport ahead." But he chastised mainstream parties for their efforts "to fawn upon us and call us the bone and sinew of the country" while making policies that would "use us until there was nothing but bone and sinew left of us." While Walsh argued that any sense of democracy in the antebellum party system was a charade, Whigs and Democrats deployed the sporting metaphor and elements of sporting culture to counter his claim by creating experiences that made their democratic rhetoric seem more real, and by linking their candidates (and supporters) to the sporting manhood many workingmen respected. Walsh's own future revealed the major parties' success. He eventually gave in, became a party man, and went to Congress as a Democrat in the 1850s.[71]

The sporting mode of electoral politics contained dissent so well that writers synthesizing reform and capitalist culture actually borrowed its central metaphor and put it to work protecting their vision of the economy as a system that justly rewarded superior individuals. "That farmer must play a losing game who will not adapt his business to circumstances and location," opined one typical article, conveniently ignoring the costs and risks of adaptation. Of course, such ignorance was purposeful. As in electoral politics, the sporting metaphor's application to the economy removed unequal means from the discussion. Rising inequality and shrinking opportunity were cloaked by thinking about profits or losses as the products of competition on an open and level playing field. No wonder Emerson preceded his attribution of "a reason in the man for his good or bad fortune" by arguing that "commerce is a game of skill, which every man cannot play, which few men can play well." Like the structure of antebellum politics, arguments about the morality of wealth gained legitimacy from a sporting metaphor that implied democratic opportunity and meritocracy.[72]

"To the Opera House"

Yet the power of a more unified and wealthier elite was not complete. Negotiation and contest, the bedrock principles of sporting culture since the colonial period, remained inescapable and not inconsiderable concessions. No single event demonstrates these facts better than the Astor Place Riot. On May 10, 1849, three days after refuse thrown from the audience forced him off the stage of New York's Astor Place Opera House, English actor William

Charles Macready was urged by his wealthy supporters to take the stage again. His well-connected backers had the police sent to protect the performance, but their presence only piqued Macready's opponents and led to an assault on the Opera House. Stones and other debris were raining down on the building when authorities called in the militia to quell the disturbance. The crowd then targeted the militiamen as well as the structure. After several soldiers were injured in their first fifteen minutes on the scene, the militia fired into the crowd. At least twenty-two were killed, and more than one hundred were wounded by shots or debris. As the most violent and most studied episode of early American sporting culture, the Astor Place Riot provides a fitting conclusion to this history because it underscores the negotiated nature of sporting culture.

Most historians would disagree with this characterization of the riot's importance, since most studies present it as a failure of negotiation, an expression of uncompromising nationalism, class conflict, or a combination of the two.[73] Certainly, these elements appear in the documentary evidence. Leaflets printed by Isaiah Rynders, a gang leader similar to Mike Walsh, mobilized rioters by layering class onto national identity. "WORKINGMEN, SHALL AMERICANS or ENGLISH RULE," he asked before urging action to protect "free expression of opinion to all Public men! WORKINGMEN! FREEMEN!!" The day after the riot, Walsh led a rally that attracted several thousand participants. His speech there blamed the episode on "the spirit of pride and presumption of the nabobs of the fifteenth ward," using a pejorative term for elites to describe Macready's supporters and referencing the posh part of the city where many of them lived. After his speech, at least 1,500 people marched with Walsh back to the Opera House, where they hurled insults and more stones at the militia. They stopped when the soldiers responded by again leveling their muskets. The units then cleared the streets by marching with fixed bayonets, ending the demonstration for good.[74]

But while class tensions clearly appeared in the rhetoric tied to the disturbance, class does not appear to have defined the rioters. Occupations and residences are known for forty-two of the men killed and wounded during the event. Of these forty-two casualties, thirteen belonged to the militia and police; eleven were "skilled" craftsmen such as butchers, carpenters, or printers; seven were "unskilled" workers, including carters, domestic servants, and sailors; and eleven held jobs increasingly seen as "white-collar": clerks, merchants, lawyers, brokers, and one "speculator." Several of the last group lived at upscale addresses on Wall Street, Broadway, and uptown. Their percentage differs little if only the killed are counted, making clear the cross-class composition of the crowd that was closest to the militia and most antagonistic toward them.[75]

Even the record of incendiary comments suggests that Rynders and Walsh may have used patriotism to breach class lines rather than reinforce them. After all, the initial leaflet couched its final reference to "workingmen" between calls to "all Public men" and "Freemen." White men of all classes were included. In particular, the phrase "public men" reached out to the broad swath of white males engaged in America's contested public sphere, of which sporting culture was a significant component. Another rejoinder referred to elite foes but did not tag its protagonists with a class reference at all, asking "whether English ARISTOCRATS!!! And FOREIGN RULE! Shall triumph in this AMERICA'S METROPOLIS, or whether her own SONS" would "allow themselves to be deprived of the liberty of opinion so dear to every true American." It is hard to see any narrow identification of the rioters in this call to action, as even a nativist reading of "America's sons" would be odd given the broadside's intent to mobilize people for a rally featuring the Irish-born Walsh. The casualty list and language of mobilization suggest that the Astor Place rioters constituted a sporting crowd more than a working-class crowd. They protested to defend the right of assertion that had become central to American sporting culture.[76]

As we have seen, playhouses throughout the country had often been sites for asserting individual status or party superiority. Even after parties stopped rallying their supporters at theatres, conflicts continued to arise between audiences and professionals over the content of a show, the delivery of lines, and the hiring or firing of actors. The majority of these disputes blended nationalistic and class antagonism. As in the attack on New York's theatre in 1766, later episodes targeting actors who "used certain opprobrious epithets and expressions against this Country" equated such statements with an elitist lack of respect for average Americans. Aggrieved audience members typically calmed down once actors or managers responded to their demands by apologizing, hiring, firing, or changing content to suit them. Real damage and assaults only followed in the rare cases when pros denied the crowd's voice. Such disregard became less common after a string of riots in the 1810s and 1820s, triggered by managers who told their audiences that "the theatre was no place for debating" their decisions. Although pits and galleries had reputations for housing rioters, some managers thought "disorderly conduct was invariably confined to the boxes" and spread after it "came principally from two or three would-be gentlemen" there who were "dressed in good broad cloth coats." In sum, the language of theatre riots painted conflict in nationalistic and class colors, but could arise from anyone sitting anywhere in the house.[77]

Nor were these practices limited to theatres. Historically, racecourses witnessed far fewer riots than theatres, but the number grew as racing became less tied to hierarchies of ownership and more of a mass sporting event where the general population expected access and equality. For instance, when the managers of the Long Island course raised grandstand ticket prices to ten dollars for a marquee match race in 1842, mobs of men furious at the price hike fought their way into the stands. Similar assaults arose when Cadwallader Colden's financial difficulties with New York's jockey club forced him to cancel races in 1831. To "give satisfaction to the populace" he returned all admission fees, a tactic theatre managers also used to quell anger at canceled performances. At both theatres and racecourses, negotiations involved audiences expressing their discontent and managers assuaging it or rejecting it and facing the consequences.[78]

At first, the Astor Place episode followed this standard model. Charles Macready faced an angry crowd on his opening night in New York because he had insulted American theatre on his last visit and then traded insults with popular American-born star Edwin Forrest. In many ways, his first show in New York only built on the hisses Macready already had heard in Boston and Philadelphia in preceding weeks. When dissent from the cheap-seat gallery prevented anyone from hearing the show, Macready stepped forward in traditional style to personally address the audience, but received "a deluge of assafoedita" instead of an opportunity to speak. The crowd then shouted down his supporters when they tried to calm things at intermission, and evidence of broadening opposition came from chairs launched toward the stage from box seats during the final act. Fearing real harm as the missiles became more dangerous and antagonism rained down from more sections of the house, Macready exited the stage and told the stage manager he "should now remain no longer" in New York. This was probably the dissenters' goal. Per the rules of sporting culture, they had won.[79]

Then the six investors in the Opera House, along with forty-two of their friends, signed and published a petition pledging to defy the crowd. Their decision spurred a wide range of sporting men to take bolder action to defend the right of assertion won at sporting events over the course of the preceding century. While several studies blame the resulting violence on divergent class cultures, approaching the riot from the perspective of sporting culture suggests that the dispute actually centered on a disagreement over whether the Opera House was a sporting space. Opened in 1847 with funds raised from subscribers who were repaid in tickets rather than cash dividends, the Astor Place Opera House featured a paneled wood interior, carpeted floor, and mahogany-backed seats in the parquette and boxes. As one reviewer noted upon the opening of an earlier opera house, their magnificent interiors made him think "of the contrast of the soiled benches worked and begrimed by the Goths and Vandals who remorselessly stand upon them at the theatres." The critic's language is telling, for he described opera houses in contrast to "the theatres," putting them in separate categories.[80]

The exclusivity of seating at Astor Place also distinguished it from theatres. Gallery tickets cost an affordable fifty cents, but places in the parquette or two tiers of boxes cost a dollar or more. The popular press reprimanded the venue's investors for creating a new class of performance venue that violated the principle of "first come first served," by which "seats have been open . . . without distinction of profession or class." By contrast, the Astor's pricing structure clearly made "the opera aristocracy" out "to be exclusives and superior to the rest of the world." Yet these critiques did not ignite riots or dissent, because sporting men understood that the opera house was not a theatre. It did not look or operate like accessible commercial theatres. As a less sporting space, nonelite operagoers did not take action against exclusion there.[81]

However, the Astor's status as something other than a theatre was complicated by financial difficulties. Before its inaugural season was over, poor attendance and high production costs left payroll obligations unmet. The subscribers infused a small amount of additional cash, but losses came to a head in March 1849 when the manager succumbed to over $20,000 in debts. A few months earlier, he had stopped reserving the finest seats for investors and cut the price of tickets to the "amphitheater," or gallery, in half, from fifty to twenty-five cents. The subscribers contracted William Niblo to take over, and the lecture hall-pleasure garden impresario made an even bigger change when he reopened the house in May with the "legitimate theatre," drama instead of opera. Niblo's choice to open the new program was the controversial Macready, whose presence promised to pack the house with supporters as well as opponents.[82]

Niblo must have made money that night, though his profits came at the cost of making the Astor Place Opera House seem more like a theatre. The small corps of elite backers resisted such an interpretation, while the dissenters in the house assumed it. This was the discrepancy at the heart of the conflict. Unquestionably, the subscribers had built the Opera House to construct class distinction and cultural authority. But nobody had opposed this. Only when the venue seemed more like a theatre, and thus more a part of sporting culture, did audiences assert themselves as they did at other sporting events and then defend their right to such assertion. In the context of sporting culture and sporting space, the Astor Place Riot appears to be something more complex than the expression of class conflict between workers and men of capital. Rather, it pitted a wide range of white men eager to defend sporting culture against a small cadre of elites who did not think the rules of sporting culture applied in this case.

Indeed, large-scale class conflict rarely erupted among the audiences at antebellum sporting events, because the accessibility of mass sport diffused class tension into individual confrontations. Group action tended to focus on challenging the alleged elitism of professional performers or managers and securing the right to self-assertion in sporting settings, while individual attendees argued and fought over the degree to which class impaired their claims to genteel or physical manly status. The opportunity to assert status and opinion may seem like something small, in comparison to the power of an elite that secured and legitimated its position in part through sporting culture's emphasis on individualism, accessible competition, and risk-taking, but the cross-class crowd at Astor Place fought to defend those opportunities because they seemed to be in jeopardy. They thought the democratic gains from a century of negotiation over sporting culture might still be lost.

If we view the aftermath of Astor Place in terms of what the sporting crowd wanted to defend, rather than as a statement by workingmen only, our conclusions also change. Instead of seeing the riot as emblematic of workingmen's defeat, marking the end of an era of negotiated public life and the rise of a more stratified, orderly, and policed society, the sporting focus makes clear how the rioters won in at least a couple of ways. For one thing, the Astor Place Opera House failed. Its investors could not support its losses, so it sank to hosting traveling animal shows, then closed in 1854, was sold, and became a library for aspiring clerks. The city's next opera house, the Academy of Music, opened the same year and avoided the fate of the Astor by quickly opening up the vast majority of its seats for fifty cents or less. Eighteen exclusive boxes were sold outright to some of the city's leading families, but virtually the rest of the house was accessible. Once again, greater accessibility diffused class animus into opportunities for individual assertion. The Academy became an upscale version of Niblo's lecture hall, a place where almost everyone could play the gentleman for a night. Only with the rise of the philanthropically funded symphonies and opera companies of the Gilded Age, backed with industrial riches that did not exist before the Civil War and were enough to make them less dependent on ticket sales, did exclusive "highbrow" venues separate from cross-class sporting culture become a sustainable part of America's entertainment landscape.[83]

Equally important is the fact that contentious cross-class sporting experiences persisted. At billiard halls, racetracks, and in a range of new venues, from the concert saloon to the burlesque theatre and the boxing ring, the manly

democracy of sporting culture continued to be divided into commercial settings where white men could express themselves in unvarnished ways and ones
where they exerted a more refined—if not "respectable"—version of self-
assertion. For over a century, this culture had faced resistance from elites and
reformers trying to limit or eliminate it. By the 1850s, reform culture had marginalized it in print, but neither reformers nor elites could reduce its centrality in real life. Its popularity helped establish cultural mobility and the fluid
movement between multiple identities associated with modern individualism
while framing how elections were understood in the young republic. At the
same time, though, elites applied the opportunity for democratic challenge
in sporting settings to perpetuate the notion that equal opportunity and competition remained cornerstones of American life, and that the rich and powerful were therefore winners who deserved to be vastly more rich and powerful.
Sporting culture's lasting impact on the country was its function as a venue
for contesting and limiting elites' social authority while ultimately supporting
their economic and political power.[84]

Epilogue
Change and Persistence

The Los Angeles Dodgers opened the 2011 Major League Baseball season by hosting their archrivals, the San Francisco Giants, on a record-setting ninety-two-degree day at the end of March. The game was hotly contested, too, as the Dodgers scored late and then held off a Giants rally in the last inning to win 2–1. But it was the feverish fans who stole the headlines. Taunting from both sides throughout the day resulted in seventy-two arrests and three reported cases of assault and battery. One of those attacks left forty-two-year-old Brian Stow temporarily unconscious and with permanent brain damage. Stow was a paramedic and father of two who had traveled three hundred miles from the Bay Area to support the Giants. His attackers, thirty-year-old Marvin Norwood and twenty-nine-year-old Louis Sanchez, worked in carpentry and auto detailing, respectively. They were about to become brothers-in-law, after Norwood's upcoming marriage to Sanchez's sister. Court records show that all three men had engaged in "trash talk" at the stadium, but not with each other. Sanchez made an impromptu decision to target Stow after seeing him in a Giants jersey as the men exited the ballpark. A taped phone conversation after their arrest recorded Sanchez apologizing to Norwood for initiating the confrontation. "That happens, bro," Norwood replied. "I mean, what kind of man would I have been if I hadn't jumped in and tried to help you?"[1]

One episode is not enough to support a claim that men still attend sporting events to prove their masculinity. But the behavior at Dodger Stadium in 2011 was hardly singular. Police had arrested 132 people at the previous year's opening game, and the increasing frequency of threats and fights at all kinds of sporting events across the country—or at least their increased visibility in an age of social media—has sparked a number of studies from psychologists, sociologists, and anthropologists in the last ten years. Taken together, the accumulated evidence and analysis of behavior at contemporary sporting events reveals the lingering influence of sporting culture's formative years. The development of mass sport since 1860 has done little to alter its function as a proving ground of masculine status.[2]

And yet the changes are what most Americans recognize, because the breakdown of sport's gender and racial barriers is a celebrated part of the narrative of increasing equality over the course of the twentieth century. To be sure, that change has been real, though it was not a linear process. For example, descriptions and images of spectators at early baseball games in the 1840s regularly described women in attendance, but their disappearance from the 1870s to the 1890s led teams to try to woo them with discounted tickets and special "ladies days."[3] Then reputable women became more prominent again as physical activity and sporting consumerism became a part of the "New Woman" movement at the turn of the century. This time, women made gains as both spectators and athletes. Starting with newly popular genteel sports like tennis and golf, white women and then women of color steadily pushed into other types of activities. Meanwhile, spectatorship at these events grew to the point that, by the end of the twentieth century, women's soccer sold out the Rose Bowl and several universities' women's basketball teams outdrew their male counterparts. In recent years, women also have made up more than 50 percent of the crowds at women's soccer and basketball games, and rates of reported violence and arrests are far lower at these events than at those featuring male team sports. In sum, more women are in the stands and on the field, yet their effect on encouraging genteel behavior recalls their role in early American sport. The growing presence of women at sporting activities has essentially multiplied the number of events and spaces that are akin to pleasure gardens and lecture halls, where anyone could get in and claim respectability.[4]

The democratization narrative asserts that African Americans have registered even greater gains. Whereas white women were never formally excluded from rough sporting spaces, generations of African American men and women were segregated out of genteel venues in the North and the South unless they were working in a service capacity. Moreover, as another reminder that the process of undoing discrimination was not linear or uniform, black pros actually lost ground before they gained it back. Black men were banned from professional ranks only after their success as free men threatened to undermine sporting culture's support of white male superiority. Upholding the racial order had become more central to sporting culture than even the profit motive, as evidenced by the fact that profitable winning was not enough to protect black pros' jobs once slavery's demise made their status and earnings a more serious social challenge to the racial hierarchy. In fact, both racehorse and baseball team owners started removing black athletes years before Louisiana enacted the law legalizing segregation that was then upheld by the Supreme Court in 1896. In the wake of a Civil War that had divided white men, their long-standing control over sporting culture helped reunite them by providing venues where they could again draw lines of exclusion that they later entrenched in law.[5]

The resulting exclusion of black pros and continuing segregation of black spectators only began to break down in the years around World War II. African American efforts to point out the hypocrisy of domestic racism in the context of the fight against Nazism, combined with rising disposable income among blacks who won new opportunities associated with the war effort, pushed white owners and managers to bring back black performers and open more seating to black spectators willing to pay to see them. If the possible gain from winning with black pros was not enough to secure their place, the promise of steady profit from more numerous black spectators was. Black athletes' success then earned them more places in integrated sport. By the 1980s, African Americans were overrepresented (compared to their percentage of the overall population) in America's top three spectator sports, and the last thirty years have seen steady, if slow, growth in the number of black coaches, front office staff, and owners.[6]

So the story of democratization is real. It was animated by African Americans and white women, from Jackie Robinson and Billie Jean King to Curt Flood and Serena Williams, who seized sporting culture's historic reputation for challenge, negotiation, and political activism to push for greater opportunity on and off the field. Some studies even cite survey data suggesting that a more inclusive sporting culture has made fans less racist and sexist. But, as in the past, focusing only on democratization obscures how sporting culture also perpetuates older hierarchies and inequalities. For instance, looking in the stands instead of on the field reveals the persistence of white men's dominance. According to nationwide data from Ticketmaster, one of the leading retailers of sporting event tickets, men made up 61 percent of all sporting event spectators in 2014, and whites accounted for 71 percent. African Americans were underrepresented at just 8 percent, given that they make up more than 13 percent of the total population. Even in several popular sports featuring female or black athletes, such as women's professional golf and men's pro basketball, white men made up the majority of the spectators watching in person.[7]

Another reflection of unbalanced access is the decreasingly cross-class composition of audiences due to rising ticket prices. The 2014 Ticketmaster data lists the average annual household income of a sporting event spectator at just under $80,000. With the exception of a few cities such as Washington, DC, and San Francisco (New York, Chicago, and Los Angeles are not exceptions here), that sum ranks in the top third of the local population. Those earning less than $50,000, who make up almost 50 percent of most urban populations, accounted for just a third of all ticket holders, and were an even smaller minority at major professional sporting events. Certainly, the exclusivity produced by elevated ticket prices helps explain the preponderance of white men, who are three times more likely than black men to make more than the average income of a sports ticket buyer.[8] As a result, it should come as no surprise that a Philadelphia judge in 2002 claimed that "95 percent of the people arrested" at the city's professional football games "live in the suburbs and the majority are college educated." Brian Stow's attackers did not fit this bill. Neither Norwood (who is white) nor Sanchez graduated from college, though their backgrounds might explain why they were so explicit about the role of manhood in motivating their assault. Instigators with better claims to respectability have tended to try to defend that status by avoiding disreputable justifications for their actions based on rough masculinity. Instead, they have echoed Isaac Mickle's shamefulness by stating that "I try to do what's right" but "I got caught up in something I wish I hadn't got caught up in."[9]

As in early America, wealthier spectators today can choose which brand of masculinity they want to assert. On one hand, they can pay enormous sums to access private "luxury" boxes, where finer décor and food service mandate more refined attire and polite behavior. In truth, many box attendees do not even have to pay for these seats because many boxes are rented by companies who cultivate clients by offering them access—using these seats for precisely the kind of exclusive business networking early American investors had pursued. On the other hand, if their goal is to prove a rougher virility, spectators of means can choose to sit in the cheapest seats, where violence and confrontation are more likely. In between boxes and bleachers are field-level seats, which are not inexpensive and which attract a mix of families, well-behaved adults, and rougher types. Venue and team owners claim to want to promote respectability and order in these seating areas, in part to attract the patronage of rich families with kids, but the sections closest to the action often host aggressive supporters who don special outfits and taunt opposing players and fans in an effort to prove their place as superior supporters. Hourly wageworkers are a rare sight here. For example, the leaders of the rabid fan section in the end zone of Cleveland's football stadium, called the "Dawg Pound," are a sports marketer, a general contractor, and an artist.[10]

That the artist is a woman, known as "The Bone Lady" because she wears a skirt adorned with small dog bones, might underscore the narrative of increasingly democratic access. However, an ethnography of women who are fans of the National Football League describes how she is regularly targeted for her "dirty skirt" by hypermasculine fans rooting for the same team in the same seating section. In Cleveland and elsewhere, the ethnographers report calls of "Get back in the kitchen!" and the physical molestation women face when they assume a traditionally male posture by being vocal or otherwise prominent in the stands, even if their self-assertion comes in support of the same team as their male castigators.[11]

Just as in earlier periods, recent studies indicate that the desire to prove rough masculine status—including dominance over women as well as physical superiority among other men—remains a leading motivator for aggressive behavior among male spectators. One overview of the literature places "thrill-seeking" atop a list of nine factors contributing to spectator violence at sporting events. Linking the enjoyment of risk-ridden physical confrontation to the same status and values it proved in early America, the author concludes that "fighting is basically about masculinity." It "is a central source of meaning, status, or 'reputation,'" in a world where rising unemployment, increased leisure time, and a mainstream culture that eschews risk-taking (inherited from reform-minded antebellum respectability) means a wide range of "males are likely to experience failure, intense competition, or boredom, which drive them to seek more satisfying and exciting experiences in their leisure lives."[12]

While broad surveys of sporting violence describe how manly status motivates aggressive spectators in both Europe and America, comparative studies have identified a key difference. Most European sporting violence tends to take place in large groups bound together by class identity expressed through affiliation with teams, especially soccer clubs. Often, those teams possess historic ties to working-class neighborhoods and boast long histories of supporting working-class politics. In contrast, as the largest study of North American violence explains, "the majority of incidents of fan-to-fan violence occurring at North American sports involve individuals or small groups of spectators." America's long history of individualized sporting confrontations over status was reinforced by the emergence of commercial team sports at the end of the nineteenth century. Infused with sport's profit-oriented past in America, in contrast to aristocratic beneficence and communitarian clubs in Europe, owners pursued the largest following possible by identifying their teams with entire cities rather than neighborhoods, and they formed monopolistic leagues or moved their franchises to limit competition in the same city. As with the regional horse races of the early nineteenth century, emphasizing a shared geographic identity united men across class lines. The scale of the new stadiums and fan bases also heightened anonymity. The result was a reduced chance of concerted class action and the persistence of individualized challenges over manly status. Recent changes to ticket prices have only further reduced class identity as a factor in sporting confrontations. Sport may now feature a more diverse pool of athletes, but they perform before audiences that remain more concerned with individual status than class action and are increasingly less diverse. Nonelites who remain see cultural mobility again becoming the preserve of the wealthiest men, who are the only ones able to move between exclusive box seats and cheaper seating sections.[13]

If the opportunity to prove genteel masculine status at venues has shrunk, attendance is nevertheless a relatively narrow lens for considering sporting culture participation in an age of mass media. The rise of radio, television, and film over the course of the last century has permitted a broader range of fans to follow sporting events. At first, mass media coverage of sport augmented live attendance by bringing events into homes where families consumed it together. Indeed, family outings to sporting events were not at all common before radios and televisions. Today, with the rising cost of tickets causing family attendance to decline again, sporting events have become so popular on television that they drive the cost of cable and satellite packages. Even on standard national networks, all but one of the forty most-watched programs of 2014 were live sporting events. Besides encouraging respectable family viewing, access via mass media allows a range of fans to follow events they can no longer afford to attend. For example, African Americans are more than twice as likely to watch NBA games on TV as whites, though they are underrepresented in the stands at NBA games (compared to their percentage of the local population). Of course, homes are not the only places where fans watch on television. Viewing at bars—which run the gamut from reputable to rough, but generally cater more to men than women—has been linked both to individualized confrontations like those inside stadiums and large-scale, cross-class (and largely white) rioting that is rare at venues but more common in the streets as an expression of male fans' excitement or frustration after major victories or losses.[14]

The emergence of mass media has also had a crucial impact on sporting culture by altering its composition. Several types of theatres and theatrical content already had begun to become "sacralized" or "feminized" in the antebellum period, processes that removed them from sporting culture by creating spaces, performances, and behavioral norms designed to reduce the sense of competition and opportunity for self-assertion among spectators. Later, the increasing affordability and popularity of radio, television, and cinema undermined forms of theatre that still belonged to sporting culture, most notably the vaudeville shows where audience interaction and individual confrontations in the gallery had continued to be part of the experience. With vaudeville's decline, only burlesque theatres remained, along with the raunchier strip clubs that descended from them but now vastly outnumber them.[15]

Music venues like concert saloons and the earliest jazz clubs acquired reputations similar to the old traditional theatres. The subsequent invention of the phonograph, followed by radio, heightened access to a diverse range of music that encouraged rather than detracted from attendance at these venues. The result of this evolution is that today, concerts at bars, clubs, and stadiums are as much a part of sporting culture as athletic events. The two activities share many of the same features, including majority-white male audiences, a range of genteel and rough spectator spaces, and a growing reputation for violence in their rougher domains. As with athletic sports, episodes of physical aggression particularly correlate with male performers in genres associated with unvarnished manhood, such as country music and hip-hop. In effect, then, mass media has altered what kinds of activities belong to sporting culture without drastically altering the available types of sporting experience.[16]

Emphasizing the democratization of sport in the twentieth century has obscured this continuity and perpetuated sporting culture's role as a keystone supporting the economic and political influence of capitalism. Contemporary media and athletes themselves often paint professional sporting success as the result of developing superior skill through superior dedication, of having "a relentless drive and the will to do whatever it takes to be successful at whatever you put your mind to," as Stephen Curry put it when he accepted the NBA's Most Valuable Player award in 2015. Yet some athletes enjoy undeniable physical advantages, and other advantages can be inherited as well— Curry's father was an NBA player, for instance, and so he could provide a level of personal coaching and financial support that many striving young basketball players can only envy. This is not to say that sporting culture does not create rags-to-riches stories, or that its stars do not work hard. But less than one percent of high school athletes ultimately play professionally, with the odds of reaching that plateau estimated at 500 to 1. Musicians face similar odds against getting a major record label deal or making enough money from their music to make it their only employment. So when a sporting culture music star like Jay Z, who was not born into wealth, describes "the gift, the spirit, and the work" as being equally responsible for his success, he is espousing a version of the reform-capitalist synthesis that ties great ability and great wealth to great character. Such logic both justifies stars' wealth and makes attaining it seem more possible than it is. As Jay Z once recalled, "growing up where I grew up, we looked to athletes" who "get paid millions of dollars to play the game they love," because "they came from the same places we came from." Today's sporting stars continue to make opportunity seem palpable, not just for aspiring athletes but for everyone, and their explanations for their success essentially repeat the old arguments that blame failure on personal traits without recognizing systemic ones.[17]

Sporting stars' function as evangelists for opportunity and meritocracy explains their growing presence as politicians. As income inequality has increased and chances of mobility have not improved, leaders and backers of the major political parties have seen sporting stars' success stories as ever more important to maintaining conviction in the culture and political system shaped by capitalism. As a result, half of the twenty-five former professional athletes to hold major elected office (federal, governorship, or major mayoral) since 1900 have served since 1990. Musicians whose performances fit into sporting culture have been less prominent in office, though they have donated on a par with athletic sports stars, and given concerts in support of their favored candidates. Meanwhile, sporting investors have continued to be political backers. Seventy-five percent of major sports franchise owners donate to the major political parties, and they gave a cumulative total of nearly $30 million in the four-year election cycle that ended in 2012. The owners of the Chicago Cubs almost matched that figure themselves in 2016, with one member of the family reaching the governorship of Nebraska and another appointed to the Commerce Department under Donald Trump. Sporting prowess and sporting businesses remain paths to political influence because they generate followers and revenue.[18]

While sporting investors have consistently involved themselves in politics over time, the rise of sporting pros as prominent campaigners and candidates signifies the return of a more palpable "sportified" politics following several decades of decline. Starting in the late nineteenth century, a series of election reforms filtered out many of the sporting elements that had become part of political culture between 1760 and 1860. Calling elections "races" was just about all that remained after stricter registration laws, secret ballots, and stronger enforcement of bans on election gambling and the distribution of alcohol near polling places combined to make campaigning and voting more sober experiences. These laws were passed at the behest of vocal reform culture adherents, who argued that respectable voters did not participate in the old sporting political culture and so its continuance drowned out their voices in favor of the new African American and immigrant citizens attracted by raucous electioneering. In fact, data suggests that the regulations sharply reduced voter turnout among the targeted demographics as well as, albeit to a lesser degree, middle- and upper-class white male voters. As historian Michael McGerr has noted, "Through newspapers and spectacular campaigns, partisanship had initiated the young into politics, simplified public life, invested the act of voting with multiple significance, and made the vote a reflection of enduring party attachments as much as interest in issues, candidates, or close elections." A wide range of voters had connected to politics through its sporting elements. When those elements disappeared, turnout dropped across a number of demographics. The expansion of the franchise to women only crystallized this shift, because women's rights activists staked part of their claim to suffrage on their moral influence, which they promised would counter the crude hypermasculinity they blamed for rampant political corruption. In the years after these changes, politicians threw out ceremonial first pitches from their exclusive box seats at baseball games, but they stopped appearing as baseball players on baseball cards (see figure E.1). For the first time in over one hundred years, links to sporting pros became more damaging than advantageous for politicians, and sport itself became seen as ideally apolitical.[19]

Over the last twenty-five years or so, however, parties and politicians have reinserted into politics some of the confrontation and spectacle of sporting culture. Not only are sporting stars more visibly engaged as candidates and partisans, but the rise of explicitly partisan news channels and their debate-style programming has returned an air of aggressive contest and sporting experience to political culture. If parties and their candidates still do not campaign by buying drinks for voters or naming racehorses for their causes, they nevertheless have encouraged coverage and mobilization techniques geared to urge voters to pick a side and defend their choice by heightening the sense of conflict and risk involved in elections. Candidates have resurfaced on baseball cards (see figure E.2), and even election gambling has returned as a multimillion-dollar industry run from offshore websites capable of skirting the laws against it. Through the partisanship of a favorite entertainer, a wager, hourly debates on cable news networks, or a call-in to a talk radio program, the recent sportification of politics heightens the sense of competition and difference between

THE PRESIDENTIAL B. B. CLUB.

HONEST LONG CUT CHEWING AND SMOKING.

W. DUKE, SONS & CO., N. Y.

FIGURE E.1. *Benjamin Harrison,* Presidential Base Ball Club Series, Duke & Sons Tobacco Company (1888), courtesy Robert Edward Auctions.

the parties, as well as the sense of popular engagement and impact in an age when investors actually have more influence over elections than ever before. Perhaps not coincidentally, voter turnout rose for three straight presidential and midterm election cycles from 2000 to 2008 for the first time since the 1930s, and peaked in 2008 with the best turnout since the 1960s. Slight but steady declines since 2012, however, may indicate the limits of this approach.[20]

In any event, evidence of more democratic participation does not imply greater equality. The recent sportification of politics carries a remarkably masculine bias, as it did in early America. Although women have consistently turned out to vote at a higher rate than men since 1980, the vast major-

Figure E.2. *John McCain*, Presidential Predictors Series (2008), courtesy Upper Deck Company.

ity of pundits in cable news debates are white men, and all of the sporting stars who have become candidates are men. Moreover, as sportified politics has taken root in the last fifteen years, the percentage of women in the United States' national legislature has slipped from ranking fifty-ninth to ninety-eighth in the world, while the percentage of women holding statewide elected office has actually declined. Donald Trump's candidacy for the presidency was emblematic of all these developments. He rallied a cross-class but overwhelmingly white male following by drawing on an image of success cultivated from his popular television series that sportified business, as well as by deploying a rhetoric crafted around "winning" and encouraging physical confrontation. His victory as an "outsider" despite his enormous wealth and history as a political backer is perhaps the most telling evidence of sporting culture's persistence as a vehicle for expressing democratic opportunity while confirming the privilege and power of wealth, race, and gender.[21]

Notes

Abbreviations

BPL	Boston Public Library
CWM	Special Collections Research Center, Earl Gregg Swem Library, College of William and Mary
Duke	David M. Rubenstein Rare Book and Manuscript Library, Duke University
HSP	Historical Society of Pennsylvania
LCP	Library Company of Philadelphia
LOC	Library of Congress
LV	Library of Virginia
MDHS	Maryland Historical Society
NJA	New Jersey State Archives
NJHS	New Jersey Historical Society
NYHS	New-York Historical Society
NYPL	New York Public Library
SCA	South Carolina Department of Archives and History
SCHS	South Carolina Historical Society
SCL	South Caroliniana Library, University of South Carolina
SHC	Southern Historical Collection, Louis Round Wilson Special Collections Library, University of North Carolina—Chapel Hill
UVa	Albert and Shirley Small Special Collections Library, University of Virginia
VHS	Virginia Historical Society
Winterthur	The Joseph Downs Collection of Manuscripts and Printed Ephemera, Winterthur Museum

Introduction

1. Benjamin Henry Latrobe to Philip Mazzei, December 19, 1806, in *Philip Mazzei: Select Writings and Correspondence*, ed. Filippo Mazzei, Margherita Marchione, and Stanley J. Idzerda (Prato, Italy, 1983), 439.

2. John C. Van Horne, ed., *The Journals of Benjamin Henry Latrobe* (New Haven, CT, 1977), 2:325–27.

3. Edward Carter II, John C. Van Horne, and Charles E. Brownell, eds., *Latrobe's View of America, 1795–1820: Selections from the Watercolors and Sketches* (Baltimore, 1985), 13–14. Francis Baily, *Journal of a Tour in Unsettled Parts of North America in 1796 and 1797* (London, 1856), 99–104.

4. Isaac Weld, *Travels through the States of North America* (New York, 1968 [orig. 1795]), 1:191. Robert Waln, *The Hermit in America on a Visit to Philadelphia* (Philadelphia, 1819), 192. *New England Courant*, February 26, 1726. See also George G. Foster, *Celio: Or, New-York Above-Ground and Under-Ground* (New York, 1850), 16.

5. Louis F. Tasistro, *Random Shots and Southern Breezes* (New York, 1842), 63. For similar lines from racing spectators, see Minutes, September 29, 1768, Register Book, Philadelphia Jockey Club Papers, HSP; Matilda Charlotte Fraser, *Hesperos; or, Travels in the West* (London, 1850), 72.

6. This book explores the relationship between egalitarian, or "democratic," social experiences in sporting culture settings and the nature of popular sovereignty, or formal political "democracy," in order to explain the enduring power of wealthy "elites" in American society. The central problematic takes its inspiration from Edmund S. Morgan's celebrated book, *Inventing the People: The Rise of Popular Sovereignty in England and America* (New York, 1988). In particular, Morgan's chapter on "Elections and Electioneering" notes how "sports competitions offer a parallel" to understanding the relationship between egalitarian settings and hierarchies of political power, though his analogy does not detail the depth of the connection between sport and politics that is revealed in the evidence here. For more on "elites," see note 9 below.

7. Patricia Cline Cohen, Timothy J. Gilfoyle, and Helen Lefkowitz Horowitz, *The Flash Press: Sporting Male Weeklies in 1840s New York* (Chicago, 2008). Timothy J. Gilfoyle, *City of Eros: New York City, Prostitution, and the Commercialization of Sex, 1790–1920* (New York, 1992), 92–122; Helen Lefkowitz-Horowitz, *Rereading Sex: Battles over Sexual Knowledge and Suppression in Nineteenth-Century America* (New York, 2002), 159–93; Guy Reel, *The National Police Gazette and the Making of the Modern American Man, 1879–1906* (New York, 2006), 91–176.

8. Even the literature on public entertainment that does not specifically address sporting culture overwhelmingly sees its commercial origins and broad appeal emerging in the decades of the 1820s–40s, with the exception of taverns. For examples, see Bluford Adams, *E Pluribus Barnum: The Great Showman and the Making of U.S. Popular Culture* (Minneapolis, 1997); Melvin L. Adelman, *A Sporting Time: New York City and the Rise of Modern Athletics, 1820–1870* (Urbana, IL, 1990); Neil Harris, *Humbug: The Art of P. T. Barnum* (Chicago, 1973); Bruce A. McConachie, *Melodramatic Formations: American Theatre and Society, 1820–1870* (Iowa City, 1992); Steven A. Riess, *City Games: The Evolution of American Urban Society and the Rise of Sports* (Urbana, IL, 1986). For a counterpoint on theatre, see Heather Nathans, *Early American Theatre from the Revolution to Thomas Jefferson: Into the Hands of the People* (Cambridge, UK, 2003).

9. Throughout this book, the term "elite" encompasses wealthy or "moneyed" men who possessed significant capital and used it to maximize their political influence, as well as the men of lesser means they let into their business and social circles. The term reflects how sporting culture helped link authority to membership in status groups that were not strictly defined by wealth or class. For the theoretical framework behind

this thinking, see C. Wright Mills, ed., *From Max Weber: Essays in Sociology* (London, 1948), 181–96; Jan Pakulski, "The Weberian Foundations of Modern Elite Theory and Democratic Elitism," *Historical Social Research* 37 (2012): 38–56; Max Weber, *Economy and Society: An Outline of Interpretive Sociology*, ed. Guenther Roth (New York, 1968), chap. 3. For "moneyed men," see Michael Merrill and Sean Wilentz, eds., *The Key of Liberty: The Life and Democratic Writings of William Manning, "A Laborer," 1747–1814* (Cambridge, MA, 1993), xiii, 4–32.

10. This argument has been made for twentieth-century sport, but not earlier periods. See Pamela Grundy, *Learning to Win: Sports, Education, and Social Change in Twentieth-Century North Carolina* (Chapel Hill, NC, 2001).

11. For the best summary of the theoretical approach to modern definitions of "sport," "game," and "play," see Kendall Blanchard, *Anthropology of Sport: An Introduction* (Westport, CT, 1995), 42–50.

12. Samuel Johnson, *A Dictionary of the English Language* (London, 1770), 1:308, 2:170–71, 362. Joseph Hamilton, *Johnson's Dictionary of the English Language in Miniature* (New York, 1817), 73, 170, 195. Noah Webster, *A Dictionary for Primary Schools* (New York, 1831), 90, 216, 275.

13. William Alexander Duer, *Reminiscences of an Old Yorker* (New York, 1867 [orig. 1847]), 42–43. John Spencer Bassett, ed., *Correspondence of Andrew Jackson* (Washington, DC, 1926–35), 3:267. William Milnor, *Memoirs of the Old Schuylkill Fishing Company and Gloucester Hunting Club* (Philadelphia, 1830), 21, 36–37. Charles Fraser, *Reminiscences of Charleston* (Charleston, 1969 [1854]), 88. Charles William Janson, *The Stranger in America* (London, 1807), 101.

14. Edward Lloyd to John Cadwalader, December 27, 1772, Gen. John Cadwalader Series, Cadwalader Papers, HSP. For similar examples, see John Tayloe II to John Baylor, March 21, 1771, Baylor Family Papers, UVa; Benjamin Franklin Taylor to Richard Singleton, December 29, 1824, Benjamin Franklin Taylor Papers, SCL; "Diary of Robert Gilmor," February 27–March 1, 1827, *Maryland Historical Magazine* 17 (September 1922): 262–64. The monthly racing reports in the "Sporting Intelligence" section of the *American Turf Register and Sporting Magazine* (hereafter cited as *Turf Register*), 1829–44, also use the term in this way.

15. *New York Mercury*, April 11, 1763. Sol Smith, *The Theatrical Apprenticeship and Anecdotal Recollections of Sol. Smith* (Philadelphia, 1846), 151–52.

16. Robert Bailey, *The Life and Adventures of Robert Bailey, from His Infancy Up to December, 1821* (Richmond, 1822), 66–67. See also Jonathan Harrington Greene, *Gambling Unmasked!* (Baltimore, 1844), 49–50, 86; Jackson Lears, *Something for Nothing: Luck in America* (New York, 2003), 100–109.

17. *Turf Register*, April 1830, 412; March 1835, 320–21. *Christian Advocate* (New York), January 13, 1827, 74. For earlier phrasing of "theatrical sports," see William Griggs, ed., *Shakespeare's Midsummer Night's Dream: The First Quarto, 1600* (London, 1880), 30; Lionel Gatford, *Logos Alexipharmakos; Or, Hyperphyiscall Directions in Time of Plague . . .* (Oxford, 1645), 19.

18. Van Horne, *Latrobe Journals*, 1:328. Meriwether Jones had been the district's elected representative until about a year before Latrobe's visit, when he had to abandon his seat in the General Assembly after that body elected him to the governor's Privy Council at the end of 1796. It is not clear that Latrobe knew this, but Jones actively campaigned on behalf of his allies, so Latrobe's analysis remains salient.

W. Hamilton Bryson, *Virginia Law Books: Essays and Bibliographies*, Memoirs of the American Philosophical Society, vol. 239 (Philadelphia, 2000), 534–35.

19. In proposing that sport was a "tool" or a "social technology" used to achieve various political ends, I am applying a notion of sport's political functionality that has largely been noted in later periods. For a prominent example and discussion of this concept, see Mark Dyreson, *Making the American Team: Sport, Culture, and the Olympic Experience* (Urbana, IL, 1998), 2–5. For a rare example covering early America, see Rhys Isaac, *The Transformation of Virginia, 1740–1790* (Chapel Hill, NC, 1982), 88–114.

20. Alexis de Tocqueville, *Democracy in America* (London, 1840), 2:216.

21. John Smail, "Credit, Risk, and Honor in Eighteenth-Century Commerce," *Journal of British Studies* 44, no. 3 (July 2005): 455. Alexandra Shepard, "Manhood, Credit, and Patriarchy in Early Modern England, 1589–1640," *Past & Present* 167 (May 2000): 83–84. *New-Yorker*, August 25, 1838. Toby L. Ditz, "Shipwrecked; Or, Masculinity Imperiled: Mercantile Representations of Failure and the Gendered Self in Eighteenth-Century Philadelphia," *Journal of American History* 81 (June 1994): 60–69. Dana D. Nelson, *National Manhood: Capitalist Citizenship and the Imagined Fraternity of White Men* (Durham, NC, 1998), 29–46. Scott Sandage, *Born Losers: A History of Failure in America* (Cambridge, MA, 2005), 24–43. For a theoretical approach to masculinity as an ideology constructed to maintain power through multiple "modes" defined by discourse and practice (such as the "genteel" and "rough" modes of sporting culture described in this book), see Todd W. Reeser, *Masculinities in Theory: An Introduction* (Malden, MA, 2010), 20–39.

22. In effect, chapters 3 and 4 argue that elites maintained authority in the new republic by conceding some of their "status power" as cultural arbiters for society at large and replacing it with status claimed through a new economic culture that borrowed heavily from sport and lauded them as champions in the great game of life. For the differences and relationships among status, economic, and political power, and the ways each can be negotiated to legitimate power relationships in a given society or state, see Norman Uphoff, "Distinguishing Power, Authority, and Legitimacy: Taking Max Weber at His Word by Using Resources-Exchange Analysis," *Polity* 22 (December 1989): 295–322. For the importance of the late eighteenth and early nineteenth centuries as the moment in Western nations when this kind of negotiation and construction of legitimacy was crafted, see Mark Haugaard, "Democracy, Political Power, and Authority," *Social Research* 77 (December 2010): 1049–74.

I use the term "capitalism" to refer to an economic system in which the ownership of the means of production is concentrated in the hands of a relatively small percentage of the population. I do not argue that capitalism is an apt description for the American economy during the entire period under investigation, and I do not wade into the debate among historians over the details of its evolution. Rather, I suggest that so-called moneyed men favored a capitalist economic system from at least the end of Revolution onward, and sporting culture helped incubate values that made the system more popular and ensured its rise over the course of the early nineteenth century. For more on this approach to capitalism and the historiographic debate over it, see Andrew Shankman, *Crucible of American Democracy: The Struggle to Fuse Egalitarianism and Capitalism in Jeffersonian Pennsylvania* (Lawrence, KS), 33–40, 225–46; Merrill and Wilentz, *The Key of Liberty*, 81–86.

23. Several studies have located sporting culture activities within "popular culture," and trace an evolution from "popular" to "mass" culture. However, recent work has made it clear that popular culture reached across class lines, so using the class-based term "popular" remains problematic for describing such practices and values. As a result, I discuss sporting culture as a subset of "public culture," and see mass culture as arising from this description of practices and values rooted in cross-class interaction and public space. For sources leading to these decisions, see David Brigham, *Public Culture in the Early Republic: Peale's Museum and Its Audience* (Washington, DC, 1995); Tim Harris, "Problematizing Popular Culture," in Tim Harris ed., *Popular Culture in England, 1500–1800* (London, 1998), 1–21; Brendan McConville, "Pope's Day Revisited, 'Popular Culture' Reconsidered," *Perspectives in Early American Culture* 4 (2000): 258–80.

24. This argument suggests that white men in early America recognized emerging class lines but saw sporting culture as a locus for challenging them by individually asserting their inclusion in the empowered status group of white men—in part because investors and managers constructed the discourse and experience of sporting culture to emphasize the individual pursuit of wealth and status. The modes of expressing masculine status were closely associated with class identity, so that "rough" manhood often connoted working-class rank and "genteel" manhood reflected the possession of capital. However, for reasons that evolved over time and that will be discussed throughout the book, white men of all classes increasingly saw sporting events as places where they could claim the benefits of asserting equality or superiority in both modes, regardless of their actual class position. In effect, then, the potential for "class consciousness" in the Marxist sense was defused by (and diffused into) the individual pursuit of manly "status," a term Max Weber used to describe a form of identity that crosses class lines because it is rooted in cultural values and "lifestyle" rather than only economic means. See Max Weber, *Economy and Society: An Outline of Interpretive Sociology*, ed. Guenther Roth (New York, 1968), 212–301; and Mills, *From Max Weber*, 181–94.

25. Tayloe to Baylor, March 21, 1771.

26. *The Cynick* (Philadelphia), September 21, 1811, 6.

27. For examples of works presenting a shift from a social order emphasizing class order to one emphasizing race and gender, see, most famously, Edmund Morgan's *American Slavery, American Freedom* (New York, 1975); but also Stephanie McCurry, *Masters of Small Worlds: Yeoman Households, Gender Relations, and the Political Culture of the Antebellum South* (New York, 1995); and David Waldstreicher, *In the Midst of Perpetual Fetes: The Making of American Nationalism, 1776–1820* (Chapel Hill, NC, 1997), 208–45, 332–48.

28. Adelman, *Sporting Time*, 186. For other studies of specific sporting activities positing the argument of increasingly class-specific sporting pursuits, see Stuart Blumin, *The Emergence of the Middle Class: Social Experience in the American City, 1760–1900* (New York, 1989); Peter Buckley, "To the Opera House: Culture and Society in New York City, 1820–1860" (Ph.D. dissertation, SUNY Stony Brook, 1984); Patricia Click, *The Spirit of the Times: Amusements in Nineteenth-Century Baltimore, Norfolk, and Richmond* (Charlottesville, VA, 1989); Elliott Gorn, *The Manly Art: Bare-Knuckle Prize Fighting in America* (Ithaca, NY, 1986); Lawrence Levine, *Highbrow/Lowbrow: The Emergence of Cultural Hierarchy in America* (Cambridge, MA, 1988); Scott C. Martin, *Killing Time: Leisure*

and Culture in Southwestern Pennsylvania, 1800–1850 (Pittsburgh, 1995); Bruce A. McConachie, *Melodramatic Formations: American Theatre and Society, 1820–1870* (Iowa City, 1992); Riess, *City Games*; Nancy Struna, *People of Prowess: Sport, Leisure, and Labor in Early America* (Urbana, IL, 1996), 119–42; Peter Thompson, *Rum Punch and Revolution: Taverngoing and Public Life in Eighteenth-Century Philadelphia* (Philadelphia, 1998). A handful of studies diverge from this trend, and so provide models for my analysis. In particular, see David Conroy, *In Public Houses: Drink and the Revolution of Authority in Colonial Massachusetts* (Chapel Hill, NC, 1995); Ann Fabian, *Card Sharps, Dream Books, and Bucket Shops: Gambling in Nineteenth-Century America* (Boston, 1990); Heather Nathans, *Early American Theatre from the Revolution to Thomas Jefferson: Into the Hands of the People* (Cambridge, UK, 2003).

29. Gilfoyle, *City of Eros*, 104. The second quote paraphrases a line from Stuart Hall that is the centerpiece of George Lipsitz's article "The Struggle for Hegemony," *Journal of American History* 75 (June 1988): 146–50. See also Gareth Stedman-Jones, "Class Expression versus Social Control? A Critique of Recent Trends in the Social History of Leisure," *History Workshop* 4 (1977): 162–70. For the links between Gramscian "hegemony" and Weberian "legitimacy," which explain how the pursuit of status could work to defuse class conflict, see M. F. N. Giglioli, *Legitimacy and Revolution in a Society of Masses: Max Weber, Antonio Gramsci, and the Fin-de-Siècle Debate on Social Order* (New Brunswick, NJ, 2013), 163–232.

30. Cohen et al., *Flash Press*, 39–53, 91.

31. My consideration of space as a framework for social interaction considers the evidence in light of two schools of thought. First, architectural historians have long claimed that the act of building is a "method of encoding and relating meanings for their efficient transfer to audiences." This communicative function of material culture establishes normative expectations but cannot completely force people to abide by its dicta. The normative patterns in the evidence, which correlate behavior with different categories of sporting space, then reflect sociologist Erving Goffman's concept of "social frames." Goffman argues that humans determine their social behavior from their interpretation of "frames," or categories of social interaction. People determine which frame is in play based on cues ranging from dress to tone of voice. Goffman does not pay much attention to space as a determinant, but the evidence of behavior in sporting space suggests that floor plan, architectural finish, and furnishings constituted a "grammar" that also communicated social frames to sporting participants. For architecture as language, see Bill Hillier and Julienne Hanson, *Decoding Homes and Houses* (Cambridge, UK, 1998), 22–27; Dell Upton, "Toward a Performance Theory of Vernacular Architecture: Early Tidewater Virginia as a Case Study," *Folklore Forum* 12 (1979): 173–96; Dell Upton, *Holy Things and Profane: Anglican Parish Churches in Colonial Virginia* (Boston, 1986), 101–62. For frames, see Erving Goffman, *Frame Analysis: An Essay on the Organization of Experience* (Cambridge, MA, 1974).

32. The literature proclaiming the influence of reform culture discipline in nineteenth-century America is vast. For examples portraying its influence on sport and the containment of risk in particular, see Blumin, *Emergence*, 190–230; Steven A. Riess, "The Rise of Respectable Sporting Culture, 1840–1870," in *The New American Sport History: Recent Approaches and Perspectives*, ed. S. W. Pope (Urbana, IL, 1997), 173–79; Richard Stott, *Jolly Fellows: Male Milieus in Nineteenth-Century America* (Baltimore, 2009). Much better at showing its incomplete influence, and thus supporting

my interpretation of the evidence in the coming pages, are Fabian, *Card Sharps*; Jackson Lears, *Something for Nothing: Luck in America* (New York, 2003); and Sandage, *Born Losers*.

33. The most prominent interpretations of gentility as a successful tool in the process of constructing deference to elite authority in the colonial period are Gordon Wood, *The Radicalism of the American Revolution* (New York, 1991), 24–92; and Richard L. Bushman, *The Refinement of America: Persons, Houses, Cities* (New York, 1993), 3–180.

34. *A Dialogue Shewing What's Therein to Be Found* (Philadelphia, 1725), and Robert Beverley to Landon Carter, August 1, 1763, both cited in Michael Zuckerman, "Tocqueville, Turner, and Turds: Four Stories of Manners in Early America," *Journal of American History* 85, no. 1 (June 1998): 22–23. See also Alan Tully, *Forming American Politics: Ideals, Interests, and Institutions in Colonial New York and Pennsylvania* (Baltimore, 1994), 370–73.

35. Joseph Dennie to his parents, April 25, 1793, cited in Gordon Wood, *The Radicalism of the American Revolution* (New York, 1992), 233; see also 305–25. Francis Grund, *The Americans in Their Moral, Social, and Political Relations* (London, 1837), 148; Thomas Hamilton, *Men and Manners in America* (London, 1834), 2:4. Horace Greeley, *Art and Industry: As Represented in the Exhibition at the Crystal Palace, New York* (New York, 1853), 231.

36. While I reject purely structural definitions of "sport" because they do not comport with evidence from the period, the traits described here do. For more about the freedom to engage as a distinguishing characteristic, see the following discussions of "play theory," all of which consider "sport" as a subtype of "play": Blanchard, *Anthropology of Sport*, 42–50; Roger Caillois, *Man, Play, and Games* (New York, 1961), 1–5; Johann Huizinga, *Homo Ludens: A Study of the Play-Element in Culture* (Boston, 1950), 7–12; Richard Schechner and Mady Schuman, eds., *Ritual, Play, and Performance: Readings in the Social Sciences/Theatre* (New York, 1976), 67–73, 89–96.

1. The Rise of Genteel Sport

1. *South Carolina Gazette*, February 13, 1762; June 5, 1762; January 29, 1763; November 12, 1764; August 31, 1765; March 21, 1768; March 30, 1769; August 2, 1770. Nicholas M. Butler, *Votaries of Apollo: The St. Cecilia Society and the Patronage of Concert Music in Charleston, South Carolina, 1766–1820* (Columbia, SC, 2007), 115–17, 132–34. Samuel Fisher Diary and Account Book, January 1, 1773, HSP. Alexander Mackraby to Sir Philip Francis, June 13, 1768, in "Philadelphia Society before the Revolution: Extracts from Letters of Alexander Mackraby to Sir Philip Francis," *Pennsylvania Magazine of History and Biography* 11 (1887): 281–82.

2. *South Carolina Gazette*, April 12, 1762; September 28, 1765; March 18, 1766; January 4, 1768; April 26, 1768; December 20, 1768. Benjamin Backhouse Inventory, Charleston County Inventory Books, 10:223–30, Charleston Public Library.

3. Bernard Bailyn, *Voyagers to the West: A Passage in the Peopling of America on the Eve of the Revolution* (New York, 1986), 24–28, 355–59; John J. McCusker and Russell R. Menard, *The Economy of British America, 1607–1789* (Chapel Hill, NC, 1985), 60, 129, 176, 186–87, 205, 320–21, 357. For Dillon's arrival, see *South Carolina Gazette*, February 13, 1762.

4. Elaine G. Breslaw, *Dr. Alexander Hamilton and Provincial America: Expanding the Orbit of Scottish Culture* (Baton Rouge, LA, 2008), 63–113.

5. Albert Bushnell Hart, ed., *Hamilton's Itinerarium; Being a Narrative of a Journey from Annapolis, Maryland, through Delaware, Pennsylvania, New York, New Jersey, Connecticut, Rhode Island, Massachusetts and New Hampshire, from May to September, 1744, by Doctor Alexander Hamilton* (St. Louis, MO, 1907), online at the Early Americas Digital Archive, http://mith.umd.edu//eada/html/display.php?docs=hamilton_itinerarium.xml, 58.

6. Ibid., 66.

7. Ibid., 579.

8. Ibid., 68, 64.

9. *South Carolina Gazette*, February 22, 1735. *New England Courant*, February 26, 1726.

10. "Diary of Samuel Sewall," *Collections of the Massachusetts Historical Society* (Boston, 1879), ser. 5, 6:419–21. Peter Thompson, *Rum Punch and Revolution: Taverngoing and Public Life in Eighteenth-Century Philadelphia* (Philadelphia, 1998), 103, 129–32; Nancy L. Struna, *People of Prowess: Sport, Leisure, and Labor in Early Anglo-America* (Urbana, IL, 1996), 153. Darrett B. Rutman and Anita H. Rutman, *A Place in Time: Middlesex County, Virginia 1650–1750* (New York, 1984), 138–41.

11. Jill Lepore, *New York Burning: Liberty, Slavery, and Conspiracy in Eighteenth-Century Manhattan* (New York, 2005), 5–15, 138–41. Philip D. Morgan, *Slave Counterpoint: Black Culture in the Eighteenth-Century Chesapeake and Lowcountry* (Chapel Hill, NC, 1998), 413–16. Sharon Salinger, *Taverns and Drinking in Early America* (Baltimore, 2002), 236.

12. Salinger, *Taverns and Drinking*, 48–50, 151–81. Thompson, *Rum Punch*, 51–74. Hart, *Hamilton's Itinerarium*, 13.

13. David W. Conroy, *In Public Houses: Drink and the Revolution of Authority in Colonial Massachusetts* (Chapel Hill, NC, 1995), 96–98. Thompson, *Rum Punch*, 93. Paton Yoder, "Tavern Regulation in Virginia: Rationale and Reality," *Virginia Magazine of History and Biography* 87 (July 1979): 259–64.

14. Peter Thompson, "'The Friendly Glass': Drink and Gentility in Colonial Philadelphia," *Pennsylvania Magazine of History and Biography* 113 (October 1989): 549–73. Hart, *Hamilton's Itinerarium*, 300, 455, 498.

15. *Diary of John Adams*, May 19, 1760, in *The Works of John Adams*, ed. Charles Francis Adams (Boston, 1850), 2:85. *New York Journal*, July 18, 1737. *Independent Reflector*, July 5, 1753. Robert Wormeley Carter Diaries, April 1, 1776, December 31, 1775, Carter Papers, CWM. Edmund S. Morgan, *Inventing the People: The Rise of Popular Sovereignty in England and America* (New York, 1988), 174–208.

16. Peter Clark, *The English Alehouse: A Social History, 1200–1830* (London, 1983), 131–51. Salinger, *Taverns and Drinking*, 220–26.

17. Marylynn Salmon, *Women and the Law of Property in Early America* (Chapel Hill, NC, 1986), 41–57. Alexandra Shepard, "From Anxious Patriarchs to Refined Gentlemen? Manhood in Britain, circa 1500–1700," *Journal of British Studies*, 44 (April 2005), 288–91. Nancy E. Wright, Margaret W. Ferguson, and A. R. Buck, eds., *Women, Property, and the Letters of the Law in Early Modern England* (Toronto, 2004), 66–94, 121–36.

18. J. Thomas Scharf and Thompson Westcott, *History of Philadelphia* (Philadelphia, 1884), 1:157. *American Weekly Mercury*, February 3, 1736.

19. Hart, *Hamilton's Itinerarium*, 146. Durand of Dauphine, *A Huguenot Exile in Virginia* (New York, 1934 [orig. The Hague, 1687]), 129.

20. *Statutes at-Large of Pennsylvania from 1682 to 1801* (Harrisburg, 1896), 5:108–11, 445–48. J. Thomas Jable, "Pennsylvania's Early Blue Laws: A Quaker Experiment in the Suppression of Sport and Amusements, 1682–1740," *Journal of Sport History* 1 (October 1974): 107–21. Struna, *People of Prowess*, 148–61.

21. J. Charles Cotton, *The Compleat Gamester; or, Instructions How to Play at All Manner of Usual and Most Genteel Games* (Barre, MA, 1970 [original 1674]). Louis B. Wright and Marion Tinling, eds., *The Secret Diary of William Byrd of Westover, 1709–1712* (Richmond, VA, 1941), 140–45, 441. H. Plumb, *The Commercialization of Leisure in Eighteenth-Century England* (Reading, UK, 1973), 12–19. Shepard, "Patriarchs to Gentlemen," 292–95.

22. Cotton, *Compleat Gamester*, 27–33. *Boston News-Letter*, October 7, 1731. *Pennsylvania Gazette*, September 4, 1760.

23. "Extracts from the Diary of Daniel Fisher, 1755," *Pennsylvania Magazine of History and Biography* 17 (October 1893): 264.

24. Brooks McNamara, *The American Playhouse in the Eighteenth Century* (London, 1969), 28–69. John Hervey, *Racing in America* (New York, 1944), 1:21–45, 97–108. *New York Mercury*, December 14, 1767.

25. For taverns, see Richard L. Bushman, *The Refinement of America: Persons, Houses, Cities* (New York, 1993), 160–61; Robert Graham, "The Taverns of Philadelphia," *Transactions of the American Philosophical Society* 43 (1953): 321–24. For theatres, see McNamara, *American Playhouse*, 49. For horse racing, see Minutes, September 8, 1767, September 26, 1769, Register Book, Philadelphia Jockey Club Papers (PJC), HSP.

26. *Boston News-Letter*, March 3, 1748. Odai Johnson, *Absence and Memory in Colonial American Theatre* (New York, 2006), 124–31. Alexander Mackay-Smith, *The Colonial Quarter Race Horse* (Richmond, 1983), 58–70. *New York Mercury*, July 2, 1753.

27. James Bullocke v. Matthew Slader, York County Deeds, Wills, and Orders, 1671–95, 84. Jonathan Andrews v. Thomas Davis, January 16, 1666, Accomack County Orders, 1666–70, 9, LV. Miles Cary v. Enos McIntosh, Warwick County Papers, Virginia Counties Collection, CWM. W. W. Hening, *The Statutes At-Large, Being a Collection of All the Laws of Virginia*, 18 vols. (Richmond, 1809–23), 4:46. T. H. Breen, "Horses and Gentlemen: The Cultural Significance of Gambling among the Gentry of Virginia," *William and Mary Quarterly* 3rd ser., 34 (April 1977): 242–50. Mackay-Smith, *Colonial Quarter Race Horse*, 5–18.

28. M. A. Bower, M. G. Campana, M. Whitten, C. J. Edwards, H. Jones, E. Barrett, R. Cassidy, E. R. Nisbet, E. W. Hill, C. J. Howe, and M. Binns, "The Cosmopolitan Maternal Heritage of the Thoroughbred Racehorse Breed Shows a Significant Contribution from British and Irish Native Mares," *Biology Letters* 7 (April 2011): 316–20. Struna, *People of Prowess*, 126–27.

29. *Pennsylvania Gazette*, May 10, 1770. Pierre-Joseph Boudier de Villemert, *The Ladies Friend, from the French of Monsieur de Gravines* (Philadelphia, 1771), 14–15. Minutes, September 8, 1767, Register Book, PJC. The literature on gentility is extensive, but for an overview of it in the colonial context, see Bushman, *Refinement*, 3–180; C. Dallett Hemphill, *Bowing to Necessities: A History of Manners in America, 1620–1860* (New York, 1999), 111–18; David S. Shields, *Civil Tongues and Polite Letters in British America* (Chapel Hill, NC, 1997), 99–179.

30. William Eddis, *Letters from America* (Cambridge, MA, 1969 [orig. 1792]), 48–49. *Pennsylvania Chronicle*, October 12, 1767. *Pennsylvania Packet*, March 21, 1774. *South Carolina Gazette*, April 18, 1761. Minutes, November 13, 1766, Register Book, PJC.

31. John Brewer, *The Pleasures of the Imagination: English Culture in the Eighteenth Century* (New York, 1997), 22, 82–84. Bushman, *Refinement*, xv, 69–74, 100–138.

32. *Independent Reflector*, July 5, 1753. For background on the DeLanceys, see Cathy D. Matson, *Merchants and Empire: Trading in Colonial New York* (Baltimore, 1998), 135, 168, 220; Alan Tully, *Forming American Politics: Ideals, Interests, and Institutions in Colonial New York and Pennsylvania* (Baltimore, 1994), 120–42, 242–46.

33. William Smith, *History of the Province of New-York* (London, 1757), 2:244–45. *New York Journal*, June 14, 1770. Bills and Receipts, March 14, 1768, April 27, 1768, April 12, 1768, James DeLancey Papers, NYHS. Francis Hopkinson, "The Cockfighter," unpublished ms. poem, 1770, NYHS.

34. Thomas Doerflinger, *A Vigorous Spirit of Enterprise: Merchants and Economic Development in Revolutionary Philadelphia* (Chapel Hill, NC, 1986), 41–42. Edward Countryman, "The Uses of Capital in Revolutionary America: The Case of the New York Loyalist Merchants," *William and Mary Quarterly*, 3rd ser., 49 (January 1992): 11–19. Robert Hull bill, December 1771–July 1772, Bills and Receipts, James DeLancey Papers, NYHS.

35. John Hervey, *Racing in America, 1655–1865* (New York, 1944), 1:30–47, 281–97. Minutes, September 26, 1769, October 10, 1770, 1773 Race Report, Register Book, PJC.

36. *New York Journal*, June 3, 1773. A Political Creed for the Day (New York, 1768).

37. Doerflinger, *A Vigorous Spirit*, 43–44. Jack Lindsay, "The Cadwalader Family: Art and Style in Early Philadelphia," *Philadelphia Museum of Art Bulletin* 91 (1996): 6–12.

38. Memorandum Book, October 17, 1771; Edward Lloyd to John Cadwalader, December 27, 1772, Gen. John Cadwalader Series, Cadwalader Family Papers, HSP. Minutes, July 1, 1768, December 28, 1772, Register Book, PJC.

39. For the first references to Cadwalader's racing, see John Craggs to John Cadwalader, March 11, 1785; Henry Ward Pearce to John Cadwalader, November 2, 1785, Gen. John Cadwalader Series, Cadwalader Family Papers, HSP.

40. For taverns, see Samuel Cardy v. Backhouse, April 17, 1763, Colonial Judgment Rolls, SCA; *Pennsylvania Gazette*, March 28, 1765; Thompson, *Rum Punch*, 64–72. For theatres, see Johnson, *Absence and Memory*, 61, 99, 107; McNamara, *American Playhouse*, 33, 45–47. For racing, see the annual expenses in Accounts, 1766–73, Register Book, PJC; *New York Gazette*, January 31, 1763; *South Carolina Gazette*, February 2, 1767. Here and throughout the book, sums are listed in colonial pounds unless designated as "sterling."

41. Doerflinger, *A Vigorous Spirit*, 65–66. Aubrey C. Land, "Economic Behavior in a Planting Society: The Eighteenth Century Chesapeake," *Journal of Southern History* 33 (November 1967): 473. In South Carolina, the wealthiest colony, the £300 sum was about the size of the average *estate*, amassed over a lifetime. Richard Waterhouse, "Economic Growth and Changing Patterns of Wealth Distribution in Colonial Lowcountry South Carolina," *South Carolina Historical Magazine* 89 (October 1988): 207.

42. Jessica Choppin Roney, *Governed by a Spirit of Opposition: The Origins of American Political Practice in Colonial Philadelphia* (Baltimore, 2014), 23–32, 95–96; Shields, *Civil Tongues*, 189–96.

43. Minutes, November 10, 1766, April 26, 1769, Register Book, PJC. *Maryland Gazette*, October 4, 1770. Edward Papenfuse, *In Pursuit of Profit: The Annapolis Merchants in the Era of the American Revolution, 1763–1805* (Baltimore, 1975), 32–34; James Haw, *Stormy Patriot: The Life of Samuel Chase* (Baltimore, 1980), 29.

44. *New York Mercury*, July 2, 1753. *Pennsylvania Gazette*, July 12, 1759. *New York Journal*, August 27, 1772. *Statutes at-Large of Pennsylvania*, 5:108–11. Salinger, *Taverns and Drinking*, 124–36, 148–50. Papenfuse, *In Pursuit of Profit*, 12, 31.

45. For subscribers, see Minutes, November 10, 1766, September 8, 1767, Register Book, PJC; *Maryland Gazette*, October 4, 1770; Deed, August 28, 1773, Charleston Land Records, Charleston Public Library.

46. Richard Lloyd to John Cadwalader, September 16, 1770, Gen. John Cadwalader Series, Cadwalader Family Papers, HSP. Accounts with Lyonel Lyde, Presly Thornton, and Charles Carter of Parke, John Tayloe II Account Book, 1749–68, Tayloe Family Papers, VHS.

47. William Milnor, *Memoirs of the Old Schuylkill Fishing Company and Gloucester Hunting Club* (Philadelphia, 1830), 1:31–36, 2:7–13. Samuel Morris Ledger, 1756–82, vol. 51, pp. 233–34, Morris Family Papers, HSP. John Cadwalader correspondence files for John Inglis, James Mease, George Mead, Robert Morris, and George Russell, Gen. John Cadwalader Series, Cadwalader Family Papers, HSP.

48. In sport as in business, what was reckless or wise was typically determined after the fact by the result, not at the moment the wager was laid. For this tendency in business, see Scott Sandage, *Born Losers: A History of Failure in America* (Cambridge, MA, 2005), 90–91.

49. Accounts, 1766–73, Register Book, PJC, HSP. *Maryland Gazette*, October 4, 1770; Thompson, *Rum Punch*, 106; Roney, *Spirit of Opposition*, 70–79.

50. *South Carolina Gazette*, August 17, 1773. Philadelphia Jockey Club members listed in Minutes, November 10, 1766, Register Book, PJC, were cross-referenced with the 1769 Proprietary Tax Roll and the 1774 Provincial Tax Roll for Philadelphia County, where thirty-five of eighty-two members were listed. The breakdown reveals many young members of middling wealth (who hailed from families of middling wealth and later became very wealthy), and a handful of older members with substantial wealth:

	OVER 30	UNDER 30	TOTAL
Over £115 (top 10% of wealth)	8	3	11
£17–£115 (next 23%)	3	6	9
18p–£17 (bottom 66%)	4	8	12
no tax	1	2	3
TOTAL	16	19	35

For the tax rolls, see *Pennsylvania Archives* (Harrisburg, 1852–1935), ser. 3, 14:149–303. For the divisions between deciles of taxable wealth, see Gary Nash, "Urban Wealth and Poverty in Pre-Revolutionary America," *Journal of Interdisciplinary History* 6 (April 1976): 552, 568.

51. For the partners, see Dunlop and Glenholme to Messrs. Bigger and Hulbert, July 4, 1767; Dunlop and Glenholme to Capt. James Blair, July 23, 1767, Orr, Dunlop, and Glenholme Letterbook (ODG), HSP; Doerflinger, *A Vigorous Spirit*, 12–15; Thomas

Truxes, *Irish-American Trade, 1660–1783* (Cambridge, UK, 2004), 69–71, 86–87. For Nesbit, Mease, and Morris, see Truxes, *Irish-American Trade*, 70–71, 117–22; Kerby Miller, Arnold Schrier, Bruce D. Boling, and David N. Doyle, eds., *Irish Immigrants in the Land of Canaan: Letters and Memoirs from Colonial and Revolutionary America, 1675–1815* (London, 2003), 538–39; Samuel Morris Ledger, 1756–82, 109, Morris Family Papers, HSP.

52. George Dunlop and William Glenholme to Andrew Orr, July 6, 1767, ODG. On the sporting presence of Nesbit, Mease, and Morris, see Minutes, November 10, 1766, Register Book, PJC; Milnor, *Memoirs*, 2:7.

53. William Glenholme to Andrew Orr, December 28, 1767, ODG. For Galloway, see Selim Studbook, 1763–83, Maryland State Archives, Annapolis; accounts with "Stewart and Richardson" in Samuel Galloway Ledger, 1753–79, Cheston-Galloway Papers, MDHS.

54. George Dunlop and William Glenholme to Andrew Orr, September 23, 1767, November 9, 1767, ODG.

55. Allan Silver, "Friendship in Commercial Society: Eighteenth-Century Social Theory and Modern Sociology," *American Journal of Sociology* 95 (May 1990): 1476–77, 1487.

56. "Reminiscences of Petersburg," *Petersburg Index*, October 10, 1868. Mike Huggins, *Flat Racing and British Society, 1790–1914: A Social and Economic History* (London, 2000), 129–31. For gambling laws, see National Institute for Law Enforcement and Criminal Justice, *The Development of the Law of Gambling, 1776–1976* (Washington, DC, 1977), 15–17, 238–47.

57. George Hume to Jonathan Hume, Aug. 22, 1754, in "Letters From and to George Hume," *Virginia Magazine of History and Biography* 20 (October 1912): 412–13. For regional conditions promoting this kind of gambling, see Doerflinger, *A Vigorous Spirit*, 47–57; John G. Kolp, *Gentlemen and Freeholders: Electoral Politics in Colonial Virginia* (Baltimore, 1998), 59–80.

58. Charles Jones, *Hoyle's Games Improved* (London, 1814), 465, 468. The rules printed here were passed by the Jockey Club at Newmarket in 1767, and governed racing in America and Britain until the 1830s. Dennis Brailsford, *A Taste for Diversions: Sport in Georgian* (Cambridge, UK, 1999), 152–64.

59. William Glenholme to Andrew Orr, December 16, 1767, ODG.

60. Truxes, *Irish-American Trade*, 69–71, 86, 113–15. William Glenholme to George Dunlop Sr., December 16, 1767; Glenholme to Greg, Cunningham, and Co., December 15, 1767, May 31, 1768, September 11, 1768, all in ODG.

61. Glenholme to Greg, Cunningham, and Co., December 15, 1767, September 11, 1768, October 18, 1768; Glenholme to Daniel McCormick, October 18, 1768, ODG. For more typical loans of horses, see John Tayloe II to John Baylor, August 14, 1770, Miscellaneous Papers, VHS; John Tayloe III to Charles Carnan Ridgely, June 21, 1794, Ridgely Family Papers, MDHS.

62. Glenholme to Greg, Cunningham, and Co., December 15, 1767, May 31, 1768, [undated] June 1768, September 24, 1768, October 18, 1768, ODG.

63. Glenholme to George Dunlop Sr., February 27, 1769, ODG. *Pennsylvania Gazette*, March 9, 1769.

64. For examples of professions that more clearly achieve goals of wealth and prestige by crafting a "professional" monopoly over certain types of work, see Paul Starr, *The Social Transformation of American Medicine* (New York, 1982); Richard Levy, "The

Professionalization of American Architects and Civil Engineers, 1865–1917" (Ph.D. dissertation, University of California–Berkeley, 1980). Most studies of professionalization indicate processes that begin in the middle of the nineteenth century. As sporting pros knew, being labeled a "professional" before that time was often more derogatory than complimentary.

65. Errol Hill, *The Jamaican Stage, 1655–1900: Profile of a Colonial Theatre* (Amherst, MA, 1992), 22–23, 76; Odai Johnson and William Burling, *The Colonial Stage, 1665–1774: A Documentary Calendar* (Cranbury, NJ, 2001), 184–85.

66. *Boston Gazette*, September 18, 1761. *New York Mercury*, July 2, 1753; October 16, 1758; November 6, 1758.

67. *New York Mercury*, November 6, 1758; December 11, 1758.

68. Alexander Garden to David Colden, February 1, 1764, reprinted in Johnson and Burling, *Colonial Stage*, 234. Johnson, *Absence and Memory*, 93–117; McNamara, *American Playhouse*, 46–69.

69. *Pennsylvania Gazette*, November 1, 1759; May 28, 1767. Deed, August 28, 1773, Charleston Land Records, Charleston Public Library.

70. *Virginia Gazette*, October 24, 1751. Johnson, *Absence and Memory*, 26–30.

71. Johnson, *Absence and Memory*, 31–37.

72. David Douglass to Philadelphia City Council, October 5, 1769, reprinted in Johnson and Burling, *Colonial Stage*, 349. Douglass to Thomas Bradford, June 2, 1770, unbound correspondence, Bradford Collection, HSP.

73. Johnson, *Absence and Memory*, 84–89.

74. Account with John William and James McCall, John Tayloe II Account Book, 1749–68, Tayloe Family Papers, VHS. Samuel Lyde to John Baylor, October 25, 1754, Baylor Family Papers, UVa. John Cadwalader, correspondence and accounts with John Hynson, 1769, Gen. John Cadwalader Series, Cadwalader Family Papers, HSP.

75. For the rise of black horsemen and integration among grooms and jockeys, see Edward Lloyd to Cadwalader, December 27, 1772; 1773 Race Report, Register Book, PJC; Mackay-Smith, *Colonial Quarter Race Horse*, 4. For the epithet of "jockey," see Gervase Markham, *The Complete Jockey; Or the Most Exact Rules and Methods to Be Observed for the Training Up of Race-Horses* (London, 1695), 48; *Pennsylvania Gazette*, June 7, 1759; July 18, 1765; July 28, 1773. For ads claiming runaway servants were posing as grooms, see *Pennsylvania Gazette*, November 29, 1756; August 6, 1761; June 3, 1773; *New York Post Boy*, January 8, 1750; *New York Mercury*, October 10, 1763; January 11, 1773. Runaway slaves did not pose as grooms, presumably because there were few free black grooms, and so posing as one would identify a runaway as a slave.

76. Account with William and McCall, John Tayloe II Account Book, 1749–68, Tayloe Family Papers, VHS. John Tayloe II to John Baylor, March 21, 1771, Baylor Family Papers, UVa.

77. John Tayloe II to John Baylor, August 14, 1770, VHS. John Cragg to John Cadwalader, March 11, 1785, Cadwalader Family Papers, HSP. *Maryland Gazette*, March 9, 1786; December 1, 1791; March 21, 1793.

78. *Federal Gazette* (Baltimore), April 26, 1800; July 8, 1800. James Long v. Andrew Buchanan, John H. Stone, and Walter Dorsey, December 28, 1799; Edward Edwards v. Andrew Buchanan, John H. Stone, and Walter Dorsey, May 17, 1800, Chancery Court Records, Maryland State Archives.

79. Allen Jones Davie, "Quarter Racing of the Olden Time," *American Turf Register and Sporting Magazine*, May 1832, 450–52; Katherine C. Mooney, *Race Horse Men: How Slavery and Freedom Were Made at the Racetrack* (Cambridge, MA, 2014), 1–18.

80. Minutes, October 10, 1772, Register Book, PJC. Jacob Cox Parsons, ed., *Extracts from the Diary of Jacob Hiltzheimer of Philadelphia, 1765–1798* (Philadelphia, 1893), 6, 11, 13–15, 26, 153. Jacob Hiltzheimer Diary, February 16, 1771, May 20, 1771, October 12, 1771, March 2, 1772, HSP.

81. Parsons, *Extracts from Hiltzheimer*, 21; Milnor, *Memoirs*, 13. For the derogatory appellation of "gentleman horse jockey," see William Taplin, *The Gentleman's Stable Directory* (Philadelphia, 1794), 13.

82. For Dillon's previous career, see Letters, Navy Board Records, Records of the Admiralty, 106/1110/30, August 18, 1753, National Archives (UK), Kew. For his legal actions, see Robert Dillon v. Richard King, April 1, 1765; Dillon v. Robert Middleton, October 20, 1767; Dillon v. Luke Stotenburgh, October 3, 1769; Dillon v. Peter Valton, May 5, 1772, all in Colonial Judgment Rolls, SCA. *South Carolina Gazette*, May 10, 1770. For Dillon's acquisition of land, see South Carolina Deed Abstracts, D3:337, March 29, 1765, G3:379, May 21, 1767, R3:69, July 5, 1770, Charleston Public Library.

83. *Backhouse*, April 17, 1763; James Moultrie v. Backhouse, November 17, 1763; William Piper, Thomas Williamson, and Joseph White v. Benjamin Backhouse, March 1, 1765; and Benjamin Backhouse v. Benjamin Matthews, June 1, 1767, Colonial Judgment Rolls, SCA. *South Carolina Gazette*, September 4, 1767. Will of Katherine Backhouse, October 23, 1767, Charleston Will Books 11:186, SCA.

84. *New York Post-Boy*, June 3, 1751. Samuel Galloway Ledger, 1748–58, 72, Cheston-Galloway Papers, MDHS. Hunter Dickinson Farish, ed., *Journal and Letters of Philip Vickers Fithian: A Plantation Tutor of the Old Dominion, 1773–1774* (Charlottesville, VA, 1957), 244–45.

85. Mary Harriman to John Baylor, January 28, 1757, Baylor Family Papers, VHS.

86. *South Carolina Gazette*, February 9, 1769.

87. *South Carolina Gazette*, February 9, 1769, February 16, 1769.

88. Robert Gay Accounts, 1769–73; John Hynson to John Cadwalader, April 13, 1769, Gen. John Cadwalader Series, Cadwalader Family Papers, HSP.

89. 1773 Race Report, Register Book, PJC. *South Carolina Gazette*, February 9, 1769.

90. 1773 Race Report, Register Book, PJC. Thomas Jones Account, 1775–80, James DeLancey Papers, NYHS.

91. George C. Rogers and David R. Chesnutt, eds., *The Papers of Henry Laurens* (Columbia, SC: 1976), 5:28. Maurie D. MacInnis, *In Pursuit of Refinement: Charlestonians Abroad, 1740–1860* (Columbia, SC, 1999), 112.

2. A Revolution in Sporting Culture

1. *South Carolina Gazette*, October 31, 1765.

2. *South Carolina Gazette*, October 31, 1765. Henry Laurens to Joseph Brown, October 22, 1765, in *The Papers of Henry Laurens*, ed. George C. Rogers and David R. Chesnutt (Columbia, SC, 1976), 5:27–28.

3. Laurens to Brown, October 22, 1765, October 28, 1765, *Papers*, 5:27–28, 29–32; Laurens to John Lewis Gervais, January 29, 1766, *Papers*, 5:52. Daniel J. McDonough,

Christopher Gadsden and Henry Laurens: The Parallel Lives of Two American Patriots (Cranbury, NJ, 2000), 101, 109, 197–200.

4. *South Carolina Gazette*, October 31, 1765.

5. G. D. Scull, "The Montresor Journals," *Collections of the New-York Historical Society* 14 (1881): 357–58. *New York Mercury*, May 5, 1766. Odai Johnson, *Absence and Memory in Colonial American Theatre* (New York, 2006), 193–98.

6. Undated playbill quoted in Johnson, *Absence and Memory*, 196. *New York Gazette*, November 7, 1765.

7. Scull, "Montresor Journals," 358. Gary Nash, *The Urban Crucible: Social Change, Political Consciousness, and the Origins of the American Revolution* (Cambridge, MA, 1979).

8. *New York Post-Boy*, May 8, 1766. John Watts to Robert Monckton, December 30, 1765, quoted in Joseph S. Tiedemann, *Reluctant Revolutionaries: New York City and the Road to Independence, 1763–1776* (Ithaca, NY, 1997), 83.

9. *New York Post-Boy*, May 8, 1766. *New York Gazette*, May 12, 1766. *Maryland Gazette*, May 22, 1766. Scull, "Montresor Journals," 364.

10. For the tactics and goals of crowd action, see George Rudé, *The Crowd in History: A Study of Popular Disturbances in France and England, 1730–1848* (London, 1981), 235–61.

11. *New York Mercury*, May 3, 1762; May 3, 1773. *Pennsylvania Gazette*, October 28, 1772; December 10, 1772.

12. Ticket requests, "Miscellaneous" Folders, Unbound Correspondence, Bradford Collection, HSP. *Pennsylvania Gazette*, December 22, 1768; November 4, 1772. Minutes, September 29, 1768, Register Book, Philadelphia Jockey Club Papers (PJC), HSP.

13. Henry Laurens to James Smith, February 8, 1769, *Papers*, 6:267–68. Charles Cotton, *The Compleat Gamester; or, Instructions How to Play at All Manner of Usual and Most Genteel Games* (Barre, MA, 1970 [orig. 1674]), 32–33. Richard Seymour, *The Compleat Gamester* (London, 1739), 270. For the range of society in the public rooms of coffeehouses and upscale taverns, see advertisements to apply for jobs and travel, as in *New York Mercury*, October 7, 1772; Peter Thompson, *Rum Punch and Revolution: Taverngoing and Public Life in Eighteenth-Century Philadelphia* (Philadelphia, 1998), 91–93.

14. Jack P. Greene, ed., *Diary of Landon Carter of Sabine Hall, 1752–1778* (Charlottesville, VA, 1965), August 12, 1778, 2:1143.

15. Donald Jackson, ed., *The Diaries of George Washington* (Charlottesville, VA, 1976), 1:99, 2:247. Lucia C. Stanton, ed., *Thomas Jefferson's Memorandum Books: Accounts, with Legal Records and Miscellany, 1767–1826* (Princeton, NJ, 1997), 73–81. Thomas Bradford, Memo Book, December 6, 1766; January 30, 1767; February 13, 1767; April 1767, Bradford Collection, HSP. Thompson, *Rum Punch*, 89–98.

16. Lincoln Macveagh, ed., *The Journal of Nicholas Cresswell, 1774–1777* (New York, 1924), 52–53. Hunter Dickinson Farish, ed., *Journal and Letters of Philip Vickers Fithian: A Plantation Tutor of the Old Dominion, 1773–1774* (Charlottesville, VA, 1957), 73–75, 232–33. *Essex (MA) Gazette*, January 24, 1769. Peter Thompson traces how drunkenness became considered ungenteel in "'The Friendly Glass': Drink and Gentility in Colonial Philadelphia," *Pennsylvania Magazine of History and Biography* 113 (October 1989): 569–73.

17. Minutes, November 13, 1766, August 18, 1767, May 12, 1772, Register Book, PJC. *South Carolina Gazette*, April 4, 1768.

18. Cotton, *Compleat Gamester*, 27–33. Edward Hotaling, *The Great Black Jockeys: The Lives and Times of the Men Who Dominated America's First National Sport* (Rocklin, CA, 1999), 297–98. Joseph Addison, Richard Steele, and Eustace Budgell, *The Spectator* (London, 1737), 182. *Pennsylvania Gazette*, January 22, 1767.

19. Richard L. Bushman, *The Refinement of America: Persons, Houses, Cities* (New York, 1993), 100–127, 169–80; Dell Upton, *Holy Things and Profane: Anglican Parish Churches in Colonial Virginia* (New Haven, CT, 1997), 101–73.

20. *New York Mercury*, March 8, 1762. Johnson, *Absence and Memory*, 68–69; Brooks McNamara, *The American Playhouse in the Eighteenth Century* (London, 1969), 48, 52–58, 69.

21. Minutes, September 8, 1767, September 22, 1767, Register Book, PJC. David W. Conroy, *In Public Houses: Drink and the Revolution of Authority in Colonial Massachusetts* (Chapel Hill, NC, 1995), 257–58; John L. Cotter, Daniel G. Roberts, and Michael Parrington, *The Buried Past: An Archaeological History of Philadelphia* (Philadelphia, 1994), 162–70.

22. *Maryland Gazette*, June 13, 1771. Minutes, November 10, 1766, August 18, 1767, June 12, 1769, December 28, 1772, Register Book, PJC.

23. "Quaker Address," January 4, 1770, Petitions, HSP. "A Tender and Affectionate Caution from Our Yearly Meeting of Ministers and Elders," September 24, 1764, Pemberton Papers, HSP. *South Carolina Gazette*, February 28, 1774. Joseph Taylor to Peter Taylor, June 27, 1764, Taylor Family Papers, SCL.

24. Odai Johnson and William Burling, *The Colonial Stage, 1665–1774: A Documentary Calendar* (Cranbury, NJ, 2001), 46, 55. Selim Studbook, Maryland State Archives.

25. John Tayloe II Account Book, 1749–68, Tayloe Papers, VHS. John Tayloe II to John Baylor, August 14, 1770, VHS. Edward Lloyd to John Cadwalader, December 27, 1772, General John Cadwalader Series, Cadwalader Family Papers, HSP.

26. Ellen Carter Bruce Baylor Commonplace Book, 1752–1906, 27, VHS. Thomas Katheder, *The Baylors of Newmarket: The Decline and Fall of a Virginia Planter Family* (Bloomington, IN, 2009), 1–13.

27. Account folios 114, 119, 124, 133, John Baylor Ledger, 1732–55, Baylor Family Papers, UVa. John Baylor to Lyonel Lyde, June 17, 1752; Baylor to G. [Alexander] Spotswood, June 28, 1763; and Baylor to Thomas Hales, August 3, 1761, John Baylor Letterbook, LV. Edmund Jenings to S. Bordley, February 26, 1755, Edmund Jenings Letterbook, 1753–69, VHS.

28. Not all of the £3,000 sum was due to horse business, but the introduction of commercial breeding drastically increased the income expected from that line of work. John Baylor to Messrs. Sydenham and Nodgson, August 6, 1763; Baylor to John Backhouse, September 3, 1764, Baylor Letterbook, LV. For planters' income, see Aubrey C. Land, "Economic Behavior in a Planting Society: The Eighteenth Century Chesapeake," *Journal of Southern History* 33 (November 1967): 472–73.

29. Samuel Lyde to John Baylor, October 25, 1754, Baylor Family Papers. John Baylor to John Backhouse, August 28, 1768; Baylor to G. Spotswood, August 6, 1763; and Baylor to John Backhouse, June 24, 1763, Baylor Letterbook, LV.

30. Katheder, *Baylors*, 27. Baylor Commonplace Book, 19–26. W. W. Hening, *The Statutes At-Large, Being a Collection of All the Laws of Virginia*, 18 vols. (Richmond, 1809–23), 7:563–69.

31. John Baylor to Messrs. Flowerdew and Norton, September 16, 1760; and Baylor to John Backhouse, July 18, 1764, September 3, 1764, Baylor Letterbook, LV.

32. Baylor Commonplace Book, 20. "Grandeur in Caroline," *Virginia Historical Society Bulletin* 9 (October 1964): 3–4. For the regional economy in the 1760s, see Allan Kulikoff, *Tobacco and Slaves: The Development of Southern Cultures in the Chesapeake, 1680–1800* (Chapel Hill, NC, 1986), 120–31.

33. John Hervey, *Racing in America* (New York, 1944), 1:281–90. John Randolph of Roanoke, Studbook, 25, VHS. *Virginia Gazette,* April 20, 1769. *Pennsylvania Gazette,* March 16, 1767; March 21, 1768. For the blockade and inflation, see Richard Buel Jr., *In Irons: Britain's Naval Supremacy and the American Revolutionary Economy* (New Haven, CT, 1998), 21–24, 35, 66–68. John J. McCusker, *How Much Is That in Real Money? A Price Index for Use as a Deflator of Money Values* (Worcester, MA, 2001), 324–25.

34. John Tayloe II Account Book. For the taxable wealth of breeding clients, I cross-referenced breeding entries in the account book with the Personal Property Tax Records for Richmond County (1782) and Charles City (1783), LV.

35. Peyton Skipwith Ledger, 1762–85, Skipwith Papers, CWM. Mecklenburg County Personal Property Tax Records, 1782, LV. Stephen Cocke Account Books, 1777–78, 1778–79, Cocke Family Papers, VHS. Amelia County Personal Property Tax Records, 1782, LV. Louisa County Personal Property Tax Records, 1782. Ledger A, 1785–97, Robert Gay Account, 129, John Steele Papers, SHC.

36. Account with John Wheldon, John Tayloe II Account Book. Robert Wormeley Carter Diary, March 22, 1777, Carter Papers, CWM.

37. "Liberty" Accounts, Lewis Holladay Account Book, 1788–92, Holladay Family Papers, VHS.

38. National Institute for Law Enforcement and Criminal Justice, *The Development of the Law of Gambling: 1776–1976* (Washington, DC, 1977), 15–17, 238–47.

39. *Boston Post-Boy,* September 9, 1754, reprinted from the satirical London newspaper *The Connoisseur,* May 9, 1754. Nancy L. Struna, *People of Prowess: Sport, Leisure, and Labor in Early Anglo-America* (Urbana, IL, 1996), 100–104.

40. The 1749 manual is reprinted in Reginald Heber, *An Historical List of Horse-Matches Run and of Plates and Prizes Run for in Great-Britain and Ireland in 1751* (London, 1752), 151–52. Robert Wormeley Carter to John Minor, June 11, 1792, Carter Papers, LV.

41. For honor, see Kathleen Brown, *Good Wives, Nasty Wenches, and Anxious Patriarchs: Gender, Race, and Power in Colonial Virginia* (Chapel Hill, NC, 1996), 166–78; Joanne Freeman, *Affairs of Honor: National Politics in the New Republic* (New Haven, CT, 2002), xiii–xxiii; Bertram Wyatt-Brown, *Southern Honor* (New York, 2007), xxxiv–xxxv, 14–34.

42. Peter Randolph to William Byrd III, September 20, 1757, William Byrd Papers, VHS. "Journal of a French Traveller in the Colonies, 1765," *American Historical Review* 26 (July 1921): 741–42. Cotton, *Compleat Gamester,* iv.

43. Marion Tinling, ed., *The Correspondence of the Three William Byrds of Westover, Virginia, 1684–1776* (Charlottesville, VA, 1977), 610–13; "Letters of the Byrd Family," *Virginia Magazine of History and Biography* 37 (October 1929): 300–314.

44. "Letters of the Byrd Family, Continued," *Virginia Magazine of History and Biography* 38 (January 1930): 59–60.

45. *South Carolina Gazette,* January 12, 1769; February 9, 1769. Keith Krawczynski, *William Henry Drayton: South Carolina Revolutionary Patriot* (Baton Rouge, 2001), 29–36.

46. Krawczynski, *William Henry Drayton,* 32–37.

47. Edward Fenwick v. William Henry Drayton, February 12, 1771; Elizabeth Holmes v. William Henry Drayton, February 12, 1771; Walter Mansell, Thomas Corbett, and William Roberts v. William Henry Drayton, February 14, 1771; and Susannah Damaris De St. Julien v. William Henry Drayton, January 1, 1771, Judgment Rolls, SCA. John Drayton to James Glen, June 15, 1770, June 11, 1771, Drayton Papers Collection, SCA. Krawczynski, *William Henry Drayton*, 36–37.

48. John Drayton to James Glen, undated [1774]; Glen to Drayton, undated [1774], Drayton Papers Collection. McDonough, *Christopher Gadsden and Henry Laurens*, 107–9. Krawczynski, *William Henry Drayton*, 36–37, 95–103.

49. *Letters of Delegates to Congress, 1774–1789* (Washington, DC, 1986), 13:135–36. *Gazette of the State of South Carolina*, October 13, 1779. Krawczynski, *William Henry Drayton*, 100, 121–22, 315–17.

50. "Letters of the Byrd Family," 310–13.

51. John Drayton, *Memoirs of the American Revolution* (Bedford, MA, 2009 [orig. 1821]), 2:212.

52. T. H. Breen, "Horses and Gentlemen: The Cultural Significance of Gambling among the Gentry of Virginia," *William and Mary Quarterly*, 3rd ser., 34 (April 1977): 243–48. Wyatt-Brown, *Honor*, 339–50. Kenneth S. Greenberg, *Honor and Slavery: Lies, Duels, Noses, Masks, Dressing as a Woman, Gifts, Strangers, Death, Humanitarianism, Slave Rebellions, the Pro-Slavery Argument, Baseball, Hunting, and Gambling in the Old South* (Princeton, NJ, 1996), 115–46; Rhys Isaac, *The Transformation of Virginia, 1740–1790* (Chapel Hill, NC, 1982), 90–110. For the suggestion that "comparable patterns" existed in the North, see Jackson Lears, *Something for Nothing: Luck in America* (New York, 2003), 70; Struna, *People of Prowess*, 120–25.

53. "A Petition from the Sundry Inhabitants of the City of Philadelphia," 1752, *Pennsylvania Archives* (Harrisburg, 1838–1935), ser. 4, 4:3483–95. *The Acts of the General Assembly of the Province of New-Jersey* (Philadelphia, 1752), 243. Thomas Cooper, ed., *The Statutes at Large of South Carolina* (Columbia, SC, 1837), 2:517–18; 4:158–62.

54. Jackson, *Diaries of Washington*, 2:99, 126, 213, 221, 3:55–56, 136. Stanton, *Jefferson's Memorandum Books*, 81, 139, 140, 147, 150, 252, 259. Robert Wormeley Carter Diary, 1768, Carter Papers, CWM. Jack P. Greene, ed., *Diary of Landon Carter of Sabine Hall, 1752–1778* (Charlottesville, VA, 1965), June 16, 1774, 830.

55. "William Gregory's Journal," *William and Mary Quarterly*, 1st ser., 13 (April 1905): 228. Jacob Hiltzheimer Diary, September 14, 1771, HSP. Thompson, *Rum Punch*, 104–5. See also Alexander Graydon, *Memoirs of a Life, Chiefly Passed in Pennsylvania within the Last Sixty Years* (Harrisburg, PA, 1811), 97.

56. *Pennsylvania Gazette*, September 4, 1760; October 9, 1760. *Gentlemen's Magazine* (London), November 1760, 593. Thompson, *Rum Punch*, 105.

57. *South Carolina Gazette*, August 22, 1771. Peter Manigault to Ralph Izard, August 24, 1771, in "The Letterbook of Peter Manigault," *South Carolina Historical Magazine* 70 (1969): 189–90.

58. *Boston Post-Boy*, July 20, 1767. Calling these taverns "private" refers to their illicit status, in contrast to calling licensed taverns "public houses."

59. *New York Gazette*, March 21, 1757. *Boston Evening Post*, September 11, 1769. *Pennsylvania Gazette*, December 27, 1764. Freeman, *Affairs of Honor*, 170–72.

60. For sporting taverns, see *Pennsylvania Gazette*, March 8, 1759; August 23, 1764; March 28, 1765; *Newport Mercury*, April 6, 1767; *Royal Gazette* (New York), July 18, 1779;

Virginia Gazette, August 4, 1774; *Maryland Gazette,* January 13, 1757. Compare them to ads for genteel taverns in the *Pennsylvania Gazette,* April 19, 1753; September 23, 1762; *New York Journal,* December 10, 1770; *Boston Evening Post,* May 17, 1762; *Virginia Gazette,* October 17, 1771. For the exception that proves the rule, see *South Carolina Gazette,* November 30, 1767, in which Henry Gray announces that he has taken over Backhouse's tavern, refers to it as "genteel," and promises to promote "civil treatment" and "good cheer." Yet Gray was short on resources and specifically noted that "it cannot be expected that the house will be furnished in the elegant manner part of it formerly was." Noting that only part of Backhouse's facility met genteel standards and then failing to clear that bar may help explain why Gray failed and left the facility less than a year later.

61. Robert Graham, "The Taverns of Philadelphia," *Transactions of the American Philosophical Society* 43 (1953): 323–24. Thompson, *Rum Punch,* 150–51. *Gentlemen's Magazine* (London), November 1760, 593.

62. *New York Journal,* February 4, 1768. *New York Gazette and Weekly Post-Boy,* March 26, 1770; October 22, 1770. *New York Gazette,* May 19, 1774. *Royal Gazette* (New York), July 18, 1779. *South Carolina Gazette,* February 24, 1732; September 4, 1767.

63. *Pennsylvania Gazette,* September 20, 1744; April 12, 1750; April 19, 1753; January 20, 1757; March 8, 1759; January 24, 1760; September 23, 1762; August 23, 1764; March 28, 1765; June 12, 1766; November 3, 1769; June 27, 1771.

64. *South Carolina Gazette,* November 30, 1767. Benjamin Backhouse Inventory, September 22, 1767, Inventory Books, 10:176–80, SCA. *Pennsylvania Gazette,* July 16, 1747; February 6, 1750; July 8, 1762; June 29, 1769. For average tenures, see Conroy, *In Public Houses,* 146; Sharon Salinger, *Taverns and Drinking in Early America* (Baltimore, 2002), 171; Struna, *People of Prowess,* 146; Thompson, *Rum Punch,* 216–17.

65. For price of secondhand billiard tables, see "Narrative of George Fisher," *William and Mary Quarterly,* 1st ser., 17 (October 1908): 133–34. Fisher's billiard table cost just five pounds less than his annual rent. For sales volumes, see Thompson, *Rum Punch,* 64–72. For Backhouse, see Benjamin Backhouse v. Robert Howard, 1765, Judgment Rolls, SCA; Salinger, *Taverns and Drinking,* 173.

66. *New York Mercury,* June 30, 1766. *New York Journal,* April 20, 1769; May 31, 1770; July 12, 1770; August 23, 1770; July 11, 1771. *New York Gazette,* May 19, 1774; May 8, 1775. *Harper's New Monthly Magazine* (March 1882): 499.

67. For the narrowing clienteles of common taverns, see Salinger, *Taverns and Drinking,* 226–39; Thompson, *Rum Punch,* 145–81.

68. Graydon, *Memoirs,* 60–61, 69–71.

69. *Virginia Gazette,* April 4, 1766. *New York Journal,* March 24, 1768; April 5, 1770; July 21, 1774.

70. *Pennsylvania Gazette,* May 19, 1773. Whitehead Humphreys, *An Epistle from Titus to Timothy* (Philadelphia, 1781). Thompson, *Rum Punch,* 174–76. Steven Rosswurm, *Arms, Country, and Class: The Philadelphia Militia and the "Lower Sort" during the American Revolution, 1775–1783* (New Brunswick, NJ, 1987), 216–17.

71. *Journals of the Continental Congress, 1774–1789* (Washington, DC, 1904–37), 1:78.

72. Josiah Tucker, *A Letter from a Merchant in London to His Nephew in America, Relative to the Present Posture of Affairs in the Colonies* (London, 1766), 28. Ann Withington, *Toward a More Perfect Union: Virtue and the Formation of American Republics* (New York, 1991), 3–19.

73. H. Trevor Colbourn, ed., "A Pennsylvania Farmer at the Court of King George: John Dickinson's London Letters, 1754–1756," *Pennsylvania Magazine of History and Biography* 86 (October 1962): 421. Johnson and Burling, *Colonial Stage*, 230. *Virginia Gazette*, April 2, 1772. *Pennsylvania Chronicle*, February 23, 1767. Jason Shaffer, *Performing Patriotism: National Identity in the Colonial and Revolutionary American Theater* (Philadelphia, 2007), 18–28, 38–100.

74. *New York Post-Boy*, April 18, 1763. *New York Gazette*, May 16, 1768. Jacob Cox Parsons, ed., *Extracts from the Diary of Jacob Hiltzheimer of Philadelphia, 1765–1798* (Philadelphia, 1893), 20.

75. *Pennsylvania Chronicle*, May 23, 1768. See also *Massachusetts Spy*, December 26, 1771; *The School for Scandal, A Comedy* (Philadelphia, 1779). This approach emerged in England a few years earlier, as outlined in Kenneth Cohen, "'Sport for Grown Children': American Political Cartoons, 1790–1850," *International Journal of the History of Sport* (May 2011): 1301–6. For analogies to theatre as opposed to racing, see Jeffrey Richards, *Theatre Enough: American Culture and the Metaphor of the World Stage, 1607–1789* (Durham, NC, 1991), 201–64.

76. *Pennsylvania Gazette*, November 20, 1766. Peter Shaw, *American Patriots and Rituals of the Revolution* (Cambridge, MA, 1981), 11–12, 193. William Pencak, "Play as Prelude to Revolution: Boston, 1765–1776," in *Riot and Revelry in Early America*, ed. William Pencak, Matthew Dennis, and Simon Newman (University Park, PA, 2002), 125–55.

77. *Massachusetts Centinel*, October 27, 1787, Allister Chang, "The Opening of Galleries at the Massachusetts House of Representatives in 1766" (undergraduate honors thesis, Tufts University, 2012), 1–16.

78. *Pennsylvania Gazette*, October 28, 1772. Thompson, *Rum Punch*, 102. Peter Saunders to Major Isaac Harleston, undated, Harleston Family Papers, SCHS.

79. *New York Chronicle*, May 15, 1769. *New York Mercury*, May 3, 1773. Bernard Bailyn, *The Ordeal of Thomas Hutchinson* (Cambridge, MA, 1976), 242.

80. John Adams to Abigail Adams, July 7, 1774, in L. Kinvin Wroth and Hiller B. Zobel, eds., *Legal Papers of John Adams* (New York, 1968) 1:40. Ann Hulton to Mrs. Lightbody, January 31, 1774 in Ann Hulton, *Letters of a Loyalist Lady* (Cambridge, MA, 1927), 69–72.

81. Tiedemann, *Reluctant Revolutionaries*, 184–219. McDonough, *Christopher Gadsden and Henry Laurens*, 133–34. Rosswurm, *Arms, Country, and Class*, 39–45. Charles Thomson to Messrs. Welsh, Wilkinson, & Co., November 7, 1765, in *Collections of the New-York Historical Society* 11 (New York, 1879): 5.

82. Thompson, *Rum Punch*, 168–71. Salinger, *Taverns and Drinking*, 151–209.

83. *New York Gazette*, December 2, 1765. *New York Journal*, May 19, 1774; June 2, 1774; July 21, 1774. *South Carolina Gazette*, October 31, 1765. McDonough, *Christopher Gadsden and Henry Laurens*, 104–8.

84. Graydon, *Memoirs*, 117–19. Conroy, *In Public Houses*, 253–309; Benjamin Carp, *Rebels Rising: Cities and the American Revolution* (New York, 2007), 62–98; Rhys Isaac, "Dramatizing the Ideology of Revolution: Popular Mobilization in Virginia, 1774 to 1776," *William and Mary Quarterly*, 3rd ser., 33 (July 1976): 364.

85. Johnson, *Absence and Memory*, 89–92. Hervey, *Racing*, 1:115. *Statutes at-Large of Pennsylvania* (Harrisburg, 1896), 9:333–38, 12:313–23. *Statutes of South Carolina*, 4:394–95, 405; *Statutes at-Large of Virginia* (New York, 1823), 10:205–6.

86. Benjamin H. Irvin, *Clothed in Robes of Sovereignty: The Continental Congress and the People Out of Doors* (New York, 2011), 133–238. David Waldstreicher, *In the Midst of Perpetual Fetes: The Making of American Nationalism, 1776–1820* (Chapel Hill, NC, 1997), 17–52, 216.

87. Benjamin Irvin, "The Streets of Philadelphia: Crowds, Congress, and the Political Culture of Revolution, 1774–1783," *Pennsylvania Magazine of History and Biography* 129 (January 2005): 12–20. Susan Klepp, "Rough Music on Independence Day: Philadelphia, 1778," in Pencak et al., *Riot and Revelry*, 156–72; John K. Alexander, "The Fort Wilson Incident of 1779: A Case Study of the Revolutionary Crowd," *William and Mary Quarterly*, 3rd ser., 31 (October 1974): 589–612; Dirk Hoerder, *Crowd Action in Revolutionary Massachusetts: 1765–1780* (New York, 1977), 354–62.

88. For the dominant emphasis on republican ideology and traditional demonstrations, such as "riding skimmington" and tarring-and-feathering, as the primary sources and models for colonial dissent, see Gordon Wood, *The Radicalism of the American Revolution* (New York, 1991), 89–195; Alfred Young, "English Plebeian Culture and Eighteenth-Century American Radicalism," in Margaret Jacob and James Jacob, eds., *The Origins of Anglo-American Radicalism* (London, 1984), 185–212. Recently, taverns have gained attention as places where these elements came to life in the resistance movement, but the broader panoply of sporting culture has not been included, and even these studies of taverns miss the sporting elements of experiences there. For examples, see Carp, *Rebels Rising*, 62–98; Conroy, *In Public Houses*; and Thompson, *Rum Punch*.

89. Christopher Gadsden to William Henry Drayton, June 15, 1778; "To the Public," May 6, 1784, in *The Writings of Christopher Gadsden*, ed. Richard Walsh (Columbia, SC, 1966), 131–33, 200–239.

3. Sport Reborn

1. Vernon F. Snow, ed., "The Grand Tour Diary of Robert C. Johnson, 1792–1793," *Proceedings of the American Philosophical Society* 102 (February 1958): 73, 76. Eliza Southgate Browne, *A Girl's Life Eighty Years Ago* (New York, 1887), 160. 1792 Tontine Agreement, reprinted in Joseph Alfred Scoville, *The Old Merchants of New York City* (New York, 1885), 4:119–24. *The Papers of Alexander Hamilton*, ed. Harold C. Syrett (New York, 1967), 12:421–23.

2. New York City Municipal Archives. *Minutes of the Common Council of the City of New York, 1784–1831* (New York, 1930), 2:150. Heather Nathans, *Early American Theatre from the Revolution to Thomas Jefferson: Into the Hands of the People* (New York, 2003), 142–43. *Diary of William Dunlap* (New York, 1931), 211.

3. Dunlap, *Diary*, 1:202–5, 211, 225, 161. New York City Property Tax Records, 1789, New York City Municipal Archives.

4. Dunlap, *Diary*, 1:202–6. For Dunlap's debts, see *Diary*, 1:76, 80, 93, 136–39, 160.

5. Dunlap, *Diary*, xx. Joseph Ellis, *After the Revolution: Profiles of Early American Culture* (New York, 1979), 137–58.

6. *Pennsylvania Evening Herald*, November 23, 1785; November 26, 1785. John Hall Diary, November 15–17, 1785, LCP. For past petitions, see *Pennsylvania Archives* (Philadelphia, 1854), ser. 1, 9:573, 10:141–43.

7. Bernard Bailyn, *The Ideological Origins of the American Revolution* (Cambridge, MA, 1992 [orig. 1967]), 344–53. Drew R. McCoy, *The Elusive Republic: Political Economy in Jeffersonian America* (Chapel Hill, NC, 1980), 48–75.

8. *Pennsylvania Evening Herald*, May 14, 1785; March 8, 1786. Johann David Schoepf, *Travels in the Confederation*, ed. Alfred J. Morrison (Philadelphia, 1911 [orig. 1784]), 380.

9. General Account of Receipts and Disbursements, New-York Theatre, 1782, NYHS. Robert Hunter, *Quebec to Carolina in 1785–1786* (San Marino, CA, 1943), 251. Leonard Marbury to William Gibbons, October 6, 1785, William Gibbons Papers, Duke. Susanne K. Sherman, *Comedies Useful: Southern Theatre History: 1775–1812* (Williamsburg, VA, 1998), 21–41, 51–72, 88.

10. Hall Diary, November 15–17, 1785.

11. Thomas Doerflinger, *A Vigorous Spirit of Enterprise: Merchants and Economic Development in Revolutionary Philadelphia* (Chapel Hill, NC, 1986), 261, 277, 297. Forrest McDonald, *We the People: The Economic Origins of the Constitution* (New Brunswick, NJ, 1991), 176. Janet Wilson, "The Bank of North America and Pennsylvania Politics: 1781–1787," *Pennsylvania Magazine of History and Biography* 66, no. 1 (January 1942): 3–28.

12. Richard Buel Jr., *In Irons: Britain's Naval Supremacy and the American Revolutionary Economy* (New Haven, CT, 1998), 151–53, 202–6, 228–39; Doerflinger, *Vigorous Spirit*, 296–310.

13. *Pennsylvania Gazette*, September 30, 1785. *Pennsylvania Packet*, March 31, 1785. *Philadelphia Independent Gazeteer*, September 3, 1785. *Pennsylvania Evening Herald*, May 10, 1786. *The Proceedings Relative to Calling the Conventions of 1776 and 1790 . . . together with the Charter to William Penn, the Constitutions of 1776 and 1790, and a View of the Proceedings* (Harrisburg, 1825), 325.

14. *Pennsylvania Gazette*, September 7, 1785. *Pennsylvania Evening Herald*, November 26, 1785.

15. Mathew Carey, ed., *Debates and Proceedings of the General Assembly, on the Memorials Praying a Repeal or Suspension of the Law Annulling the Charter of the Bank* (Philadelphia, 1786), 10, 53–54. *Pennsylvania Gazette*, September 7, 1785.

16. Jean-Christophe Agnew, *Worlds Apart: The Market and the Theater in Anglo-American Thought, 1550–1750* (New York, 1986). For the quote, see James Wilson, *Considerations on the Bank of North America* (Philadelphia, 1785), 7.

17. *Pennsylvania Evening Herald*, November 23, 1785.

18. Carey, *Debates*, 10, 21. *Pennsylvania Evening Herald*, November 23, 1785; May 10,1786.

19. *Pennsylvania Evening Herald*, February 18, 1786; September 30, 1786. *Pennsylvania Gazette*, April 7, 1786.

20. *Pennsylvania Gazette*, April 17, 1786. Wilson, "Bank of North America," 23–28.

21. Clinton Rossiter, ed., *The Federalist Papers* (New York, 1961 [orig. 1788]), 77–83. Benjamin Hichborn, *An Oration, delivered July 5th 1784 . . . in Celebration of the Anniversary of American Independence* (Boston, 1784), 19. *Pennsylvania Gazette*, February 17, 1789.

22. Rossiter, *Federalist Papers*, 188, 377. This interpretation avoids the sense of dramatic partisan differences over a transition from "republicanism" to "capitalism" that dominated much of the scholarship on the political economy of the early republic during the 1980s and 1990s. It builds on works that focus on the political origins of capi-

talism and its values, rather than the philosophical roots of the system or the debate over the degree to which it was realized in this era. For key examples, see Mark E. Kann, *A Republic of Men: The American Founders, Gendered Language, and Patriarchal Politics* (New York, 1998), 14–15, 119–21; Dana D. Nelson, *National Manhood: Capitalist Citizenship and the Imagined Fraternity of White Men* (Durham, NC, 1998), 45–48; and Andrew Shankman, *Crucible of American Democracy: The Struggle to Fuse Egalitarianism and Capitalism in Jeffersonian Pennsylvania* (Lawrence, KS), 33–40, 225–46.

23. *The Speech of John Gardiner, Esq; Delivered in the House of Representatives, on Thursday the 26th of January, 1792, on the Subject of the Report of the Committee Appointed to Consider the Expediency of Repealing the Law against Theatrical Exhibitions within This Commonwealth* (Boston, 1792), 4–6. William Haliburton, *Effects of the Stage on the Manners of a People and the Propriety of Encouraging and Establishing a Virtuous Theatre* (Boston, 1792), 29–30, 36. T. A. Milford, "Boston's Theater Controversy and Liberal Notions of Advantage," *New England Quarterly* 72 (March 1999): 61–88; For examples from other cities, see *City Gazette* (Charleston, SC), February 28, 1787; *Pennsylvania Packet*, February 17, 1789.

24. "Proposals by Messers Wignell and Reinagle for Erecting a Theatre in Philadelphia," October 17, 1791, Chestnut Street Theatre, Society Small Collection, HSP. *New Theatre Resolutions and Articles of Agreement Entered into and Adopted by the Proprietors* (Philadelphia, 1799). *Maryland Journal and Baltimore Advertiser*, August 19, 1794. "Hallam & Hodgkinson Proposal," ca. 1794–95, NYHS. Elisha Sigourney Account, 1796–98, Box D33, Federal Street Theatre Papers, Boston Theatre Collection, BPL. Martin Staples Shockley, "The Proprietors of Richmond's New Theatre of 1819," *William and Mary Quarterly*, 2nd ser., 19 (July 1939): 302–3.

25. *American Citizen and General Advertiser* (New York), February 16, 1801. Petition for Racing from Bergen, Somerset, Middlesex, and Hunterdon Counties, Petitions, October 1822, NJA. *Poulson's American Daily Advertiser* (Philadelphia), October 15, 1811. *Boston Gazette*, October 17, 1811. Colonial jockey clubs had used "improvement of the breed" to justify their existence but had not gone so far as to insert that purpose into their organizations' titles. For an example, see *Pennsylvania Gazette*, August 31, 1761.

26. "Subscription for the Race Ground," Tappahannock Jockey Club Record Book, Tayloe Papers, VHS. "Abstract of Title," South Carolina Jockey Club Records, SCHS. *City Gazette* (Charleston, SC), January 15, 1793. See also "Petersburg Jocky Club Book, 1785," *William and Mary Quarterly*, 2nd ser., 18 (April 1938): 210–11; *Alexandria Times*, May 14, 1798.

27. Minutes, May 9, 1826, Richmond Jockey Club Records, VHS. *Richmond Enquirer*, October 18, 1805; October 10, 1806; April 17, 1807; September 30, 1807; April 22, 1808; May 3, 1808; September 6, 1811. *Petersburg Intelligencer*, September 9, 1808. Annual Financial Statements, St. Stephen's Jockey Club Records, 1791–1853, SCHS. "Subscription for the Race Ground," Tappahannock Jockey Club Record Book. *Rules and Regulations of the Easton Jockey Club* (Easton, MD, 1818), 4–6. Minutes, October 9, 1826, Norfolk Jockey Club Minute Book, VHS.

28. *Richmond Enquirer*, September 24, 1805. Minutes, October 19, 1826, Norfolk Jockey Club Minute Book, VHS. *Rules and Regulations of the Easton Jockey Club*, 4–5, 6. John Tayloe III to William Weatherby, June 1, 1801, John Tayloe III Letterbook, Tayloe Papers, VHS. William Taplin, *The Gentleman's Stable Directory* (Philadelphia, 1794), 7–14. *Correspondence of Andrew Jackson*, ed. John Spencer Bassett, (Washington, DC, 1926–35), 1:111.

29. For natural aristocracy, see Kann, *Republic of Men*, 115–19; Gordon Wood, *Empire of Liberty: A History of the Early American Republic, 1789–1815* (New York, 2009), 234.

30. Brooks McNamara, *The American Playhouse in the Eighteenth Century* (London, 1969), 104–54. Dunlap, *Diary*, 1:225. "Proposals by Messers Wignell and Reinagle." Nathans, *Early American Theatre*, 51–60.

31. *Pennsylvania Gazette*, September 5, 1792. *New York Magazine* (April 1794): 3–4. Moreau de St. Mery, *Moreau de St. Mery's American Journey, 1793–1798* (Garden City, NJ, 1947), 345–47. *Columbian Centinel* (Boston), January 29, 1794. McNamara, *American Playhouse*, 104–26. For these distinctions continuing into the 1810s, see Joseph Cowell, *Thirty Years Passed among the Players in England and America* (1979 [orig. 1844]), 57.

32. *Dunlap's American Daily Advertiser* (Philadelphia), February 4, 1793; McNamara, *American Playhouse*, 124.

33. *Boston Gazette*, October 7, 1811; October 17, 1811. *City Gazette* (Charleston, SC), February 26, 1816. Minutes, November 22, 1797, Tappahannock Jockey Club Record Book. See also *Rules and Regulations of the Easton Jockey Club*, 4–5; *Rules and Regulations of the Washington Jockey Club* (Washington, DC, 1821), 5–6.

34. *Boston Gazette*, October 17, 1811.

35. *Pennsylvania Packet*, February 17, 1789.

36. For lists of trustees and other subscribers, see Nathans, *Early American Theatre*, 173–80. "Proposals by Messers Wignell and Reinagle"; Bill on Bank of North America, April 13, 1792; and "At a Meeting of the Subscribers . . . ," June 22, 1792, Chestnut Street Theatre, Society Small Collection, HSP. *New Theatre Resolutions*. Minutes, Proprietors' Meeting, December 10, 1796, Box C10, Federal Street Theatre Papers, Boston Theatre Collection, BPL. *Olympic Theatre Proceedings, Resolutions, Deeds and Declaration of Trust* (Philadelphia, 1819). Shockley, "Proprietors," 302–3; Richard Philip Sodders, "The Theatre Management of Alexandre Placide in Charleston, 1794–1812" (Ph.D. dissertation, Louisiana State University, 1983), 92. Tappahannock Jockey Club Record Book. St. Stephens Jockey Club Records, SCHS. "Abstract of Title," South Carolina Jockey Club Records, SCHS. "Petersburg Jocky Club Book, 1785," 210–14. *Rules and Regulations of the Washington Jockey Club*, 11–12. I cross-referenced these rosters against the following tax lists and property assessments: Philadelphia City Property Tax Records, 1791, 1799, 1823, HSP; New York City Property Tax Records, 1789, New York City Municipal Archives; Boston Tax Assessors Books, 1792, 1795 (microfilm, BPL); and Richmond City Personal Property Tax records, 1819, LV. In South Carolina, where tax records from the period no longer exist, I used property evaluations in the 1790 and 1800 South Carolina Censuses, Charleston and St. James Goose Creek Schedules.

37. A. Glenn Crothers, "Banks and Economic Development in Post-Revolutionary Northern Virginia, 1790–1812," *Business History Review* 73 (April 1999): 1–39. Naomi Lamoreaux, *Insider Lending: Banks, Personal Connection, and Economic Development in Industrial New England* (New York, 1994), 11–23. Robert E. Wright, "Bank Ownership and Lending Patterns in New York and Pennsylvania, 1781–1831," *Business History Review* 73 (April 1999): 40–60.

38. Nathans, *Early American Theatre*, 173–80. For the term "merchant-planter" and the related term of "planter-businessman," see Laura Croghan Kamoie, *Irons in the Fire:*

The Business History of the Tayloe Family and Virginia's Gentry, 1700–1860 (Charlottesville, VA, 2007), 1–40.

39. *City Gazette* (Charleston, SC), February 13, 1793. For Morris, see "Proposals by Messers Wignell and Reinagle," October 17, 1791, and "Trustees New Theatre" Account Book, 1791–92, Chestnut Street Theatre, Society Small Collection, HSP; John Brown Account Book, 1774–76, 1783–87, HSP; Robert Morris to James Gibson, February 16, 1799, June 14, 1799, June 19, 1799, James Gibson Papers, HSP; Ronald M. Baumann, "John Swanwick: Spokesman for 'Merchant-Republicanism' in Philadelphia, 1790–1798," *Pennsylvania Magazine of History and Biography* 97 (April 1973): 131–82; Doerflinger, *Vigorous Spirit*, 296–329.

40. *Columbian Herald* (Charleston, SC), February 14, 1788. *City Gazette* (Charleston, SC), October 10, 1790; March 21, 1793. *Petersburg Intelligencer*, October 26, 1802. Stateburgh Jockey Club Papers, 1786–88, Singleton Papers, SHC. Tappahannock Jockey Club Record Book. St. Stephens Jockey Club Records, SCHS.

41. Timothy Tickler, *The Philadelphia Jockey Club; or, Mercantile Influence Weighed* (Philadelphia, 1795). This pamphlet borrowed its title and message from a similar polemic published in London. *Easton Jockey Club*, 4. *Richmond Enquirer*, March 24, 1808. *Constitution of the Missouri Association for the Improvement of the Breed of Horses* (St. Louis, 1835), 7. Annual Accounts, St. Stephen's Jockey Club Papers, 1811–36. For the cost of theatre subscriptions, see "Trustees New Theatre" Account Book; Nathans, *Early American Theatre*, 139.

42. John Hood, *Index of Colonial and State Laws of New Jersey, 1663–1903* (Camden, NJ, 1905), 53, 549. *Acts of the General Assembly of the State of New Jersey* (Trenton, NJ, 1797), 193–94.

43. *Report of the Trials of Dr. John Strattan, Dr. Benjamin Budd, Joseph Merit, Jesse White, and Samuel Hewlings Who Were Brought before Josiah Foster Esq. on an Information for Being Concerned in Horse-Racing* (Burlington, NJ, 1803), 3.

44. Hood, *Laws of New Jersey*, 193–94. *Report of the Trials*, 5, 8.

45. *Report of the Trials*, 6–10. Harriet Russell Stratton, *A Book of Strattons, Being a Collection of Stratton Records . . .* (New York, 1908), 235.

46. *Report of the Trials*, 9–10.

47. John Lardner to Alexander Graydon, May 26, 1792, John Lardner Series, Lardner Family Papers, HSP. *Statutes-at-Large of Pennsylvania* (Harrisburg, 1911), 12:313. Hood, *Laws of New Jersey*, 550–52. See also Charleston Grand Jury Presentments, 1798, SCA.

48. *Pennsylvania Evening Herald*, August 20, 1785. 1796 Evesham Township Tax Assessment, and Burlington County Tax Ratables, General Assembly Records, NJA.

49. John Tayloe II to George William Fairfax, December 14, 1773, Tayloe Papers, VHS. Laura Croghan Kamoie, "Three Generations of Planter-Businessmen: The Tayloes, Slave Labor, and Entrepreneurialism in Virginia, 1710–1830" (Ph.D. dissertation, College of William and Mary, 1999), 159–60.

50. Julian Ursyn Niemcewicz, *Under Their Vine and Fig Tree; Travels through America in 1797–1799, 1805, with Some Further Account of Life in New Jersey* (Elizabeth, NJ, 1965), 75.

51. Niemcewicz, *Under Their Vine*, 19. For Tayloe's annual gross income from horses for 1802, see his Account Book, 1801–4, 11, 52, 66, 139, Tayloe Papers, VHS. For the comparison to land rents, see Kamoie, "Three Generations," 166, 208.

52. John Tayloe III to William Weatherby, June 1, 1801, July 15, 1801, John Tayloe III Letterbook, Tayloe Papers, VHS. John Hoomes to Robert Burton, November 2, 1802; Hoomes to James Brown, October 5, 1801, John Hoomes Papers, Duke.

53. Stud Broadside, "Young Emperor" (Platt Kill, NY, 1796), Zinman Collection of Broadsides, HSP. "Liberty" Accounts, Holladay Family Papers, VHS.

54. Peyton Skipwith to Ezekial Smith, April 30, 1785, Correspondence, Skipwith Papers, CWM. For other examples demonstrating the national scope of this trend, see *Virginia Herald*, April 17, 1797; *City Gazette* (Charleston, SC), March 2, 1798; Stud Broadsides for "Feather" (Goshen, CT, 1797) and "Creeper" (Litchfield, CT, 1797), Zinman Collection, LCP.

55. Kamoie, "Three Generations," 160-212.

56. Jean B. Russo, "A Model Planter: Edward Lloyd IV of Maryland, 1770-1796," *William and Mary Quarterly*, 3rd ser., 49 (January 1992): 62-88. Slave Lists and Inventories, V6, Lloyd Family Papers, MDHS.

57. Minutes, May 8, 1797, May 13, 1799, June 20, 1800, Tappahannock Jockey Club Record Book, 1786-1801. John Tayloe III Account Book, 1793-1800, 71; John Tayloe III Account Book, 1801-4, 14, 18; John Tayloe III Daybook, 1798, passim, Tayloe Papers, VHS. For other examples, see Henry Ravenel Jr. Daybook, October 23, 1809, September 4, 1817, October 20-22, 1817, March 16-17, 1818, Thomas P. Ravenel Collection, SCHS. Annual reports, 1817-22, St. Stephen's Jockey Club Records, 1791-1853, SCHS. Stateburgh Jockey Club Papers, 1786-88, Singleton Family Papers, SHC.

58. For crops, see John Tayloe III Account Book, 1801-4, 14; "Gwinfield" and "Old House" annual crop sales, John Tayloe III Account Book, 1789-1828, Tayloe Papers, VHS; Kamoie, "Three Generations," 172. For training, see John Tayloe III to William Fitzhugh, June 10, 1801; Tayloe to J. Butter, June 12, 1801; and Tayloe to John Stith, July 15, 1801, John Tayloe III Letterbook, Tayloe Papers, VHS. John Tayloe III Daybook, November 8, 1798, Tayloe Papers, VHS.

59. Thomas Cooper, ed., *The Statutes at Large of South Carolina* (Columbia, SC, 1837), 4:405. Virginia was one of the few states that never illegalized racing, only gambling on races. William Waller Hening, *The Statutes at-Large . . . of Virginia* (New York, 1823), 10:205. There were northern leading owners, just not many. Most northern thoroughbreds came from the South rather than England, fueling the Southern majority of leading owners. But for examples of two Northerners, Abraham Skinner and John Hunt, who did import and operate like leading owners, see "Comet" (East Hartford, CT, 1795), "Creeper" (Litchfield, CT, 1797), "Creeper" (Hardwick, MA, 1799), and "All Fours" (Claverack, CT, 1800), Zinman Collection, LCP; Ralph Phillips account with John W. Hunt, 1803-6, Unger Collection, HSP.

60. John Tayloe III to Charles Carnan Ridgely, June 21, 1794, Charles Carnan Ridgely Papers, Ridgely Family Papers, MDHS. Tayloe to William Weatherby, June 1, 1801, John Tayloe III Letterbook, Tayloe Papers; John Hoomes to Lamb and Younger, June 15, 1801, Hoomes Papers, Duke. For independent grooms in this era besides Craggs, see *Columbian Herald* (Charleston, SC), March 30, 1789; *Maryland Journal*, May 11, 1790.

61. John Tayloe III to Charles Carnan Ridgely, June 21, 1794, William Alston Studbook, 87, SCHS. John M. Garrard to Andrew Jackson, July 2, 1805, in *Correspondence of Andrew Jackson*, ed. John Spencer Bassett (Washington, DC, 1926-35), 1:116. John Tayloe III Daybook, April 7, 1798; Mount Airy Inventory Book, 1808-27, Tayloe

Papers, VHS. James Chesnutt to Richard Singleton, March 4, 1809, Richard Singleton Correspondence, Singleton Family Papers, SHC.

62. For Tayloe's total investment, see John Tayloe Inventory Book, 1808–27, Tayloe Papers, VHS; Mutual Assurance Policy #228, February 27, 1797, LV. For the other men's similarity to Tayloe, see Deed of Sale, March 20, 1820, "Horse Notes," Steele Papers, SHC; Allen Davie to Richard Singleton, January 1, 1810; Harry Heth to Richard Singleton, August 23, 1819, Family Correspondence, Singleton Family Papers, SHC. Wade Hampton to John Bynum, September 9, 1803, in *Family Letters of the Three Wade Hamptons, 1782–1901*, ed. Charles E. Cauthen (Columbia, SC, 1953), 6. "John Hoomes' Stud Book," *American Turf Register and Sporting Magazine*, November 1830, 99–104.

63. Peter O'Kelly to John Tayloe III, December 10, 1798, John Tayloe III Correspondence, Tayloe Papers, VHS. For race results, see "Horse Notes," Steele Papers, SHC; *Richmond Enquirer*, October 10, 1806, May 5, 1809, May 10, 1811, October 8, 1811; *Virginia Gazette & General Advertiser*, March 9, 1805 (report from Charleston). For more variety among winners before the leading owners consolidated their dominance, see William Bolling Diaries, May 27–29, 1794, May 28–30, 1795, VHS; *City Gazette* (Charleston, SC), February 16, 1792, February 15, 1793, February 18, 1796.

64. John N. Davis to Richard Singleton, November 24, 1819. Jonathan R. Spann to Richard Singleton, August 27, 1819, Correspondence, Singleton Family Papers, SCL. George P. Tayloe to William Henry Tayloe, January 1, 1833, William Henry Tayloe Correspondence, Tayloe Papers, VHS. Melvin L. Adelman, *A Sporting Time: New York City and the Rise of Modern Athletics, 1820–1870* (Urbana, IL, 1990), 34–38.

65. For examples of lesser and marginal owners' buying and breeding from leading owners, see Ledger A, 1785–97, John Steele Papers, SHC; Robert A. Jones Account Book, 1817–29, 336, SHC. John Randolph of Roanoke, Studbook, 11–16, 41–47, VHS. Stateburgh Jockey Club Papers, 1786–88, Singleton Family Papers, SHC. "Comet" (East Hartford, CT, 1795); "Creeper" (Hardwick, MA, 1799); and "All-Fours" (Claverack, NY, 1800), Zinman Collection, LCP. Daniel Brodhead Stud Book, 1799–1802, Brodhead Family Papers, Winterthur.

66. Stud broadsides, "Horse Notes," Steele Papers, SHC. See also "Young Herod" (Connecticut, 1800), Zinman Collection.

67. Kamoie, "Three Generations," 160–212; For sales of export goods to fund horse purchases, see John Tayloe III Account Book, 1793–1800, 50, 170; Account Book, 1801–4, 19, Tayloe Papers. Robert Ackerman, *Wade Hampton III* (Columbia, SC, 2007), 5.

68. Hallam to Bradford, August 24, 1785. Indenture for the Theatre, April 1, 1785, Legal Documents, Bradford Family Papers, HSP.

69. Lewis Hallam Jr. to Thomas Bradford, undated (1793–94); Hallam to Bradford, undated (February 17, 1785–91); Hallam to Bradford, undated (September 16, 1793–94); Hallam to Bradford, undated (April 19, 1794–96); and Hallam to Bradford, undated (August 21, 1785–1800), Unbound Correspondence, Bradford Collection, HSP. Hallam to Bradford, August 29, 1794, Dreer Collection, HSP.

70. Hallam to Bradford, undated (August 31, 1785–88); Hallam to Bradford, undated (November 15, 1785–90), Unbound Correspondence, Bradford Collection, HSP.

71. "Memoirs and Recollections by Thomas Bradford," Bradford Collection; Eric Foner, *Tom Paine and Revolutionary America* (New York, 1976), 192–203.

72. "Memoirs and Recollections by Thomas Bradford." John Hodgkinson, *A Narrative of his Connection with the Old American Company from the Fifth September 1792 to*

the Thirty-First of March 1797 (New York, 1797), 7–8. Hallam to Bradford, undated (November 1785–94); Hallam to Bradford, undated (November 15, 1785–94), Unbound Correspondence, Bradford Collection.

73. Hallam to Bradford, undated (November 15, 1785–94), Unbound Correspondence, Bradford Collection. James S. Bost, *Monarchs of the Mimic World; or, The American Theatre of the Eighteenth Century through the Managers—The Men Who Made It* (Orono, ME, 1977), 144–45; "Proposals by Messers Wignell and Reinagle."

74. Peter Early to James Gibson, January 17, 1793, Society Collection, HSP. Dunlap, *Diary*, 1:49, 51, 216. Hodgkinson, *Narrative*, 5.

75. For the failed subscription, see Hallam to Bradford, undated (June 27, 1794–95), Unbound Correspondence, Bradford Collection, HSP; "Hallam & Hodgkinson" Broadside, ca. 1794–95, NYHS. For Hallam's buyout, see Dunlap, *Diary*, 1:47, 52, 216, 218.

76. Hallam to Bradford, August 5, 1801, Unbound Correspondence, Bradford Collection, HSP. Dunlap, *Diary*, 1:278.

77. Thomas Bradford to Mr. North, August 8, 1801, Unbound Correspondence, Bradford Collection. William Dunlap, *History of the American Theatre* (New York, 1832), 2:159, 234–39.

78. Charles William Janson, *The Stranger in America* (London, 1807), 253. John Bernard, *Retrospections of America, 1797–1811* (New York, 1887), 76, 312, 340–43. James Fennell, *An Apology for the Life of James Fennell* (Philadelphia, 1814), 342–56, 360–63.

79. Dunlap, *Diary*, 1:77. For investors prioritizing short-term dividends, see Elisha Sigourney Account, 1796–98, BPL; Leases, April 7, 1800, March 21, 1806, Boxes C14–18, Federal Street Theatre Papers, Boston Theatre Collection, BPL. *Olympic Theatre Proceedings, Resolutions, Deeds and Declaration of Trust* (Philadelphia, 1819), 25; *1821 Alterations and Amendments to the Olympic Theatre Declaration of Trust* (Philadelphia, 1821), 9; Francis C. Wemyss, *Twenty-Six Years of the Life of an Actor and Manager* (New York, 1846), 233, 325–26; William B. Wood, *Personal Recollections of the Stage* (Philadelphia, 1855), 248.

80. Hood, *Laws of New Jersey*, 267–68. *The Statutes at Large of South Carolina* (Columbia, SC, 1837), 5:431–33. *Statutes-at-Large of Pennsylvania*, 15:115. John Haywood, ed., *A Manual of the Laws of North Carolina* (Raleigh, NC, 1819), 250–53. Samuel Shepherd, *The Statutes at Large of Virginia, 1792 to 1806* (New York, 1970), 2:75–76. Victor Stein and Paul Rubino, *The Billiard Encyclopedia* (Minneapolis, MN, 1996), 22–23. For the arguments against gambling, see Ann Fabian, *Card Sharps, Dream Books, and Bucket Shops: Gambling in Nineteenth-Century America* (Boston: 1990), 39–56, 66.

81. *Massachusetts Magazine*, August 1789, 508–12. *Olive Branch* (Sherburne, NY), October 22, 1806. *Statutes-at-Large of Pennsylvania*, 15:113–15. *Statutes of South Carolina*, 5:432–33.

82. Charleston Grand Jury Presentments, 1817, SCA. Isaac Weld, *Travels through the States of North America* (New York, 1968 [orig. 1799]), 1:191. John Lardner to Alexander Graydon, May 26, 1792, John Lardner Series, Lardner Family Papers, HSP. *New Haven Gazette*, August 16, 1787.

83. As one example, eight charges were brought in New York City in 1807, but none in 1808 or 1809. *Minutes of the Common Council of the City of New York, 1784–1831* (New York, 1930), 4: 571, 575, 663, 677. Similar binges occurred in the South, too. See "Halifax County, Virginia, Indictments, 7 Apr. 1809," *Southsider Genealogy Magazine* 1 (1982):

13–23. For connected players and tavernkeepers escaping charges, see William P. Palmer, ed., *Calendar of State Papers of Virginia* (New York, 1968) 4:436.

84. Jacob Cox Parsons, ed., *Extracts from the Diary of Jacob Hiltzheimer, of Philadelphia, 1765–1798* (Philadelphia, 1893), 145. Paul B. Moyer, *The Public Universal Friend: Jemima Wilkinson and Religious Enthusiasm in Revolutionary America* (Ithaca, NY, 2015), 67–78, 94–100.

85. *Philadelphia Gazette*, December 14, 1797. *Claypoole's Gazette* (Philadelphia), August 6, 1785; July 4, 1799.

86. *Boston Gazette*, July 4, 1814. Thomas Garrett, "A History of Pleasure Gardens in New York City, 1700–1865," (Ph.D. dissertation, New York University, 1978). Geraldine A. Duclow, "Philadelphia's Early Pleasure Gardens," in *Pleasure Gardens*, ed. Stephen M. Vallillo and Maryann Chach (New York, 1998), 1–11.

87. *New York Evening Post*, August 15, 1804. *Claypoole's Advertiser* (Philadelphia), October 18, 1791. *Federal Gazette* (Philadelphia), February 28, 1798. Duclow, "Pleasure Gardens," 5–11. Peter Thompson, *Rum Punch and Revolution: Taverngoing and Public Life in Eighteenth-Century Philadelphia* (Philadelphia, 1998), 182–204.

88. Robert Bailey, *The Life and Adventures of Robert Bailey, from His Infancy Up to December, 1821* (Richmond, 1822), 160. *American Watchman* (Wilmington, DE), March 5, 1814. Robert C. Smith, "A Portuguese Naturalist in Philadelphia, 1799," *Pennsylvania Magazine of History and Biography* 78 (January 1954): 91. *New York Public Advertiser*, July 14, 1812. *Common Council of New York*, 4:571, 677, 6:788, 8:651.

89. *New York Herald*, August 31, 1808.

90. Duclow, "Pleasure Gardens," 1–11; Garrett, "Pleasure Gardens in New York," 205–377; Katy Matheson, "Niblo's Garden and Its 'Concert Saloon,' 1828–1846," in Vallillo and Chach, *Pleasure Gardens*, 82–83. For differences in the South, see Nicholas M. Butler, *Votaries of Apollo: The St. Cecilia Society and the Patronage of Concert Music in Charleston, South Carolina, 1766–1820* (Columbia, SC, 2007), 176–77; Susanne K. Sherman, *Comedies Useful: Southern Theatre History: 1775–1812* (Williamsburg, VA, 1998), 161–62, 196; Sodders, "Theatre Management," 137, 158, 192, 252.

91. For Soria, see *Poulson's Advertiser* (Philadelphia), August 8, 1801; *Public Advertiser* (New York), October 16, 1807; I. Harold Sharfman, *Jews on the Frontier* (Chicago, 1977), 139–40. For others, see Bailey, *Life and Adventures*, 48–49, 160; *Charleston (SC) Courier*, February 14, 1809; *Common Council New York*, 4:571, 575, 663, 677; Smith, "Portuguese Naturalist," 91.

92. *Latrobe Journals*, 1:100–105. Stephen Ravenel Diary, October 24–26, 1803, Thomas Porcher Ravenel Papers. *Virginia Gazette and Petersburg Intelligencer*, June 10, 1794; January 10, 1804.

93. For Wise, see James Mackay III, "Built for a Tavern: A Brief History of Gadsby's Tavern Museum," *1992 Historic Alexandria Antique Show Catalogue* (Alexandria, VA, 1992); Virginia Property Tax Records, Alexandria City, 1785–97, LV. For the mixed society at billiard tables, see "Observations on the Badness of the Times," *South Carolina Weekly Museum*, January 21, 1797, 76; John C. Van Horne, ed., *The Journals of Benjamin Henry Latrobe*, (New Haven: 1977), 2:325–27; and Francis Baily, *Journal of a Tour in Unsettled Parts of North America in 1796 & 1797* (London, 1856), 99–104.

94. Mutual Assurance Company Policies, 1796, 1:94 (Wise); 10:31 (Armistead); Policy #2351, 13 June 1817 (Hallam), Mutual Assurance Company Records, LV. William

Henry Dabney, *Sketch of the Dabneys of Virginia: With Some of Their Family Records* (Richmond, 1888), 95–96.

95. *Richmond Enquirer*, March 26, 1805; September 1, 1809. "The Dumfries Masonic Lodge, 1797," *William and Mary Quarterly*, 2nd ser., 4 (April 1924): 120–22. Esme Smock deed to John Fox, November 2, 1809, Hustings Deeds, 1807–10, LV. Fox v. Wilde, 1822, in Thomas Johnson Michie, *Reports of the Court of Appeals of Virginia* (Richmond, 1904), 1:165–68.

96. Mackay, "Built for a Tavern." Doris E. King, "The First-Class Hotel and the Age of the Common Man," *Journal of Southern History* 23 (May 1957): 183–84. Seth Rockman, *Scraping By: Wage Labor, Slavery, and Survival in Early Baltimore* (Baltimore, 2009), 111–12; John Thomas Scharf, *History of Baltimore City and County, from the Earliest Period to the Present Day* (Philadelphia, 1881), 252, 470, 492, 514.

97. For McCrady, see *City Gazette* (Charleston, SC), August 7, 1790; August 16, 1790; November 12, 1790; For the Eagle, see *Virginia Gazette*, September 25, 1798. *Richmond Enquirer*, June 9, 1809; August 4, 1809.

98. Sandoval-Strausz, *Hotel: An American History* (New Haven, CT, 2007), 13–74. Thompson, *Rum Punch*, 190–96; Jane Kamensky, *The Exchange Artist: A Tale of High-Flying Speculation and America's First Banking Collapse* (New York, 2008), 222–29.

99. Ira Berlin, *Many Thousands Gone: The First Two Centuries of Slavery in America* (Cambridge, MA, 1998), 279–85, 319–20. Peter Kolchin, *American Slavery, 1619–1877* (New York, 2003), 77–95.

100. For the importance of physical prowess to "mastery" in the South, see Elliott J. Gorn, " 'Gouge and Bite, Pull Hair and Scratch': The Social Significance of Fighting in the Southern Backcountry," *American Historical Review* 90 (February 1985): 18–43; Kenneth S. Greenberg, *Honor and Slavery: Lies, Duels, Noses, Masks, Dressing as a Woman, Gifts, Strangers, Death, Humanitarianism, Slave Rebellions, the Pro-Slavery Argument, Baseball, Hunting, and Gambling in the Old South* (Princeton, NJ, 1996), 1–35, 135–46. For "respectability," see Richard Bushman, *The Refinement of America: Persons, Houses, Cities* (New York, 1992), xv, 231–37.

4. Prestige or Profit

1. *Diary of William Dunlap* (New York, 1931), 1:205–6.

2. William Dunlap, *A History of the American Theatre* (New York, 1832), 1:129, 2:361–62. William Dunlap, "Theatrical Register," *New York Magazine*, November 1794, 654.

3. Dunlap, *Diary*, 1:142, 119. Dunlap, "Theatrical Register," 654.

4. Dunlap, "Theatrical Register," 654. For *André*, see Joseph Ellis, *After the Revolution: Profiles of Early American Culture* (New York, 1979), 141–44. Bryan Waterman, *Republic of Intellect: The Friendly Club of New York City and the Making of American Literature* (Baltimore, 2007), 174–77.

5. *The Argus* (New York), April 3, 1798. Dunlap, *Diary*, 236–39.

6. John Daly Burk, *Bunker Hill; or, The Death of General Warren* (New York, 1891 [orig. 1797]), 41, 46–47, 61. S. E. Wilmer, *Theatre, Society, and the Nation: Staging American Identities* (New York, 2002), 53–65.

7. William W. Clapp, *A Record of the Boston Stage* (Boston, 1853), 55. Dunlap, *History*, 1:312–16.

8. Dunlap, *History*, 2:81. Ellis, *After the Revolution*, 152–56; David Grimsted, *Melodrama Unveiled: American Theater and Culture, 1800–1850* (Chicago, 1968), 9–21.

9. *The Tickler* (Philadelphia), May 9, 1810.

10. Minutes, Proprietors' Meeting, December 10, 1796, Box C10, Federal Street Theatre Papers, Boston Theatre Collection, BPL. For competition driving up costs for managers, see Dunlap, *Diary*, 1:160–61, 201, 262; James Fennell to Miss [Caroline] Westray, June 18, 1799, Gratz Collection, HSP; Heather Nathans, *Early American Theatre from the Revolution to Thomas Jefferson: Into the Hands of the People* (New York, 2003), 106–21; Susanne K. Sherman, *Comedies Useful: Southern Theatre History: 1775–1812* (Williamsburg, VA, 1998), 95–153. For playhouse costs exceeding budgets, see "Trustees New Theatre" Account Book, 1791–92; and "Articles of Agreement," Chestnut Street Theatre, Society Small Collection, HSP; *At a General Meeting of the Subscribers to the New Theatre* (Philadelphia, 1795); Dunlap, *Diary*, 1:211, 225–26, 228; *City Gazette* (Charleston, SC), January 9, 1793; *Pennsylvania Gazette*, February 14, 1798; Nathans, *Early American Theatre*, 51.

11. Elisha Sigourney Account, 1796–98, and Leases, April 7, 1800, March 21, 1806, Box C10, Federal Street Theatre Papers, Boston Theatre Collection, BPL. *Olympic Theatre Proceedings, Resolutions, Deeds and Declaration of Trust* (Philadelphia, 1819), 25. *1821 Alterations and Amendments to the Olympic Theatre Declaration of Trust* (Philadelphia, 1821), 9. Francis C. Wemyss, *Twenty-Six Years of the Life of an Actor and Manager* (New York, 1846), 233, 325–26.

12. *New York Daily Advertiser*, March 7, 1794. For the standardization of ticket prices, see *City Gazette* (Charleston, SC), February 23, 1795; *Philadelphia Gazette*, February 16, 1795; *Aurora* (Philadelphia), March 30, 1805; *Republican Gazeteer* (Boston), January 29, 1803; *Virginia Patriot*, January 9, 1810; *Columbian* (New York), August 13, 1811; *American Beacon* (Norfolk, VA), November 6, 1817. For wages, see Billy G. Smith, *The "Lower Sort": Philadelphia's Laboring People, 1750–1800* (Ithaca, NY, 1990), 109–12; Seth Rockman, *Scraping By: Wage Labor, Slavery, and Survival in Early Baltimore* (Baltimore, 2009), 91–92.

13. John Lardner to Alexander Graydon, December 10, 1784, John Lardner Series, Lardner Family Papers, HSP.

14. *Philadelphia General Advertiser*, February 19, 1794; February 24, 1794. *United States Gazette*, November 9, 1811; October 30, 1811. *The Cynick* (Philadelphia), September 28, 1811, 20.

15. *The Cynick* (Philadelphia), September 28, 1811, 6, 78, 29. *United States Gazette*, September 18, 1811.

16. *State Gazette of South Carolina*, February 21, 1800. James Cronin, ed., *The Diary of Elihu Hubbard Smith* (Philadelphia: 1973), 157, 242, 244. Edward Lloyd VI Diary, November 13, 1826, Lloyd Family Papers, MDHS.

17. Charles William Janson, *The Stranger in America* (London, 1807), 255. *Succinct Account of the Disturbance which Occurred at the Charleston Theatre* (Charleston, 1817), 5–8.

18. Aeneas Mackay Diary, November 28, 1810, NYHS. Washington Irving, *Letters of Jonathan Oldstyle, Gent.* (Boston, 1977 [orig. 1802–3]), 12. For the French seamen, see *City Gazette* (Charleston, SC), March 19, 1794; *Columbia* (SC) *Gazette*, March 28, 1794.

19. Matthew Carey, *The Thespian Monitor and Dramatick Miscellany* (Philadelphia, 1809), 17.

20. Henry Bradshaw Fearon, *A Narrative of a Journey of Five Thousand Miles through the Eastern and Western United States of America* (London, 1818), 87. For another print showing women in the pit in British theatres, see Thomas Rowlandson, "Orchard Street Theatre," *Comforts of Bath*, Plate 8 (London, 1798).

21. *The Cynick* (Philadelphia), October 19, 1811, 81–82. Kenneth Roberts and Anna Roberts, eds., *Moreau de St. Mery's American Journey* (Garden City, NY, 1947), 347. Rosemarie K. Bank, *Theatre Culture in America, 1825–1860* (New York, 1997), 125–38; Christine Stansell, *City of Women: Sex and Class in New York: 1789–1860* (Urbana, IL, 1987), 94–100.

22. Benjamin Rush, "On Manners: Excerpts from a Diary Traveling through France," in *The Selected Writings of Benjamin Rush*, ed. Dagobert D. Runes (New York, 1947), 384. For gendered traits, rights, and behavior, see Nancy Folbre, *Greed, Lust, and Gender: A History of Economic Ideas* (New York, 2009), 35–70; Dana D. Nelson, *National Manhood: Capitalist Citizenship and the Imagined Fraternity of White Men* (Durham, NC, 1998), 29–46; Robert J. Steinfeld, "Property and Suffrage in the Early American Republic," *Stanford Law Review* 41 (January 1989): 355–60, 375. C. Dallett Hemphill, *Bowing to Necessities: A History of Manners in America, 1620–1860* (New York, 2002), 104–19.

23. *The Cynick* (Philadelphia), October 19, 1811, 81–82. Frances A. B. Hoffman to Bridget Wickham, March 26, 1829, Villiers-Hatton Papers, NYHS. Sarah Rose, *For All the Tea in China: Espionage, Empire, and the Secret Formula for the World's Favourite Drink* (London, 2010), 27.

24. Roberts and Roberts, *St. Mery's Journey*, 347. Petition to the General Assembly of South Carolina, November 22, 1855, SCA.

25. Simon Snipe, *Sports of New-York, Containing an Evening at the African Theatre Also a Trip to the Races with Two Appropriate Songs* (New York, 1823), 3–15; Shane White, *Stories of Freedom in Black New York* (Cambridge, MA, 2002), 74–86; Marvin McAllister, *White People Do Not Know How to Behave at Entertainments Designed for Ladies and Gentlemen: William Brown's African and American Theatre* (Chapel Hill, NC, 2003), 131–66. *City Gazette* (Charleston, SC), November 21, 1821.

26. Thomas Jefferson, *Notes on the State of Virginia* (London, 1787), 231–32. Nelson, *National Manhood*, 52–60.

27. *City Gazette* (Charleston, SC), March 17, 1795. Nathans, *Early American Theatre*, 106–11.

28. Tappahannock Jockey Club Record Book, 1786–1801, Tayloe Papers, VHS.

29. John Tayloe III to William Herndon, June 10, 1801, John Tayloe III Letterbook, VHS; Minutes, May 1801, Tappahannock Jockey Club Record Book, Tayloe Papers.

30. Tayloe to Herndon, June 10, 1801.

31. "The Celebrated American Racehorse Leviathan," *American Turf Register and Sporting Magazine* (hereafter cited as *Turf Register*), July 1834, 551.

32. "Petersburg Jocky Club Book, 1785," *William and Mary Quarterly* 18 (April 1938): 210–14. William Haxall Correspondence, 1787–1831, Haxall Family Papers, VHS. *Virginia Gazette and Petersburg Intelligencer*, January 18, 1787, May 3, 1787; August 30, 1787; November 1, 1787. Personal Property Tax Records, Petersburg City and Dinwiddie County, 1785, LV.

33. "Petersburg Jocky Club Book," 212.

34. Records and newspaper coverage suggest the only members to enter their own horses were Haxall and Bolling, and they did so sporadically and never won the most prestigious four-mile race. For prize money and entrants, see "Petersburg Jocky Club Book," 211–16; *Virginia Gazette and Petersburg Intelligencer*, March 29, 1793, December 12, 1798, October 26, 1802; *Richmond Enquirer*, October 18, 1805; *City Gazette* (Charleston, SC), February 13, 1799.

35. Edward C. Carter II, ed., *The Papers of Benjamin Henry Latrobe, Journals 1795–1820* (New Haven, 1977), 1:100–101. Charles Fraser, *Reminiscences of Charleston* (1969 [orig. 1854]), 61–63. James Burchill Richardson to William Sinkler, March 3, 1803, Sinkler Family Papers, SCHS.

36. For the importance of Southside in American thoroughbred breeding, see *Petersburg Intelligencer*, September 9, 1808; *Turf Register*, June 1832, 505; John Hervey, *Racing in America* (New York, 1944) 1:150–60. For stock sales at the Petersburg track, see newspaper advertisement collection, 1809–20, Horse Notes, Haxall Family Papers, VHS.

37. Subscription List, 1824, Richmond Jockey Club Records, 1824–38, VHS; *Rules and Regulations of the Washington Jockey Club* (Washington, DC, 1821), 11–12.

38. Annual Accounts, St. Stephen's Jockey Club Papers, 1811–36, SCHS; Raymond A. Mohl, ed., "'The Grand Fabric of Republicanism': A Scotsman Describes South Carolina, 1810–1811," *South Carolina Historical and Genealogical Magazine* 71 (July 1970): 186; *Turf Register*, May 1831, 505. For proprietors who paid rent to clubs in return for managing the track and keeping any profits above the rent, see chapter 3.

39. William Taplin, *The Gentleman's Stable Directory* (Philadelphia, 1794), 9, 12. Richard Mason, *The Gentleman's New Pocket Farrier* (Richmond, 1825), 15.

40. *National Advocate*, October 1818. The article was reprinted elsewhere, suggesting its portrayal resonated widely. For an example, see *American Beacon* (Norfolk, VA), November 17, 1818. For the function of second-floor front rooms, see Bernard L. Herman, *Town House: Architecture and Material Life in the Early American City, 1780–1830* (Chapel Hill, NC, 2005), 58–71.

41. *Alexandria Gazette*, October 31, 1817; February 5, 1818. Janson, *Stranger in America*, 209–10.

42. Snipe, *Sports of New-York*, 17–20. *New York Journal*, May 27, 1773.

43. Snipe, *Sports of New-York*, 28–30. The second quote comes from a report recounting the 1823 race in the *American Sporting Magazine*, July 3, 1830, reprinted in Frank Forester, *The Horses of America* (New York, 1857), 1:191.

44. Janson, *Stranger in America*, 208–10. *Washington Federalist*, October 5, 1803. James W. Camp to William Purnell, November 18, 1809, in *Papers of Andrew Jackson*, ed. Sam B. Smith and Harriet C. Owsley (Knoxville, 1980), 2:224–25. While episodes of violence exercised in defense of masculine status were a motif of published travel narratives, the pattern also appears in court records, newspaper reports, personal correspondence, and unpublished diaries, as the vignettes from this chapter and others make clear. So while not all of these episodes may have actually happened, some of them did, and taken together, the pattern expresses the *belief* that violent manly challenge was part of the experience in rougher sporting spaces (and, increasingly in this period, even in genteel ones as well). For more on the literary motifs, see Elliot J. Gorn, "'Gouge, Bite, Pull Hair, and Scratch': The Social Significance of Fighting in the Southern Backcountry," *American Historical Review* 90 (December 1985): 23–33.

45. Henry Garret and John Amis, August 1819; Cornelius Johnson, June 8, 1812; and Abyah Rembert, February 18, 1813, Richard Singleton Accounts, Singleton Family Papers, SHC. For Garrett, see the Census for Hillsborough and Orange County, NC, in 1800 (p. 510), 1810 (p. 1), and 1820 (p. 121).

46. A. T. B. Merritt to Richard Singleton, July 1, 1833; and Boyce, Henry, and Waller to Singleton, November 26, 1833, Family Correspondence, Singleton Family Papers, SHC. For more on "hiring out," see John J. Zaborney, *Slaves for Hire: Renting Enslaved Laborers in Antebellum Virginia* (Baton Rouge, LA, 2012); Seth Rockman, *Scraping By: Wage Labor, Slavery, and Survival in Early Baltimore* (Baltimore, 2009), 1–74, 231–60.

47. Allen Davie to Richard Singleton, June 30, 1819; and John Amis to Richard Singleton, June 30, 1819, Family Correspondence, Singleton Family Papers, SHC. Accounts with Henry Garret and John Amis, August 1819; Account with John Amis, 1821, Richard Singleton Accounts, Singleton Family Papers, SHC. For slaves at spas, see Charlene M. Boyer Lewis, *Ladies and Gentlemen on Display: Planter Society at the Virginia Springs, 1790–1860* (Charlottesville, VA, 2001), 63, 196–99.

48. Luzborough Account, April 15, 1834, Richard Singleton Accounts, Singleton Family Papers, SHC. Wade Hampton II to Richard Singleton, August 1, 1834, Richard Singleton Papers, SCHS.

49. Joseph Cotton to Jonathan Singleton, June 21, 1820; and A. T. B. Merritt to Richard Singleton, July 1, 1833, Family Correspondence, Singleton Family Papers, SHC. Benjamin Franklin Taylor to Richard Singleton, August 18, 1832, Benjamin Franklin Taylor Papers, SCL.

50. Cornelious Johnson to Richard Singleton, October 6, 1810, Family Correspondence, Singleton Family Papers, SHC.

51. Bill of Sale, John Charles Steedman to Richard Walls in Trust for Cornelius Johnson, February 16, 1813, Miscellaneous Records, SCA. For Walls, see Edmund L. Drago, *Charleston's Avery Center: From Education and Civil Rights to Preserving the African American Experience* (Charleston, 2006), 31–32. For more on trust purchases, see Amrita Chakrabarti Myers, *Forging Freedom: Black Women and the Pursuit of Liberty in Antebellum Charleston* (Chapel Hill, NC, 2011), 67–73, 121.

52. John Tayloe III Daybook, April 7, 1798; December 23, 1808; January 1, 1809; and John Tayloe III Account Book, 1801–4, 52, Tayloe Papers, VHS. John M. Garard to Andrew Jackson, July 2, 1805, in *Correspondence of Andrew Jackson*, ed. John Spencer Bassett (Washington, DC, 1926–35), 1:116. *Turf Register*, March 1832, 358.

53. Katherine C. Mooney, *Race Horse Men: How Slavery and Freedom Were Made at the Racetrack* (Cambridge, MA, 2014), 1–6, 33–38, 74–88. For wealthy men's willingness to mingle slave and free labor, see Rockman, *Scraping By*, 7–12, 45–74. Scholarship on "whiteness" also has made clear that the line was fine, if hardening, between being Irish and being black in this period. Most notably, see Noel Ignatiev, *How the Irish Became White* (London, 1995), and David Roediger, *The Wages of Whiteness: Race and the Making of the American Working Class* (London, 1999).

54. Mooney, *Race Horse Men*, 53. For the role of racism in preventing a united working class, see Rockman, *Scraping By*, 9–12, 70; Roediger, *Wages of Whiteness*, 43–165; and Edmund Morgan's classic *American Slavery, American Freedom* (New York, 1975).

55. Jacob Motte Alston Autobiography Ms., 2:71, Alston Family Papers, SCHS. Benjamin Franklin Taylor to Richard Singleton, August 18, 1832, Benjamin Franklin Taylor Papers, SCL.

56. John Tayloe III to John Rose, July 16, 1801, John Tayloe III Letterbook, Tayloe Family Papers, VHS. For Dunwoody, see John M. Garrard to Andrew Jackson, July 2, 1805, *Correspondence*, 1:116; Andrew Jackson to Hardy Cryer, January 10, 1830, *Correspondence*, 4:1167–70; Jackson to Andrew Jackson Jr., March 25, 1836, *Correspondence*, 5:394.

57. Annie Porter, ed. "My Life as a Slave," *Harper's New Monthly Magazine* (October 1884): 732. For sales of horsemen and especially young boys, see Pollard Brown to Richard Singleton, February 29, 1823, George Coffin Taylor Papers, SHC; Account, October 20, 1802, "Racing Reminiscences," Alston-Pringle-Frost Papers, SCHS; Mount Airy Inventory Book, 1808–27, Tayloe Papers, VHS; Bills of Sale, January 1, 1829, undated (1831), Pegram-Johnson Papers, LV; Tucker R. Woodson to William Ransom Johnson, January 13, 1844, Johnson Family Papers, VHS.

58. Herbert H. Breck and William Frederic Worner, "Horse Racing in Lancaster County," *Lancaster County Historical Society Papers* 37 (1933): 45. Henry Ravenel Jr. Daybook, November 19, 1819, Thomas P. Ravenel Collection, SCHS.

59. Charles P. Lee to William Henry Tayloe, February 26, 1835; June 9, 1835, William Henry Tayloe Correspondence, Tayloe Papers, VHS.

60. Jonathan R. Spann to Singleton, August 17, 1819, Correspondence, Singleton Family Papers, SCL. D. W. Goodman to Richard Singleton, June 25, 1825, Richard Singleton Correspondence, Singleton Family Papers, SCL. Jack Leftwich to Joel Leftwich, June 16, 1819, Horse Papers, Papers of Joel Leftwich, UVa.

61. Donald Jackson, ed., *The Diaries of George Washington* (Charlottesville, VA, 1976), 5:50. *National Advocate*, October 1818. Mrs. Smith Journal, March 5, 1793, Duke.

62. Isaac Weld, *Travels through the States of North America* (New York, 1968 [orig. 1799]), 150. Andrew Jackson to William B. Lewis, August 5, 1828, *Correspondence*, 3:418–19. William Read to Jacob Read, February 14, 1800, Read Family Papers, SCHS.

63. Robert Bailey, *The Life and Adventures of Robert Bailey, from His Infancy Up to December, 1821* (Richmond, 1822), 344–48.

64. Ibid., 25–27.

65. Ibid., 48–49, 61.

66. Ibid., 66–67, 47.

67. Ibid., 48–50, 125, 132–133, 160, 241.

68. Ibid., 64–65, 72–73.

69. Ibid., 72–73, 174–75.

70. Thomas Anburey, *Travels through the Interior Parts of America* (London, 1789), 2:347–48. Gorn, "Gouge," 19–22.

71. Bailey, *Life and Adventures*, 74.

72. Ibid.

73. *Poulson's American Daily Advertiser* (Philadelphia), August 12, 1793. Robert Waln, *The Hermit in Philadelphia, Second Series* (Philadelphia, 1821), 77–79.

74. *Laws of the State of North Carolina* (Raleigh, NC, 1839), 32. Richard C. Wade, *Slavery in the Cities: The South, 1820–1860* (New York, 1964), 85–90, 149–60; David Wiggins, "Good Times on the Old Plantation: Popular Recreations of the Black Slave in the Antebellum South, 1810–1860," *Journal of Sport History* 4 (October 1977), 274.

75. *The Repertory* (Boston), May 29, 1804. *Raleigh Star*, January 17, 1815. Lewis Beebe Journal, 17, HSP. Elkanah Watson, *Men and Times of the Revolution; or, Memoirs of Elkanah Watson* (Boston, 1856), 261.

76. *New York Spectator*, January 19, 1821. (New York) *Freedom's Journal*, June 22, 1827. New York had slavery until 1821, and passed a law against slaves gambling in 1811. See *Minutes of the Common Council of the City of New York, 1784–1831* (New York, 1930), 6:546–47.

77. Bailey, *Life and Adventures*, 103. Jeffrey Forret, *Race Relations at the Margins: Slaves and Poor Whites in the Antebellum Southern Countryside* (Baton Rouge, LA, 2006), 56–70. For the racial lines of "honor," see Kenneth S. Greenberg, *Honor and Slavery: Lies, Duels, Noses, Masks, Dressing as a Woman, Gifts, Strangers, Death, Humanitarianism, Slave Rebellions, the Pro-Slavery Argument, Baseball, Hunting, and Gambling in the Old South* (Princeton, NJ, 1996), x–xx, 135–46.

78. *The New Mirror for Travellers, and Guide to the Springs* (New York, 1828). "Laws of Honor," *The Stranger*, January 29, 1814, 245. "Letter of Advice to a Young Friend," *Boston Weekly Magazine*, June 2, 1804, 125–26. "Address to Those Who Are of Service Either as Apprentices or for Wages," *Piscataqua Evangelical Magazine*, March 1808, 60. "Introductory Discourse to the Mercantile Library of Philadelphia," *The Register of Pennsylvania*, November 14, 1829, 310. Scott Sandage, *Born Losers: A History of Failure in America* (Cambridge, MA, 2005), 35–39. For the rise of "respectability," see Stuart Blumin, *The Emergence of the Middle Class: Social Experience in the American City, 1760–1900* (Cambridge, UK, 1989), 192–229; Richard Bushman, *The Refinement of America: Persons, Houses, Cities* (New York, 1992), 238–352.

79. Robert Wormeley Carter to John Minor, June 11, 1792, Carter Papers, LV. John Browne Cutting, *Argument Delivered before the Judges of the Court of Appeals in Richmond, Virginia in the Case of Carter's Executors* (Fredericksburg, VA, 1817), 17–18.

80. Landon Carter to John Brown Cutting, January 18, 1819, Robert Wormeley Carter Correspondence, Carter Papers, CWM.

81. *Boston Gazette*, October 17, 1811. *New York Patriot*, May 28, 1823; Sandage, *Born Losers*, 44–69.

82. *The Philadelphiad; or, New Pictures of the City* (Philadelphia, 1784), 56–59. John C. Van Horne, ed., *The Journals of Benjamin Henry Latrobe* (New Haven, CT, 1977), 2:328.

83. Breck and Worner, "Racing in Lancaster," 45, 50. William Alston Studbook, 1789–1809, 18, SCHS. *Turf Register*, June 1832, 523–25.

84. Articles of Agreement, William B. Vinson and Andrew Jackson, June 1809, in Smith and Owsley, *Papers of Andrew Jackson*, 2:217–18. Statement, February 1, 1806; Jackson to Thomas Swann, February 10, 1806, *Correspondence*, 1:122–30. For Bailey, see *Life and Adventures*, 125; results under "Robert Bailey" in *A New Nation Votes: American Election Returns, 1787–1825*, http://elections.lib.tufts.edu/. The same site reveals that leading owners Richard Singleton and John Tayloe III, as well as theatre trustees John Swanwick and Perez Morton, among others, won election to their state assemblies. As these four examples suggest, the list spans party and regional lines.

85. *Boston Patriot*, May 28, 1804. *Aurora* (Philadelphia), February 21, 1806. "Reminiscences of Petersburg," *Petersburg Index*, October 10, 1868. Henry Augustine Tayloe to William Henry Tayloe, July 16, 1835, William Henry Tayloe Correspondence, Tayloe Family Papers.

86. Donald Ratcliffe, "The Right to Vote and the Rise of Democracy," *Journal of the Early Republic* 33 (July 2013), 219–54. Sean Wilentz, *The Rise of American Democracy: Jefferson to Lincoln* (New York, 2006), 116–25.

87. Griswold to Cooper, November 22, 1796, cited in Alan Taylor, "'The Art of Hook & Snivey': Political Culture in Upstate New York during the 1790s," *Journal of American History* 89 (March 1993): 1386; see also 1371–96.

88. *Aurora* (Philadelphia), February 21, 1806. For Griswold's reward, see Nathaniel Soley Benton, *A History of Herkimer County* (Albany, NY, 1856), 316.

89. *Spirit of the Press* (Philadelphia), October 5, 1805. *Boston Patriot*, May 28, 1804.

90. Tyrone Power, *Impressions of America* (London, 1836), 1:127–28, 2:58–59. Arney R. Childs, ed., *Rice Planter and Sportsman: The Recollections of J. Motte Alston, 1821–1909* (Columbia, SC, 1953), 19–20. In contrast, women participated in domestic card games and lotteries just as men did. Linda L. Sturtz, "The Ladies and the Lottery: Elite Women's Gambling in Eighteenth-Century Virginia," *Virginia Magazine of History and Biography* 104 (April 1996): 165–84. On women's property rights, see Marylynn Salmon, *Women and the Law of Property in Early America* (Chapel Hill, NC, 1986), 81–140, 188–93. For women's expanded participation in political events, and subsequent exclusion from them, see Rosemarie Zagarri, *Revolutionary Backlash: Women and Politics in the Early American Republic* (Philadelphia, 2008), 148–81.

91. Zagarri, *Revolutionary Backlash*, 60–70, 148–81.

92. *The New-Yorker*, August 25, 1838.

93. Joanne Melish, "The 'Condition' Debate and Racial Discourse in the Antebellum North," *Journal of the Early Republic* 19 (December 1999): 651–72. Christopher Malone, *Between Freedom and Bondage: Race, Party, and Voting Rights in the Antebellum North* (New York, 2008); David Waldstreicher, *In the Midst of Perpetual Fetes: The Making of American Nationalism, 1776–1820* (Chapel Hill, NC, 1997), 230–31, 308–48.

94. For the classic definition of "status politics," see Gerard A. Brandmeyer and R. Serge Denisoff, "Status Politics: An Appraisal of the Application of a Concept," *Pacific Sociological Review* 12 (April 1969): 5–11. Although Brandmeyer and Denisoff, along with historians such as Richard Hofstadter, discuss "status politics" in terms of voting patterns on issues that would sustain or recover a certain group's status, the evidence of sport's application to politics in the early republic suggests that the act of engaging in politics and voting could satisfy the same purpose. This is not to say that parties and issues did not matter, of course, but that the act of participating in electoral politics also carried meaning. Richard Hofstadter, *The Age of Reform: From Bryan to F.D.R.* (New York, 1955), 284–91. For another example of how a mode of action (in this case, modern bureaucracy) could serve the ends of status, see Robert Wiebe, *The Search for Order, 1877–1920* (New York, 1967).

95. *National Gazette* (Philadelphia), July 7, 1792. Jeffrey L. Pasley, *"The Tyranny of Printers": Newspaper Politics in the Early Republic* (Charlottesville, VA, 2001), 64–71, 229–57; Saul Cornell, *The Other Founders: Anti-Federalism and the Dissenting Tradition in America, 1788–1828* (Chapel Hill, NC, 1999), 172–219.

96. William Priest, *Travels in the United States of America, 1793–1797* (London, 1802), 165–66. Nathans, *Early American Theatre*, 106–14.

97. *Philadelphia General Advertiser*, February 24, 1794. For the tax data, I used the investor rosters (with political affiliations) in Nathans, *Early American Theatre*, 80, 173–80, and cross-referenced them with the Boston Tax Assessors Books, 1792, 1795 (microfilm), BPL. For the divisions of taxable wealth in Boston in 1790, see Alan Kulikoff, "The Progress of Inequality in Revolutionary Boston," *William and Mary Quarterly*, 3rd ser., 28

(July 1971): 380. In Philadelphia, where assessments were lower, only ten of thirty identifiable original shareholders were assessed over $1,000 in 1791, though by 1799 the number was up to 50 percent, showing consolidation of shares among the wealthiest risk-takers. Philadelphia City Property Tax Records, 1791, 1799, HSP.

98. William B. Wood, *Personal Recollections of the Stage* (Philadelphia, 1855), 323.

99. *New York Daily Advertiser*, March 7, 1794. *Independent Chronicle and Universal Advertiser*, January 23, 1794. 14. Sarah L. Flucker to Lucy Knox, February 15, 1794, Henry Knox Papers, BPL, cited in Nathans, *Early American Theatre*, 80.

100. *Gazette of the United States*, April 28, 1798. *Morning Chronicle* (New York), January 27, 1803. Nathans, *Early American Theatre*, 157.

101. *New York Daily Advertiser*, March 7, 1794. Dunlap, *Diary*, 1:304. For other examples of anticipating that conflict would sell tickets, see John Anderson Diary, March 13, 1794, NYHS; *City Gazette* (Charleston, SC), April 29, 1793.

102. *Charleston Courier*, March 10, 1803. *A New Farce Acted on Wednesday Evening Last, at the New Theatre in the Town of Hoosack, Called, Pandemonium in Dishabille; or, Pretended Republicanism Put in Practice* (Hoosack Falls, NY, 1808). *Federalism Triumphant in the Steady Habits of Connecticut; or, the Turnpike Road to a Fortune, A Comic Opera or Political Farce in Six Acts* (New Haven, CT, 1802).

103. For leading Democratic-Republicans supporting natural aristocracy, see Thomas Jefferson to John Adams, October 18, 1813, in *The Adams–Jefferson Letters*, ed. Lester J. Cappon (Chapel Hill, NC, 1988), 352; Cornell, *Other Founders*, 80, 176.

104. Lewis Beebe Journal, 2:8–12, HSP. John Randolph of Roanoke Diaries, April 14–28, 1817, VHS. J. T. Lomax to Robert Wormeley Carter, March 16, 1821, Robert Wormeley Carter Correspondence, Carter Papers, CWM.

105. Margaret Bayard Smith to Jane Bayard Kirkpatrick, March 13, 1814, Margaret Bayard Smith Papers, LOC; Catharine Akerly Mitchell to Margaret Akerly Miller, December 19, 1808, Catharine Akerly Mitchell Papers, LOC, both cited in Christine Allgor, *Parlor Politics: In Which the Ladies of Washington Help Build a City and a Government* (Charlottesville, VA, 2000), 115–18. William Alexander Duer, *Reminiscences of an Old Yorker, Addressed to the St. Nicholas Society, 1849* (New York, 1867), 77.

5. A Mass Sporting Industry

1. Camden Jockey Club Agreement, July 11, 1836, Stud Records, Pegram-Johnson-MacIntosh Papers, VHS.

2. Petition from Bergen, Somerset, Middlesex, and Hunterdon Counties, October 1822; and Petition from New Brunswick, October 1822, NJA, Trenton. *Washington Whig* (Bridgeton, NJ), December 10, 1825; November 21, 1829.

3. "Horse Notes," John Steele Papers, SHC. *American Turf Register and Sporting Magazine* (hereafter cited as *Turf Register*), November 1829, 118; January 1831, 246; July 1832, 568–70; February 1832, 267–68. John J. McCusker, *How Much Is That in Real Money? A Price Index for Use as a Deflator of Money Values* (Worcester, MA, 2001), 327.

4. *Turf Register*, May 1830, 438. *Acts of the Fifty-Ninth General Assembly of the State of New Jersey* (Trenton, NJ, 1835), 169. Melvin L. Adelman, *A Sporting Time: New York City and the Rise of Modern Athletics, 1820–1870* (Urbana, IL, 1990), 41–42.

5. Adelman, *Sporting Time*, 42. Camden Jockey Club Agreement. *Turf Register*, August 1832, 637; September 1832, 38; September 1833, 46.

6. Harry Heth to Richard Singleton, August 23, 1819, Family Correspondence, Singleton Family Papers, SHC. *Turf Register*, May 1830, 466; January 1831, 243; March 1838, 100. *Spirit of the Times* (New York), October 20, 1838.

7. Callendar Irvine to Daniel Parker, January 20, 1836, Daniel Parker Papers, Zaccheus Collins Collection, HSP. *Turf Register*, August 1836, 537; May 1830, 467; July 1830, 560.

8. My definition of "mass culture" as standardized, indiscriminate, accessible, and hegemonic is based on the classic "Frankfurt School" definitions in Theodore Adorno, *The Culture Industry: Selected Essays on Mass Culture* (London, 1991), 53–114; Dwight MacDonald, "A Theory of Mass Culture," in *Mass Culture: The Popular Arts in America*, ed. Bernard Rosenberg and David Manning White (Chicago, 1956), 59–73; and C. Wright Mills, *The Power Elite* (New York, 1956), 298–24. Yet, because the initial mass culture I am describing was rooted in live sporting experiences rather than mass media, I contend that the hegemony constructed through it resulted from more active negotiation between producers and consumers, a negotiation that demanded real concession from the early American "power elite." For other examples of this negotiation, see David Henkin, *City Reading: Written Words and Public Spaces in Antebellum New York* (New York, 1998), 1–30; David Anthony, *Paper Money Men: Commerce, Manhood, and the Sensational Public Sphere in Antebellum America* (Columbus, OH, 2009), 21–26.

9. John Tayloe III will, 1828; William Henry Tayloe to Henry Augustine Tayloe, September 17, 1828; Henry Greenfield Southeron Key to Benjamin Ogle Tayloe, December 31, 1832; and Henry Augustine Tayloe to William Henry Tayloe, February 7, 1833, William Henry Tayloe (WHT) Correspondence, Tayloe Papers, VHS. George Plater Tayloe to William Henry Tayloe, November 8, 1832, March 30, 1834, WHT Correspondence, Tayloe Papers, VHS. Oakley Stables Accounts, 1832–34, Horse Papers, Tayloe Papers.

10. George Plater Tayloe to William Henry Tayloe, March 30, 1834; February 2, 1838, December 16, 1837; Henry Augustine Tayloe to William Henry Tayloe, April 5, 1837, WHT Correspondence, Tayloe Papers, VHS.

11. For a summary of the differences, see John Henry Watson to William Henry Tayloe, July 14, 1838, WHT Correspondence, Tayloe Papers, VHS.

12. For Johnson's father, see John Eisenberg, *The Great Match Race: When North Met South in America's First Sports Spectacle* (New York, 2006), 44–49. For his land speculation, see Deed of Sale, 1806, Pegram-Johnson Papers, Brock Collection, Huntington Library (microfilm), LV. For his early ownership, see Elizabeth Blanchard and Manly Wellman, *The Life and Times of Sir Archie* (Chapel Hill, NC, 1958), 32, 65; Horse Notes, 1809, Haxall Family Papers, VHS. For his move to Petersburg and shift to racing as a full-time business, see John Dizikes, *Sportsmen and Gamesmen* (Boston, 1981), 24–25; Plan of Dissolution, July 19,1827, and Accounts of Purchases, January 21, 1829, November 1829, 1831, Pegram-Johnson Papers, Brock Collection Huntington Library (microfilm), LV. For later diversification, see William S. Archer to William Ransom Johnson, March 4, 1818; Woolridge to William Ransom Johnson, July 2, 1838; and Eggleston Cheatham to Johnson, March 24, 1846, William Ransom Johnson Papers, UVa. For the concluding quotes, see "A Peep at the Old Dominion," *Turf Register*, June 1832, 521–22.

13. Sales Notice, ca. 1820, Horse Papers, Papers of Joel Leftwich, UVa. "John Hoomes Will," *Virginia Magazine of History and Biography* 38 (1930): 78.

14. For Ariel, see William Bolling Diary, May 10, 1827, Bolling Papers, VHS; *Turf Register*, June 1832, 518. Johnson had to split the purses with the owner possessing the other half-share in the horse, reducing his net gain. Shared care for the animal probably lowered his profit by another $100. For another example, follow William Wynn's ownership of the mare Kate Kearney in *Turf Register*, November 1829, 153–63; February 1830, 311; November 1830, 138; February 1831, 267. Planter income varied widely from place to place and year to year based on crop prices, so the comparison here is a rough one at best. For its sources, see John H. Moore, *The Emergence of the Cotton Kingdom in the Old Southwest: Mississippi, 1770–1860* (Baton Rouge, LA, 1988), 115–23; Frederick Law Olmsted, *The Cotton Kingdom: A Traveller's Observations on Cotton and Slavery* (London, 1861), 1:5–18, 2:204–42.

15. Minutes, 1824, Richmond Jockey Club Records, 1824–38, VHS. Cadwallader R. Colden, *An Expose of the Measures Which Caused Suspension of the Races on the Union Course in October 1830* (New York, 1831), 9, 38. *Rules and Regulations Adopted by the New York Jockey Club* (New York, 1836), NYPL.

16. Samuel Ringgold to George Cadwalader, May 18, 1833, Gen. George Cadwalader Series, Cadwalader Family Papers, HSP. *Turf Register*, February 1830, 311; August 1830, 618–20; July 1837, 459–77; April 1843, 224.

17. Colden, *Expose*, 9, 13, 38. *Turf Register*, November 1829, 149–52; January 1832, 248; Statement of Receipts and Disbursements, February 1836–February 1837, South Carolina Jockey Club Records, SCHS. Henry Augustine Tayloe to William Henry Tayloe, February 1, 1838, WHT Correspondence, Tayloe Papers, VHS.

18. Robert M. Cahusac to William Porcher, February 17, 1822, SCHS. *Turf Register*, October 1831, 89. John S. Corbin, broadside advertising 1838 Fairfield Races, WHT Correspondence, Tayloe Papers, VHS. For turfmen's dominance on the track, see the monthly installments of "Sporting Intelligence" in the *Turf Register*.

19. In lieu of proprietors, South Carolina jockey clubs incorporated, paid their treasurers to invest club funds broadly, and ran their events themselves with the income earned from these investments. See South Carolina Jockey Club Rules, 1828, 8–12; and St. Stephen's Jockey Club Records, 1846–47, SCHS. Jockey Club Petitions and Judgments, ca. 1826, #557; December 7, 1826, #85; December 1, 1835, #64; #4604, SCA. The Pendleton, Camden, Congaree, and Sumter Jockey Clubs have similar petitions in same collections. For the greater wealth of major cotton planters, see Gavin Wright, "'Economic Democracy' and the Concentration of Agricultural Wealth in the Cotton South, 1850–1860," *Agricultural History* 44 (January 1970): 75–85.

20. Cadwallader R. Colden Deposition (vs. John D. Dickinson), 1818; Indenture between Cadwallader and Eliza Colden and Lynde Catlin, June 1, 1820; "Rules and Regulations of the New York and Vermont Northern Association," September 1, 1823; Cadwallader R. Colden Deposition (vs. Alexander Colden), 1827; "Valuable Farms at Auction," September 23, 1826, Cadwallader R. Colden Papers, NYHS. *Turf Register*, August 1834, 597; April 1837, 364; April 1844, 243.

21. Richard Ten Broeck to William Ransom Johnson, July 29, 1844, William Ransom Johnson Correspondence, Pegram-Johnson-MacIntosh Papers, VHS. Dizikes, *Sportsmen and Gamesmen*, 144–53.

22. *Turf Register*, August 1832, 632.

23. Henry Key to William Henry Tayloe, January 14, 1835, WHT Correspondence, Tayloe Papers, VHS.

24. *Petersburg Intelligencer,* undated (1826); Ephraim Conrad, *An Authentic History of the Celebrated Horse American Eclipse* (New York, 1823), 10. *Turf Register,* February 1832, 305. *American Farmer,* November 12, 1824, 270.

25. For farmers' incomes, see Jeremy Atack and Fred Bateman, "Marketable Farm Surpluses: Northeastern and Midwestern United States, 1859 and 1860," *Social Science History* 8 (October 1984): 382; G. Melvin Herndon, "Elliott L. Story: A Small Farmer's Struggle for Economic Survival in Antebellum Virginia," *Agricultural History* 56 (July 1982): 516–27. For price "tiers" in the market, see Stud Notices, Miscellaneous Papers Concerning Horses, Burwell Family Papers, VHS; Robert Wormeley Carter Stable Accounts, August 1821, Carter Papers, CWM; Unaddressed letter, December 8, 1833, George Coffin Taylor Papers, SHC; "Stud Account," 1821–22, Robert A. Jones Account Book, SHC; Busiris Account, 1835–37, and Expences, 1829–37, Daniel Parker Papers, Zaccheus Collins Collection, HSP; William B. Randolph Account Book, May 28, 1822, VHS; William Rust Baskerville Account Book, October 1, 1822, Baskerville Family Papers, VHS; *Turf Register,* December 1829, 167; Drew Gilpin Faust, *James Henry Hammond and the Old South: A Design for Mastery* (Baton Rouge, LA, 1987), 159. For a comparison of breeding clients, consider the Tayloes' accounts for second-tier Tychicus and top-tier Autocrat, who both bred near Leonardtown, Maryland, in 1833–34. Only one client bred to both horses, and while both sets of owners came from relatively wealthy backgrounds, all of Autocrat's clients came from outside the county where he was breeding, while Tychicus attracted some locals of middling wealth who owned land in nearby towns but no slaves. Accounts, 1833–34, William Henry Tayloe Account Book, 1818–44, Tayloe Papers, VHS. Maryland Censuses, 1830 and 1840; Tax Assessments, 1783–1848, St. Mary's County, St. Mary's County Historical Society, Leonardstown, MD.

26. George Plater Tayloe to William Henry Tayloe, January 16, 1835, WHT Correspondence, Tayloe Papers, VHS.

27. Callendar Irvine to Daniel Parker, November 1, 1836; March 8, 1839, Daniel Parker Papers, Zaccheus Collins Collection, HSP. L. P. Cheatham to Richard Singleton, January 28, 1832, Richard Singleton Correspondence, Singleton Family Papers, SCL.

28. Bernard Hewitt, "'King Stephen' of the Park and Drury Lane," in *The Theatrical Manager in England and America: Player of a Perilous Game,* ed. Joseph W. Donohue (Princeton, NJ, 1971), 87–90. For the quotes, see William Dunlap, *A History of the American Theatre* (New York, 1832), 1:287–88

29. Hewitt, "'King Stephen,'" 92–136. Francis C. Wemyss, *Twenty-Six Years of the Life of an Actor and Manager* (New York, 1846), 85–86.

30. Reese D. James, *Old Drury of Philadelphia: A History of the Philadelphia Stage, 1800–1835, Including the Diary or Daily Account Book of William Burke Wood, Co-Manager with William Warren of the Chestnut Street Theatre* (Philadelphia, 1932), 33–246. Cooper Engagement, January 1807, Box D87, Federal Street Theatre Papers, Boston Theatre Collection, BPL. James Fennell, *An Apology for the Life of James Fennell* (Philadelphia, 1814), 372–73, 476.

31. William B. Wood, *Personal Recollections of the Stage* (Philadelphia, 1855), 391–96. Wemyss, *Twenty-Six Years,* 94–95, 191–92, 260. Joseph Cowell, *Thirty Years Passed among the Players in England and America* (Hampden, CT, 1979 [orig. 1844]), 59.

32. Wemyss, *Twenty-Six Years,* 108. Wood, *Personal Recollections,* 155, 259, 304, 393, 399. James, *Old Drury,* 314.

33. For guaranteed contracts, see Junius Brutus Booth Account Book, Richmond, 1821, NYPL; *Boston Recorder*, October 16, 1840, 168; *The Whip* (New York), January 8, 1842; Wemyss, *Twenty-Six Years*, 166, 332–33; Wood, *Personal Recollections*, 351–52; Nan Louise Stephanson, "The Charleston Theatre Management of Charles Gilfert, 1817–1822," (Ph.D. dissertation, University of Nebraska–Lincoln, 1988), 503. For the quotes, see Wood, *Personal Recollections*, 132, 394.

34. Wemyss, *Twenty-Six Years*, 172. Wood, *Personal Recollections*, 394. Louis F. Tasistro, *Random Shots and Southern Breezes* (New York, 1842), 141. For ticket prices, see Expenses and Receipts, 1828–30, Box E28, Federal Street Theatre Papers, Boston Theatre Collection, BPL; *Baltimore Patriot*, October 27, 1830; *New York American*, January 6, 1832; *Philadelphia Inquirer*, October 11, 1832.

35. Sol Smith, *The Theatrical Apprenticeship and Anecdotal Recollections of Sol Smith* (Philadelphia, 1846), 54–63. For Gilfert, see Charles Gilfert v. Proprietors of the Charleston Theatre, February 14, 1824; Proprietors of the Charleston Theatre v. James Lynch, February 12, 1825, Judgment Rolls, SCA; Cowell, *Thirty Years*, 68, 71; Wemyss, *Twenty-Six Years*, 110; Stephanson, "Charleston Theatre Management," 503, 519.

36. For the boom years, see John Ashley Deposition, June 13, 1824; "Statement of Account," Wood v. Peters Case Papers, Legal Papers, Judge John Cadwalader Series, Cadwalader Family Papers, HSP. *Maryland Journal and Baltimore Advertiser*, August 19, 1794. Accounts, 1819–20, Box DD207, Federal Street Theatre Papers, Boston Theatre Collection, BPL. For declines in the ensuing decades, see Martin Staples Shockley, "The Proprietors of Richmond's New Theatre of 1819," *William and Mary Quarterly*, 2nd ser., 19 (July 1939): 304; Accounts, 1823–33, Box E142, Federal Street Theatre Papers, Boston Theatre Collection, BPL; *The Dramatic Mirror*, December 1, 1829; "An Act to Incorporate the Baltimore Theatre and Circus," February 27, 1830, *The Laws of Maryland, 1818–1836* (Annapolis, 1836). Also see the theatre entries in Richard Sylla, Jack Wilson, and Robert E. Wright, eds., "Price Quotations in Early U.S. Securities Markets, 1790–1860," http://www.icpsr.umich.edu/icpsrweb/ICPSR/studies/4053.

37. Baltimore Theatre Record Book, 1813–48, MDHS. Shockley, "Proprietors," 306. 1829 Assessment, Box DD258, Tremont Theatre Papers, Boston Theatre Collection, BPL. Shares Certificates, 1819–21, Boxes DD209–20, and Minutes, July 21, 1828, November 3, 1828, Boxes P135–36, Federal Street Theatre Papers, Boston Theatre Collection, BPL. Only one of the remaining Federal Street shareholders possessed an estate worth less than $10,000 in 1828, while 30 percent stood below that benchmark in the 1790s, despite deflation in the years between. Boston Tax Assessors Book, 1827 (microfilm), BPL.

38. J. R. Ingersoll to Richard Peters, May 19, 1830; H. D. Gilpin to Richard Peters, July 29, 1831; and Ingersoll to Peters, September 17, 1835, Wood v. Peters Case Papers, Legal Papers, Judge John Cadwalader Series, Cadwalader Family Papers, HSP. Wemyss, *Twenty-Six Years*, 197. Wood, *Personal Recollections*, 352–53.

39. Cowell, *Thirty Years*, 64, 71. Wemyss, *Twenty-Six Years*, 110; Stephanson, "Charleston Theatre Management," 557–59.

40. For bans and blacklisting, see Cowell, *Thirty Years*, 64; *New York Mirror*, November 23, 1833; Wood, *Personal Recollections*, 200; Hewitt, "'King Stephen,'" 136–37. For his personality, see William Toynbee, ed., *Diaries of William Macready* (London, 1912), 1:45. Philip Hone Diary, January 22, 1840, NYHS.

41. Washington Irving to Peter Irving, March 16, 1832, in *The Life and Letters of Washington Irving*, ed. Pierre Irving (New York, 1862), 416, 483. Cowell, *Thirty Years*, 64. Arthur Herman Wilson, *A History of the Philadelphia Theatre 1835 to 1855* (Philadelphia, 1935), 25–27. Hewitt, "'King Stephen,'" 110–34.

42. Park Theatre Leases, August 31, 1821; May 1, 1834, April 19, 1834, Deeds, Astor Papers, NYHS. Park Theatre Circular, Edmund Simpson, April 14, 1828, Nicholas Low Papers, NYHS.

43. *New Theatre Resolutions and Articles of Agreement Entered into and Adopted by the Proprietors* (Philadelphia, 1799), 10. Wemyss, *Twenty-Six Years*, 124–25, 134, 318. See also Cowell, *Thirty Years*, 84–85; Wood, *Personal Recollections*, 350.

44. Emmett Robinson, ed., "Dr. Irving's Reminiscences of the Charleston Stage," *South Carolina Historical and Genealogical Magazine* 51 (October 1950), 197, 200–204. William Gilmore Simms to James Lawson, November 15, 1843, in *Letters of William Gilmore Simms*, ed. Mary C. Simms Oliphant, Alfred T. Odell, and T. C. Duncan Eaves (Columbia, SC, 1952–82), 1:387–89. William Pelby, *Letters on the Tremont Theatre* (Boston: 1830), 26–27. "Management of Theatre by Committee," 1828, Box P19, Federal Street Theatre Papers, Boston Theatre Collection, BPL.

45. For Peters and Freeman, see *Philadelphia Directory*, 1825; *DeSilver's Philadelphia Directory* (Philadelphia, 1837); 1830 Census, Philadelphia County, Locust Ward. For Bradbury and Coolidge, see *The Boston Directory* (Boston, 1827); 1827 Boston City Tax, City Records Office, Boston, MA; Edward Pessen, *Riches, Class and Power before the Civil War* (Lexington, MA, 1973), app. C, 331–32. For the Cohens, see Summary, Cohen Collection Finding Aid, MDHS.

46. Wood, *Personal Recollections*, 331. Tasistro, *Random Shots*, 114.

47. For Pratt, see Wemyss, *Twenty-Six Years*, 164, 174; *Philadelphia Directory* (Philadelphia, 1825); Lewis Pratt and Francis Wemyss to Robert Pullen and Thomas De Silver, June 3, 1829, Wood v. Peters Case Papers, Legal Papers, Judge John Cadwalader Series, Cadwalader Family Papers, HSP. For Dana, see Francis W. Dana to Charles Bradbury, July 10, 1829; William Dinneford to Charles Bradbury, July 24, 1829, Boxes DD264–68, Federal Street Theatre Papers, Boston Theatre Collection, BPL; *The Boston Directory* (Boston, 1827). For Annapolis, see "Agreement in Reference to the Theatre," September 24, 1833, Ridout Papers, Maryland State Archives.

48. Stephen Price to unknown, September 14, 1827, in Dr. John W. Francis, *Old New York: Or, Reminiscences of the Past Sixty Years* (New York, 1865–72), 4:65. For slight changes and continuing similarities in content and performance, see Samuel Francis Ward Mss, January 16, 1821, NYHS; David Grimsted, *Melodrama Unveiled: American Theater and Culture, 1800–1850* (Chicago, 1968), 170–248; Bruce A. McConachie, *Melodramatic Formations: American Theatre and Society, 1820–1870* (Iowa City, 1992), 29–63, 119–42.

49. For Dana, see William Dinneford to Charles Bradbury, July 13, 1829, July 24, 1829, Boxes DD264–68; and Lease, December 24, 1832, Boxes E133–35, Federal Street Theatre Papers, Boston Theatre Collection, BPL; *Dramatic Mirror*, October 16, 1829. For Pratt, see Wemyss, *Twenty-Six Years*, 174, 329; Wilson, *History*, 11–20.

50. For Pratt, see Wilson, *History*, 11–20. For Dana, see William W. Clapp, *A Record of the Boston Stage* (Boston, 1853), 262, 305. For Charleston, see Thomas Hatcher v. Proprietors of the Charleston Theatre, February 2, 1839, Judgment Rolls, SCA; James H. Dormon, *Theatre in the Antebellum South, 1815–1861* (Chapel Hill, NC, 1967), 133–35,

162. For Baltimore, see Thomas Ward to the Trustees of the Holliday Street Theatre, November 27, 1839, Vertical File, MDHS; Gordon W. Wilson, "The Holliday Street Theatre, Baltimore: Chapters from Its History" (M.A. thesis, Johns Hopkins University, 1949), 65–66.

51. Jessica Lepler, *The Many Panics of 1837: People, Politics, and the Creation of a Trans-atlantic Financial Crisis* (New York, 2013), 8–156. Robert A. Margo, *Wages and Labor Markets in the United States, 1820–1860* (Chicago, 2000), 146–48; Peter L. Rousseau, "Jacksonian Monetary Policy, Specie Flows, and the Panic of 1837," *Journal of Economic History* 62 (June 2002): 457–88.

52. *The Knickerbocker; or New York Monthly Magazine*, September 1837, 268–70. *Spirit*, May 20, 1837, 112. *The Christian Reflector*, April 26, 1839, 3. *Turf Register*, November 1837, 555.

53. Wemyss, *Twenty-Six Years*, 297, 306, 334. *Spirit*, September 15, 1838; July 13, 1839. Peter Buckley, "To the Opera House: Culture and Society in New York City, 1820–1860," (Ph.D. dissertation, SUNY Stony Brook, 1984), 144. Dormon, *Theatre in the Antebellum South*, 133, 146.

54. *Spirit*, September 30, 1839. Wood, *Personal Recollections*, 407. For the changing yet uniform content, see Rosemarie K. Bank, *Theatre Culture in America, 1825–1860* (Cambridge, UK, 1997), 98–118; McConachie, *Melodramatic Formations*, 91–155; Dormon, *Theatre in the Antebellum South*, 256–74.

55. For northern theatre closings, see Wemyss, *Twenty-Six Years*, 318–19; *The Sporting Whip* (New York), March 4, 1843; Wilson, *History*, 9–26; *New York Mirror*, January 23, 1841; *Ladies' Companion*, June 1837, 95. For the South, see *Hatcher v. Proprietors*, February 2, 1839, Judgment Roll, SCA; *Spirit*, September 12, 1840, 336; Wilson, "Holliday Street," 66; Dormon, *Theatre in the Antebellum South*, 133–48, 155.

56. Richard Adams to Richard Singleton, February 8, 1832, Family Correspondence, Singleton Family Papers, SHC. Thomas Barry to William Henry Tayloe, December 16, 1835, WHT Correspondence, Tayloe Papers, VHS. Callendar Irvine to Daniel Parker, March 2, 1839, Daniel Parker Papers, Zaccheus Collins Collection, HSP. Henry Augustine Tayloe to William Henry Tayloe, June 23, 1838, WHT Correspondence, Tayloe Papers, VHS. Sketches from the Washington Races in October 1840 by an Eye Witness, Marion du Pont Scott Collection, UVa. Tyrone Power, *Impressions of America during the years 1833, 1834, and 1835* (London, 1836), 1:127–29, 2:58, 193. The growing number of shorter races from 1830 to 1840 appears in the *Turf Register*'s race reports, printed under the headline "Sporting Intelligence."

57. *Spirit*, June 8, 1839. William P. Stewart to Governor James Thomas, May 10, 1837, Mrs. T. Rowland Thomas Collection, MDHS. For former leading owners leaving the market, see Inventory Books, 1837–40 and 1837–61, Tayloe Papers, VHS; G. B. Mayo to William Gibbons, September 17, 1850, Gibbons Family Papers, NJHS; *Turf Register*, March 1838, 127–29; November 1838, 482–83; November 1841, 636–41; Adelman, *Sporting Time*, 78; Lynn Hastings, "A Sure Bet: Thoroughbreds at Hampton," *Maryland Historical Magazine* 89 (Spring 1994): 26, 33–35.

58. "Utilitarian," John H. Cocke, 1837, Broadsides, UVa. Adelman, *Sporting Time*, 55–73.

59. For attendance, see *Turf Register*, November 1837, 556; May 1838, 229. For purses, sales prices, and breeding fees staying high through 1837 and 1838, see *Turf*

Register, January 1838, 31; March 1838, 115, 127; July 1839, 423–24; Robert Wormeley Carter Stable Accounts, March 26, 1838, Carter Papers, CWM.

60. John Sawbridge Corbin to Robert Wormeley Carter, July 1, 1842, Robert Wormeley Carter Correspondence, Carter Papers, CWM. For Tayloe, see Henry Augustine Tayloe to William Henry Tayloe, March 13, 1836; February 25, 1837; June 15, 1840, WHT Correspondence, Tayloe Papers, VHS; "Sale of Personal Property," May 16, 1843; and Indenture, January 1847, Henry Augustine Tayloe Accounts, Tayloe Papers, VHS. For Johnson, see "Public Sale," March 25, 1845; Account with Thomas Branch and Sons, June 26, 1845, William Ransom Johnson Accounts, Johnson Family Papers, VHS. For translating past sums to values in 2014, see the inflation calculator at https://www.measuringworth.com/uscompare/.

61. Wemyss, *Twenty-Six Years*, 304, 311, 334, 351. *Spirit*, September 12, 1840. Dormon, *Theatre in the Antebellum South*, 177; Wilson, *History*, 25–27; Wilson, "Holliday Street," 66–67.

62. Wood, *Personal Recollections*, 436; David L. Rinear, *The Temple of Momus: Mitchell's Olympic Theatre* (Metuchen, NJ, 1987), 83–86, 187–95.

63. *New-York Mirror*, January 23, 1841. For ticket prices, see *Ladies' Companion*, May 1842, 68–70; *Spirit*, September 3, 1842, 324; *New York Herald*, September 5, 1842; *Southern Patriot* (Charleston, SC), November 18, 1844 (Charleston's box seats were reduced to seventy-five cents); Wood, *Personal Recollections*, 365, 402; Wemyss, *Twenty-Six Years*, 326. On the difficulties for company actors, see Faye Dudden, *Women in the American Theatre: Actresses and Audiences, 1790–1870* (New Haven, CT, 1994), 62; Bank, *Theatre Culture*, 92–96. Leading company actors could still do well. Thomas A'Becket netted about $400 in 1844, but made a fourth of his profit by doing odd jobs such as copying scripts and giving music lessons. Laborers did well to make $200 in the same period. See Thomas A'Becket Diaries, NYPL (Performing Arts). For wages, see Margo, *Wages and Labor Markets*, 146–48; Richard B. Stott, *Workers in the Metropolis: Class, Ethnicity, and Youth in New York City* (Ithaca, NY, 1990), 69.

64. *Advocate of Moral Reform*, November 15, 1838. *The Knickerbocker; or, New York Monthly Magazine*, May 1841, 441–43; *Ladies' Companion*, May 1842, 68–70; February 1843, 210. Rosemarie K. Bank, "The Bowery Theatre as a Mode of Historical Information," in Ron Engle and Tice L. Miller, eds. *The American Stage: Social and Economic Issues from the Colonial Period to the Present* (New York, 1993), 50–58.

65. Frances Milton Trollope, *Domestic Manners of the Americans* (London, 1832), 339–40; James Boardman, *America and the Americans* (London: 1833), 79–80, 203–5; Power, *Impressions*, 1:141; Godfrey Vigne, *Six Months in America* (London, 1832), 1:14; Walt Whitman, "The Old Bowery," in *Prose Works* (Philadelphia, 1862). For interpretations of class-specific theatre in the 1830s and 1840s based on these reports, see Buckley, "To the Opera House," 148–49; Richard Butsch, *The Making of American Audiences: From Stage to Television, 1750–1990* (New York, 2000), 46–60; Bruce A. McConachie, "The Theatre of the Mob," in *Theatre for Working Class Audience in the United States, 1830–1890*, ed. A. Bruce McConachie and Daniel Friedman (Westport, CT, 1985), 19–21; Sean Wilentz, *Chants Democratic: New York City and the Rise of the American Working Class, 1788–1850* (New York, 1984), 257–58.

66. *Sunday Flash*, October 17, 1841; October 24, 1841. *The Whip* (New York), January 1, 1842. *The Sporting Whip* (New York), February 11, 1843.

67. *Spirit*, March 30, 1839. For respectable visitors to the Bowery, see *Spirit*, May 25, 1839; November 4, 1843; Philip English Mackey, ed., *A Gentleman of Much Promise: The Diary of Isaac Mickle, 1837–1845* (Philadelphia, 1977), 470; Brewster Maverick Diary, July 6, 1847, November 2, 1847, May 31, 1848, NYHS.

68. *Life in Boston and New England Police Gazette*, April 6, 1850. For ticket prices, see *Spirit*, September 1, 1838; *New York Herald*, October 13, 1848.

69. For the evolution of content and targeting women, see Bluford Adams, *E Pluribus Barnum: The Great Showman and the Making of U.S. Popular Culture* (Minneapolis, 1997), 116–63; Buckley, "To the Opera House," 145; Richard Butsch, "Bowery B'hoys and Matinee Ladies: The Re-Ordering of Nineteenth Century American Theatre Audiences," *American Quarterly* 46 (September 1994): 373–403. For distinctions among theatres in the South, see Patricia C. Click, *Spirit of the Times: Amusements in Nineteenth Century Baltimore, Norfolk, and Charleston* (Charlottesville, VA, 1989), 45–56.

70. Thomas Ward to Trustees of Holliday St. Theatre, November 27, 1839, MDHS; *Dramatic Mirror*, September 29, 1829; Buckley, "To the Opera House," 248–56.

71. *The American Musical Journal*, October 1834, 17. *New York Mirror*, December 28, 1833. Nicholas B. Wainwright, ed., *A Philadelphia Perspective: The Diary of Sidney George Fisher Covering the Years 1834–1871* (Philadelphia, 1967), 268. Katherine K. Preston, "To the Opera House? The Trials and Tribulations of Operatic Production in Nineteenth-Century America," *Opera Quarterly* 23 (January 2007): 39–49.

72. *Albion* (New York), November 1847, 576. Power, *Impressions*, 1:164, 170–71.

73. T. H. Morrell, *Sketch of the Life of James William Wallack* (New York, 1865), 44–60. Martin Banham, *The Cambridge Guide to Theatre* (New York, 1995), 1183. Dudden, *Women*, 60–63. Wilson, "Holliday Street," 67–69. "Restoration of Ford's Theatre," Historic Structures Report, National Park Service (Washington, DC, 1963), 10. Lawrence Levine, *Highbrow/Lowbrow: The Emergence of Cultural Hierarchy in America* (Cambridge, MA, 1988), 143–242.

74. Cowell, *Thirty Years*, 77. *Stephen H. Branch's Alligator* (New York), July 10, 1858; Thomas Bogar, *Backstage at the Lincoln Assassination: The Untold Story of the Actors and Stagehands at Ford's Theatre* (Washington, DC, 2013), chap. 13.

75. For a greater range of society in the stands, see James Franklin Beard, ed., *Letters and Journals of James Fenimore Cooper* (Cambridge, MA, 1960–68), 1:99–103; *Spirit*, April 21, 1838; March 22, 1845; April 13, 1850; *The New World*, June 18, 1842, 25; *Camden Mail*, June 4, 1845. For ticket prices, see *Spirit*, March 10, 1838; January 7, 1843; April 27, 1844; June 1, 1844; Adelman, *Sporting Time*, 50; Dale Somers, *The Rise of Sports in New Orleans, 1850–1900* (Baton Rouge, LA, 1972), 25–30.

76. For "the Great North-South Match Race" of 1823 that initiated the trend of interregional races, see Beard, *Letters and Journals*, 1:99–103; Eisenberg, *Great Match Race*. For later renditions, see *Turf Register*, June 1831, 506; March 1840, 116; March 1842, 130–36; July 1842, 367–81; February 1844, 118.

77. John Morris, *Wanderings of a Vagabond* (New York, 1873), 267, 134–35. Adelman, *Sporting Time*, 88–89. Steven Riess, *City Games: The Evolution of American Urban Society and the Rise of Sports* (Urbana, IL, 1989), 181–82.

78. For Johnson, see Account with Thomas Branch, December 20, 1844–July 3, 1845; William Ransom Johnson Estate Account, April 15, 1850, William Ransom Johnson Accounts, Johnson Family Papers, VHS. For Ten Broeck, see Dizikes, *Sportsmen and Gamesmen*, 144–58. For western tracks, see *Spirit*, March 18, 1843; September 18, 1847.

79. Cornell Law Project, *The Development of the Law of Gambling: 1776–1976* (Washington, DC, 1977), 145–46. *Supplement to the Revised Statutes of Massachusetts* (Boston, 1850), 487–88. *Revised Statutes of Massachusetts* (Boston, 1859), 435–36. *Laws of Pennsylvania Passed in the Year 1847* (Harrisburg, PA, 1847), 111–13.

80. For the demise of renowned sporting taverns, see Virginius Dabney, *Richmond: The Story of a City* (Charlottesville, VA, 1990), 102; Martha A. Zierden and Jeanne A. Calhoun, "Urban Adaptation in Charleston, South Carolina, 1730–1820," *Historical Archaeology* 20 (April 1986): 30.

81. *Doggett's New York Directory* (1847, 1851, 1860). *Trow's Directory of New York* (1857–59). *McElroy's Philadelphia Directory* (1850, 1851, 1859). *Cohen's Philadelphia Directory* (1860). *Cohen's New Orleans Directory* (1846–54, 1859). Security Bonds, 1852, Records of the Office of the Mayor, New Orleans Public Library. Riess, *City Games*, 17.

82. *Barre Gazette*, July 12, 1844. *Western Recorder* (New York), September 12, 1826, 147. *Boston Recorder and Religious Telegraph*, September 8, 1826, 144. South Carolina presentments and petitions, S165010 and S165015, SCA. Ann Fabian, *Card Sharps, Dream Books, and Bucket Shops: Gambling in Nineteenth-Century America* (Ithaca, NY, 1990), 74–82.

83. The forty-nine managers named in the directories in n. 81 above, in newspaper advertisements in those three cities, or in the Security Bonds for licensing a hotel, billiard table, bowling alley, or restaurant, in the Records of the Office of the Mayor at the New Orleans Public Library, were cross-referenced with Real Estate Tax Valuations, Manhattan, 1845, 1856, Municipal Archives, New York City; and Census Records, New York City, Philadelphia County, New Orleans Parish, 1850 and 1860.

84. For the number of tables in halls, see Michael Phelan, *Rise and Progress of the Game of Billiards* (New York, 1860), 22–30; Frank St. Clair, *Six Days in the Metropolis; or Phases of Life in Town* (Boston, 1854), 41–45. For the cost of tables, see Ferry Company Accounts, September 3–17, 1822, Stevens Family Papers, NJHS; Thurston and Company Catalog (London, 1840); "Billiard Table Price List," Brunswick Corporation Catalog (Cincinnati, 1868).

85. For table makers sponsoring halls, see *New York Enquirer*, September 18, 1831; *New York Arena*, May 24, 1842; "Billiards Now and Then," *New York Times*, November 14, 1878; Phelan, *Rise and Progress* (New York, 1857), 67–72; *New Orleans Times-Picayune*, September 24, 1842, B. Antognini for Lucas Orlich, Security Bonds, 1852, New Orleans Mayor's Office, New Orleans Public Library. For brewers, see Jon M. Kingsdale, "The 'Poor Man's Club': Social Functions of the Urban Working-Class Saloon," *American Quarterly* 25 (October 1973): 475–78.

86. Phelan, *Rise and Progress*, vi–viii; Michael Phelan, *Billiards without a Master* (New York, 1850), 3.

87. Security Bonds, 1836, 1852–53, New Orleans Mayor's Office. Morris, *Wanderings of a Vagabond*, 106. Joseph Holt Ingraham, *The South-West, by a Yankee* (New York, 1835), 1:129.

88. Jonathan Harrington Greene, *Gambling Unmasked!* (Baltimore, 1844), 106. Fabian, *Card Sharps*, 29–38. Morris, *Wanderings of a Vagabond*, 106, 267, 460–62.

89. *Spirit*, March 1, 1851, 18. *Doggett's New York Directory* (1847, 1851). For other examples of matches making "friends," see *Spirit*, July 11, 1840, 222; August 4, 1849, 290; *The Sporting Whip*, February 11, 1843.

90. For his publications, see Phelan, *Billiards without a Master; Charleston Courier*, November 5, 1851. For his departure and return, see *Boston Herald*, April 20, 1852; *New York Irish American*, November 10, 1853; *San Francisco Daily Placer Times*, October 31, 1854; January 29, 1855; *New York Evening Post*, April 14, 1855.

91. Phelan, *Rise and Progress*. For the 1858 matches, see *Spirit*, September 25, 1858; *Frank Leslie's Illustrated Newspaper*, December 25, 1858.

92. *Spirit*, April 16, 1859. *Frank Leslie's Illustrated*, February 5, 1859, 154–55; February 19, 1859, 187; February 26, 1859, 203–4; May 7, 1859, 364.

93. George G. Foster, *New York in Slices* (New York, 1849), 25–30; George G. Foster, *New York by Gas-Light and Other Urban Sketches* (New York, 1850), 18–24.

94. Thomas Nicholas, *Ellen Ramsay; or, the Adventures of a Greenhorn in Town and Country* (New York, 1843). *Times-Picayune* (New Orleans), January 7, 1848. *New York Times*, March 26, 1864. For the accuracy of observations in sensational works, see J. Paul Erickson, "New Books, New Men: City-Mysteries Fiction, Authorship, and the Literary Market," *Early American Studies* 1 (April 2003): 4–5.

95. Policy #7022, September 10, 1846; Policy #116, March 31, 1830, Franklin Fire Insurance Company Records (FFI), HSP. For similar examples, see Morris, *Wanderings of a Vagabond*, 106–7; Ingraham, *South-West*, 1:127–29.

96. Policy # 4731, October 16, 1843, FFI. Inventory of Estate of M. M. Miller, September 25, 1868, Second District Court Records, New Orleans Public Library. Reginald T. Townsend, *Mother of Clubs: Being the History of the First Hundred Years of the Union Club of New York* (New York, 1936), 54–57. *The Century, 1847–1946* (New York, 1947), 8.

97. The connection between classical architecture and virtue dated back to the colonial period. See Dell Upton, *Holy Things and Profane: Anglican Parish Churches in Colonial Virginia* (Boston, 1986), 163–66. For the need to build trust among patrons in an increasingly anonymous antebellum society, see Karen Halttunen, *Confidence Men and Painted Women: A Study of Middle-Class Culture in America, 1830–1870* (New Haven, CT, 1982), 1–32.

98. Robert Bailey, *The Life and Adventures of Robert Bailey, from His Infancy Up to December, 1821* (Richmond, 1822), 160. *Republican Crisis* (New York), August 25, 1807. *Christian Watchman* (Boston, MA), June 2, 1821. For prominent friends who help prevent getting busted, see St. Clair, *Six Days in the Metropolis*, 52.

99. Aida DiPace Donald and David Donald, eds., *The Diary of Charles Francis Adams* (Cambridge, MA, 1964), 1:195. Policy #18153, May 13, 1853, FFI. Adlard Welby, *A Visit to North America* (London, 1821), 167–68. Francis Grund, *The Americans in Their Moral, Social, and Political Relations* (London, 1837), 119. Foster, *New York in Slices*, 27.

100. Foster, *New York in Slices*, 30. Foster, *New York by Gas-Light*, 20–21. Morris, *Wanderings of a Vagabond*, 264. Grund, *Americans*, 231–33. Power, *Impressions*, 2:195.

101. Policy #14955, December 22, 1851, FFI. *Signs of the Times* (Albany, NY), August 2, 1828.

102. Donald and Donald, *Diary of Charles Francis Adams*, 1:231–32, 274–75. Anonymous, *Law and Laziness; or, Students at Law of Leisure* (New York, 1846), 12–13, 47.

103. Morris, *Wanderings of a Vagabond*, 232. *McElroy's Philadelphia Directory* (1850, 1851, 1859). Greene, *Gambling Unmasked!*, 9–12, 65–66. Foster, *New York in Slices*, 27. For Jalbert, see Security Bonds, 1852, New Orleans Mayor's Office, New Orleans Public Library; *Cohen's New Orleans Directory*, 1846–54, 1859; 1850 and 1860 Census, New Orleans Parish.

104. For billiard game costs, see Adelman, *Sporting Time*, 226; Riess, *City Games*, 17. For the length of games, see Phelan, *Billiards without a Master*, 7.

105. *Turf Register*, May 1836, 423. Michael Zakim, *Ready-Made Democracy: A History of Men's Dress in the American Republic, 1760–1860* (Chicago, 2003), 69–84, 185–211.

6. Sporting Cultures

1. Isaac Mickle Diary, 1838, 36, Mickle Family Papers, Camden County Historical Society. *Appeal of the People of the County of Gloucester* (Camden, NJ, 1840), 27.

2. Mickle Diary, 1838, 29.

3. Stuart Blumin, *The Emergence of the Middle Class: Social Experience in the American City, 1760–1900* (Cambridge, UK, 1989), 190–218. Steven Mintz, *Moralists and Modernizers: America's Pre-Civil War Reformers* (Baltimore, 1995), 1–78. Ronald G. Walters, *American Reformers, 1815–1860* (New York, 1978), 1–30.

4. *Southern Sentinel*, February 14, 1852. J. Paul Erickson, "New Books, New Men: City-Mysteries Fiction, Authorship, and the Literary Market," *Early American Studies* 1 (April 2003): 273–312. T. Gregory Garvey, *Creating the Culture of Reform in Antebellum America* (Athens, GA, 2006), 34–38. Isabelle Lehuu, *Carnival on the Page: Popular Print Media in Antebellum America* (Chapel Hill, NC, 2000), 36–58. Maria Carla Sanchez, *Reforming the World: Social Activism and the Problem of Fiction in Nineteenth-Century America* (Iowa City, IA, 2008), 1–27.

5. Mickle Diary, 1838, 36–37.

6. Philip English Mackey, ed., *A Gentleman of Much Promise: The Diary of Isaac Mickle, 1837–1845* (Philadelphia, 1977), 116, 179, 187, 251–52, 342, 405, 507.

7. Ibid., xix, 264–65, 507. Mickle, Diary, February 5, 1844; May 28, 1844. *Camden Mail*, July 2, 1845.

8. Mickle Diary, February 22, 1844; Samuel Foster to Isaac Mickle, August 18, 1844; Isaac Mickle to Clara Mickle, August 6, 1853, Mickle Family Papers. *Camden Mail*, June 4, 1845. For another synthesis of reform culture and sporting culture, emphasizing how reformers made certain expressions of physicality respectable, see Steven A. Riess, "Sport and the Redefinition of Middle-Class Masculinity in Victorian America," in *The New American Sport History: Recent Approaches and Perspectives*, ed. S. W. Pope (Champaign, IL, 1997), 173–97.

9. For examples of continuing to use the term "genteel" to describe refined sporting settings, see George G. Foster, *New York by Gas-Light* (New York, 1850), 21; Harry Hazel, *The Belle of Boston: Or, the Rival Students of Cambridge* (Boston, 1841), 28; Jonathan Harrington Greene, *Gambling Unmasked!* (Baltimore, 1844), 49–50; John Morris [pseud. O'Connor], *Wanderings of a Vagabond* (New York, 1873), 267; *Ely's Hawk and Buzzard* (New York), September 1, 1832; *The Theatrical World*, July 12, 1845. Because of this usage, I have maintained references to "genteel" sport and sporting spaces, even though some patrons may have considered themselves to be asserting refined (if not reform) "respectability" there.

10. *The Theatrical World*, July 12, 1845. Patricia Cline Cohen, Timothy J. Gilfoyle, and Helen Lefkowitz Horowitz, *The Flash Press: Sporting Male Weeklies in 1840s New York* (Chicago, 2008).

11. The Camden racetrack: *Camden Mail*, June 4, 1845; *McElroy's Philadelphia Directory*, 1845. Matilda Charlotte Fraser, *Hesperos; or, Travels in the West* (London,

1850), 72. George G. Foster, *New York in Slices* (New York, 1849), 26–27. For a classic interpretation of workingmen using reform culture organizations to claim respectability, see Paul E. Johnson, *A Shopkeeper's Millennium: Society and Revivals in Rochester, New York, 1815–1837* (New York, 1978), 104–27.

12. For the ability of clear architectural patterns to influence behavior, see Henry Glassie, *Material Culture* (Bloomington, IN, 1999), 48–67; Bernard Herman, "The Bricoleur Revisited," in *American Material Culture: The Shape of the Field*, ed. Ann Smart Martin and J. Ritchie Garrison (Knoxville, TN, 1997), 41–55; Bill Hillier and Julienne Hanson, *Decoding Homes and Houses* (Cambridge, UK, 1998); Dell Upton, *Holy Things and Profane: Anglican Parish Churches in Colonial Virginia* (Boston, 1986), 101–62.

13. Aida DiPace Donald and David Donald, eds., *The Diary of Charles Francis Adams* (Cambridge, MA, 1964), 1:231–32, 274–75. Anonymous, *Ps and Qs* (Boston, 1828), 60–61. Mackey, *Promise*, 252, 384, 388, 405. Benjamin Brown French Diary, June 21, 1831, January 22, 1838, May 7, 1838, May 18, 1838, LOC. *Ely's Hawk and Buzzard* (New York), July 3, 1830.

14. *American Turf Register and Sporting Magazine* (hereafter cited as *Turf Register*), May 1836, 423. *Camden Mail*, May 28, 1845; June 4, 1845.

15. Morris, *Wanderings of a Vagabond*, 230–32. *Ely's Hawk and Buzzard* (New York), July 3, 1830.

16. J. Henry Smith, *The Green Family; or, The Veil Removed* (Springfield, MA, 1849), 112. *The Whip* (New York), January 29, 1842. Francis Grund, *Aristocracy in America* (London, 1839), 2:191–99. Morris, *Wanderings of a Vagabond*, 264, 269, 322.

17. For other studies of "cultural mobility," see Michael Emmison, "Social Class and Cultural Mobility: Reconfiguring the Cultural Omnivore Thesis," *Journal of Sociology* 39 (September 2003): 211–30; Peter Bailey, " 'Will the Real Bill Banks Please Stand Up?' Towards a Role Analysis of Working-Class Respectability," *Journal of Social History* 12 (April 1979): 336–53; Mike Huggins, "More Sinful Pleasures? Leisure, Respectability, and the Male Middle Classes in Victorian England," *Journal of Social History* 33 (Spring 2000): 585–600.

18. For leading examples of this argument, see Melvin L. Adelman, *A Sporting Time: New York City and the Rise of Modern Athletics, 1820–1870* (Urbana, IL, 1990); Stuart Blumin, *The Emergence of the Middle Class: Social Experience in the American City, 1760–1900* (New York, 1989), 190–230; Peter Buckley, "To the Opera House: Culture and Society in New York City, 1820–1860" (Ph.D. dissertation, SUNY Stony Brook, 1984); Patricia Click, *The Spirit of the Times: Amusements in Nineteenth-Century Baltimore, Norfolk, and Richmond* (Charlottesville, VA, 1989); Susan Davis, *Parades and Power: Street Theater in Nineteenth-Century Philadelphia* (Philadelphia, 1986); Paul Gilje, *The Road to Mobocracy: Popular Disorder in New York City, 1763–1834* (Chapel Hill, NC, 1987); Elliott Gorn, *The Manly Art: Bare-Knuckle Prize Fighting in America* (Ithaca, NY, 1986); Lawrence Levine, *Highbrow/Lowbrow: The Emergence of Cultural Hierarchy in America* (Cambridge, MA, 1988), 26–70; Bruce A. McConachie, *Melodramatic Formations: American Theatre and Society, 1820–1870* (Iowa City, IA, 1992).

19. For the spread of etiquette manuals, see C. Dallett Hemphill, *Bowing to Necessities: A History of Manners in America, 1620–1860* (New York, 1999), 129–213. My interpretation of architecture's power to communicate behavioral norms considers different

types of spaces as distinct "frameworks" encouraging certain behaviors over others. For the concept of behavioral "frames," see Erving Goffman, *Frame Analysis: An Essay on the Organization of Experience* (Cambridge, MA, 1974).

20. John Mack Faragher, *Sugar Creek: Life on the Illinois Prairie* (New Haven, CT, 1986), 181–98; Daniel Walker Howe, *What Hath God Wrought: The Transformation of America, 1815–1848* (New York, 2007), 538–39; Allan Kulikoff, *The Agrarian Origins of American Capitalism* (Charlottesville, VA, 1992), 41–46; James Oakes, *The Ruling Race: A History of American Slaveholders* (New York, 1982), 230; Edward Pessen, *Riches, Class and Power before the Civil War* (Lexington, MA, 1973), 73–89, 130–67; Stephan Thernstrom, *Poverty and Progress: Social Mobility in a Nineteenth-Century City* (Cambridge, MA, 1967), 96–97; Gavin Wright, *The Political Economy of the Cotton South: Households, Markets, and Wealth in the Nineteenth Century* (New York, 1978), 15–37.

21. George G. Foster, *New York Naked* (New York, 1855), 143. For laborers' wages, see Robert A. Margo and Georgia C. Villaflor, "The Growth of Wages in Antebellum America: New Evidence," *Journal of Economic History* 47 (December 1987): 880. For workingmen's "leisure preference," see Gorn, *Manly Art*, 138–40; Bruce Laurie, "Nothing on Compulsion: Life Styles of Philadelphia Artisans, 1820–1850," *Labor History* 15 (July 1974): 337–66; Christine Stansell, *City of Women: Sex and Class in New York: 1789–1860* (Urbana, IL, 1987), 90–94.

22. *Ely's Hawk and Buzzard* (New York), July 3, 1830; September 21, 1833. See also *The Anglo-American* (Philadelphia), July 15, 1843; *The Sporting Whip* (New York), January 28, 1843.

23. Kenneth S. Greenberg, *Honor and Slavery: Lies, Duels, Noses, Masks, Dressing as a Woman, Gifts, Strangers, Death, Humanitarianism, Slave Rebellions, the Pro-Slavery Argument, Baseball, Hunting, and Gambling in the Old South* (Princeton, NJ, 1996), 1–23, 124–46. Stephanie McCurry, *Masters of Small Worlds: Yeoman Households, Gender Relations, and the Political Culture of the Antebellum South* (New York, 1995), 208–76. Bertram Wyatt-Brown, *Southern Honor* (New York, 1982), 154–64, 339–66.

24. Edward Tailer Diary, December 2, 1848, NYHS. Nicholas B. Wainwright, ed., *A Philadelphia Perspective: The Diary of Sidney George Fisher Covering the Years 1834–1871* (Philadelphia, 1967), 34, 107. *Turf Register*, November 1844, 674–78. For the reform critique of white-collar masculinity and its effects, see Harvey Green, *Fit for America: Health, Fitness, Sport, and American Society* (New York, 1986), 10–31, 85–90; Brian P. Luskey, *On the Make: Clerks and the Quest for Capital in Nineteenth-Century America* (New York, 2010), 107–18; Scott Sandage, *Born Losers: A History of Failure in America* (Cambridge, MA, 2005), 55–58.

25. Godfrey Vigne, *Six Months in America* (London, 1832), 1:15. Foster, *New York Naked*, 44. *The Whip* (New York), April 9, 1842.

26. David Anthony, *Paper Money Men: Commerce, Manhood, and the Sensational Public Sphere in Antebellum America* (Columbus, OH, 2009), 6–23. Edward J. Balleisen, *Navigating Failure: Bankruptcy and Commercial Society in Antebellum America* (Chapel Hill, NC, 2001), 100–134. Joshua R. Greenberg, *Advocating the Man: Masculinity, Organized Labor, and the Household in New York, 1800–1840* (New York, 2009), 119–210. Paul Goodman, "The Emergence of the Homestead Exemption in the United States: Accommodation and Resistance to the Market Revolution, 1840–1880," *Journal of American History* 80 (September 1993): 470–98.

27. Mickle Diary, January 14, 1844. Neil Harris, *Humbug: The Art of P. T. Barnum* (Chicago, 1973), 70–88. This playful approach to being cheated was more likely in the North than the South, as noted in Greenberg, *Honor and Slavery*, 1–23.

28. Richard Butsch, "Bowery B'hoys and Matinee Ladies: The Re-Ordering of Nineteenth Century American Theatre Audiences," *American Quarterly* 46 (September 1994), 382–403.

29. George G. Foster, *Celio; or, New-York Above-Ground and Under-Ground* (New York, 1850), 16. *Turf Register*, May 1836, 423. For the persistence of interracial gambling in southern dives, see Jeffrey Forret, *Race Relations at the Margins: Slaves and Poor Whites in the Antebellum Southern Countryside* (Baton Rouge, LA, 2006), 56–70. Richard C. Wade, *Slavery in the Cities: The South, 1820–1860* (New York, 1964), 85–90, 149–60.

30. For theatre, see Theatre Petition, November 22, 1855, Petitions, South Carolina Archives; *Colored American*, May 10, 1834; Fanny Trollope, *Domestic Manners of the Americans* (London, 1832), 350; James H. Dorman, Jr., *Theater in the Antebellum South, 1815–1861* (Chapel Hill, NC, 1967), 233–37. For "black Broadway," see *Frederick Douglass Newspaper*, February 26, 1852; *The North Star* (Rochester, NY), December 5, 1850.

31. Annie Porter, "My Life as a Slave," *Harper's New Monthly Magazine*, October 1884, 730–38. For former slaves providing different insights depending on their interviewer, see John Blassingame, "Using the Testimony of Ex-Slaves: Approaches and Problems," *Journal of Southern History* 41 (November 1975): 473–92. For fears of superior black prowess at the time of the article, see Gail Bedermann, *Manliness and Civilization: A Cultural History of Gender and Race in the United States, 1880–1917* (Chicago, 1995), 1–44.

32. Porter, "My Life as a Slave," 731–33.

33. Ibid., 733–36.

34. Ibid., 734–35.

35. Ibid., 736–37.

36. Peter Kolchin, *American Slavery, 1619–1877* (New York, 2003), 128. Katherine C. Mooney, *Race Horse Men: How Slavery and Freedom Were Made at the Racetrack* (Cambridge, MA, 2014), 74–88, 213–45.

37. *New York American*, November 11, 1823. *Saturday Evening Post*, April 17, 1835. *Hudson River Chronicle*, July 10, 1838. Francis C. Wemyss, *Twenty-Six Years of the Life of an Actor and Manager* (New York, 1846), 324, 291–92. Gorn, *Manly Art*, 108–28. Edward Hotaling, *They're Off: Horse Racing at Saratoga* (New York, 1995), 60–65.

38. *New York Times*, November 20, 1890. Wemyss, *Twenty-Six Years*, 122. Sol Smith, *The Theatrical Apprenticeship and Anecdotal Recollections of Sol Smith* (Philadelphia, 1846), 73, 94.

39. Bluford Adams, *E Pluribus Barnum: The Great Showman and the Making of U.S. Popular Culture* (Minneapolis, 1997), 41–74. Faye E. Dudden, *Women in the American Theatre: Actresses and Audiences, 1790–1870* (New Haven, CT, 1994), 27–55, 75–103. In some ways, Cushman benefited from an era that saw her lesbianism as "chaste romantic friendship," as Lisa Merrill points out in *When Romeo Was a Woman: Charlotte Cushman and Her Circle of Female Spectators* (Ann Arbor, MI, 2000), xvii–xviii, 80–137.

40. William Alcott, *The Young Man's Guide* (Boston, 1834), 160. *How to Do Business: A Pocket Manual of Practical Affairs and Guide to Success in Life* (New York, 1857), 10, 147–48. Ann Fabian, *Card Sharps, Dream Books, and Bucket Shops: Gambling in Nineteenth-Century America* (Ithaca, NY, 1990), 12–107. Jackson Lears, *Something for Nothing: Luck in America* (New York, 2003), 22–98. Sandage, *Born Losers*, 22–98.

41. R. Hildreth, *Banks, Banking, and Paper Currencies* (Boston, 1840), 159–60. Ralph Waldo Emerson, "Wealth," in *The Conduct of Life* (Boston, 1860), 86. Balleisen, *Navigating Failure*, 25–48. Sandage, *Born Losers*, 24–35, 44–64, 84–92.

42. Greenberg, *Honor and Slavery*, 141.

43. Morris, *Wanderings of a Vagabond*, 106–8. *Turf Register*, January 1830, 255–57; November 1843, 648; November 1844, 658.

44. Cadwallader R. Colden, *An Expose of the Measures Which Caused Suspension of the Races on the Union Course in October 1830* (New York, 1831), 1–16, 40–41.

45. Colden, *Expose*, 16–28. Adelman, *Sporting Time*, 39–42.

46. John Sawbridge Corbin to Robert Wormeley Carter, June 30, 1840, July 22, 1840, February 28, 1842; William Henry Tayloe to Robert Wormeley Carter, November 6, 1846, Robert Wormeley Carter Correspondence, Carter Papers, CWM. John Sawbridge Corbin to William Henry Tayloe, May 8, 1838, William Henry Tayloe (WHT) Correspondence, Tayloe Papers, VHS. For the rules on paying entrance fees, see *Rules and Regulations Adopted by the New York Jockey Club* (New York, 1836), 7–8.

47. John Sawbridge Corbin to Robert Wormeley Carter, August 18, 1840, March 6, 1843, July 30, 1845; Carter to Corbin, September 18, 1840, Robert Wormeley Carter Correspondence, Carter Papers, CWM.

48. John Sawbridge Corbin to William Henry Tayloe, May 15, 1846, WHT Correspondence, Tayloe Papers, VHS.

49. *Southern Quarterly Review*, January 1853, 59. *Ely's Hawk and Buzzard* (New York), August 1, 1833. Wyatt-Brown, *Southern Honor*, 345–46. Cohen, et. al., *Flash Press*, 2–8, 55.

50. Isaac Mickle to Clara Mickle, August 6, 1853, Mickle Family Papers. Wemyss, *Twenty-Six Years*, 324.

51. *Ely's Hawk and Buzzard* (New York), September 1, 1832. McConachie, *Melodramatic Formations*, 70–90; Gorn, *Manly Art*, 129–47.

52. Andrew Jackson, "Nullification Proclamation," December 10, 1832, in *State Papers on Nullification* (Boston, 1834), 75–97. Daniel Webster, "Editorial: The Treaty of Washington," August 22, 1842, in *The Papers of Daniel Webster: Diplomatic Papers*, ed. Kenneth E. Shewmaker (Hanover, NH, 1983), 1:693–95. *The Crime against Kansas: Speech of Hon. Charles Sumner of Massachusetts; In the Senate of the United States, May 19, 1856* (New York, 1856), 3.

53. John H. Schroeder, "Major Jack Downing and American Expansionism: Seba Smith's Political Satire, 1847–1856," *American Quarterly* 50 (June 1977): 214–20.

54. *Rutland (VT) Herald*, September 12, 1810. *Connecticut Courant*, August 26, 1828. For the rise of "sporting political cartoons," I examined the print catalogues at the Library of Congress (LOC) and American Antiquarian Society (AAS). At LOC, 39 of 273 political cartoons (14 percent) in the American Cartoon Prints Collection published between 1820 and 1860 contained sporting themes. At (AAS), 41 of 411 items (10 percent) in the same period fit the category. For the catalogues, see www.loc.gov/rr/print/catalog.html and catalog.mwa.org/.

55. Thomas Brothers, *The United States of America as They Are; Not as They Are Generally Described: Being a Cure for Radicalism* (London, 1840), 301–2. *Western Monthly Magazine*, September 1834, 479. Robert Corbin to Robert Wormeley Carter, April 16, 1840; William Henry Tayloe to Carter, August 28, 1840, Robert Wormeley Carter

Correspondence, Carter Papers, CWM. See also Daniel Dupre, "Barbecues and Pledges: Electioneering and the Rise of Democratic Politics in Antebellum Alabama," *Journal of Southern History* 60 (August 1994): 490–99; Ronald P. Formisano, *The Transformation of Political Culture: Massachusetts Parties, 1790s–1840s* (New York, 1983), 295–303.

56. Edwin A. Miles, "President Adams' Billiard Table," *New England Quarterly* 45 (March 1972): 31–43.

57. Walter Dean Burnham, "Those High Nineteenth-Century American Voting Turnouts: Fact or Fiction?," *Journal of Interdisciplinary History* 26 (October 1985): 613–44.

58. Glenn Altschuler and Stuart Blumin, *Rude Republic: Americans and Their Politics in the Nineteenth Century* (Princeton, NJ, 2000), 83.

59. J. B. Dunlop, "'The Grand Fabric of Republicanism': A Scotsman Describes South Carolina, 1810–1811," *South Carolina Historical and Genealogical Magazine* 71 (July 1970): 180. John Davis, *Travels of Four Years and a Half in the United States of America during 1798, 1799, 1800, 1801, and 1802* (New York, 1909 [orig. 1803]), 97–98. See also Edmund S. Morgan, *Inventing the People: The Rise of Popular Sovereignty in England and America* (New York, 1988), 174–208; Andrew W. Robertson, "Voting Rites and Voting Acts: Electioneering Ritual, 1790–1820," in *Beyond the Founders: New Approaches to the Political History of the Early American Republic*, ed. Jeffrey Pasley, Andrew Robertson, and David Waldstreicher (Chapel Hill, NC, 2004), 69–71.

60. Wainwright, *Philadelphia Perspective*, 104. Thomas J. McCormack, ed., *Memoirs of Gustave Koerner* (Cedar Rapids, IA, 1909), 2:434, cited in William E. Gienapp, "'Politics Seem to Enter into Everything': Political Culture in the North, 1840–1860," in *Essays on American Antebellum Politics, 1840–1860*, ed. Stephen E. Maizlish and John J. Kushma (Dallas, TX, 1982), 32. See also Altschuler and Blumin, *Rude Republic*, 46–86; Formisano, *Transformation of Political Culture*, 252–78.

61. Virginia K. Jones, ed., "A Great Day for the Whigs of Alabama, the Diary of Hardy Vickers Wooten," *Alabama Historical Quarterly* 25 (Fall 1963): 259–60. Levi Lincoln Newton Diary, June 17, 1840, July 3, 1840, AAS. "Life and Journal of John Sutherland," *Mississippi Valley Historical Review* 4 (1917–18): 362–70. "Narrative of a Journey through the United States, 1821–24," anonymous diary, 238–50, NYHS. Wainwright, *Philadelphia Perspective*, 106. Parades became more orderly over time, as Susan Davis outlines in *Parades and Power: Street Theater in Nineteenth-Century Philadelphia* (Philadelphia, 1986).

62. Benjamin Drake, *Tales and Sketches from the Queen City* (Cincinnati, 1838), 88. Charles Sealsfield, "Annexation, or, Sport for Grown Children" (New York, 1845), AAS. Altschuler and Blumin, *Rude Republic*, 33, 37, 46, 62–63, 83. Burnham, "Voting Turnouts," 613–44.

63. Drake, *Tales and Sketches*, 76. Altschuler and Blumin, *Rude Republic*, 22–37.

64. Newton Diary, May 28, 1840, June 11–13, 1840, AAS. Formisano, *Transformation of Political Culture*, 285–309; Robert E. Mutch, "The First Federal Campaign Finance Bills," *Journal of Policy History* 14 (March 2002): 30–48. Pessen, *Riches, Class and Power*, 285–99.

65. Levi Lincoln Newton Diary, May 28, 1840, June 11–13, 1840, AAS. William A. Brewer, *A Few Thoughts for Taxpayers and Voters* (New York, 1853), 74. Altschuler and Blumin, *Rude Republic*, 67–69. Pessen, *Riches, Class and Power*, 285–99.

66. Altschuler and Blumin, *Rude Republic*, 106–7, 119–28, 135–37. Gienapp, "Politics," 43.

67. Richard Franklin Bensel, *The American Ballot Box in the Mid-Nineteenth Century* (New York, 2004), 57–77. Morris, *Wanderings of a Vagabond*, 315. See also Gorn, *Manly Art*, 135–36; David Grimsted, *American Mobbing, 1828–1861* (New York, 1998), 182–97.

68. Formisano, *Transformation of Political Culture*, 262–73. Joel H. Silbey, *The American Political Nation, 1838–1893* (Stanford, CA, 1991), 63–70.

69. Sarah J. Hale, *Traits of American Life* (Philadelphia, 1835), 121. Altschuler and Blumin, *Rude Republic*, 89–105. Formisano, *Transformation of Political Culture*, 307–9.

70. Bensel, *Ballot Box*, 57–63. For the continued use of sporting sites for separate political events, see R. C. Long and A. C. Smith, "National Convention of Whig Young Men" (Baltimore, 1840), MDHS.

71. *Hudson River Chronicle*, July 10, 1838. *Subterranean*, September 2, 1843. Michael Walsh, "Speech at Tammany Hall," *Sketches of the Speeches and Writings of Michael Walsh* (New York, 1843), 10. Sean Wilentz, *Chants Democratic: New York City and the Rise of the American Working Class* (New York, 1984), 328–56. Gorn, *Manly Art*, 129–47.

72. T. J. Carmichael, "Why the East Cannot Compete with the West," *The Plough, the Loom and the Anvil*, January 1849, 438. Ralph Waldo Emerson, *The Conduct of Life* (Boston, 1860), 86.

73. Most notably, see Buckley, "To the Opera House," 25–63; Levine, *Highbrow/Lowbrow*, 56–81; McConachie, *Melodramatic Formations*, 145–55.

74. *New York Herald*, May 11, 1849; May 12, 1849. Buckley, "To the Opera House," 12–18.

75. The most comprehensive roster of casualties is in Buckley, "To the Opera House," 5–6.

76. *New York Herald*, May 12, 1849.

77. J. R. Anderson, "To the Public," November 15, 1831, Broadside Collection, AAS. *New York Mercury*, October 19, 1831. *Succinct Account of the Disturbance Which Occurred at the Charleston Theatre* (Charleston, 1817), 6–8. Wood, *Recollections*, 321–23. *The Theatrical Contributions of Jacques to the United States Gazette* (Philadelphia, 1826), 42.

78. *Spirit*, May 21, 1842. *The New World*, June 18, 1842. Colden, *Expose*, 32.

79. Buckley, "To the Opera House," 57–61.

80. *New York Mirror*, December 28, 1833, 377–78.

81. *Albion* (New York), November 1847, 576. *New York Herald*, February 17, 1849; March 10, 1849. For examples of opera staged in theatres triggering violence much like that sparked by drama in theatres, see Levine, *Highbrow/Lowbrow*, 88–93.

82. *New York Herald*, November 1, 1848; March 10, 1849. *The Weekly Herald*, May 5, 1849.

83. Buckley, "To the Opera House," 77–78; Karen Ahlquist, *Democracy at the Opera: Music, Theater, and Culture in New York City, 1815–1860* (Urbana, IL, 1997), 130–62; Paul Dimaggio, "Cultural Entrepreneurship in Nineteenth-Century Boston," Parts 1 (January) and 2 (October), *Media, Culture, and Society* 4 (1982): 35–50, 303–22.

84. Robert Clyde Allen, *Horrible Prettiness: Burlesque and American Culture* (Chapel Hill, NC, 1991). Brooks McNamara, *The New York Concert Saloon: The Devil's Own Nights* (Cambridge, UK, 2002). Steven Riess, *City Games: The Evolution of American Urban Society and the Rise of Sports* (Urbana, IL, 1989), 171–202.

Epilogue

1. Lee Jenkins, "The Day That Damned the Dodgers," *Sports Illustrated*, August 29, 2011, 50–59. Ian Lovett, "Two Plead Guilty in Beating of Giants Fan," *New York Times*, February 20, 2014.

2. Steven J. Swenson, "Unsportsmanlike Conduct: The Duty Placed on Stadium Owners to Protect against Fan Violence," *Marquette Sports Law Review* 23 (Fall 2012), 135–41.

3. Dorothy Seymour Mills, *Chasing Baseball: Our Obsession with Its History, Numbers, People, and Places* (Jefferson, NC, 2010), 137. Steven A. Riess, *Touching Base: Professional Baseball and American Culture in the Progressive Era* (Urbana, IL, 1999), 33–37.

4. Michael K. Bohn, *Heroes and Ballyhoo: How the Golden Age of the 1920s Transformed American Sports* (Washington, DC, 2009), 299–301. Annemarie Farrell, Janet S. Fink, and Sarah Fields, "Women Sports Spectatorship: An Exploration of Men's Influence," *Journal of Sport Management* 25 (2011): 190. D. C. Funk, D. F. Mahoney, M. Nakazawa, and S. Hirakawa, "Development of Sport Interest Inventory (SII): Implications for Measuring Unique Consumer Motives at Sporting Events," *International Journal of Sports Marketing and Sponsorship* 3 (2001), 291–316. Kevin Young, *Sport, Violence, and Society* (New York, 2012), 161–71.

5. Ryan A. Swanson, *When Baseball Went White: Reconstruction, Reconciliation, and Dreams of a National Pastime* (Lincoln, NE, 2014), 100–5, 177–19. Katherine C. Mooney, *Race Horse Men: How Slavery and Freedom Were Made at the Racetrack* (Cambridge, MA, 2014), 224–30.

6. Andrew Yiannakis and Merill J. Melnick, eds., *Contemporary Issues in the Sociology of Sport* (Champagne, IL, 2001), 212–16.

7. Eric Bain-Selbo, *Game Day and God: Football, Faith, and Politics in the American South* (Macon, GA, 2009), 27–52. Ticketmaster LiveAnalytics, "U.S. Live Event Attendance Study," June 2014, 12. Farrell et al., "Women Sports Spectatorship," 190–91. Yiannakis and Melnick, *Contemporary Issues*, 216.

8. Jeremy White, Robert Gebeloff, and Ford Fessenden, "What Percent Are You?," *New York Times*, January 14, 2012. Ticketmaster, "Attendance Study," 12. Mark Robert Rank, Thomas A. Hirschl, Kirk A. Foster, *Chasing the American Dream: Understanding What Shapes Our Fortunes* (New York, 2014), 124–28.

9. For the judge's quote, see Young, *Sport, Violence, and Society*, 54. The second quote comes from Bryant Jackson, a father of six and resident of suburban Detroit who was convicted of throwing a chair at an NBA player during a fight between players and fans in 2004, cited in Jonathan Abrams, "The Malice at the Palace: An Oral History of the Scariest Moment in NBA History," ESPN *Grantland*, March 20, 2012, http://grantland.com/features/an-oral-history-malice-palace/.

10. B. J. Srinivasaraju, *Sports Sociology* (New Delhi, 2012), chap. 9. Marla Ridenour, "Fans to Meet with Lerner," *Akron Beacon-Journal*, November 2, 2009.

11. Anne Cunningham Osborne and Danielle Sarver Coombs, *Female Fans of the NFL: Taking Their Place in the Stands* (New York, 2016), 146–48.

12. Michael K. Ostrowski, "The Social Psychology of Alcohol Use and Violent Behavior among Sports Spectators," *Aggression and Violent Behavior* 19 (2014): 303–9.

13. Young, *Sport, Violence, and Society*, 54. Wray Vamplew, *Pay Up and Play the Game: Professional Sport in Britain, 1875–1914* (Cambridge, UK, 1988), 77–111.

14. Gerry Smith, "Why Your Cable Bill Is Going Up Again—Sports," *Bloomberg Tech*, January 7, 2015. Steve Baron, "NFL TV Recap," *TV by the Numbers*, January 9, 2015. Nate Silver, "The Clippers, Like Many NBA Teams, Have a Majority-Minority Fan Base," *FiveThirtyEight*, April 29, 2014. Young, *Sport, Violence, and Society*, 58–63.

15. Lawrence Levine, *Highbrow/Lowbrow: The Emergence of Cultural Hierarchy in America* (Cambridge, MA, 1988). M. Alison Kibler, *Rank Ladies: Gender and Cultural Hierarchy in American Vaudeville* (Chapel Hill, NC, 1999), 24–49. Robert Clyde Allen, *Horrible Prettiness: Burlesque and American Culture* (Chapel Hill, NC, 1991), 241–58.

16. Ticketmaster, "Attendance Study," 18–19. Emily Yahr, "Violence, Tragedy, Mass Arrests: What Is Going On with Country Music Concerts This Summer?," *Washington Post*, August 7, 2014. Tamara D. Madensen and John E. Eck, "Spectator Violence in Stadiums," U.S. Department of Justice, Problem Oriented Guides for Police, 54 (2008), 6–11. For the long history of certain genres of music merging into sporting culture, see Glenn Altschuler, *All Shook Up: How Rock 'n' Roll Changed America* (New York, 2003), 1–6, 110; Brooks McNamara, *The New York Concert Saloon: The Devil's Own Nights* (New York, 2002).

17. For the quotes see, Jerry Barca, "NBA MVP Stephen Curry Seizes the Moment and Delivers His Message," *Forbes*, May 8, 2015; "Oprah Talks to Jay-Z," *O Magazine*, October 2009; Anthony DeCurtis, "Not a Businessman—A Business, Man," *Men's Health*, October 5, 2010. For the odds of lucrative success, see the NCAA's "Probability of Competing beyond High School," http://www.ncaa.org/about/resources/re search/probability-competing-beyond-high-school, accessed February 2, 2016; Moses Avalon, "What Are the Vegas Odds of Success on Today's Major Label Record Deal?," http://www.mosesavalon.com/what-are-the-vegas-odds-of-success-on-todays-major-label-record-deal/, accessed February 2, 2016.

18. Raj Chetty, Nathaniel Hendren, Patrick Kline, Emmanuel Saez, and Nicholas Turner, "Is the United States Still a Land of Opportunity? Recent Trends in Intergenerational Mobility," National Bureau of Economic Research Working Paper, January 2014. Kenneth Cohen, "The Manly Sport of American Politics; or, How We Came to Call Elections Races," *Common-Place*, April 2012, http://www.common-place-archives.org/vol-12/no-03/cohen/, accessed February 2, 2016. Sporting investors' political contributions are trackable through the Sunlight Foundation at www.sunlightfoundation.com, and have received attention in more than a dozen articles, including Louis Serino, "Grammy Winners on the Political Party Trail," *Political Party Time*, February 12, 2013, http://politicalpartytime.org/blog/2013/02/12/grammy-winners-on-the-political-party-trail/; Louis Serino, "Baseball's (Political) Heavy Hitters, *sunlightfoundation.com*, March 29, 2013, http://sunlightfoundation.com/blog/2013/03/29/politics-mlb-teams-are-heavy-hitters-republicans/; Seth Cline, "All-Star Politics of the NBA," *OpenSecrets.org*, February 24, 2012, http://www.opensecrets.org/news/2012/02/nba/; Elliot Smilowitz, "Political Football," *Washington Examiner*, September 5, 2013; Sara Burnett, "Cubs Owners Active in Politics, Though Loyalties Divided," *NBC Chicago*, October 28, 2016, http://www.nbcchicago.com/news/local/Cubs-Owners-Also-Active-in-Politics-Though-Loyalties-Split-399022531.html.

19. Michael McGerr, *The Decline of Popular Politics: The North, 1865–1928* (New York, 1986), 205–6. Walter Dean Burnham, "Theory and Voting Research: Some Reflections on Converse's 'Change in the American Electorate,'" *American Political Science*

Review 68 (September 1974): 1002–23; Liette Gidlow, *The Big Vote: Gender, Consumer Culture, and the Politics of Exclusion, 1890s–1920s* (Baltimore, 2004), 1–24.

20. Patrick Hruby, "The SportsCenter-Ization of Political Journalism," *Atlantic*, January 4, 2012. John L. Jackson Jr., "Media Reform, 2008's Presidential Election, and the Sportification of Politics," *International Journal of Communication* 3 (2009): 42–46. Melonyce McAfee, "Are 'Political Futures' Illegal?," *Slate*, April 27, 2007. For recent turnout data, see the United States Elections Project, online at http://www.electproject .org/home/voter-turnout/voter-turnout-data (accessed March 18, 2017).

21. Rob Savillo and Oliver Willis, "Diversity on Evening Cable News," *Media Matters Reports*, May 13, 2013, http://mediamatters.org/research/2013/05/13/report-diversity-on-evening-cable-news-in-13-ch/194012. Steven Hill, "Why Does the U.S. Still Have So Few Women in Office?," *The Nation*, March 7, 2014. Donald Trump, Speech, Jacksonville, FL, October 24, 2015, http://edition.cnn.com/TRANSCRIPTS/1510/24 /cnr.03.html.

Index

risk, 15, 33, 38, 51, 81, 160–161, 191–193, 202–203, 235, 243, 249. *See also* capitalism: economic culture of; gambling

rough sport, 11–12, 15, 55, 76, 233, 236, 248–251; and cultural mobility, 133–138, 142–145, 171, 184, 200, 207–214; and taverns, 23–30, 35, 71–72, 79–83, 126–127, 153–155, 200. *See also* masculinity; sporting space

roulette, 120, 124

saloons. *See* taverns

Singleton, Richard, 114–115, 145–148, 150, 175–177, 229

slaves, 10, 69, 70, 73, 111, 153, 205; and horse racing, 47–52, 112–114, 145–151, 172, 192, 215–219, 247; and taverns or gambling houses, 24–25, 124–127, 155–156; and theatre, 138

Sons of Liberty, 22, 34, 54–58, 75, 79, 81–82, 88

South. *See* sporting culture: regional comparisons of

South Carolina, 74–75, 85, 109, 114, 120–121, 133, 145, 149, 158–159, 166, 170, 175, 192, 194, 226, 229. *See also* Charleston

spectators. *See* participants: audiences

sporting culture: definition of, 4–8; regional comparisons of, 5, 28, 37, 61, 76–77, 109, 121–127, 138, 148, 155–157, 185–186, 193, 199, 205, 210–212, 223, 226, 246. *See also* genteel sport; rough sport; sporting space

sporting professionals, 11, 12, 31, 43–53, 59, 85, 120, 121, 126, 129, 131, 152, 219–220, 229, 235, 243, 247, 252–253. *See also* actors and actresses; gambling; horsemen; taverns: financing and management of; theatres: financing and management of

sporting space, 9–11, 15–16, 33, 78–82, 155–156, 171, 188–191, 197–203, 241–244; accessibility of, 13, 30–32, 58–59, 88, 132–138, 143–145, 151, 214–215, 229, 246–247; architecture of, 4, 30, 62–65, 102–104, 122–126; behavior in, 12, 26, 54–55, 61, 80, 85, 87, 126, 139, 144, 153, 205, 207–213, 250–251, 262n31. *See also* genteel sport; rough sport

status, 13, 26, 47, 49, 60, 70, 81–82, 138, 141, 145, 206–207, 229, 240, 246, 248–249, 258n9, 260n22; and class, 132, 135, 143, 210–213, 215, 243, 250, 261n24; and gentility, 11, 46, 55, 151–155; and honor, 10, 76–77, 155–156, 220–225; "status politics," 85–86, 161–164, 234–235

subscribers. *See* investors

subscriptions, 36–38, 45, 63–66, 81, 93–95, 102, 106–107, 112, 128, 140–141, 200–202, 223, 235

suffrage, 8, 55, 159, 161, 250, 253

taverns: evolution of, 121–127, 193, 197, 199; financing and management of, 36–37, 48–50, 59, 80–81, 120–121, 141, 194–195; and politics, 33–34, 54–56, 81–83, 87–89, 158, 237; social experience of, 1–3, 8–9, 11–12, 16, 21–33, 59–60, 63–65, 72, 77–82, 86, 151, 153–155, 199, 205. *See also* gambling

Tayloe, John, II, 13, 35, 47–48, 67, 69–70, 110

Tayloe, John, III, 110–115, 139–140, 148–150, 171

Tayloe, William Henry, 172, 175–176, 186, 223–224

Tennessee, 120, 115, 158, 176, 192

theatres, 5–8, 21; financing and management of, 30, 36–38, 43–46, 61–63, 66, 93–95, 101–103, 116–120, 132, 138–139, 177–185, 187–191, 241–244; opposition to, 65–66, 83–84, 95–97, 207; performance material, 32, 61, 129–131, 162–164, 177; and politics, 56–58, 83–85, 96–101, 117, 158, 162–166, 225, 231, 233, 237, 240; social experience of, 3, 58–60, 87, 128–139, 143–144, 162–163, 188–191, 206–209, 212–215, 239–244, 251

thoroughbreds. *See* horse racing; racehorses

Trump, Donald, 252, 256

turfmen, 175–177, 184–187, 191–193, 206–207, 217, 222–224, 229

violence, 28, 60, 77–79, 138, 144–145, 150, 153–156, 166, 246, 251. *See also* protests

Virginia, 1–3, 25, 41, 60, 67–68, 70–73, 82, 85, 101, 104, 113–115, 121, 124–125, 133, 139–143, 146–147, 152, 159, 170–172, 185–186, 192, 216, 229. *See also* Richmond, VA

CPSIA information can be obtained
at www.ICGtesting.com
Printed in the USA
LVOW07*0814110118

562686LV00003B/34/P